Economics Evolving

*

Economics Evolving

A HISTORY OF ECONOMIC THOUGHT

*

AGNAR SANDMO

PRINCETON UNIVERSITY PRESS

PRINCETON AND OXFORD

Originally published in Norwegian as Samfunnsøkonomi—en idéhistorie
by Universitetsforlaget AS, Sehesteds gate 3,
P.O. Box 508 Sentrum, NO-0105 Oslo, Norway

English translation copyright © 2011 by Princeton University Press
Published by Princeton University Press, 41 William Street,
Princeton, New Jersey 08540
In the United Kingdom: Princeton University Press,
6 Oxford Street, Woodstock, Oxfordshire OX20 1TW

press.princeton.edu

Library of Congress Cataloging-in-Publication Data

Sandmo, Agnar.
[Samfunnsøkonomi—en idéhistorie. English]
Economics evolving : a history of economic thought / Agnar Sandmo.
p.   cm.
Includes bibliographical references and index.
ISBN 978-0-691-14063-6 (hardcover : alk. paper) —
ISBN 978-0-691-14842-7 (pbk. : alk. paper)
1. Economics. I. Title.
HB75.S293165 2011
330.1—dc22   2010018664

British Library Cataloging-in-Publication Data is available

This book has been composed in Palatino

Printed on acid-free paper. ∞

Printed in the United States of America

7   9   10   8   6

* Contents *

CONTENTS

* Preface *

T HE HISTORY OF ECONOMIC THOUGHT may be approached from several different perspectives. The title of this book suggests one such perspective: the scientific study of economics is a developing field where economists of the past have strived to extend their understanding of the workings of the economic system and of the policies and institutions whose adoption might seem likely to improve its performance. What is true of the past is true of the present, so that knowledge of the history of the subject makes one better able to appreciate the fact that the science of economics is still a developing one, driven forward by the realization that there are still large gaps both in theoretical insights and empirical knowledge concerning how the economy functions and how it could be made to function differently. The present financial crisis is an illustration of this, but it is in a historical perspective only one of many events that have led to revisions of the research agenda of economists.

Every history of economic thought has to be selective, both regarding time periods and personalities. The present book focuses on the period from the time of Adam Smith in the late eighteenth century to the beginning of the 1970s. The reasons for this focus are explained in the text; at this point it need only be said that this is the time when the foundations of modern economics were laid and the period whose literature can still be studied without serious difficulties by the modern reader. In terms of personalities the book is selective in giving most attention to the major economists in every period, sometimes to the neglect of lesser figures who may still have given valuable contributions to economic knowledge.

Selectivity is also an issue with regard to the topics covered. Economics is a large field and not every aspect of it can be discussed in a single book. The central core of economic theory, such as the theory of prices and markets, income distribution and employment, must obviously be included. In addition, I present some of the major economists' thoughts on problems of economic policy and social welfare and some of their reflections on wider issues such as the choice between alternative economic systems.

The style of exposition is basically nontechnical, and an attempt has been made to make the book accessible to readers who have

PREFACE

little formal training in economics but who are still interested in the history of economic ideas. There are some diagrams and a very few examples of the use of mathematical symbols, but these can easily be skipped by the reader who is not familiar with their use.

Each chapter closes with some suggestions for further reading. These are deliberately very selective; the idea is to offer some suggestions for reading the original works of the authors covered and to provide some references to the secondary literature that to me seem especially well suited for those who wish to follow up the discussion of the present text. References are given in the familiar form of "Keynes (1936)." In some cases, a book has come out in several editions; in such cases it is referred to in the form illustrated by "Jevons (1871; 1970)." Here 1871 is the year of the original publication, while 1970 is the date of the edition that I quote from. I use this form even when, as in this case, the 1970 edition is based on the second edition of Jevons's book, which came out in 1879. The reason for this is just practical: I like to keep 1871 in the reader's mind as the year of first publication, while it is obviously important to give exact page references to the edition that I use. To be precise about the different editions would have required references of the form "Jevons (1871; 1879; 1970)," and this seems excessively pedantic.

The book is partly a translation, partly a revision and extension, of a book that was written in Norwegian and published by Norwegian University Press in 2006. I received valuable comments on the manuscript of that book from many people; of these, Dagfinn Føllesdal, Einar Lie, Kalle Moene, Preben Munthe, and Erling Sandmo should be especially mentioned as well as my editor, Erik Juel. In addition, some friends and colleagues have given me advice and encouragement regarding the English edition; these include Avinash Dixit, Ray Rees, Bo Sandelin, and David Wildasin. Both my editor at Princeton University Press, Richard Baggaley, and two anonymous reviewers have given me much useful advice regarding the English version of the book. Astrid Oline Ervik helped me with the diagrams. To all of these I am extremely grateful. Last but not least my wife Tone has as always been a source of inspiration and support.

Agnar Sandmo
Bergen, December 2009

Economics Evolving

*

A Science and Its History

This is a book about the history of economic thought and the thinkers behind it. It is natural to begin such a history with some reflections on the nature of economics as a scientific discipline: What is the essential nature of economics as a field of research and study? Over the years several attempts have been made to formulate a definition of the subject that would capture its essence in a single sentence, at once striking and deep. Possibly the most famous example of such a definition was proposed by the English economist Lionel Robbins in the 1930s according to which economics was the study of human behavior as a relationship between given ends and scarce means that have alternative uses. The formulation is a perceptive one that clearly goes to the core of a set of problems that economists are interested in. Sixty years earlier, Alfred Marshall had written that economics was the study of men "in the ordinary business of life," another interesting definition that communicates something of the special nature of the field. Nevertheless, most economists would probably feel that if a noneconomist were to ask them the question "What is economics?" both Robbins's and Marshall's definitions would be much too abstract and obscure to provide the outsider with a helpful answer. A more informative response would be to reply that economics is the study of the functioning of economic life in society, adding some illustrations of central issues that economists are concerned with: What determines the prices of goods and services? What are the causes of unemployment? Which factors decide the distribution of income between individuals and families in society? Why are some countries rich and some poor? What are the effects of public policy such as taxes and public expenditure on prices and the distribution of income? What are the determinants of trade flows between countries? An answer of this kind, although longer and less elegant than the definitions of Robbins and Marshall, is certain to give the outsider a much better idea of what economics is all about.

1

The list of specialized areas could obvious be made much longer and more detailed, and if we compare such a list with the set of topics that have engaged economists over the last two and a half centuries we will quickly discover that over time a number of interesting changes have occurred regarding the focus of economic research. On the one hand, the list of topics has expanded: with the development of analytical tools, economists discovered that their discipline could be applied to a wider set of issues than before, so that a number of specializations emerged within the field. Health economics, energy economics, and financial economics are examples of specializations that have grown up during the last decades of the twentieth century. On the other hand, with the passage of time, economics has been more sharply delimited toward other fields of science, with the result that in some respects it has become narrower. Thus the economists of the eighteenth and early nineteenth centuries did not draw any clear borderlines between economics and the field that is presently known as political science, and in general expositions of the subject they also took up many problems that we now think of as belonging to philosophy, sociology, or psychology. It is also worth noting that the relative importance of subfields has varied substantially over time. The conviction of the classical economists that the study of population movements belonged to the core of economics has left few traces in modern textbooks of economics. John Maynard Keynes's analysis of the problem of unemployment in the 1930s became so influential that it led to a change in the research agenda of economics that lasted for decades. The current interest in the economic aspects of environmental problems has no counterpart in the economics literature of the nineteenth century.

A book on the history of economic thought that was written with the ambition to cover all of the special fields within the subject could hardly be written, and certainly not as a one-man undertaking; it also seems doubtful whether it would attract many readers. A more modest and reader-friendly ambition is to give an impression of the history of ideas within the most central areas of economic theory. One such central area is the functioning of the market mechanism. The problem of price determination for goods and services and the question of whether the market mechanism can be said to work for the common good have been at the core of the subject throughout its existence. Another central area is the role of the public sector in the economy, its interactions with the private sector, and the determination of a rational balance between the market and the state. A third important area of research is the study of the time path of economic development: economic fluctuations between good and bad times, unemployment, inflation, and growth of productivity and the standard of living. Broad problems of this kind will be at the center of attention in the chapters that follow.

ECONOMICS AS A SOCIAL SCIENCE

The view of economics on which this book is based is that economics is one of the social sciences that study how society works. It is possible, however, to take a broader view of the subject by considering all applications of the methods of economic theory and method. In that case it would also be necessary to cover the history of applications of economics to problems that are internal to the individual business firm, but this large and important field will be left out here. The same holds true for the discipline of accounting, which is also in the nature of a tool for better decision making within firms and organizations. Although the basic theory and analytical methods of these areas have much in common with economics as usually understood, the objective of the analysis is different: in business applications the role of economic methods is to provide a more solid foundation for decisions that further the objectives of the firm, not to lead us to better understanding of the economic life of society as a whole. Of course, the borderlines between the areas are not entirely fixed. To understand the functioning of the market mechanism, it is sometimes important for economists to try to understand the internal workings of the firm. Similarly, for business economists who study the strategic decisions in firms, it is often essential to understand the properties of the markets in which the firms operate.

The term *economics* has been used in English as a name for the subject since the 1890s. Before then, the name commonly used for it was *political economy*. The older name indicated the connections between the study of the economy and the political life and institutions of society—in modern usage between economics and political science—but it also served as a reminder that many writers on economics believed that one of its central tasks was to provide governments with a better foundation for the design of economic policy. Today, "political economy" survives partly in the name of one of the leading economic journals (*Journal of Political Economy*) and partly as a term denoting a particular approach to the study of economic policy. In several other languages there has been a similar movement away from terms that gave the impression of economics as mainly a line of inquiry in the direct service of the government.

WHY STUDY THE HISTORY OF ECONOMIC THOUGHT?

In many countries, the study of the history of economic ideas was previously considered to be an indispensable part of the training of an economist.[1] This point of view, however, has been losing ground for a number of years. Many contemporary economists take no interest in the history of their subject, and some are decidedly doubtful about the value of acquiring historical knowledge. There may be several explanations for this, but a main reason is probably that modern economists more than their predecessors regard economics as a cumulative science in which new research and new insights are based on existing knowledge that is constantly being extended and improved. In a cumulative science, therefore, new insights will always tend to make the views of earlier scientists dated and erroneous. The science as it appears today is, according to this view, the result of a systematic process of sorting whereby the valid elements of earlier thinking have been preserved, while the parts of it that were wrong or uninteresting have been discarded. If we go back fifty or a hundred years in time, however, it would have been more difficult to argue in this way. This is because, first, economic theories

[1] A British economist who got his first university position at the end of the 1940s told me that during his first interview with the department chairman he was asked, "What is your period?" In this department the position of the history of economic thought was apparently so strong that it was expected of every member of the staff that he had some kind of expertise on a particular period. However, this young economist thought that the question reflected an obsolete view of the subject and answered with great self-confidence, "It is the future!"

were formulated with a much lower degree of logical precision than is presently the case and, second, that the opportunities for systematic empirical testing of the theories were considerably poorer. It was accordingly a much more complicated issue that it now is to decide on the exact assumptions on which a theory was based, whether its construction was logically rigorous, and if it was consistent with our knowledge of empirical reality. The old views therefore tended to live on beside the new, and a well-educated economist ought therefore to have some knowledge of the economic thought of earlier times.

The adherents of the cumulative science view of economics regard this question in a different light. They see themselves primarily as problem solvers, either because they wish to contribute to the advancement of academic research or because they have a desire to contribute to practical problems of economic policy. Whichever line of problem solving they wish to pursue, it may seem clear that what they need in the form of scientific training is knowledge of the present contents of economics. That knowledge can be obtained by reading the best modern textbooks and getting acquainted with the research literature of the last twenty to thirty years. But a study of the older literature is only likely to convince one that what is valid in it has been restated later in a better, clearer, and more general way. The American economist Kenneth Boulding (1971) has told the story of an economist who said that he had no interest in the history of thought because it was only about "the wrong opinions of dead men."

It is clearly undeniable that economics has many of the features of a cumulative science, so that it may be worth reflecting on the question of why it should be worthwhile to spend time on the study of its intellectual history. Here are some reasons why it might reasonable to use some time and effort getting to know the history of economics.

1. It is fun. Anyone with some familiarity with modern economics should find it interesting to read about the thinkers and theories of the past, and some will no doubt feel that time spent on the history of economic ideas does not need any further justification. The opinions of dead men may be fascinating to study even if one believes them to be wrong. Einstein's discoveries did not turn Newton into an irrelevant character in history; in a

5

similar vein, Paul Samuelson and other twentieth-century economists did not make the life and work of Adam Smith a subject of no relevance and interest.

2. Some knowledge of the history of thought should form part of the liberal education of an economist. In books and articles—sometimes even in the popular press—one comes across terms like "Adam Smith's invisible hand," "Walrasian equilibrium," "Pareto optimality," "Pigouvian taxes," and "Keynesian policies." A well-educated economist clearly ought to know something about the persons that the terms refer to.

3. Some familiarity with the history of thought contributes to a better understanding of the fact that the discipline of economics is in a permanent process of change and development, thereby leading to a better understanding of the nature of economic research. The common nonhistorical way of teaching economics may easily give a false impression of the subject as one that has found its final form. The history of thought makes one realize that economic science has always progressed through the efforts of people who have seen that it contains deficiencies and errors.

These are three good reasons for studying the history of economic thought. Regarding the last of the three, there can be little doubt that economics in general and economic theory in particular have never been as well developed as they now are. Students who read modern textbooks in macro- and microeconomics, public finance, and international trade clearly acquire more solid knowledge and better analytical skills than those who read the textbooks of fifty or one hundred years ago.[2] One of the benefits to be gained by getting acquainted with the older literature is a better understanding of the internal dynamics of the subject. The concepts and theories that today's students encounter during their first year are the results of the work of earlier generations of economists on the frontiers of research.

---

[2] A small reservation may be in order at this point: they get a better insight in the problems that are taken up *in today's textbooks*. But if one goes back to a book like Marshall's *Principles of Economics* from 1890, one will find that this book considers a number of issues that do not receive much attention in modern expositions. A comparison of then and now that focuses exclusively on the treatment of modern topics in the older literature will therefore be systematically biased in favor of the present.

Consider the following example: one of the first theoretical concepts that one encounters in the study of economic theory is the demand curve, that is, the graphical representation of the connection between the quantity demanded and the price of a commodity. But the demand curve is not something that actually exists "out there"; it is a theoretical construction created by economists to understand how markets function. When in 1838 the demand curve was drawn (or at least appeared in print) for the first time it was a great scientific breakthrough! The realization that concepts and theories that today are regarded as elementary and obvious were once major intellectual challenges for the sharpest minds among economists gives us an important insight into the nature of the research process. It also shows that what presently appears to be simple elements in the theory may not in fact be quite as self-evident as we tend to believe, and this recognition may in turn come to deepen our insights in the modern version of economic theory.

The understanding that economics has developed as a continuous process which continues today is in itself an inspiration for those who wish to attempt to gain a better knowledge of the subject and perhaps even contribute to its further development. In addition, it could even be the case that the study of the older literature may encourage new research by the discovery and reconsideration of problems and fruitful insights that have been neglected in contemporary work.

STYLES IN THE HISTORY OF ECONOMIC THOUGHT

There are several ways to present the history of economic thought. One possibility is to analyze the changing nature of economic theory in conjunction with the social and economic development of society, while another is to emphasize economic thinking as part of the main currents of philosophical and political ideas. Yet another alternative is to emphasize the internal dynamics of the science where new insights and results emerge as a consequence of economists' awareness of the shortcomings of the present state of the subject. The main emphasis in the following will be on the third of these perspectives, but in a number of cases it is also necessary to draw on other approaches to reach a clear understanding of why a particular theoretical reorientation took place. When in the 1930s John Maynard Keynes worked out his new analysis of the causes of unemployment it was in part motivated by what he saw as the weaknesses of existing theory but to a large extent also by the mass unemployment that he observed both in Britain and other countries. If in addition we are to understand the background of some of his policy proposals for a way out of the crisis it is also useful to have some knowledge of the attitudes to social engineering and expert rule that were so influential in the intellectual and political climate of the interwar period.

In earlier times it was common to judge the thought of previous generations of economists from what one considered to be their own preconditions without relating them to modern theory. This approach easily leads to what one may call scientific *relativism:* all theories become correct and valuable relative to the context in which the authors lived and worked. This point of view may come to imply a complete denial of the cumulative nature of economics and consequently of the possibility of progress in economics, a point of view that most people today would consider to be an unreasonable position to hold. However, as late as 1931 the historian of thought Alexander Gray was able to write that "economic science, if it be a science, differs from other sciences in this, that there is no inevitable advance from less to greater certainty; there is no ruthless tracking down of truth which, once unbared, shall be truth to all times to the complete confusion of any contrary doctrine" (Gray 1931; 1980, pp. 2–3).

Gray's meaning may perhaps not be entirely clear. If he simply means to say that the search for eternal truths is made difficult or impossible by the fact that the economy and its institutions are in a process of constant change, it is not difficult to agree with him in principle. But if he is to be interpreted more generally as saying that there is no scientific progress in economics, it becomes more problematic to support his view. On the contrary, the following chapters will present a number of examples of how economists have been able to achieve a more secure understanding of the assumptions underlying their theories and of the connections between their assumptions and conclusions. Moreover, there can be no doubt that great progress has occurred in regard to the production of knowledge about the empirical facts of economic life.

Beginning in the 1960s, the common approach to the history of economic thought changed as many authors began to describe the theories of past economists in a modern theoretical framework so as to make them more easily comprehensible to modern readers.[3] This makes it in a sense easier to understand the relationship between new and old economic theories and to use one's insights from the study of the history of thought to understand the modern version of the subject. At the same time, this may easily foster an attitude of scientific *absolutism:* one reads the work of the older authors as if they were exam papers written by students who have had no opportunity of getting acquainted with the contents of the reading list.

It is not practically feasible to judge the work of past economists entirely on the basis of the state of the subject in their own time; it is simply not possible for us as moderns to disregard our knowledge of all that has happened during the period between their own time and ours. A pure relativist attitude is therefore impossible. However, scientific absolutism is an approach with its own difficulties. One may to an excessive degree come to regard the past through the lenses of the present, although this might result in an incomplete understanding of the historical foundations of economic thought. It may be argued that this does not matter as long as the interpretations are interesting. But in taking this line one runs the risk of overlooking other contributions by these authors that are as interesting as the ones that can be "translated" into modern scientific language and that might possibly provide more valuable suggestions for future research. A more fruitful attitude consists of combining elements of relativism and absolutism and approaching the older literature in the same way that one ought to approach the new: understanding but critical.

Theories and Facts

An economic theory is a set of hypotheses about the functioning of parts or the whole of the economic system. A particular

---

[3] A textbook that did much to change the literature on the history of thought in this direction is Mark Blaug's *Economic Theory in Retrospect* that appeared in its first edition in 1962.

theory may concern a limited set of questions, like the reactions of consumer demand to changes in prices and income, or it may be a more comprehensive analysis of how prices are determined in an economy with many producers, consumers, and markets. Theoretical research aims to improve current theories in terms of generality and logical standards and to develop new theories that either concern novel aspects of economic life or types of economic activity that have so far escaped the attention of theorists. Empirical research can simply take the form of producing data or have the more ambitious aim of testing economic theories—deciding whether or not the theories fit the facts.

The history of economic thought has traditionally been a history of economic *theories*. This is not because economics is nothing but theory. Anyone who has turned the pages of Adam Smith's *Wealth of Nations* (1776) will have discovered that his arguments are based on an impressive array of historical and institutional facts, and a perusal of the most recent volumes of a selection of academic journals will show clearly that empirical analysis occupies a prominent place in modern economic research. Nevertheless, a historical review of the empirical findings of economists through the ages would easily become both excessively long and probably not very interesting. The main reason for this is that the results of empirical research are time specific and heavily dependent on the political and institutional setting of the time. Still, there is a good deal of empirical research that is of more general interest and some of this will be covered in the chapters to follow. Moreover, there is a significant degree of interaction between theory and empirical findings. Although some economic theorists have received most of their inspiration simply from reading the works of other theorists, in the last resort all theories derive from empirical observations that economists feel that they have a need to explain and understand. The theories that emerge from this process will in turn suggest new hypotheses about the functioning of the economy, which can be tested against new observations. Indirectly, therefore, empirical facts and judgments do enter into the development of economic theories, although we will not always be able to account in detail for the specific facts that have inspired the theorists.

It was not until the twentieth century that some economists began to interest themselves more systematically in the statistical problems that arise when one tries to put economic theories to the test. Their efforts led to the recognition that the interpretation of empirical relationships involved a series of methodological problems that needed to be solved before one could draw firm conclusions from the study of the statistical material. Some of the work that was done on these problems will be reviewed in chapter 16.

A SPECIAL FIELD

From one point of view, the history of economic thought is a field of specialization within economics in the same way as are international economics, public finance, or labor economics. The literature is written partly by specialists in the field, partly by economists who primarily work in other areas but who take an interest in the history of the subject (as when a public finance specialist writes about some nineteenth-century contribution to the theory of taxation). But most of the contributors to the literature are specialists on the history of economic thought who have their own specialized journals, research conferences, and scientific organizations. There is a steady flow of new publications in the form of articles and books that contribute to new insights in the history of economics as a science.

However, the history of economic thought is a *special* special field. It encourages one to reflect on the contents and development of the subject, while a review of its historical development may serve as an introduction to economics that is different from that of the standard introductory textbook. This introduction must necessarily be organized in a particular way: instead of presenting a first view of economics in terms of the inherent logic of the subject matter, it proceeds in terms of the chronology of theoretical innovations. The chronology of course has its own internal logic by the fact that each generation of researchers relate to the body of knowledge that already exists. The study of the history of economic ideas is therefore a natural supplement to the standard program of study, while at the same time it can function as an introduction to economics for noneconomists.

Any account of the history of economic thought must be selective, not only in terms of topics but also in terms of persons: the number of individuals who have made significant contributions to economics is much too large for a discussion of them to be contained within a single book. In the present book, the guiding principle behind the selection of authors has been that the chief interest of modern economists lies in being informed about the thinkers that have had the greatest influence on the subject as we know it today. As an example, one of the reasons why David Ricardo is a central figure in this context is that he is regarded as the originator of the theory of comparative advantage, which is familiar to anyone with an elementary knowledge of the theory of international trade. All modern treatments of international economics refer to Ricardo as the father of the theory, although some historians of thought have argued that the basic elements in Ricardo's theory can be found in the works of earlier authors. It is an interesting research project to clarify the contributions of Ricardo's forerunners, but this type of problem will not receive much attention here. Whatever others may have thought about comparative advantage, Ricardo's name is the one that is familiar to modern economists; it is therefore the natural focus of interest for a history of thought. (In addition there are, as we shall see later, a number of other reasons to pay attention to Ricardo.)

In this book, therefore, we shall concentrate our attention on the great names in the development of economics—on individuals like Adam Smith, David Ricardo, Léon Walras, and Irving Fisher. In a more complete coverage one ought also to discuss the contributions of a series of economists whose work in a historical context may be of great interest even though they do not have the same scientific status. The neglect of some important economists becomes more glaring as we get close to our own times, above all because the number of economists who are active in research is larger than ever before. But the ambition to include more names would, in a relatively short exposition, easily lead to a situation where more elaborate discussions of individuals and ideas get crowded out in favor of brief mention of names, titles, and dates. Hopefully, the reader will be encouraged to follow up some of the references to the literature and go on to further study of particular authors or periods. In that case, maybe he or she will discover some of the pleasure in the study of economics that Keynes expresses when he describes it as, "our own most agreeable branch of the moral sciences, in which theory and fact, intuitive imagination and practical judgement, are blended in a manner comfortable to the human intellect" (Keynes 1933, p. 239).

FURTHER READING

There are a number of good expositions of the history of economics. The towering classic in the field is the book by Joseph Schumpeter (1954) whose work will be further considered in chapter 14. It is an impressive book, although many are likely to feel that it contains too much detail. As a reference, especially as regards the older (pre–Adam Smith) literature, it is extremely useful.

A light and entertaining exposition is Heilbroner (1999) where the emphasis is on economists' broader visions of society and the conduct of economic policy and less on their contributions to science in a more specific sense. Comprehensive treatments in modern textbooks are provided by Spiegel (1991) (which has particularly extensive references to the literature), Ekelund and Hébert (1997), Backhouse (2002), and Screpanti and Zamagni (2005). Blaug (1962; 1997) is a more analytic exposition, containing modern mathematical representations of older theories; the book also includes reader's guides to some of the great books of the past. The volume by Niehans (1990) goes further in the direction of mathematical modeling of past theories; this book has a particularly good coverage of the period 1940–80. To proceed even further along the mathematical road one may consult Negishi (1989), but this book only covers the literature until the beginning of the twentieth century. A highly personal treatment is the book by Lionel Robbins (1998), which is based on his lectures in his legendary course at the London School of Economics. The style is informal and amusing, and the lectures include advice to students about the purchase of first editions of economics books from the eighteenth century. Steven G. Medema and Warren J. Samuels have edited a volume, *The History of Economic Thought: A Reader* (2003), that contains selections from the works of a number of writers from Aristotle to Keynes.

Palgrave's Dictionary of Political Economy was first published in the 1890s, and a revised edition came out in the 1920s. A new and much enlarged edition of this important work of reference was published in 1987 as *The New Palgrave Dictionary of Economics,* and the second edition of this was published in 2008 under the editorship of Steven N. Durlauf and Lawrence E. Blume. This eight-volume work is available both on paper and on the internet (at www.palgrave.com) and contains numerous excellent articles on individual economists and special topics, often with a historical perspective. Leading journals in the field include *History of Political Economy, Journal of the History of Economic Thought,* and *European Journal of the History of Economic Thought.* A comprehensive website for the history of economic thought is operated by the Center for the History of Political Economy at Duke University; see www.econ.duke.edu/CHOPE. This site also provides numerous links to related websites.

CHAPTER 2

Before Adam Smith

Descriptions and analyses of economic decisions and the economic organization of society can be traced far back in history; examples can be found in the Bible and in the works of Plato and Aristotle. Production and trade have always been important parts of the life of society, and after social development had reached the stage that allowed time for analysis and reflection, it was natural that some individuals would devote themselves to systematic thinking about issues related to economics. It is not unreasonable, however, to maintain that it was only in the eighteenth century that the field of economics emerged as a separate discipline, a different field of specialization from those of philosophy, history, and law. Adam Smith's *The Wealth of Nations* (1776) may be the first general work in which the modern economist will find it easy to recognize the field and be able to relate the exposition to the present understanding of economics. In order to give an account of the development of economic thought that may help the reader to acquire a broader perspective and deeper understanding of modern economics, it might therefore be natural to start with Smith. But to draw an exact starting line for the history of ideas is obviously impossible. We begin, therefore, with a bird's-eye and selective view on economic thought before Adam Smith.

Economic Thought in Ancient Times

Some elementary economic theories have been known and generally accepted for centuries, and we can find expressions of them in some of the oldest written sources that we possess. A famous example from the Old Testament is the story of Joseph in Egypt. Joseph interpreted one of Pharaoh's dreams as a prediction that seven fat years would be followed by seven lean years. Acting on the authority of the pharaoh, he used the prediction as a basis for purchasing and building up stores of grain during the fat years. This is described in Genesis 41:

And he gathered up all the food of the seven years which were in the land of Egypt, and laid up the food in the cities; the food of the field, which was round about every city, laid he up in the same.

By acting in this way he managed to have grain for distribution to the people when the lean years actually arrived:

And the famine was over all the face of the earth; and Joseph opened all the storehouses and sold unto the Egyptians. And the famine waxed sore in the land of Egypt.

The story can be understood as an example of the analysis of price formation as a result of the interplay of supply and demand. Joseph saw that a reduction in the future supply of grain would lead to higher prices and economic hardship, and he used this insight to buy grain when prices were low in order to provide a greater supply when the lean years arrived. Through this policy it would be possible to achieve the result of lower prices and higher consumption than would otherwise have been possible in a situation of crop failure. It should be emphasized that the Bible's perspective on Joseph's actions is not that he was a successful grain speculator; what he wished was to help those who would otherwise starve during the period of the lean years. Nevertheless it is natural to argue that Joseph's strategy of buying and selling makes little sense unless one assumes that he had reflected on the underlying economic mechanisms.

In ancient Greece it is especially in the works of the philosopher Aristotle (approx. 384–322 BC) that we find examples of reasoning about economic issues.[1] The best known may be his attempt to analyze exchange transactions between two individuals. In his *Ethics* he recognizes that exchange, or trade, can only come about if there is a potential surplus from the transaction in which both parties can share. He understands the importance of money as a means to simplify exchange transactions by allowing all prices to be expressed in the same unit. His work also contains formulations that, with some good will, can be seen as an early statement of the principle of diminishing marginal utility. But neither Aristotle nor the other philosophers of ancient Greece or Rome

---

[1] The word *economy* comes from Greek, where *oikonomia* can be taken to mean "domestic management" or "management of a household" (*oikos* means house, while *nomia* is derived from *nemein*—to manage).

made any attempt to understand the economic system as a whole. Many of them do demonstrate an interest in economic questions, but it would be misleading to argue that these authors had developed systematic theories about the functioning of the economy.[2] Their economic theories remain fragments that have not been integrated into any wider framework of economic theory.

The Scholastics

The group of thinkers known as the scholastics, or schoolmen, were mostly priests and teachers at medieval universities from the thirteenth century onward. Their approach to the study of the market economy was from the beginning an ethical one. As priests, their task was among other things to provide guidance regarding the determination of the just price. In order to understand their interest in this question, it is not sufficient just to focus on their theological background. It is also important to keep in mind that economic transactions in medieval times as a rule did not take place within the framework of well-organized markets. In such markets one could count on competition to keep a check on prices and see to it that buyers and sellers could trade under the same conditions. However, many transactions took place between individual buyers and sellers who operated in relative isolation from other economic agents. Under such conditions it was clearly possible for one of the parties to a transaction to exploit the other through a stronger bargaining position or better information. To determine a just price is then no simple matter, for the buyer is interested in a price that is as low as possible, while the seller is interested in the highest possible price. The point of view taken by the scholastics was that the question of the just price had to be answered on the basis of a concept of the interests of society. It is remarkable that the scholastics were not satisfied with an answer that was founded solely on moral and theological principles. Gradually, they also found it necessary to acquire

---

[2] The Roman author Pliny the Elder (AD 24–79) expressed a way of thinking that reminds one of the modern economic theory of optimization when, in his great work on natural history, he wrote, "One must cultivate well, but not too well, because this brings losses."

empirical knowledge of how transactions actually occurred and how the markets functioned. Their studies in this area led them to the view that the just price was "the natural price." The natural price was that which would emerge under free and effective competition, unaffected by monopoly, unnecessary resource waste, or deceitful behavior. In the writings of the scholastics one can also find the view that this price is not only determined by the cost of production, but that the consumers' perception of the utility of a good also plays a role for the natural price. The respective roles of cost and utility in price determination became one of the central themes of research in economic theory in later times, and the issue was not resolved until the later part of the nineteenth century.

Posterity has focused much attention on the attitude of the scholastics—and more generally of the church—to the charging of interest. Originally, the Catholic Church had, like Islam, a prohibition against interest. Interest was seen as exploitation of the weak (the debtor) by the strong (the creditor). But the scholastics gradually developed a more balanced view of this question. Interest was justified if it reflected actual costs, such as the risk incurred by the creditor in lending money, or even in the form of the rate of return that the creditor had to forego by not being able to undertake investments on his own account.

Even if the economic theories of the scholastics were fragmentary, they nevertheless represent an attempt to establish a more systematic body of economic thought, and because of this they deserve a place in the history of economic ideas. Possibly their most important contribution is the idea that economic life obeys certain laws that can be studied by scientific methods. It is in this respect that their thinking represents the greatest step forward relative to that of their great teacher in secular matters, Aristotle.

MERCANTILISM

The concept of mercantilism as a characterization of the economic policy regime that dominated Europe in the seventeenth and eighteenth centuries originated with Adam Smith, and his use of it formed part of his criticism of the predominant views of economics and economic policy in his own time. Mercantilism was a political ideology rather than a theoretical system, and the term may easily give a misleading impression of general agreement among a large group of writers on economics who in many respects had relatively little in common. Nevertheless, they shared some fundamental convictions that justify the common view of them as a particular school of thought. Moreover, mercantilism is of importance in the history of thought because of its role as a point of reference for Adam Smith and in more recent debates about international trade, where some types of trade policies have been characterized as neomercantilist.

Mercantilism was above all a set of economic policy prescriptions for rulers whose aim was to promote their country's interests, its wealth, and power relative to other nations. But the "country" and "nation" was in the world of the mercantilists the same as the state or the individuals in power; the time had not yet come when the interests of the country were to be identified with those of the people or the general public. A crucial element of mercantilist thinking was that the production of all goods ought primarily to take place, when at all possible, in the country itself. Imports ought to be restricted as much as possible and above all to raw materials, which could then be further processed in the domestic economy. For the domestic economy to thrive it was essential that there be sufficient money to support the payments system, and money was identified with the precious metals of gold and silver. If the country did not possess its own sources of gold and silver it would have to acquire them through international transactions, and a central aim of economic policy was therefore to create a surplus in the balance of trade that would imply an inflow of gold and silver from abroad. To modern economists this line of thought may appear to be fundamentally wrongheaded if the aim of the government is to promote the welfare of the nation. However, it makes more sense if one reads it as a set of guidelines for rulers who are intent on promoting their country's military and economic power relative to that of other countries.

The popular view of the economic policy of the mercantilists has been that they identified the country's wealth with its stores of precious metals. Is this view justified? The answer must be yes, but with some qualifications. There were mercantilist writers who emphasized that the wealth of a country also included natural resources and real capital, but this was an insight that was often overshadowed by the attention that was focused on the accumulation of gold and silver. An implication of the dominant view was that the government ought to pursue an active economic policy to stimulate export and nurture domestic industries that competed with foreign firms in the same industry while limiting imports.[3] It was against this aspect of mercantilist thinking that Adam Smith above all came to direct his polemic.

The ideology of mercantilism was not erected on a unified theoretical basis, and among the many authors who discussed economic issues during this period, one can identify a variety of views about the functioning of the economic system. Some of them promote views that can be seen as early signs that a shift in theory and ideology was under way, one that we now associate with Adam Smith and the classical school. One of the most important of the persons representing this period of transition was Richard Cantillon.

RICHARD CANTILLON

Richard Cantillon (168?–1734) was Irish by birth but led a vagrant life in several European countries. He lived for many years in Paris where during the years 1715–20 he accumulated a great personal fortune by trading in stocks and foreign exchange. Besides his practical activities he also pursued his intellectual interests. He was very well read, and he also found time to write down his thoughts regarding economic life in his book *Essai sur la nature du commerce en général* (*Essay on the Nature of Commerce*). The circumstances surrounding the publication of this book are slightly mysterious. It did not appear until 1755, twenty years after the death of its author, and it has never become quite clear whether the French version is the original one or if it is the translation of an earlier English manuscript that has never been found.

---

[3] Thomas Mun, who was identified by Adam Smith as one of the leading mercantilist authors, wrote in 1664 that "the ordinary means therefore to encrease our wealth and treasure is by Forraign Trade, wherein wee must ever observe this rule; to sell more to strangers yearly than wee consume of theirs in value" (Mun 1664; 1895, p. 7).

Cantillon's *Essay* contains several important contributions to economic theory. First of all he develops a theory about the determination of relative prices. Starting from the assumption that there are two basic factors of production, capital and agricultural land, he argues that the structure of the economy—the allocation of resources between agriculture and manufacturing—as well as the prices of agricultural and manufacturing goods are determined by the technology of production. Cantillon was also interested in the distribution of income between what he saw as the three economic classes in society: landowners, farmers, and workers. In order to explain this distribution he developed a theoretical framework for analysis of the economic circulation in the economy. In this framework the economy's aggregate demand is always equal to the sum of incomes. It terms of promoting a better understanding of the interrelationships of economic life, this was a big step forward relative to earlier writers, and many historians of economic thought have emphasized that Cantillon can be said to have been the first to formulate a general equilibrium model of the economy. The characteristic feature of such a model is that, at least in principle, it describes all relationships between consumption and production in the economy. In modern terminology we might say that he had developed an early version of an input-output model, although in a highly simplified form. He was not himself capable of giving analytical shape to this model, but modern historians of economics have shown that it is possible to construct a mathematical model that represents the verbal reasoning in Cantillon's work.

Cantillon's practical experience from the world of finance made it especially natural for him to reflect on the roles played by money and financial assets in the economy. In this area also he provided a number of important insights. He distinguished clearly between short-term and long-term effects of changes in the stock of money, and he studied the relationship between the domestic money market, the balance of payments, and the rates of exchange. As we would have said today, he had a clear understanding of the distinction between real and monetary magnitudes in the economy. In spite of this, in his general attitude to economic issues Cantillon remained a mercantilist: a successful economic policy was, in his view, one that led to a large domestic stock of gold and silver.

21

David Hume

David Hume (1711–76) is best known as one of the great names in the history of philosophy, with *A Treatise of Human Nature* (1741–42) as his most important single work. But like many of the great Enlightenment intellectuals, he was interested in a number of different fields of study, and in his book *Political Discourses* (1752) he also wrote about economic problems. One would perhaps imagine that someone whose interests lay in the theory of knowledge and moral philosophy would select his economic topics from areas that were somehow related to these, but this is not what Hume did. His most important contributions, which have ensured that his name is still mentioned in modern textbooks, are concerned with monetary theory for an open economy. In contrast to Cantillon, Hume had no practical experience from financial transactions. His analysis was important above all because its simplifications made the theoretical structure of his reasoning stand out much more clearly than in the work of previous authors. This may explain some of his appeal to later generations of abstract model builders.

What is the effect of changes in the stock of money on the real economy? Hume was the first to provide a clear and simple answer: none! Prices, including the prices of the factors of production such as wages, will be proportional to the stock of money: the larger the quantity of money in relation to the volume of transactions, the higher will prices be. But this cannot possibly have any real economic consequences. Hume compares the effects of different nominal price levels with the transition from Roman to Arabic numerals, which does not affect the elementary principles of arithmetic. So what is the essential role of money? Money, says Hume, is not itself a wheel in the economic machinery of society; it is the oil that makes the wheels turn more quickly—just like the Arabic system makes it easier to carry out calculations. In this line of reasoning we see for the first time the contours of what later became known as the quantity theory of money.

But the simple theory is only valid in the long run. In the short run, according to Hume, the relationship between prices and the quantity of money is more complex, since it takes time before all prices fully adjust to a change in the stock of money. During the process of adjustment there will accordingly be real economic effects of changes in the quantity of money. An increased stock of money will stimulate economic activity, while a fall will lead to a contraction. The best-known part of Hume's theory in this area is his analysis of international adjustment following an increase in the domestic money stock. He assumes that there are two countries, the domestic, or home, country and the foreign country, both of which have monetary systems that are based on gold and whose price levels to begin with are the same. Suppose now that the domestic quantity of money increases, following an increase in the country's stock of gold. This leads to an increase of the domestic price level, which implies that the home country's goods become more expensive abroad, while the foreign country's goods become more competitive in the domestic economy. The home country accordingly experiences a deficit in the balance of trade, which must be financed through an outflow of gold. This means that the quantity of money in the home country falls, while it increases in the foreign country. Accordingly, the domestic price level falls while foreign prices increase. This process will continue until the price levels at home and abroad are once more the same. Hume was not the first to describe this so-called specie-flow mechanism, but his exposition of it was so clear and pointed that it had a great influence on the thinking of later economists—in spite of the strong simplifications that it involved, particularly in abstracting from transactions costs.

That a philosopher like Hume should concern himself with questions of this kind, throws an interesting light on the status of economics, or political economy, at that time. It was not yet recognized as a separate science, and Hume obviously did not feel that he moved outside the borders of "his own field" when he explored this area of the social sciences. Academic specialization was not yet so entrenched that a thinker and scientist endowed with talent and intellectual curiosity could not engage in philosophy (in the more narrow modern sense), history, and political science as well as economics. As a matter of fact, his broad field of interest was one that Hume shared with some of his great predecessors among English philosophers: both Thomas Hobbes (1588–1679) and John Locke (1632–1704) wrote about economic issues. One of Hobbes's interests was taxation (he argued in favor of taxing consumption rather than income), while Locke among other things was an early contributor to the quantity theory of money and prices.

François Quesnay and the Physiocrats

François Quesnay (1694–1774) is one of the most remarkable characters in the history of economic thought. He worked as a physician in Paris, and his reputation was so high that he came to be consulted by individuals of the very highest ranks within the French nobility. In 1749 he took up residence in the royal palace at Versailles, where he became the personal physician of Madame de Pompadour, the mistress of King Louis XV. He established close contacts with some of the leading intellectuals of the Enlightenment and began gradually to develop an interest in economic questions. His first contribution to the literature of economics appeared in the form of an article in Diderot's famous *Encyclopédie* in 1756, at the mature age of sixty-two. His later fame rests entirely on his *Tableau Economique* (1759), a sort of tabular construction showing the flows of commodities and incomes in the economy.[4] It is related to the earlier model of Cantillon, but it is more detailed, and Quesnay also made an attempt to estimate the coefficients in the model on the basis of empirical knowledge of the French economy. With a little good will we may thus regard Quesnay as a forerunner both of modern national accounting and input-output analysis and as an early econometrician. He also believed that his tables could be used to analyze the effects of public policy, to the extent that political intervention changed the fixed coefficients on which his model was based.

As a supplement to his tables, Quesnay wrote down a series of "maxims" for economic policy. One of these maxims was that the government must be aware that agriculture was the main foundation of economic wealth. Consequently, a policy that was good for agriculture was also good for France. More influential was another maxim which said that the best economic system that the government could promote was free competition and

---

[4] "Tableau" can be translated as "table" but also as "panorama" or "view," words that may be better in capturing the intention behind Quesnay's geometric constructions.

free trade—"laissez faire, laisser passer," as some of his disciples expressed it.[5] Quesnay must probably have meant that the former maxim was consistent with the latter, but he gave no justification for this view, nor did he develop a more systematic economic theory to support his maxims. But he became the center of an enthusiastic group of followers, and it was this group of liberal thinkers that became known as the physiocrats and may be the first example of a clearly defined "school" of economic thought. During the 1760s and 1770s this group had considerable influence on economic policy in France and other European countries. Adam Smith visited the group during his stay in Paris in the 1760s, and the discussions that he had with them were clearly important for his own analysis of economic policy in the *Wealth of Nations*.

Evaluations of Quesnay's importance for the development of economics have varied considerably. Some writers have considered his *Tableau* as an important forerunner of modern general equilibrium theory, and Joseph Schumpeter called him one of the giants of science. Others have seen his efforts more as an interesting but peculiar sidetrack. As an early representative of quantitative economic model building he has in any case secured a name for himself in the history of economic thought.

A.R.J. TURGOT

Anne Robert Jacques Turgot (1727–81) is usually considered to have been a member of the physiocratic school, and at any rate he was in deep sympathy with the liberal economic attitudes of the physiocrats. He studied theology, but he later resigned from his position in the church and entered the civil service. There he embarked on a brilliant career that reached its peak when he was appointed minister of finance under Louis XVI, the last king before the great revolution. However, his ideas about economic reform, which went in the direction of deregulation and liberalization of economic life, did not achieve sufficient political accep-

---

[5] A direct translation of this expression would be something like "let it go, let it pass," which sounds awkward and artificial. But the translation is actually superfluous, for "laissez-faire" has become an international term to characterize a policy that leaves the economy to the free play of market forces.

tance, and in 1776 he had to resign after only a couple of years in his ministerial position.

Many of Turgot's writings reflect his preoccupation with concrete practical problems that he encountered in his capacity as a civil servant, and these are of less interest today. But while he was the chief administrative officer of the district of Limoges he wrote a book that is of more general interest. His *Réflexions sur la formation et la distribution des richesses* (*Reflections on the Formation and Distribution of Wealth*, 1766) is said to have originated as a sort of roadmap for two Chinese students, Ko and Yong, who had come to France to study its economy and society. It builds in part on physiocratic ideas, but it also contains parts that are truly original and have ensured that Turgot, in addition to his position in the political history of France, also occupies a prominent place in the history of economics.

The original elements in the book concern the analysis of investment and production, where Turgot moved beyond the basically static analysis in the work of Quesnay and the physiocrats. In Quesnay's *Tableau* it had been assumed that the input of capital per unit of land was constant. Turgot assumed instead that it was variable: saving contributed to capital accumulation, which in turn increased capital intensity and productivity, both in agriculture and other industries. But with increasing capital intensity there will come a decline in the rate of return on new investment. This is an example of a more general law of production, the law of decreasing returns, that Turgot probably was the first to formulate in a clear and precise manner. He writes that to sow seed on an unploughed piece of land in general is a waste, but when it has been ploughed once, the yield increases, and it increases further when the land has been ploughed a second or third time. Up to a certain point the yield will increase more than in proportion to the input of labor and capital, but beyond this point the increase will become less, and the soil will eventually become so exhausted that there will be no further increase in yield.

What is the optimal use of capital in agriculture?[6] Turgot points out that it would be a mistake to believe that the optimum would

---

[6] Ploughing implies the use of both labor and capital, but Turgot seems in this connection to assume that the ratio of capital to labor is constant, so that the extent of ploughing can be measured via the use of capital.

correspond to the level of input that maximizes the increase in production, or to use the modern term, the marginal productivity. The correct conclusion, he argues, is that the greatest surplus is attained when the value of production minus the interest on capital is as large as possible. This means that the use of capital should be increased as long as the marginal productivity is greater than the rate of interest. The optimum would then be achieved at the point where the two are equal.

In this analysis Turgot is far ahead of his time, but otherwise he did not make any significant contributions to the development of economic theory. He probably had the intellectual resources to do so, but his busy administrative and political life did not allow him the time. To call him, as Schumpeter (1954, p. 247) does, "one of the greatest scientific economists of all times," is a drastic exaggeration. The scientific contribution that he did make was, however, of great importance for the development that took place with the work of Adam Smith and his successors.

AUTHORS OF PARADOXES: DANIEL BERNOULLI AND THE MARQUIS DE CONDORCET

The economic thinkers that we have presented so far in this chapter made their contributions in the most central fields of economics: the theory of price formation, the role of money in the economy, and the theory of growth and development. But there were some individuals that took an interest in more specific and narrow problems where they provided an analysis of a depth and significance that have secured them a permanent place in the history of economics. Prominent persons of this kind are Daniel Bernoulli and the Marquis de Condorcet, each of whom formulated a paradox that would present a challenge to later theorists.

Daniel Bernoulli (1700–82) was born in the Netherlands and educated as a mathematician and scientist. In 1725 he was called to a position at the imperial Russian court in St. Petersburg, and it was there that he was confronted with a problem concerning the valuation of a game of money. The structure of the game is as follows: Peter asks Paul to participate in a game of gambling against the payment of a fee. The game begins by Peter tossing a coin; if it comes up heads at the first toss, Paul is paid 2 ducats, and the game is over. If the coin comes up tails at the first toss, Peter tosses it once more. If heads come up, Paul is paid $2^2 = 4$ ducats; if tails come up the game continues and gives Paul a gain of $2^3 = 8$ ducats if heads come up at the third toss. Thus the game continues. The problem is now: What is the value of participating in the game, or in other words, what is the size of the fee that Paul should be willing to pay to participate in the game? Some people had maintained that the fee should be computed as the mathematical expectation of the game. But here the paradox arises: the probability of heads at the first toss is equal to ½, for heads to come up for the first time at the second toss is $(1/2)^2$ and so on. When we compute the expected gain, we easily see that it is equal to

$$(1/2) \times 2 + (1/2)^2 \times 2^2 + (1/2)^3 \times 2^3 = 1 + 1 + 1 + \ldots,$$

which is a sum that does not converge to any finite number. Therefore, according to this view Paul should be willing to pay a fee of any size—e.g. a million ducats—to be allowed to participate, since the expected gain would in any case be larger than the fee. But this conclusion, which is known as the St. Petersburg paradox, clearly goes against common sense and practical experience: nobody would believe that Paul would actually be willing to pay more than a rather small amount to take part in the game. Bernoulli's pathbreaking contribution was the hypothesis that he introduced in order to make the theory consistent with observed facts. He assumed that Paul's valuation of the game would be based not on the expected monetary gain but on the expected *utility*. His postulate was that utility was a magnitude that increased with the magnitude of the gain, but less that proportionally with the amount. He assumed in other words that marginal utility was decreasing, and this would later turn out to be a central and fruitful hypothesis in economic theory. On the basis of the more special assumption that utility was proportional to the logarithm of the amount, Bernoulli (1738; 1954) showed that Paul's willingness to pay would only be a rather modest amount.

Marie Jean Antoine Nicolas de Caritat, Marquis de Condorcet, (1743–94) was a French mathematician and philosopher who also took a strong interest in political science and economics. His most famous contribution (Condorcet 1785) concerned an issue that is most naturally thought of as a problem in political science,[7] but which almost two hundred years later was taken up and developed further by the American economist Kenneth Arrow (see chapter 17). The question that he raised was whether majority voting—as in a committee or a parliamentary assembly—would lead to rational decisions from a collective or social viewpoint. Condorcet analyzed the problem through the following example: a committee is to make a choice between a certain number of alternatives; in the example there are three committee members and three alternatives, denoted A, B, and C. Let us further assume that the three members' preferences over the alternatives (from the best to the worst) are given by the rankings (A-B-C), (B-C-A) and (C-A-B), respectively. If, in the first round of voting, the two alternatives are A and B, A will be chosen by two votes to one, and alternative B has accordingly been eliminated. In the next round the alternatives are A and C, and here C will be chosen, also with two votes to one. According to common procedure, C will now be declared to be the committee's choice. But—and here comes the paradox—in a vote between B and C, B would have won by two votes to one! It is easy to see that the outcome of the two-stage procedure depends on the voting sequence; the way the example has been constructed implies that it is the alternative left out of the first round of voting that will be chosen after the second round. The example raises more general doubts about the rationality of the process of majority voting, and Condorcet himself proposed several modifications of pure majority voting that would avoid paradoxes of this type. However, it is the paradox as such that is the main source of his fame, and it is through this that he has influenced later research on collective decisions within economics and political science.

Periods and Schools

The physiocrats were a scientific community, or "school," in a very concrete sense: they were a group of people who lived ap-

[7] A partial translation of this work as well as extracts from Condorcet's other writings have been made by Iain McLean and Fiona Hewitt (Condorcet 1994). This book also contains a long introduction that surveys his life as well as his writings both on the theory of voting and on human rights.

proximately in the same place and at the same time, and they shared a common vision about the functioning of the economic system and about the effects of economic policy. However, concepts like schools or periods in intellectual history are commonly used in a much wider sense, often to characterize long periods in the history of a subject or groups of individuals who lived far apart from each other, both in time and space.

The use of these concepts is part of the theory developed by the historians of thought, and there is much to be said in favor of such attempts to create a theoretical structure in the study of the history of economic thought. At the same time it has to be realized that it is difficult to draw up clear dividing lines between periods and schools. This is illustrated by the fact that there is considerable variation in the literature regarding the use of central concepts, and there are many cases of significant overlaps between them. We shall, for instance, use the term the *classical school* about the economists (especially the British economists) from Adam Smith to John Stuart Mill, and this is common usage among modern historians of thought. It has also been usual to refer to the economists who began to dominate the subject from the 1870s as the "neoclassical" or "marginalist" school and to draw a sharp line between these and the classics. But as we shall gradually realize, during the classical period there were several economists who developed theories that by their content ought really to be classified as belonging to the neoclassical school. Furthermore, there were economists who even after the 1870s continued to write in the tradition of Smith and Ricardo. The concepts of periods and schools must not be interpreted as more than they are—fairly inaccurate signposts in a landscape lacking clear contours.

FURTHER READING

Most textbooks on the history of economic thought include some material on economic thinking before Adam Smith, although the weight accorded to it varies a good deal. The exposition in this chapter gives only a taste of a large literature, and many important names have been neglected.

Many of the writers discussed in the present chapter are represented by extracts from their works in the book edited by Medema and Samuels (2003). Among these are Cantillon, Quesnay, Turgot, and Hume as well as some writers who have been left out or only received brief mention in the present chapter: Aristotle, St. Thomas Aquinas, William Petty, Thomas Mun, John Locke, and Bernard Mandeville. Although these extracts are imperfect substitutes for the originals, one also has to admit that economic writings from the early period are more difficult to penetrate for the modern reader than the literature from Adam Smith onward, and this makes a book of readings particularly useful. The essential contributions by Bernoulli and Condorcet, which have been translated into English as Bernoulli (1738; 1954) and Condorcet (1994) are well worth the attention of a modern reader.

Some expositions of the history of economic thought pay particularly close attention to early writings in economics and are therefore particularly well suited as supplementary reading. Outstanding examples of such books are Schumpeter (1954) and Robbins (1998). Schumpeter devotes more than 250 pages to the early periods, and Robbins's lectures also cover economic thinking from Plato and Aristotle to Smith in some detail.

Odd Langholm has written extensively on the economic thinking of the scholastics and its basis in the work of Aristotle; see, for example, Langholm (1998). The classic study of the mercantilist economic system is by the Swedish economic historian Eli Heckscher (1931; 1935). A broad view of the economic and social thought of Marquis de Condorcet is presented by Rothschild (2001).

Adam Smith

ADAM SMITH (1723–90) was born in the small town of Kirk-caldy in Scotland. During the years 1737–40 he studied at Glasgow University, which at that time was one of the leading universities in Britain. He was a good student and received a grant that enabled him to go to Balliol College, Oxford, where he spent the years 1740–46 studying the classical languages, literature, and philosophy. He was not particularly impressed by the quality of the teaching at the university: many years later he remarked that the professors at Oxford had even stopped pretending to teach. But there were first-class libraries that Smith used extensively, and he left the university as a knowledgeable and well-read man, especially in the fields of English and French literature.

After completion of his studies he returned to Scotland, where at first he had problems finding a suitable position. However, he made a name for himself by a series of lectures on rhetoric and literature that he gave in Edinburgh, and this led to his appointment as professor at the University of Glasgow. At first he held a position in logic, while later on his field became that of moral philosophy. Moral philosophy was defined very broadly, and Smith's lectures included subjects as varied as rhetoric, literature, ethics, law, and economics—or political economy, as the subject was then called. His first book, for which for a long time he was chiefly known, was the philosophical treatise *The Theory of Moral Sentiments* (1759), where he discusses the foundations of man's moral attitudes. Some later writers have tended to see a contradiction between the Adam Smith of *The Theory of Moral Sentiments* and the author of the later work *The Wealth of Nations*. The first book advances a view of man as basically a moral and altruistic being, while the second emphasizes self-interest as the driving force behind human action. One explanation for the alleged contradiction is that, during the seventeen years that lay between the publication of the two works, Smith changed his basic views on moral and social questions. But there is little reason to believe that he should have undergone such a deep-seated intellectual change. First, it is clearly possible both to hold the view that man is a moral being and that in many arenas of his life he is motivated by the pursuit of self-interest. Second, whatever the view of later commentators, Smith himself was apparently unaware of any such contradiction between the basic messages of the two books, for he published two new editions of *The Theory of Moral Sentiments* after *The Wealth of Nations* had come out. In the former book, Smith explains how the concern for justice is materialized both in formal and informal rules for acceptable social and economic behavior; within this framework of rules, there is room for the exercise of self-interest whose consequences are explored in the *Wealth of Nations*.

In 1764 Adam Smith resigned from his professorship to take up a position as tutor and travel companion for the young Duke of Buccleuch on a journey through France. From a modern perspective, the transition from university professor to private tutor looks like an academic comedown, but financially it was extremely profitable: Smith's income was very substantially increased, and in addition he was assured a generous pension for the rest of his life. The journey also enabled him to make the acquaintance of many leading French intellectuals of his time, among them the philosopher Voltaire, whom Smith greatly admired. During a longer stay in Paris, he got to know Quesnay, who introduced him to his group of physiocrats; among them, he came to know Turgot particularly well. The greater freedom that he now enjoyed, compared with his time in Glasgow, also provided him with more time for his writing, and it was during his time in France that he began writing *The Wealth of Nations*. In 1766 he moved back to Scotland to stay with his mother in Kirkcaldy. It was there, and later on during some years that he spent in London, that he finished the manuscript of his most famous book. When it was published in 1776, it became an immediate success—it came out in five editions during Smith's lifetime—and made its author famous.

In 1778 Adam Smith was appointed to a position as one of five customs inspectors in Scotland, which required him to move to Edinburgh. It might seem somewhat paradoxical that a person who was seen as such a prominent spokesman for free trade should end his career in the enforcement of tariffs, but Smith apparently had no problem with combining his role as intellectual advocate of free trade with the task of administering the trade restrictions that were a fact of life. And there are no indications that he did not faithfully serve the government in his new position.

Beyond his two great books Smith published little during his lifetime. However, a number of works that were left in manuscript form at the time of his death have later been published, and the edition of his collected works that was published at the two hundredth anniversary of the *Wealth of Nations* comprises six large volumes. His writings span a wide range of topics, but in economics his reputation rests almost solely on the *Wealth of Nations*. It is accordingly this book that we will focus on in the present chapter.

WEALTH OF NATIONS

An Inquiry into the Nature and Causes of the Wealth of Nations is a large and wide-ranging work. It contains passages that may well be described as abstract theory, although not in the form of diagrams and mathematics, but as carefully formulated logical chains of reasoning in literary form. It also contains long and detailed descriptions of social and economic institutions in Scotland, England, and the rest of the world. These are based partly on Smith's own experience from his travels, but to a large extent also on his reading (as when he tells us that Peru is more civilized than Mexico). He also takes the reader on long sweeps through history in order to illustrate his thoughts on economic development. From a thematic point of view the book therefore covers a much larger ground than the modern reader would expect to find in a textbook on economics. However, it would be highly misleading to think of it as a textbook in the modern sense of the word. A market for academic textbooks hardly existed at Smith's time, and even if he could count on some sales to students, the book was chiefly intended for the enlightened general public.

A central concern for Adam Smith is to argue against the mercantilist view of economic policy and in favor of free trade and free markets. But in order to explain how a system of free markets can be in the interests of society, he found it necessary to explore in some detail the actual functioning of markets. The analysis of this question is developed by Smith into a pathbreaking vision of

the workings of a market economy. It is accordingly his contributions to economic theory and not the more polemical parts of the
book that have left their marks on the history of thought.

The *Wealth of Nations* is divided into five "books." The first
contains what we would today call microeconomics or price
theory. It discusses the division of labor in a market economy,
the formation of prices under competition and monopoly, and
the determination of factor prices and the distribution of income.
Book II is concerned with capital accumulation and the financial
system, while book III is mainly historical, focusing on the development of agriculture in Europe since the time of the Roman Empire. Book IV is mostly about international trade and contains the
essence of Smith's criticism of mercantilism. Book V takes up the
role of the public sector in the economy, treating taxes and public
expenditure both from a theoretical and historical perspective.

ADAM SMITH'S PRICE THEORY

During the age of the classical economists, price theory, the theory
of price formation under alternative assumptions about market
structure, was known as the theory of value. The problem that
they studied was the determinants of the prices, or values, of
different goods and services. A problematic distinction that
Smith introduced at an early stage of his theoretical discussion
(book I, chapter IV) was between *value in use* and *value in exchange*. Water is more useful than diamonds, but diamonds are
more expensive; the exchange value of water, which is low compared to diamonds, does not reflect its high value in use. This
alleged paradox he did not manage to solve, but he went on to
say that his own analysis of prices would be limited to the study
of exchange value. Already at this introductory stage of the book
we get an indication of what would turn out to be the main
weakness of the classical theory of value: its failure to construct a
satisfactory theory of demand and to clarify the role of demand
in the formation of prices.

A famous passage in the *Wealth of Nations* contains an account
of the formation of prices in a primitive society of hunters, an
example obviously intended as a pedagogical simplification of
a complicated problem. There is assumed to be free access to

35

hunting grounds, and the resources needed to supply the hunt-ers with weapons and provisions are supposed to be of minor significance. The main input into the production process is ac-cordingly hours of labor in the form of hunting time. Suppose that it requires twice as many hours of hunting to kill a beaver than to kill a deer. It follows that the price of a beaver will be twice that of a deer, so that one beaver will be exchanged for two deer. Smith modifies this conclusion by pointing out that one type of hunting may require different skills than the other, and that a scarcity of people with the special skill may cause the rate of exchange to deviate from the ratio of labor time requirements. The simple case is still of interest because it illustrates the core element in the theory of price held by the classical economists, that is, the—primarily English—economists from Adam Smith to John Stuart Mill. This is known as the labor theory of value: the relative prices of commodities are determined by the relative amounts of labor needed to produce them.

For modern economists this theory seems special in that it makes no reference whatever to demand conditions. But it is straightforward to interpret it in a way that makes it fully con-sistent with modern insights. A modern textbook exposition of price formation under perfect competition is based on a diagram that shows the price as determined at the intersection of the de-mand and supply curves (we will come back to the history of this diagram in later chapters). This way of thinking was foreign to Adam Smith, but we can relate his theory to the modern view by imagining that the supply curve, which reflects the unit cost of production, is horizontal. Price will then be determined by the cost of production, while the role of demand is to determine the volume of output. Relative prices will be determined by relative costs of production, just as in the beaver-deer example. The role played by demand is to determine how many beavers and how many deer will be killed by the hunters.

Smith emphasizes that the example is special since the whole produce of labor accrues to the hunters themselves. In a more developed society the work of the laborers will be organized by people who have accumulated capital and who use it to pro-vide the hunters or laborers with the necessary tools and pay their wages in advance. The prepaid wages—known as the wage fund—was an important part of the concept of capital used by

Smith and the other classical economists. For this contribution to the production process the employer must earn a profit, which must also be paid from the value of the produce. (Smith remarks that profits may also be regarded as a wage earned from the labor of management and control.) If the hunting grounds are privately owned, the landlords will also charge a rent for the use of the land, so that the value of the produce must be distributed among the three components of cost, namely, labor, capital, and land. This perspective extends the theory of price formation from the simple labor theory of value to a more general cost-of-production theory. It continues to be the case that prices are determined by the cost of production, but cost is now a more complex concept than in the primitive society of hunters—"the early and rude state of society."

In any society, according to Smith, wages, profits, and rent all tend toward their respective normal levels, and these normal levels are what determine "the natural price." In later chapters of the book he discusses in more detail the determination of the normal levels of the cost components; this will be considered further below. In his theory of the natural price Smith uses the normal level of cost as a causal explanation of price. As many historians of thought have pointed out, this shows that Smith did not have what we now refer to as a general equilibrium perspective on price determination. In that perspective it makes no sense to say that product prices are determined by factor prices; instead, product and factor prices are mutually dependent on each other.

How much or how little of this perspective that Smith possessed is, however, a matter of judgment. In the introductory chapter to the *Wealth of Nations* we find a famous analysis of the division of labor in society, a topic that Smith obviously thought to be of great importance since he gave it such a prominent place in the book. The starting point for the discussion is the example of the organization of production in a pin factory. Smith points out that the production of a pin is a complicated and difficult task. A worker without experience from this line of work who had no access to the specialized machinery used in a modern pin factory would find it very difficult to produce a single pin in the course of a day's work. In the pin factory, on the other hand, the production of pins has been broken down into "about eighteen" separate operations, with each worker specializing in just one or a few of them. In a small factory that Smith has seen, ten men can produce 48,000 pins per day, that is, 4,800 pins per worker or 4,800 as many as could be produced by a single worker without specialization and division of labor. This implies that the unit cost of production is not only determined by technological relationship, as the beaver-deer example may suggest. First of all, it obviously depends on the organization of labor, which again depends on technological possibilities. Second, however, it depends on the size of the market. In the Scottish highlands each farmer has to be both slaughterer and baker as well as brewer, and the nearest blacksmith, carpenter, or mason is often miles away. Nor can these highland artisans afford to be very specialized. A carpenter cannot make a living by specializing in house-building or cabinet-making; he has to do both these things and also work at tasks like carving and wagon making. Since the cost of production depends on the size of the market, in other words on demand, commodity prices are not only technologically determined but also depend on factors on the demand side of the market. The further society has advanced with respect to the division of labor, the lower will prices be, especially for manufacturing goods.

Another connection between demand and prices emerges in Smith's discussion of the distinction between the *market price* and the *natural price,* as he describes it in book I, chapter VII. We have seen that the natural price is the one that corresponds to the normal level of the three components of cost—wages, profits, and rent. The market price is the actual price that prevails in the market at a given moment of time, and this can differ from the natural price both in the upward and downward direction. The market price is determined by the relationship between the quantity that is actually brought to the market and by the demand of those who are willing to pay the normal price; this is called the effectual demand. When the quantity brought to the market is less that the effectual demand, the competition between buyers will cause the price to rise until there is balance between demand and supply. If, on the contrary, the quantity supplied is greater than the effectual demand, the market price will fall to some level below the natural price. But the natural price is the central level toward which the market price will continually gravitate. How large price fluctuations there will be in any particular market de-

38

pends on the production conditions of the industry in question. In Smith's view, fluctuations will be greater in the markets for agricultural commodities than in manufactured goods markets. The reason is that the variations in output, and thereby in the supply of goods on the market, are larger in agriculture, which is subject to frequent changes in production conditions through variations in the weather.

An example that Smith uses to illustrate the deviations between market price and natural price concerns the effects of a public mourning announced on the death of a king. This increases the demand for black cloth while the quantity of cloth is limited to what the merchants have in stock. The effect of the increase in demand is therefore an increase in the price of black cloth. When everyone has acquired the cloth required by the state of mourning, the market price will fall back to its natural level.

Smith emphasizes that the market price cannot for long stay below the natural price. For this would imply that wages, profits, or rent would fall below their natural level. This would lead the owners of these resources to withdraw from the market, with the result that the volume of output falls and the price rises to its natural level. On the other hand, it is fully possible for the market price to be above the natural price for long periods. The reason for this could be the use of resources of unusual quality, for instance, vineyards of especially "happy soil and situation," or a monopoly granted by the government. Of the last example, he says, "The monopolists, by keeping the market constantly under-stocked, by never fully supplying the effectual demand, sell their commodities much above the natural price, and raise their emoluments, whether they consist in wages or profit, greatly above their natural rate" (Smith 1776; 1976, p. 78).[1] Later on, we shall take a closer look at Smith's theory of monopoly and competition.

The Returns to the Factors of Production

The natural or long-run prices of commodities are those that correspond to the natural or long-run level of the prices or returns

---

[1] All page references are to the 1976 bicentenary edition of the *Wealth of Nations*.

to the three factors of production—labor, capital, and land. So what are the long-run determinants of the prices of the factors of production?

In book I, chapter VIII, Smith begins by pointing out that when we move away from the primitive society of hunters, where each worker is his own employer, most workers will be hired by an employer at a wage they have agreed upon. The level of wages will therefore be determined by the employment contracts. Workers and employers have conflicting interests: workers desire high wages, while employers want them to be as low as possible. But in contract negotiations employers tend naturally to be the stronger participants. First, there are fewer employers than workers, so that it is easier for employers to agree between themselves to keep wages low than it is for workers to combine to push wages up. Smith writes long before the time of strong trade unions, and he remarks that there are many laws that forbid workers from organizing themselves for the purpose of obtaining higher wages, while there are none that prevent employers in cooperating for the opposite purpose. Moreover, he says, it is obvious that if a conflict occurs, the employers can hold out much longer than the workers. A factory owner or a merchant will often be able to live well for a year or two without workers, while a worker will find it difficult to survive for a week or a month if he is not employed.

However, wages are not only determined by the bargaining power of the two parties. The wage must be at least so high that the worker can survive on it, and it must actually be a good deal higher since it must be sufficient for the working class to survive. Consequently, the wage must be high enough for the worker to raise a family. Smith cites Cantillon, who pointed out that a working-class family accordingly must be able to bring up two grown children, but since the statistics show that only two out of four children reach adult age, each family must be enabled to give birth to four children. Smith himself hesitates to draw a firm conclusion as to the level of wages that this implies, but the general conclusion is clearly that the long-run wage level tends toward a subsistence level that ensures the reproduction of the working class.

In some cases, however, we observe wages that are clearly above the level of subsistence. This will be the case in countries with high economic growth, for in those countries the wage fund—the resources that employers command for the payment of wages—increases faster than population. The American colonies have a high rate of population growth,[2] but their wage fund increases even faster. Wages in America are therefore above the level in Great Britain, in spite of the fact that Great Britain is a richer country in terms of its national wealth.

In a later chapter Smith points out that the treatment of labor and wages as homogeneous is a simplification of reality. In real life wages will reflect the particular circumstances pertaining to different professions. For any particular line of work these circumstances could be such as to imply that the wage is either above or below the average for all professions. Smith mentions several causes of wage inequality. One of these is the "ease or hardship" of the employment. A blacksmith earns less in the course of a twelve-hour day than a miner does in eight hours, for the work of a blacksmith is less dirty and dangerous, and it is carried out in daylight and above the ground. Some professions are particularly honorable, and since honor is part of the reward, wages are correspondingly lower. Other professions are held in general disgrace, which has the opposite effect. The most detested of all workers is the public executioner, but relative to the hours worked, no one is better paid than he.

Smith also argues that wages will vary with how difficult and expensive it is to learn the profession, with "the constancy or inconstancy of employment," and with the amount of trust placed in the worker. His fifth and final cause of wage inequality is the probability of succeeding in one's profession. If one trains to become a shoemaker, it is virtually certain that one will be able to earn one's living by making shoes. But if one is educated as a lawyer, Smith claims, only one in twenty will be able to do well enough to live by it. To aim at the profession of a lawyer is accordingly a lottery, and since there are so few winning tickets they must carry very high prizes. However, the wage differences

[2] Smith says that the population of the American colonies has increased so fast that it is expected double within a space of 25 years. By contrast, in Great Britain and the rest of Europe it is estimated that it will take more than 500 years for the population to double. He does not cite any sources for these forecasts. The first of them turned out to be fairly accurate, while the second was way off the mark. In the case of Great Britain it took only about half a century before the population had reached twice its size at the time when Smith wrote.

in this respect are in fact less than a rational consideration of the probabilities would imply, because most people, and particularly the young, have a tendency to overestimate the probability of success. Smith argues that this explains why so many of the young among "the common people" are ready to enlist as soldiers or to go to sea.

By way of summary, Adam Smith's general theory of the wage structure is that the wages in different professions reflect noneconomic advantages and disadvantages. This theory of compensating wage differentials, as it is generally referred to, has had great influence on later research in labor economics.

The rewards for the use of capital are also variable. However, the variations will be far less than in the case of wages. The most important cause of the variation in the rate of return on capital is difference in risk. An owner of capital takes a larger risk when he invests abroad; consequently, the expected return on foreign investment must be higher. Part of the return on capital must also be seen as compensation to the owner for the work he has with the management and supervision of his business. Relative to the capital invested, therefore, this compensation must be higher for a merchant who serves a small market than for one who operates on a larger scale.

Smith emphasizes that this account of the inequalities of wages and the return on capital are based on the assumption of free and unregulated markets. In reality, however, wages and profits are strongly influenced by institutional and political circumstances, in particular by "the policies of Europe." The private restraints on competition, as represented especially by the ancient guild system, are tolerated by the authorities who thereby limit access to certain professions and push up wages to a level above that which would exist under free competition. Smith is skeptical about the value of these limitations on competition. Admittedly, they are often claimed to be in the interest of society, but such arguments are usually just camouflage for self-interest.

The third component of the natural price of a commodity is rent, and this is discussed in book I, chapter XI. Rent enters into the determination of prices in a way that is fundamentally different from wages and the return on capital (or profit). High wages and profits are *causes* of high commodity prices, says Smith, while high rents are *effects* of high prices. The landowner is by the nature of the case a monopolist, for he owns a piece of land that is different from that of other landowners. The person who has the use of the land—the tenant—must therefore pay the price that the owner demands and this will correspond to the difference between the tenant's income and the normal cost in the form of wages and profit. Adam Smith's theory of rent was further developed by the later classical economists, and we will discuss it further in chapter 4.

THE INVISIBLE HAND

If one were to carry out an opinion poll among economists concerning the most important single contribution of the *Wealth of Nations*, the probability is high that most of them would say that it is the idea of the invisible hand. No doubt there are also those that imagine that this is the real theme of the book, since many, particularly among those who have not actually read the book, have an image of the *Wealth of Nations* as basically a piece of propaganda for the market economy and a polemic against public regulation and intervention.

There is more than a grain of truth in this, but the image must still be modified in a number of respects. Let us first look at what Smith actually says about the invisible hand. This can be done rather quickly, since it is mentioned only once in this book of nine hundred pages. In book IV, chapter II, we find the central formulation:

> Every individual necessarily labours to render the annual revenue of society as great as he can. He generally, indeed, neither intends to promote the publick interest, nor knows how much he is promoting it. … He intends only his own gain, and he is in this, as in many other cases, led by an invisible hand to promote an end which was no part of his intention. Nor is it always the worse for the society that it was no part of it. By pursuing his own interest he frequently promotes that of the society more effectually than when he really intends to promote it. (Smith 1776; 1976, p. 456)

A popular summary interpretation of this statement is that what is best for the individual is also best for society, and that the invisible hand that ensures this is the system of free competition.

Is this a "correct" interpretation? Does it provide a reasonable summary of the real content of the statement? When one reads the original formulation more carefully, one quickly discovers that there are more possible interpretations than the popular short version.

In the quotation, Smith begins by stating that each individual *necessarily* works to make the national income as large as possible.[3] The reasonable interpretation of this is evidently that the individual is not aware of this, for it is obviously not his personal aim to increase the national income, nor is he aware of the connection between this and his own effort. The consequences of his actions are good for society even if he only has his self-interest in mind.

Note that Smith chooses his words with some caution. It is *not always* the worse for society that the individual pursues his self-interest, but when he does so, it happens *frequently* that he also acts in the interest of society. The rule of harmony between individual and social interests is not absolute; there is an implicit admission that the two may be in conflict. Nevertheless, the quotation seems clearly to indicate that in Smith's view the coincidence of interests is the main rule. But it is notable that he does not say directly what the invisible hand really is, and this has resulted in extensive discussions among his interpreters.

The invisible hand passage has been rendered here in a form that is common among those that quote Smith on this issue, most of whom include a dotted line in the middle of the passage to show that something has been left out. Let us now look at the complete version of the text, with the omitted lines in italics:

> Every individual necessarily labours to render the annual revenue of society as great as he can. He generally, indeed, neither intends to promote the publick interest, nor knows how much he is promoting it. *By preferring the support of domestick to that of foreign industry, he intends only his own security; and by directing that industry in such a manner as its produce may be of the greatest value,* he intends only his own gain, and he is in this, as in many other cases, led by an

[3] National income" is a natural modern translation of "the annual revenue of society," but we must obviously keep in mind that this concept, as used by Smith, does not have the precise theoretical definition and empirical content that it has today.

44

invisible hand to promote an end which was no part of his intention. Nor is it always the worse for the society that it was no part of
it. By pursuing his own interest he frequently promotes that of the
society more effectually than when he really intends to promote it.

The first version of the quotation is quite general, while the second and complete version ties the argument to a specific example, namely, the "natural" preference of a single individual or
investor in favor of domestic over foreign investment. Many of
those who cite the passage of the invisible hand leave out the reference to the specific example, preferring the abbreviated form
of the quotation. One possible explanation is that they believe
that the shorter version better represents Smith's central message.[4] Another explanation is that they read Smith in the light
of modern views of the connection between competition and social efficiency, and that they simply use the quotation to color
an otherwise dry theoretical exposition. In the latter case, those
who cite him may not actually be interested in what Smith really
meant; rather, they use the quotation as an illustration of their
own opinions. What was Smith's own view?

Let us first pose the question of whether the frequently omitted lines were intended as an essential part of the argument, or
whether, as some have suggested, they were included in the text
more or less by mistake, thereby clouding Smith's real message.
In favor of the first point of view one may refer to the context in
which the invisible hand passage occurs: it is not to be found in
a chapter on the general properties of free markets, but in one
whose subject is import restrictions. There can therefore be no
doubt that Smith considered the statement about the relationship
between domestic and foreign investment as an important part
of his argument.

A couple of pages before the passage of the invisible hand,
Smith has a somewhat different formulation of the same line of
thought, but without reference to foreign investment and without use of the famous metaphor:

[4] A statement of this view can be found in Lionel Robbins's lectures on the
history of economic thought, where he says, with reference to Smith's discussion of domestic and foreign investment, that his "praise" of the invisible hand
would have been much better if he had not used that specific example (Robbins
1998, p. 149).

Every individual is continually exerting himself to find out the most advantageous employment for whatever capital he can command. It is his own advantage, indeed, and not that of the society, which he has in view. But the study of his own advantage naturally, or rather necessarily leads him to prefer that employment which is most advantageous to the society.

In what does his own advantage consist? According to Smith, this has two aspects:

First, every individual endeavours to employ his capital as near home as he can, and consequently as much as he can in the support of domestick industry; provided always that he can thereby obtain the ordinary, or not a great deal less than the ordinary profits of stock.

Secondly, every individual who employs his capital in the support of domestick industry, necessarily endeavours so to direct that industry, that its produce may be of the greatest possible value . . . or to exchange for the greatest quantity either of money or of other goods. (Smith 1776; 1976, p. 455)

The first aspect of his own advantage is that a man of business has less control over the use of his resources if he is not present where the production activity takes place. Therefore, he will choose to invest at home rather than abroad even if the foreign rate of return on capital were higher.[5] But why would this be in the interest of society, meaning the domestic economy? The answer to this question is provided later in the chapter. Adam Smith has rightly been considered as a keen spokesman for free trade. But he deviated from his principles when it came to goods and services that were of strategic importance for the country's defense, for "defence . . . is much more important than opulence." Examples of his application of this point of view can be found in his support of the Navigation Acts, which served to protect

[5] Like the other economists of the classical school, Smith used the concept of capital in a different sense than we do today. The classical economists drew a distinction between fixed and circulating capital, circulating capital being the wages paid to workers while they were engaged in the process of production, i.e., the wage fund. Therefore, when Smith writes about the individual's employment of his capital at home and abroad, we should interpret him more generally as referring to the use of factors of production, including labor.

British shipping, and export duties on sailcloth and gunpowder. More generally, we should perhaps interpret him as saying that the use of resources at home rather than abroad is in the public interest because it strengthens the economic foundation for national defense.

Let us now look at the second aspect of individual advantage. Given the difference between the required rate of profit abroad and at home, capital will be invested in such a manner that its total rate of return will be as large as possible. It is reasonable to conclude that this provided Smith with the justification for the conclusion that self-interest tends to maximize national income. Thus, it is self-interest, as manifested in the context of market behavior, that constitutes the invisible hand, and the hand works in two ways that are both beneficial to society. One achieves a right balance between domestic and foreign investment, and the composition of domestic investment is such that it yields the greatest possible return on the nation's capital.

What is the most important result of the workings of the invisible hand? There are those who maintain that in Smith's view it was the strengthening of national defense; among spokesmen for this view are Grampp (2000) and Persky (1989). From their point of view it becomes misleading to refer to the image of the invisible hand as a general justification for the view that markets and competition are good for society. Instead, the invisible hand should be interpreted as a mechanism that helps to neutralize a weakness of markets—a case of market failure, as we would now say—in a special and limited area, and it cannot be generalized beyond that specific context. But when one considers the invisible hand passage in the context of the *Wealth of Nations* as a whole, such an interpretation becomes quite unreasonable.

THE INVISIBLE HAND AND THE MARKET ECONOMY

The fact that the invisible hand is mentioned only once in *The Wealth of Nations* may be taken as an indication that Smith himself did not regard the formulation itself as quite so fundamental as posterity has done. But this does not necessarily imply that the underlying idea was not central to Smith's way of thinking. That this was in fact the case is strongly suggested even in the complete version of the central passage, for he emphasizes that it is not only in this special case that the invisible hand works for the common good, but also "in many other cases." Moreover, we do not have to search long in the *Wealth of Nations* before we find formulations that support this view. One example is that which occurs just before the invisible hand passage and was quoted above. Another much cited formulation is the following: "It is not from the benevolence of the butcher, the brewer, or the baker, that we expect our dinner, but from their regard to their own interest. We address ourselves, not to their humanity but to their self-love, and never talk to them of our own necessities but of their advantages" (Smith 1776; 1976, p. 27).

This is fully in line with the conventional interpretation of the invisible hand: producers think primarily of their own interest and not of the welfare of their customers, but it is their self-interest that provides us with the goods and services that we demand. This and several similar formulations are strong indications that Adam Smith was convinced of the general truth expressed in the metaphor beyond the special context in which it occurs in the text.

We may conclude that it is the market mechanism and competition that are represented by the image of the invisible hand. But what kinds of markets and what type of competition is it that lead to the best outcome for society?

Free or Perfect Competition?

Adam Smith's treatise does not contain any systematic discussion of alternative concepts of competition. Present-day references to the invisible hand tend to relate Smith's insights to modern theories of the connection between economic efficiency and market equilibrium under perfect competition. But Smith's concept of competition, often referred to as "the system of perfect liberty," is far more comprehensive than the modern definition of perfect competition, which implies that each producer is so insignificant relative to the size of the market that he takes prices as given and outside his control. When one reads Smith, it becomes clear that competition first and foremost implies the absence of monopoly, and that it is this which ensures that prices tend towards their "natural" levels. The reason is that a price that lies above this level will lead to the entry of new firms and a downward pressure on the price; conversely, a price below the natural level will lead some firms to withdraw from the market so that supply goes down and the price increases. In Adam Smith's theory of competition it will only be when the price has reached its natural level that producers will face prices that are beyond their control.

The basic assumption required for this mechanism to work is that of free entry and exit, and this more or less defines the nature of free competition in the *Wealth of Nations*. Smith has a clear conception of the relationship between the monopoly price and the price that would exist in a free market:

> The price of monopoly is upon every occasion the highest that can be got. The natural price, or the price of free competition, on the contrary, is the lowest which can be taken, not upon every occasion, indeed, but for any considerable time together. The one is upon every occasion the highest which can be squeezed out of the buyers, or which, it is supposed, they will consent to give. The other is the lowest which the sellers can commonly afford to take, and at the same time continue their business. (Smith 1776; 1976, pp. 78–79)

Underlying these hypotheses about the formation of prices there is obviously an assumption that must come close to that of profit maximization on the part of producers, but Smith is not explicit on this point. Otherwise, this paragraph has a strikingly modern character: there is no significant difference between it and the comparison in modern textbooks between monopoly pricing and long-run equilibrium under perfect competition.

What about the forms intermediate between perfect competition and monopoly? Smith has not really much to say about this, although there are a few scattered references. Of particular interest is his analysis of the relationship between grocery prices and the number of grocers in a town:

> If this capital [sufficient to trade in a town] is divided between two different grocers, their competition will tend to make both of them sell cheaper, than if it were in the hands of one only; and if it were divided among twenty, their competition would be just so much

the greater, and the chance of their combining together, in order to raise the price, just so much the less. (Smith 1776; 1976, p. 361)

Thus the degree of competition increases with the number of sellers. Of particular interest is Smith's emphasis on the point that a larger number of sellers makes it less likely that they will be able to agree between themselves to restrict competition. A monopoly or other limitation of competition is then not only due to government privileges or natural cost advantages. It could equally well come from the sellers' realization that by cooperation they may be able to increase prices. A system of free competition is not, therefore, self-regulating, since sellers will have an incentive to collaborate in order to increase their market power:

> People of the same trade seldom meet together, even for merriment and diversion, but the conversation ends in a conspiracy against the publick, or in some contrivance to raise prices. It is impossible indeed to prevent such meetings, by any law which either could be executed, or would be consistent with liberty and justice. But though the law cannot hinder people of the same trade from sometimes assembling together, it ought to do nothing to facilitate such assemblies; much less to render them necessary. (Smith 1776; 1976, p. 145)

It has been a common view that Adam Smith was an extreme market liberalist who believed that it was in the interest of society to leave everything to the free play of market forces. The last quotation alone is enough to show that this opinion of him is wrong, and that the view of him as a naive believer in social harmony is misleading. The economic framework of free competition stands in constant danger of being destroyed by the market actors themselves. This type of "conspiracy against the publick" demonstrates that the self-interest of economic agents induces them to prevent the invisible hand to work for the interests of society. From a modern perspective it would be natural to classify the weaknesses of the market in regard to the public interest partly as failure to achieve *efficient use of resources*, partly as failure to attain *social justice*. Smith does not employ this classification, but he presents a number of interesting reflections concerning both aspects. We first take a closer look at what he really means by the concept of the public interest.

The Public Interest

In the selection of quotations from the *Wealth of Nations* we have encountered several references to the interest of society or the public interest. In the passage where the invisible hand is mentioned, Smith maintains that it induces the individual to act in the interest of society, but he does not actually define what that interest is. He does say, however, that the individual works to make the annual revenue of society as large as possible, and a possible interpretation is that he considers these two concepts as being equivalent. Smith's line of thought may have been that the maximization of national income would provide the population as a whole with the largest possible amount of resources for consumption, and that this was as far as one could go in terms of normative statements without invoking ethical judgments. On the other hand it is difficult to understand why Smith as a moral philosopher should be so cautious in his definition of the interest of society, and it is not quite consistent with other statements that he made about the aim and purpose of economic activity in society: "Consumption is the sole end and purpose of all production; and the interest of the producer ought to be attended to, only so far as it may be necessary for promoting that of the consumer" (Smith 1776; 1976, p. 660).

Therefore, it is in the light of the consumer's interest that we must judge the effects of the invisible hand. This creates a problem of interpretation concerning the connection between the public interest and the size of the national income. There are two possibilities. One is that Smith thought that the consumer's interest was best served by an economic system that guaranteed the largest possible national income. The other possibility is that "the annual revenue of society" is to be understood as something wider than just national income, at least in its modern sense— perhaps as something more akin to "social welfare." But if we choose that interpretation, we must also take into account that the many individual consumers in society do not necessarily have coinciding interests, and we shall have to weigh individual interests together in order to arrive at the interest of society. We do not find in Smith's work any systematic attempt at aggregation of individual interests. On the other hand we find a number of formulations that are indications of his view of the relationship between the rich and the poor. They must also be brought into the picture when we attempt to form a balanced perspective of his views on markets and competition.

One example of Smith's view can be found in his discussion of the attitude of employers regarding the connection between wages, prices, and competitiveness. He says that merchants and manufacturers frequently complain about the unfortunate effects of high wages in raising prices and diminishing the sale of their commodities both at home and abroad, while they say nothing about the effects of high profits. He finishes his chapter "On the Wages of Labor" with a sarcasm: "They are silent with regard to the pernicious effects of their own gains. They complain only of those of other people" (Smith 1776; 1976, p. 115). Another example can be found in his discussion of the system of tolls that should be charged for different types of public transport. Here he speaks out against the common principle of charging according to the weight of the carriage. Instead he recommends that tolls be levied at higher rates on luxury carriages, and at lower rates on carriages of necessity, for by that system "the indolence and vanity of the rich is made to contribute in a very easy manner to the relief of the poor, by rendering cheaper the transportation of heavy goods to all the different parts of the country" (Smith 1776; 1976, p. 725). This formulation is notable both for its substantial content and for the tone of its language, which leaves one with no doubt as to the author's sympathy and social concerns.

According to modern economic thinking the strength of the market mechanism is that under suitable conditions it leads to an efficient use of society's resources. On the other hand, it can hardly be maintained that the resulting distribution of income and resources between individuals ensures economic justice.[6] Most probably, this was also the view of Adam Smith. The reasonable interpretation of what he meant by his theory of the invisible hand was that the market leads to a use of resources that will be to the advantage of the representative or average consumer. But he was also fully aware that a free market economy could generate inequalities that were unacceptable from the

[6] The exception is provided by the view that a just distribution of resources is the one that is generated by a free market. In that case, of course, justice follows by definition.

point of view of economic justice, and that a concern for fairness might motivate public intervention in markets. Competition was good for economic efficiency, but a just distribution of resources could not be achieved by the market alone.

INTERNATIONAL TRADE

Adam Smith's arguments in favor of encouragement to the domestic production of strategic goods like gunpowder are far from being representative of his general views regarding foreign trade. On the contrary, in his view free international trade is an important aspect of the system of free markets, but the argument in favor of free trade acquires a special significance in the *Wealth of Nations,* since it is in this context that we encounter Smith's sharpest criticism of mercantilism. In book IV he first examines the view that the wealth of society can be measured by its stocks of gold and silver and argues that this is based on a false analogy between the popular way to measure the wealth of a private individual, which is based on a confusion of the concepts of wealth and money, and the measurement of the wealth of the nation as a whole. In fact, he considers the alternative view that true wealth consists in the stock of real goods to be self-evidently true: "It would be too ridiculous to go about seriously to prove, that wealth does not consist in money, or in gold and silver; but in what money purchases, and is valuable only for purchasing" (Smith 1776; 1976, p. 438).

A policy of foreign trade that starts from the objective of accumulating stocks of gold and silver is therefore likely to lead to results that go against the public interest. Mercantilist foreign trade policies consisted on the one hand in the erection of barriers to imports, particularly from countries where the trade balance was assumed to be negative, and on the other hand in the encouragement of exports either by direct subsidies or by commercial treaties with foreign countries. Smith points out that in all of these cases mercantilist trade policy prevents the market system from functioning efficiently. In the case of restrictions on imports, by imposing a high tariff that prevents the entry of foreign goods into the domestic market the government in many cases creates a monopoly for domestic producers. This will be to the advantage of the domestic producers but not to the country as a whole, for it prevents others from buying the commodities in question from the cheapest source and directs productive resources into uses that are less productive than those that would have been chosen under "the system of perfect liberty." Deviations from the system of free trade therefore impose costs on society that are of the same nature as those associated with monopoly and restraints on competition in general.

THE MARKET AND THE STATE

An aspect of the simplified view of Adam Smith as a laissez-faire economist is that he was an adherent of the view that the public sector ought to be as small as possible. A minimal, or "night watchman," state would seem to follow from the view of the market as the universally best system for the allocation of resources. It is obvious that in his polemic against the mercantilists and their belief in central planning and market regulation Smith emphasized the positive aspects of the market economy; however, it is also important to be aware that in this debate it was the mercantilists who represented the economic and social establishment. In comparison with them Smith was a reformer and, as the historian Emma Rothschild (2001) has pointed out, during the first years following the publication of the *Wealth of Nations* Smith was regarded as a radical, not least because of his connections with the intellectual environment in prerevolutionary France. It was not until some time into the nineteenth century that he gradually acquired a reputation as "the employers' economist." But as we have seen, there is hardly any foundation for the view that he should have identified the public interest with that of the employers or producers; such an interpretation is based on a superficial reading of his economics. The simplified interpretation of the image of the invisible hand as an unreserved recommendation of laissez-faire economics is largely responsible for this. Several liberalists of the nineteenth century claimed the authority of Adam Smith in support of free markets and a minimal government, thereby helping to perpetuate a misleading image of Smith among later writers and politicians who only knew his work from secondary sources.

So what role was there for the public sector to play according to the worldview of Adam Smith? According to him, the state has three functions. First, it is the duty of the state to protect society against violence and invasion from other societies. Second, the state ought to protect each single member of society against injustice and oppression from other members of it. The third duty of the state consists in

> erecting and maintaining certain publick works and certain pub-
> lick institutions which it can never be for the interest of any in-
> dividual, or small number of individuals, to erect and maintain;
> because the profit would never repay the expence to any individ-
> ual or small number of individuals, though it may frequently do
> much more than repay it to a great society. (Smith 1776; 1976, pp.
> 687–688)

At this point, it is tempting to say that Smith's exposition fore-shadows the modern theory of public or collective goods. A public good has the property that no one can be excluded from enjoying or consuming it once it has been provided. A single individual who considers the profitability of providing a public good will compare the cost with his private gain, but this is only a small fraction of the gain to society, and it is impossible for him to collect payments for the benefits enjoyed by others. The market will therefore provide too little of public goods, and the provision of this type of goods must be the responsibility of an agent who can act on behalf of "the great society." This agent is the state. Scattered around the *Wealth of Nations* one finds a series of applications of this principle, from the building of roads and canals to public concern with health and education. Thus Adam Smith does more than supply arguments why the state should refrain from interfering with free competition. He also puts forward the positive case for the state as an important sector in an otherwise market-dominated economy.

ECONOMIC GROWTH

The title of Adam Smith's economic treatise suggests that the main question that it poses is what determines a nation's level of economic development; we therefore expect the book to present us with a theory of economic growth. The analysis of the economic benefits of a system of free competition and free international trade and of a well-functioning public sector do not form parts of the theory of growth in the modern sense of the term. However, they can be read as analyses of an economic system that provides a *framework* for economic growth. The invisible hand of the market directs resources to the areas where they yield the highest return. At any time, therefore, "the system of perfect liberty" will ensure the best possible use of resources.

However, this argument does not constitute a theory of growth in the more specific sense: it does not explain how the economy grows toward a higher level of wealth. One part of this explanation can be found in the perspective of reform: by changing the economic system in the direction of more competitive markets, less restrictions on international trade, better institutions (especially with regard to securing private property rights), and more enlightened public policies the government will release productive forces that will carry society to a higher level of wealth and better standards of living for its people.

Nevertheless, for a given availability of resources there are clearly limits to how far economic development can be carried. What are the factors that cause the amount of productive resources to increase? Smith considers this question especially in book II, chapter III, where he emphasizes the role of population. Population growth is of central importance for economic development because it implies both more workers and larger markets. That more workers increase the productive capacity of the economy is the more self-evident effect of population growth. The more original part of Smith's thinking in this regard lies in his emphasis on the connection between population growth, the growth of markets, and the resulting increase in the possibilities for the division of labor, such as we have seen in his generalization of the pin factory example. The link between population, market size, and work specialization is an important explanation of the growth of productivity. But workers also become more productive if they have more real capital to work with, and an increase in the capital stock can only occur through saving. At the individual level, saving is motivated by a desire to improve one's future standard of living. The person who saves will do so by investing in real capital for his own use or by lending to

56

others who in turn will invest in real capital goods. Individual saving therefore leads to an increase of capital in the economy, and together with the growth of population the accumulation of capital implies more division of labor, improved productivity, and increasing prosperity.

There have been a number of attempts to formalize Adam Smith's ideas of the growth process in terms of simple mathematical models. Such models are interesting, although they may easily leave one with the impression that he had a separate theory of economic growth that was independent of his more general analysis of the workings of the market economy. This was not the case. Smith's analysis of saving, investment, and productivity growth was an integrated part of his total vision of the functioning of the economy. In his view, capital accumulation was a central source of growth in the wealth of nations. But at least as important was the introduction of reforms designed to improve the ability of the market mechanism to direct resources to their most productive use.

TECHNOLOGICAL PROGRESS AND THE INDUSTRIAL REVOLUTION

Like all social philosophers and scientists, Adam Smith was a child of his time, and we have seen that his theories of the market economy originated in his critical views of the economic policies of mercantilist governments. There has been some speculation in the literature whether it might not also be fruitful to see Smith's thinking as a direct offspring of the industrial revolution, for he lived not only at the time of that revolution but also in the country where it started. It would be reasonable, therefore, to imagine that the rapid industrial development must have made a deep impression on him and led him to identify technological progress as an important source of economic development.

Somewhat surprisingly, it is difficult to find convincing evidence for this view in Smith's writing. The famous description of the pin factory is actually the only direct reference to modern manufacturing and technological change to be found in the *Wealth of Nations,* and the modernity of the example is not particularly striking. Moreover, there are no references, either in this example or anywhere else, to the use of steam power, although the use of this source of energy was well under way in Smith's time—for instance, in mining. Also notable is the fact that the inventor of the steam engine, James Watt, was a personal friend of Smith who could have kept him up to date about technological developments. But what Smith might have heard or seen of the introduction of modern industrial technology cannot have made a very strong impression on him, at least not to the degree of making him incorporate this perspective in his own analysis. The industrial revolution was still, at least as regards commercial applications, in its early phase, and Adam Smith was hardly the only one who did not fully realize the nature of the technological revolution that took place during his lifetime. Maybe there is a more general point here: it is obvious that economists have always been influenced by current economic events and developments, but it was not necessarily the historical events that we today consider to be the most significant that made the greatest impression on those who lived at the time. The material development of society formed the background for Adam Smith's life and work, but it still may not be very fruitful to see his research and writing as a direct result of the changes in economic life. After all, he used more of his time reading about economics, philosophy, and history than he spent on visits to pin factories.

Further Reading

The Wealth of Nations is a book that can still be read with pleasure and profit. The present standard version forms part of the edition of Smith's collected works that was published by Oxford University Press in the years following the two hundredth anniversary of its publication in 1976. It has an extensive set of notes that provide the reader with informative references both to Smith's other books and correspondence and to the work of other authors. It also contains a highly readable introduction by the editors, R. H. Campbell and A. S. Skinner. Skinner is also the editor of the 1970 Penguin paperback edition. This also has an excellent introduction, but it contains only books I–III; a further volume containing books IV and V came out in 1999. Another paperback version with extracts from all of the five books has been edited by Kathryn Sutherland and published in the World Classics series, also by Oxford University Press, in 1993. There are also several other paperback editions of the *Wealth of Nations*. *The Theory of Moral Sentiments*, while naturally also included in the collected works, is also available in a number of different editions.

The classical biography of Smith is by John Rae (1895), which can still be highly recommended. The 1965 reprint contains a valuable introductory essay by Jacob Viner. A more recent life of Smith is by Ross (1995). A shorter biography with a survey of Smith's writings can be found in Skinner's article in *The New Palgrave*.

The literature on Adam Smith's work is overwhelmingly large. In conjunction with the publication of the collected works, Skinner and Wilson (1975) have edited a collection of essays that provide perspectives on the whole range of his writing. They cover various aspects of his moral philosophy and reflections on history and political science as well as his economics. The essays by A. W. Coats on "Adam Smith and the Mercantile System" and by George Stigler on "Adam Smith's Travels on the Ship of State" are of particular interest for economists. O'Brien (2004) is an outstanding book about the classical economists, which also includes an extensive treatment of Adam Smith's economic theories. Emma Rothschild (2001) gives a fascinating account of Smith's ideas as part of the general body of thought in the period of the Enlightenment.

* CHAPTER 4 *

The Classical School:
Thomas Robert Malthus and David Ricardo

W<small>ITH</small> A<small>DAM</small> S<small>MITH</small> we are at the beginning of the stage in the history of economic thought that is commonly referred to as the classical period. Many of the leading economists of this period who took Adam Smith's work as their point of departure show a high degree of similarity both in their analytical approach and in their views on economic policy, and this group of economic thinkers is known as the classical school. Sometimes one refers to the English classical school, but since many of its prominent members were Scottish, "British" would perhaps be a more suitable term. During the hundred years from the 1770s to the 1870s there were obviously a number of important economists outside Britain, and some of them could naturally be seen as belonging to the classical school; a prominent example is the French economist Jean-Baptiste Say (1767–1832). But there were also economists, especially in Germany and France, who did significant work somewhat apart from the classical tradition, and we will return to some of these in chapter 7. In the present and the following chapter we concentrate on a few of the greatest names of the classical school.

While Adam Smith is the first of the leading classical economists, it has been common to see John Stuart Mill as the last. In most expositions of the history of ideas the death of Mill in 1873 marks the transition to a new dominant school of thought—the neoclassical. The term *classical* has accordingly a fairly precise content, at least in terms of chronology. However, it should be kept in mind that John Maynard Keynes, in the preface to his *General Theory of Employment, Interest, and Money* (1936), wrote that he would refer to all economists who did not share his own view of the causes of unemployment as "classical." This interpretation was taken up by many of Keynes's followers, but in the present context the meaning of the term is the standard one in the history of economic thought and not that of Keynes.

To what extent is it meaningful to talk about these economists as a "school"? Taking a broad view of the period, they constitute a fairly large but rather heterogeneous group of people. Some of them were members of parliament, some were employed in public administration, while a third group earned their living in the private sector. Their interest in economic questions was for most of them something that they cultivated during their leisure time—which for a number of them was rather extensive. Few of them had any connection with academic life. For those of them who were based in London or its vicinity, their common meeting place was the Political Economy Club, founded in 1821. At its monthly gatherings one of the members talked on a topic of current theoretical or practical interest, and this was followed by a general debate. Even if the members of the school identified themselves in a broad sense with Adam Smith's approach to the subject, they were not dogmatic, and they had a number of topics and issues that they could discuss and sometimes disagree about.[1] But one of the reasons that we think of them as a specific scientific school is that they very consciously related their work to each other: Ricardo took his point of departure from Smith, while Mill built on Ricardo's formulations. The later members of the school, especially John Stuart Mill, also emphasized their dependence on the work of their predecessors and were rather reluctant to accept that their own thinking represented a break with the past. However, it is important to realize that the concept of the classical school and indeed of other schools of economic thought is an invention of later historians of the subject, being one of many concepts that they use to impose order and structure on a complex past. We will come back to this issue in the discussion of the neoclassical school and the breakthrough of "marginalist" thinking in chapters 8 and 9.

Thomas Robert Malthus and David Ricardo are two of the greatest names in the classical school, and they were the dominating characters in the community of economists at the be-

---

[1] Prominent members of the club included James Mill (1773–1836), Robert Torrens (1780–1864), and Nassau Senior (1790–1864). James Mill (the father of John Stuart Mill) was at his time best known for his work in philosophy and history. Torrens wrote on monetary questions and international trade, while Senior was among other things an early critic of Malthus's theory of population.

ginning of the nineteenth century. They shared many of Adam Smith's views concerning the social benefits of a system of free markets and also agreed with each other on many basic issues in economic theory and policy. But as we shall see, there were also areas where their opinions differed sharply.

THOMAS MALTHUS

Thomas Robert Malthus (1766–1834) grew up as the son of a lawyer and country gentleman with strong intellectual interests. The younger Malthus studied science and mathematics in Oxford while at the same time acquiring a broad knowledge of literature and history. After completion of his studies he became a fellow of Jesus College in Oxford, and he was also ordained as a priest in the Anglican Church. His positions both at the college and in the church provided him with a reasonable income and only a modest workload, so that he had good opportunities to pursue his intellectual interests. In 1805 he was appointed professor of history, politics, commerce, and finance at the East India College, a new institution that had been founded to train employees for the East India Company, the trading monopoly that governed India during a large part of the time of the English colonial rule. Malthus can therefore be said to have been the first professor of political economy or economics in England,[2] although not at a proper university. As professor, his duties were similar to those of his colleagues at the present time; he was expected to teach, carry out administrative tasks, and do research. And like his successors he thought that it was difficult to find the time to carry out all his tasks. In his correspondence we find several letters

---

[2] In comparison it may be mentioned that the first professor of economics in the Nordic countries was Anders Berch, who was appointed *juris prudentiae, oeconomiae et commerciorum professor* at Uppsala University in 1741; see Liedman and Persson (1993). In Norway, Christen Smith became professor of botany and economic sciences at the University of Christiania (now Oslo) in 1814. The combination of botany and economics may seem strange from a modern perspective, but at that time it was not uncommon in some countries to see the exploration of a country's natural resources as a central concern of economics, and from that point of view the combination of subjects might have seemed more natural.

where he complains that teaching and administration take up too much of his time; the result is that he is behind with his correspondence and has problems meeting the various deadlines set for him by editors and publishers.

The Theory of Population

Malthus is above all known for his theory of population growth, which was first presented in his book *An Essay on the Principle of Population* (1798). Few books written by an economist have received so much attention and had so much influence. It was an important source of inspiration for Charles Darwin's theory of evolution, and it left its mark on the thinking of several generations regarding the population problem and related issues, particularly poverty and birth control. It came out in six editions during Malthus's lifetime. The most substantial revision occurred with the publication of the second edition, which in many respects must be considered a new book. In the literature on Malthus the first edition is therefore often referred to as the *First Essay*, while the second and later editions are known as the *Second Essay*. In the various editions of the *Second Essay* the book increased steadily in volume, mainly because of increased emphasis on providing factual evidence for the theory. Malthus attempted to strengthen its empirical foundations through reports from his extensive travels in a number of European countries, the Scandinavian countries among them. He collected data and general observations on population questions; the basic theory, however, remained the same through all editions of the book.

The full title of Malthus's book was *An Essay on the Principle of Population as it affects the future Improvement of Society, with Remarks on the Speculations of Mr. Godwin, M. Condorcet, and other Writers*. The Marquis de Condorcet (see chapter 2) had published a book with a broad perspective on the development of mankind and a utopian vision of the future. The English writer William Godwin's book *Enquiry concerning Political Justice* (1793) belonged to the same utopian tradition. He claimed that in the human society of the future, war and crime would cease to exist, and therefore there would be no need for law enforcement. Disease, anguish, melancholy, and resentment would vanish, and each person would strive to promote the common good. Malthus and his father had long discussions about these visions of the future. The older Malthus was enthusiastic about the books and their optimistic forecasts. But the son was unable to share his father's optimism, and in his own book he set himself the task of rejecting the reasoning on which it was based. His main idea was that the tension between the growth of population and the production of food would set strict limits to how far human progress could be carried.

The first edition of Malthus' *Essay* begins with two basic postulates, which in a pointed and dramatic manner convey to the reader that he is about to read a book that is concerned with the very foundations of human existence:[3]

> I think I may fairly make two postulata. First, That food is necessary to the existence of man. Secondly, That the passion between sexes is necessary and will remain nearly in its present state. (Malthus 1798; 1970, p. 70)

It is easy to agree with the first postulate: man cannot live without food. The second may require a further comment. One of Godwin's hypotheses was that the sexual instinct—"the passion between the sexes," as Malthus says—would decline with increasing wealth. Malthus did not share Godwin's belief at this point, but we may note that he gives a small concession to Godwin's view by his use of the word *nearly*.

On the next page of the book, the core of Malthus's theory of population is presented in compact form as follows:

> Population, when unchecked, increases in a geometrical ratio. Subsistence increases only in an arithmetical ratio. A slight acquaintance with numbers will show the immensity of the first power in comparison to the second. (Malthus 1798; 1970, p. 71)

So, according to Malthus, a population which is not faced with any constraints on the availability of resources will have a tendency to grow as a geometric series of the form

$$1, 2, 4, 8, 16, \ldots$$

[3] All quotations and page references are taken from the edition of the *First Essay* that was published in the Pelican Classics series in 1970.

and the justification for this is the second postulate of the constancy of the passion between the sexes. The theoretical foundation for the assumption of geometric growth can therefore be derived from biology. Malthus also provides an empirical justification of the hypothesis by citing the development in the United States, where, according to him, there was an abundance of food, and where in fact it had turned out that population had doubled every twenty-five years. We saw in chapter 3 that Adam Smith made a similar observation about the development in the American colonies (which, during the time between the publication of *The Wealth of Nations* and Malthus's *First Essay*, had become the United States of America).

When the production of food only grows as an arithmetic series, that is, in the form of

$$1, 2, 3, 4, 5, \ldots$$

the interpretation must be that the distance in time between each element of the series is the same as in the population series. If both tendencies could develop independently of each other, we would observe a steady fall in the amount of food production per capita. But the very essence of Malthus's theory of population is that such an independent development of population and food production is impossible.

The population hypothesis is based on a clearly formulated (although stylized) biological assumption. By contrast, the theoretical justification for the arithmetic series describing food production is less evident; nor is it easy to derive it from empirical generalizations. But Malthus's intention regarding the special hypothesis of the arithmetic series is clearly to put it up as a pointed contrast to the geometric progress of the population, once we interpret the distance in time between the terms as being the same for the two series. The numbers $1, 2, 3, 4, 5, \ldots$ must therefore be considered as describing the development of production over time with a growing population. The example accordingly implies that the relative increase of food production is less then the (potential) relative increase of population. In a more modern formulation the food production hypothesis may be interpreted as an assumption that there are decreasing returns to scale in agriculture. This interpretation is supported by a statement in the *Second Essay*: "It must be evident to those who have

65

the slightest acquaintance with agricultural subjects that, in proportion as cultivation extended, the additions that could yearly be made to the former average produce must be gradually and regularly diminishing" (Malthus 1803; 1992, p. 18).[4] This formulation comes close to the one that we find in Turgot (1766), and which was discussed in chapter 2.

Malthus also argues that historical experience indicates that the arithmetic series represents an upper limit of what one may envisage for the increase of food production in England in intervals of twenty-five years. Some historians of thought have criticized Malthus for failing to provide a deeper theoretical justification for the arithmetic series and argued that it would have been better if he had used the more general assumption of decreasing returns in agriculture. Quite clearly, they have a point. On the other hand, there can be no doubt that the dramatic juxtaposition of the two series is an important explanation of the general acceptance and popular appeal of his theory.

The core of Malthus's theory is accordingly that there exists a permanent tension between the availability of food and the size of the population. The natural growth rate of population must necessarily be kept down to that of the lower rate of growth of food supply:

> By that law of our nature which makes food necessary to the life of man, the effects of these two unequal powers must be kept equal. This implies a strong and constantly operating check on population from the difficulty of subsistence. This difficulty must fall somewhere; and must necessarily be severely felt by a large portion of mankind. (Malthus 1798; 1970, p. 71)

There must be mechanisms that hold down the rate of population growth so as to keep it aligned with the development of food supply.[5] These were positive and preventive checks, which Malthus also divided into "misery and vice." Famine was the most obvious example of misery while birth control, according to Mal-

---

[4] The quotation from the *Second Essay* has been taken from the edition published by Cambridge University Press in 1992.

[5] This basic idea can also be traced back to the *Wealth of Nations*: "Every species of animals naturally multiplies in proportion to the means of their subsistence, and no species can ever multiply beyond it" (Smith 1776; 1976, p. 97).

thus's theological convictions, was the primary example of sin. In the long run, per capita food supply would be constant. The mechanisms that would ensure this were on the one hand decreasing returns in agriculture (the arithmetic series) and on the other hand an infinitely elastic supply of labor at the subsistence wage. The subsistence wage was defined, following the lines of thought of Cantillon and Smith, as the level of income that was just sufficient for the reproduction of the working class. Malthus did not deny that wages, for a number of reasons, could lie above the subsistence level for limited periods of time, but he believed that higher family incomes would increase the number of children and thereby the size of the population and the workforce. The increased supply of labor would then put downward pressure on wages, which would move back toward the subsistence level. This "iron law of wages," as it was called, was part of the explanation why the critics of economics sometimes referred to it as "the dismal science."[6]

Malthus's ideas about the forces determining population, wages, and the standard of living had a strong influence on the whole of the classical school and led many of its members to take a pessimistic view of the possibility of improving the situation for the poor of society. However, both Malthus and other economists came later on to modify the theory that he presented in

---

[6] It was the historian Thomas Carlyle (1795–1881) who first used the expression "the dismal science" to characterize economics, but it is interesting to note that he used it in a completely different connection. The expression appeared for the first time in an article that Carlyle published in 1849 on "the negro question." There his main point was that economists did not realize that society could not function without strong leadership. The economists' idea that the market mechanism could direct the use of resources to promote the common good was in Carlyle's opinion based on a total misunderstanding of human nature. The strong must necessarily lead the weak, among other things by forcing them to work more than they desired. The specific example that he used was the white plantation owners in the West Indies in relation to the black population there, but he also believed that his arguments were of more general validity. Thus, according to Carlyle, the worst form of contemporary slavery was not that of the American South, but the slavery of the strong under the weak which resulted from democracy and the market economy. It was the economists' recommendations of this type of society that made their subject deserve the epithet "the dismal science." For a further discussion of Carlyle's views see Persky (1990).

the first edition of his *Essay*. The definition of subsistence wages gradually underwent a change, so that it was conceived more as a social and psychological minimum rather than a purely physiological one. Higher wages could make people used to a higher standard of living, and this adjustment could prevent the wage from falling back to its previous subsistence level. Malthus also found that there were other checks on population than misery and vice. In the second and later editions of *Essay on Population* he introduced self-control—"moral restraint"—as a further cause of reduced population growth. He pointed out that the growth of population could be checked through late marriages, and he found that this hypothesis was confirmed by observations that he made in particular during his travels in Norway.

Seen against the background of Godwin's utopian vision of the good society that humanity could establish on the basis of scientific insight and political determination, Malthus's message was widely viewed as deeply pessimistic. Man was doomed to live in a permanent tension between population growth and food production, and in this perspective there was limited scope for economic and social reform. When regarded as a broad vision of society, the theory appeared to be strongly conservative. However, Malthus himself was probably not as conservative as he was commonly regarded in public opinion. He considered his descriptive analysis of the central problems of society also as a guideline to constructive reforms, which in his view had to be designed with a view to limiting population growth.

Economic Policy: Poverty, Free Trade, and Unemployment

A controversial aspect of Malthus's writings was his analysis of poor relief, which was derived from his theory of population and focused on the connection between income and the number of child births. A form of poor relief that led to an increase of the incomes of the poor would in his view primarily result in an increase in the number of children. Over time, this would increase the supply of labor and lead to lower wages, so that the result of higher incomes for the poor would not increase their standard of living; the standard would be the same, but there would be more people living in poverty. The best form of assistance to the poor, according to Malthus, was a social and economic policy that stimulated people to have fewer children. The existing form of poor relief in England was therefore misguided and ought to be dismantled. His stand on this question furthered strengthened his reputation as a conservative thinker with policy recommendations that were seen as going against the interests of the poor.

Another area where Malthus's participation in the public debate created considerable controversy was the debate about free trade. The free trade issue arose particularly in connection with the so-called Corn Laws, which were a central theme in the economic policy debates in England in the early nineteenth century. The purpose of the Corn Laws was to protect British agriculture by allowing for prohibition on imports when the price of wheat fell below a certain level. The consequence was naturally that this level became a minimum price of wheat, which ensured the profitability of the existing domestic wheat production. Malthus was against the abolishment of the Corn Laws. He realized that this went against the principle of free trade that was supported by Ricardo and other economists, but he argued that no principle of economic policy could claim to be universally valid, and that exceptions must be allowed under particular circumstances. In this case, his view was that the Corn Laws could be justified by the concern for national security, for it was important that Britain was self-sufficient with corn in the case of war. The question was also an important one from the point of view of distributive justice, for the high price of corn was a particularly heavy burden on the poor. Malthus's position in this controversy further increased his reputation as a spokesman for the landowners' interests and an enemy of the working classes. He protested keenly against this interpretation of his views, and in the fifth edition of his *Essay on Population* he emphasized that his primary goal as regarded economic policy was to "improve the condition and increase the happiness of the lower classes of society" (Malthus 1803; 1992, p. 386.)

Malthus was not only an expert on population. He was also a general economist with broad interests, and his other main work was *Principles of Political Economy Considered with a View to their Practical Application* (1820). Although the book was firmly rooted in the classical tradition, in a number of areas Malthus adopted views that deviated from the ideas of the other classical economists. His best-known case of heterodoxy was his belief that aggregate demand could become too low to secure full employment. This was a viewpoint which led his good friend David Ricardo to conclude that Malthus had failed to understand the most fundamental principles of economics. Many years later, however, it led John Maynard Keynes—in chapter 23 of his *General Theory* (1936)—to hail him as an important precursor of his own ideas. Malthus's theory was based on his assumption about population and wages; wages would tend toward the minimum subsistence level. However, the workers would produce far more that could be absorbed by their own demand, and there would accordingly be a latent trend toward overproduction. In other words, the aggregate demand in society would tend to be too low to absorb the aggregate supply, and a natural consequence of this would be unemployment. In Malthus's view, there would therefore be a need for a class of people who demanded the excess production without themselves making any contribution to output. In England, this role could in his view be played by the class of landowners, "the landed gentry." Ricardo was extremely skeptical both to the idea of general overproduction and to the role of landowners in the prevention of unemployment. In a letter to Malthus he wrote, "I can see no soundness in the reasons you give for the usefulness of demand, on the part of unproductive consumers. How their consuming, without reproducing, can be beneficial to a country, in any possible state of it, I confess I cannot discover" (Ricardo 1951–55, Vol. VIII, p. 301). As Robert Dorfman says in his article on the friendship between Malthus and Ricardo, one can almost see Ricardo shaking his head as he writes these words.

The Friendship with David Ricardo

The contact between the two economists was established in 1811, when Malthus wrote to Ricardo on a question concerning the causes of inflation; Malthus wished to meet Ricardo for an "amicable discussion in private," so as not to waste time on a long controversy in print. This became the beginning of their correspondence and a friendship which lasted until Ricardo's death in 1823. According to Dorfman (1989) they often met several times a week and they wrote about eighty letters to each other each way. They disagreed about a large number of issues, and they became steadily better friends. We get a good impression of the relationship between them from the last letter that Ricardo wrote to Malthus two weeks before his death. After a long discussion of a problem in the theory of value that they had disagreed about, he concludes: "And now, my dear Malthus, I have done. Like other disputants, after much discussion we each retain our own opinions. These discussions, however, never influence our friendship; I could not like you more than I do if you agreed in opinion with me" (Ricardo 1951–55, Vol. IX, p. 382).

The story of the friendship between Malthus and Ricardo is a moving one. It is also of interest from the point of view of the history of economic ideas, since it demonstrates that the classical school of economists did not only consist of people who thought alike about economic questions. They had a common approach to economics that enabled them to communicate easily with each other, and this approach was based on a shared theoretical framework. But this framework was not so narrow that it necessarily made them draw the same conclusions. After Ricardo's death Malthus reflected that if they had only had the opportunity to continue their discussions, they would in the end have reached agreement. In his speech at Ricardo's funeral he said: "I never loved anybody out of my own family so much. Our interchange of opinions was so unreserved, and the object after which we were both enquiring was so entirely the truth and nothing else, that I cannot but think we sooner or later must have agreed" (Dorfman 1989, p. 162).

DAVID RICARDO

David Ricardo (1772–1823) came from a wealthy Jewish family. His father was a commodity and securities broker, and the family had been business people for several generations, first in Spain, later in Italy and the Netherlands before they settled in England a few years before David was born. His formal schooling lasted only until he was fourteen, when he started to work for his father's firm. Gradually, frictions developed between him and his orthodox family, and the conflict became acute when he married a non-Jewish woman. He left his father's business and established himself as a stockbroker. He was very successful and quickly amassed a substantial fortune, which enabled him to retire when he was about forty. He bought a country estate outside London and lived on the income from his capital while devoting much of his time to the study of politics and social affairs, particularly economic issues. In 1819 he entered the House of Commons, not as the result of an election campaign but through the purchase of a seat in Ireland (where he never set foot). From a modern-day perspective this suggests a form of political corruption, but at the time it was an accepted practice, which apparently did not hurt Ricardo's reputation.

The story is that Ricardo's interest in economics as a science was aroused during a stay in the city of Bath, where Mrs. Ricardo was taking the waters. He was looking around for something to read and found *The Wealth of Nations* in a library—probably one of the more significant library loans in the history of the subject. Like many other members of the classical school, he was a self-taught person in the area of economics, and—in contrast to people like Smith and Malthus—he had not carried out academic studies in any other field of knowledge.

Ricardo's career as a writer on economics began with the publication of the pamphlet *The High Price of Bullion, a Proof of the Depreciation of Bank Notes* (1810).[7] Its chief argument was that the high price of gold was caused by a pronounced increase in the circulation of bank notes, thereby establishing Ricardo as an early spokesman for the quantity theory of money. This publication caused considerable attention and established Ricardo as an authority on financial and monetary questions. Gradually, he became one of the central participants in the Political Economy Club, and several of its members, among them Malthus and James Mill (the father of John Stuart Mill), strongly encouraged him to write a general exposition of the whole area of economics, or political economy. Ricardo was at first skeptical to the idea, particularly because he felt that the cost of the effort of a sustained literary exposition would be too high. He probably overestimated the cost, for he managed to complete his major work, *The Principles of Political Economy and Taxation*, in less than two years, and it was published in 1817. Later on he published little of scientific significance, but when Malthus's *Principles* came

---

[7] "Bullion" means unminted gold.

out in 1820 Ricardo sat down to write a series of comments on it that became so extensive as to correspond to the length of a book. He did not, however, wish the manuscript to go into print, and it was in fact not published until 1928 under the title of *Notes on Malthus.*

Many writers have maintained that Ricardo's most important contribution to the development of economics lies in his establishment of a certain style of theoretical research that had a strong influence on his successors. More than Adam Smith, Ricardo reasons in terms of theoretical models. He makes simplifying assumptions, he takes care to be precise about their exact content, and he derives results from the models that are directed both toward explaining the actual functioning of the economy and laying the foundations for economic policy. The models are not mathematically formulated, but the careful verbal formulations and the illustrative numerical examples make the modern reader feel that the mathematical formulations lie just below the surface of the text. Not surprisingly, therefore, Ricardo's theories have inspired a number of later theorists to try to formulate them in mathematical language. The historical examples and practical observations that are so characteristic of *The Wealth of Nations,* play a very subordinate role in Ricardo's work.

There are also other ways in which *The Principles of Political Economy and Taxation* is a totally different book from *The Wealth of Nations.* Adam Smith's aim was to write a broad theoretical and historical exposition of the whole field of economics. Ricardo's book is both shorter and narrower in terms of scope. Rather than aiming at a broad survey, he makes a selection of topics that particularly interest him, and to a large extent the book takes the form of comments on what he has read by other authors. He quickly reviews topics on which he agrees with Smith, Malthus, and others, then probes more deeply and carefully into the issues where he sees himself as having something important to contribute to economic theory.

Ricardo's *Principles* can roughly be divided into three parts. The first part discusses the foundations of the theories of price formation and income distribution, the second part is concerned with issues of taxation theory and policy, while the third part is a collection of chapters on selected topics that are only loosely interconnected.

Price and Distribution Theory: Labor and Capital

Chapter I of Ricardo's *Principles* begins with an italicized paragraph:[8]

> *The value of a commodity, or the quantity of any other commodity for which it will exchange, depends on the relative quantity of labour which is necessary for its production, and not on the greater or less compensation which is paid for that labour.* (Ricardo 1817; 1951, p. 11.)

Like Adam Smith before him, Ricardo thought of labor, capital, and land as the three basic factors of production. But the quotation suggests that his theory of relative prices took the form of a clearly formulated labor theory of value similar to what we find in Smith's work.[9] As a matter of fact, Ricardo quotes the beaver-deer example and says that it illustrates the foundation of the theory of value. However, there is evidently a problem here which Smith, in Ricardo's opinion, had not clarified in a satisfactory manner. How can there be three factors of production and yet be the case that only the use of one of them explains relative prices? The theory chapters of the *Principles* can be read as an attempt to explain how these propositions fit together. The analysis tries to make the labor theory of value more rigorous, but in the course of his discussion Ricardo also arrives at a more subtle understanding of it, introducing modifications that foreshadow theoretical developments that only became prominent in the 1870s.

Ricardo first confronts the view that commodity production needs more inputs of factors of production than just labor; therefore it cannot be the case that the use of labor alone determines value. This view, he says, is based on a too simple understanding of the theory. Let us extend the beaver-deer example by imagin-

---

[8] All references are to Piero Sraffa's edition of the *Principles*, which was published by Cambridge University Press in 1951.

[9] However, the emphasis of the irrelevance of the wage rate for relative prices raises a problem of interpretation. In the beaver-deer example the conclusion follows if one assumes that beaver and deer hunters earn the same wage rate. But in more complex settings with different types of workers who have different wages, this assumption becomes unrealistic. We must therefore imagine that what Ricardo has in mind is a stylized economy where labor as a factor of production is homogeneous and is paid the same wage rate.

ing that beaver and deer hunting require different kinds of weapons, and further that more labor is needed to produce a weapon for the beaver hunt than for the deer hunt. It will still be the case that the relative price of beaver and deer reflects the use of labor in the two activities, but when assessing their labor contents it is not enough to consider the time it takes to kill the animals. One also has to consider the indirect time use that goes to construct the weapons. The use of capital—the weapons in this example—can therefore be recalculated in terms of labor, so that the relative labor contents of commodities also takes into account all indirect use via the input of capital goods. When it is extended along these lines, the use of material factors of production does not create any problems for the labor theory of value; capital can be dissolved into units of labor. In a modern economy characterized by extensive specialization and division of labor, the more general version of the theory becomes more difficult to confront with factual observation compared to the impression that one gets from Adam Smith's example. But it becomes more general, resting on a more convincing theoretical foundation.

Ricardo also has another theoretical approach to the analysis of capital, which represents one of his most important theoretical innovations. He points out that the process of production requires different amounts of time in different industries. For a wine grower the time between the beginning and end of the production process may be several years, for the corn farmer close to a year, for the baker less than a week. The capital—which Ricardo mainly thought of as prepaid wages—will accordingly be tied up in the production process for unequal lengths of time, and the interest cost that this involves must be reflected in prices. If the direct wage costs are the same in these industries, the implication is that capital intensive goods become relatively more expensive than would follow from the simple version of the theory. Ricardo acknowledges therefore that the labor theory of value does not hold in its simple form, but he constructs some numerical examples to indicate the magnitude of the differences that arise when one takes account of the unequal length of the production processes. In these examples it turns out that the deviations in relative prices cannot exceed 6–7 percent. Ricardo uses these modest deviations to argue that for analytical purposes it may be acceptable to use the labor theory of value in its simple form—even if it strictly speaking is inaccurate. But we must conclude that he did not hold a pure labor theory of value, and the American economist George Stigler (1958; 1965) has characterized his theory as a "93 % labour theory of value" (100% minus the deviation of 6–7%.)

However, Ricardo does not drop his point about the time dimension of production. In the pure labor theory of value, it will be the case—as indicated in the introductory paragraph—that the level of wages plays no role for relative prices. Both for beaver and deer hunting the price must be equal to labor hours times the wage rate, but when we consider the relative price, given that the wage rate is the same for the two activities, this will be equal to the ratio of their respective labor requirements. But when the length of the production processes differs, the commodity that has the longest period of production must sell at a higher price than that which would follow from the simple version of the theory. Consequently, the conclusion that the level of wages is irrelevant for relative prices no longer holds. For an increase in the wage rate will have the least effect on the price of the commodity that has the longest period of production:

> The relative prices of those commodities on which such durable capital is employed, will vary inversely as wages; they will fall as wages rise, and rise as wages fall. (Ricardo 1817; 1951, p. 43)

Ricardo emphasizes that this value or price theory is a theory of *relative* prices. He also discusses the question of whether the theory can say anything about *absolute* prices, or, as he formulates it, whether there exists "an invariable measure of value." His criterion for a constant measure of value is that there must be a commodity whose labor content is constant, since such a commodity would be ideal for expressing all other prices. But such a commodity, he concludes, does not exist. Even in the case of gold, technological changes occur that influence the cost of production in terms of units of labor. On the other hand, it is obviously convenient to be able to talk about rising and falling prices without always having to specify exactly which price ratios one is referring to. The way by which Ricardo cuts through this problem is characteristic of his theoretical style. Gold is not a perfect measure of value, but we may still make the simplifying assumption that it is: "Although I fully allow that money made of gold is subject to most of the variations of other things, I shall suppose it to be invariable, and therefore all alterations in price to be occasioned by some alteration in the value of the commodity of which I may be speaking" (Ricardo 1817; 1951, p. 46).

The Theory of Rent

As we have seen, Ricardo "saved" the labor theory of value from the complications raised by the use of capital. By dissolving capital into labor units and using the 93 percent approximation, both labor and capital could be incorporated in an extended labor theory of value. But the role played by the third factor of production—land—still needed to be clarified. It was in the analysis of this factor that Ricardo made one of his most pathbreaking contributions in the form of his theory of rent. The theory is easiest to understand if we assume that the person who owns the land is different from the one who cultivates it. A farmer who rents his farmland from a landowner will have to pay him a periodic sum for the use of the land, and this is Ricardo's concept of rent. Land varies in terms of its quality or productivity. As population and with it the consumption of food increases, farmers will use land of decreasing quality. On the farm that uses the land of the poorest quality, the cost of production (in terms of labor and capital) will be exactly equal to sales revenue, and rent will be zero. The farms that use land of higher quality will, on the other hand, show a positive difference between revenue and cost, and the difference will increase with the quality of the land. This is the rent, for the difference shows the highest payment that the landowner can collect without providing the farmer with an incentive to move to a farm with a lower quality of land.[10]

How should the rent of land be incorporated in the labor theory of price formation? Will not a higher rent and thereby a higher cost also lead to a higher price? No, says Ricardo. Suppose that the farmers who occupy the land of highest productivity succeed in reducing their labor cost of production. This causes the rent to increase. But the price does not increase, for this is determined by the cost of production on the farm at the margin of cultivation,

[10] The theory of rent is discussed in detail in chapter II in the *Principles*. A short chapter III analyzes the rent from mines, but mostly by pointing out that the same principles hold for the mining of minerals as for the production of food.

where the rent is zero. Let us now assume that the price of corn (which Ricardo often uses as a synonym for food) goes up, for example, as a consequence of an increasing population. Farmers will then start to use land of poorer quality, with the implication that the rent on all other land increases. In other words, the chain of causation goes from the price of corn to the rent of land, not the other way round; rent is not an element of the cost of production. Ricardo summarizes the essence of the theory as follows:

> Corn is not high because a rent is paid, but a rent is paid because corn is high. (Ricardo 1817; 1951, p. 74)

In his exposition of the theory of rent Ricardo also arrived at another insight that marks significant progress from the treatment of Adam Smith. He pointed out that the price of corn must be determined by the cost of production on the farm with the highest cost, that is, by the farm "on the margin of cultivation." There is no necessary contradiction between this result and the labor theory of value, but this version of the theory has an interesting connection with later "marginalist" theories where the individual producer will choose a volume of production so as to equalize marginal cost and price. In Ricardo's work there is no analysis of the cost conditions on the individual farm; it is for agriculture as a whole that competition leads to equality between price and cost on the marginal land.

Ricardo's theory of value is a theory of price formation for produced goods. He points out, however, that there also exist other goods where availability does not depend on production; an example that he mentions are rare old coins. For such goods the labor theory of value is clearly irrelevant, and the only thing that Ricardo has to say about them is that their value is determined by scarcity. He also briefly discusses Adam Smith's distinction between natural and market prices but makes it clear that what he is interested in is the natural price—or the long-run equilibrium price, as we would have formulated it today.

Long-run Development and the Stationary State

Ricardo's theory of rent forms the point of departure for his theory of the long-run development of the market economy. As the population and workforce increase, the demand for agricultural goods ("corn") increases also. For this demand to be satis-fied, less-productive land must be brought into cultivation. This leads to an increase of rent on the more productive land and a larger share of rent in national income. With a constant level of real wages—as determined by the Malthusian subsistence prin-ciple—the rate of profit will fall. But with a decreasing rate of profit the incentive to invest will weaken and gradually fall to the level where further accumulation of capital comes to a halt. At this point the real growth of the economy reaches an end; we have arrived at the stationary state.[11] This idea became one of the cornerstones of classical thinking regarding the long-run pros-pects for the market economy.

Was the movement toward the stationary state an inevitable process? Not entirely, according to Ricardo. Technical progress might slow the process: "This tendency, this gravitation as it were of profits, is happily checked at repeated intervals by the improve-ments in machinery … as well as by discoveries in the science of agriculture" (Ricardo 1817; 1951, p. 120). However, technical and scientific innovation could only, in Ricardo's view, delay the dy-namic process toward a stationary state; it could not lead to any fundamental change in it. Another factor that might cause a delay in the advent of the stationary state was the abolition of restric-tions on food imports and adoption of a regime of free trade. This is part of the explanation of Ricardo's stand in the debate about the Corn Laws: importing food would decrease the pressure on land in England and thereby prevent the rate of profit from de-creasing as rapidly as it otherwise would have done. But this ef-fect too is of a temporary nature; in the long run the tendency of the rate of profit to fall and the accumulation of capital to cease is an inevitable feature of the development of the economy.

The Theory of International Trade

Ricardo's fame today rests to a large extent on his contribution to the theory of foreign trade, especially the theory of compara-tive advantage as the basis for the international division of labor. Even students who have never been exposed to the history of

[11] It should be noted that Ricardo himself did not use this term, which was adopted by his followers.

economics will associate his name with the illustrative example of trade between England and Portugal which occurs in virtually every textbook exposition of the principles of international trade.

Ricardo begins his chapter on foreign trade by maintaining that even if international trade does not directly increase "the amount of value" in a country (because the value of exports tends to be equal to the value of imports), it will nevertheless increase the standard of living: "It will very powerfully contribute to increase the mass of commodities, and therefore the sum of enjoyments" (Ricardo 1817; 1951, p. 128).

Nevertheless, foreign trade does make a real contribution to output or the amount of value, but its contribution is more indirect; it encourages specialization and the international division of labor, and this leads to a more efficient use of resources in every single country. About free trade he says that

> by increasing the general mass of productions, it diffuses general benefit, and binds together by one common tie of interest and intercourse, the universal society of nations throughout the civilized world. It is this principle which determines that wine shall be made in France and Portugal, that corn shall be grown in America and Poland, and that hardware and other goods shall be manufactured in England. (Ricardo 1817; 1951, p. 134)

So what is this principle that determines the international division of labor? One could imagine, Ricardo says, that if the rate of return on capital were higher in Portugal than in England, capital would move from England to Portugal—just as it would move from London to Yorkshire if the rate of return were higher in Yorkshire. But this argument is too simple, for experience shows that the owners of capital have a strong aversion to removing their capital and themselves to another country. This is partly because foreign investment appears to be less certain and less subject to the owner's control, partly because of the "natural disinclination" that all men have toward leaving the country of their birth.

This reasoning forms the background to the assumptions on which Ricardo builds his theory of foreign trade. The factors of production are assumed to be immobile between countries while finished goods are assumed to be perfectly mobile; a set of assumptions that would come to characterize the theory of international trade right up to our own time. The assumptions are used to demonstrate the benefits of international specialization: when each country adopts specialization in production and uses part of its output for exports—which in turn finances its imports—all countries can exploit their productive advantages in the international exchange of commodities.

How these advantages can be exploited is illuminated in the example of trade between England and Portugal, who produce and exchange two commodities, wine and cloth. The example is nowadays usually presented in the form of a table of numbers, frequently supplemented by means of equations and diagrams. Ricardo himself has nothing of this, but his exposition is still very clear and analytic. In his original version the numbers of man-years it would take to produce given quantities of wine and cloth are as follows:

	England	Portugal
Wine	120	80
Cloth	100	90

Obviously, Portugal is the most efficient country in the production of both goods.[12] In spite of this, it is to Portugal's advantage to import cloth from England instead of producing them at home:

> Though she [Portugal] could make the cloth with the labour of 90 men, she would import it from a country where it required the labour of 100 men to produce it, because it would be advantageous to her rather to employ her capital in the production of wine, for which she would obtain more cloth from England, than she could produce by diverting a portion of her capital from the cultivation of vines to the manufacture of cloth. (Ricardo 1817; 1951, p. 135)

It is accordingly not the case, as one might perhaps intuitively believe, that all production will take place in the high-productivity country. It is the relative productivity or comparative advantage that determines the location of production. For Portugal it will be in the national interest to leave the production of cloth to English producers and specialize in the production of wine. For in the

---

[12] However, modern textbooks that use a table of this type appear without exception to let England be the most efficient country.

exchange of wine against cloth Portugal will obtain more cloth for its input of labor than if the country had engaged in domestic production of cloth.[13]

In Ricardo's *Principles* there is an unresolved tension between the labor theory of value and the theory of comparative advantage. For the producers in England and Portugal to have incentives to specialize in the production of cloth and wine, the price of wine relative to cloth must deviate from the relative labor content in each of the countries; it must be higher than that of Portugal and lower than that of England. Ricardo realizes this but remarks only that the principles that determine relative prices in a single country do not hold in the context of international exchange. But what it then is that determines relative prices is a problem that he does not pursue further. As we shall see in chapter 5, its solution appeared first in a contribution by John Stuart Mill.

The theory of comparative advantage is an interesting demonstration of Ricardo's style when he writes about economic theory. In his willingness to adopt simplifying assumptions and construct stylized examples he gives a foretaste of the development of modern economics. He acknowledges that his theories represent abstractions from real life, but he defends his simplifications by the argument that they make it possible to grasp the essence of complex problems.

The Theory of Taxation

More than one fourth of Ricardo's *Principles* is concerned with taxation, and this part has a more applied character than the rest of the book. After a short introductory chapter he discusses the most important types of taxes, such as taxes on raw materials, on wages, on profits, and on housing. His main interest is in the

---

[13] There has been some discussion in the literature about which economist deserves the honour of first having formulated the theory of comparative advantage. It has been maintained that the theory appears both in works by Robert Torrens and James Mill, which appeared some years before the publication of Ricardo's *Principles*. But there seems to be general agreement that Ricardo's version of the theory is the most general one and the most clearly formulated, and that it was his exposition of it that led to its general acceptance as a cornerstone of the theory of international trade. An interesting survey of the historical debate can be found in Aldrich (2004).

incidence of taxes: Who is it that in the last instance carries the burden of taxation? His interest in this question reflects Ricardo's conviction that the explanation of the distribution of income between the different classes of society is the central problem of economic theory. Rather than take a long detour into the details of Ricardo's analysis of tax incidence, instead, I will provide a few examples of his analytical approach.

Ricardo advances the hypothesis—his formulation in fact suggests that the correctness of the hypothesis is beyond doubt—that there is a significant difference between the incidence of taxes on necessities and luxury goods. Taxes on luxuries like wine and riding horses are paid, in the form of higher prices, by those who consume them. But taxes on necessities are not necessarily paid by the workers who consume them. Because the real wage of the workers in the long run will tend toward the subsistence level, the increase in the prices of necessities that follow from taxation must be compensated by increases in nominal wages. In the long run, therefore, these taxes are not paid by the workers, but by the employers who must pay them higher wages. How large are the effects of taxes on consumer prices? According to Ricardo, they are completely shifted to consumer prices:

> A tax on hats will raise the price of hats; a tax on shoes, the price of shoes; if this were not the case, the tax would be finally paid by the manufacturer; his profits would be reduced below the general level, and he would quit his trade. (Ricardo 1817; 1951, p. 205)

This is a precise and elegant analysis. But Ricardo's conclusion is not as general as it first appears, for in other chapters he allows for the possibility that commodity taxes may also reduce producer prices. In the case of hats and shoes it is natural to suppose that all producers face the same costs. But in agriculture, as argued in his theory of rent, the situation may be different. A fall in the producer price will only lead the marginal producers, those with the highest costs, to "quit their trade," while the others will continue to produce. Hence it is possible for the burden of the tax to be shared between producers and consumers.

What are the best forms of taxation? On this point Ricardo is a little less clear. He says that "taxation under every form presents but a choice of evils" (p. 167). However, he has a somewhat ambivalent attitude to the rules for good taxation suggested by

Adam Smith in the *Wealth of Nations*. One of these rules was that the difference between the amount paid by the citizens and the amount collected by the government ought to be as small as possible. This rule is open to alternative interpretations. Smith could be referring to the desirability of low collection costs, but he could also be interpreted more generally as maintaining that the social cost of taxation, including the costs of price distortions, ought to be as low as possible. In at least one connection Ricardo appears to say that Smith's rule is meaningless, since what the citizens pay must by definition be equal to what the government receives. This is a rather narrow accounting interpretation of Smith's rule and is probably not a good expression of Ricardo's views. Elsewhere, however, he says that there are no taxes which do not weaken the economy's "power to accumulate." It is natural to read this as a statement that all kinds of taxes lead the economy to function less efficiently than it would otherwise have done.

An especially interesting element in Ricardo's theory of taxation is his analysis of the relationship between tax and loan finance of public expenditure. The discussion of this in chapter XVII is set in the context of war finance. Given that taxation imposes efficiency costs on the economy, would it not be better to finance the war by issuing a loan? Suppose that the war (assuming full certainty about the outcome) lasts for a year and costs the country 20 million pounds. The government can finance the war by collecting this amount in taxes at the beginning of the year. Alternatively, it could issue a loan at 5 percent interest and collect an annual tax of 1 million pounds to cover interest payments. But the economic realities of the alternatives are the same. The payment of interest is just a transfer between the creditor and the debtor and no cost for the nation as a whole. From the point of view of the citizens, therefore, the government might just as well have collected the 20 million in tax at the beginning of the war. If any of the taxpayers were to feel that their share of this amount was too much to pay during a single year, they could take up a private loan so as to distribute their payments over a longer time, but this transaction also is irrelevant for judging the economic position of society. In real economic terms, therefore, tax and loan finance are equivalent from the point of view of society, but it is clear from Ricardo's presentation that he believes that this point is difficult to realize for the ordinary citizen, and that loan finance in this kind of situation would be unfortunate. The reason is that loan finance induces the citizens to base their private decisions on an illusion that they are richer than they really are, since in the short run they pay only 1/20 of the tax that they would have to pay with the alternative form of finance. In other words, taxpayers tend not to realize that the real economic position both for themselves and society is the same in the two cases.

On the background of Ricardo's analysis it is something of a paradox that the expression "Ricardian equivalence" in modern macroeconomics has come to stand for a hypothesis that Ricardo definitely did not hold. The modern interpretation is that individual taxpayers actually see through the connection between tax and loan finance; they understand that whether the war is financed by loans or taxes, they have to pay the real cost of the war. Their private choices regarding consumption and saving should therefore be unaffected by which alternative the government chooses to finance the war. The modern usage could clearly be justified by the fact that Ricardo provided such a transparent explanation of the equivalence. On the other hand, however, it is clear that his view is that although *he himself* has understood the equivalence, there is no reason to believe that the general public has done so! His own view is therefore that tax finance is to be preferred because it makes people realize the true cost of the war. When modern economists invoke the economists of the past in support of their own views, they may sometimes provide a misleading impression of what the older economists actually said.

On Machinery

Principles of Political Economy and Taxation appeared in three editions during Ricardo's lifetime. Before publication both of the second and third editions he revised the text and made a number of alterations, most of which are concerned with details. But one of the changes is in fact far more than a detail. At the appearance of the third edition in 1821 Ricardo had written an entirely new chapter with the monumental title "On Machinery." In this chapter (chapter XXXI) he discusses whether the industrial revolution and the introduction of modern technology ("machinery")—now much more visible than at the time of Adam Smith—was a development that benefited all classes of society, paying special attention to the working class. In the introductory paragraph he says that in other connections he has expressed a view of this question that he now believes to be erroneous, so that "it, therefore, becomes a duty in me to submit my present views to examination, with my reasons for entertaining them" (Ricardo 1817; 1951, p. 386).

Ricardo's original conviction had been that since the introduction of machinery made it possible to produce at lower cost and sell at lower prices, the result would be a larger volume of production and greater availability of goods for all classes of society (abstracting from short-run structural problems). In his new chapter he acknowledges that this line of reasoning is not entirely correct. It is certainly true that workers will pay lower prices for consumer goods, but—and this is his new insight—the demand for labor will fall because employers will substitute machinery for human labor. It may appear as if Ricardo originally had overlooked a fairly obvious element in the analysis. But his line of reasoning had been that the labor that was replaced by machinery in some industries would be absorbed by other industries and firms. In other words, the theoretical hypothesis was that the demand for labor was constant. He now felt that this hypothesis must be rejected, and he formulated his new conclusion in a way which caused considerable attention among his contemporaries:

> That the opinion entertained by the labouring class, that the employment of machinery is frequently detrimental to their interests, is not founded on prejudice and error, but is conformable to the correct principles of political economy. (Ricardo 1817; 1951, p. 392)

When judging his readers' reactions to this proposition, it must be kept in mind that this was a time of great social unrest among English workers. There were frequent protests, some of them violent, against the introduction of new technology which, in the workers' view, deprived them of their work. Especially dramatic were the actions of the so-called Luddites (named after their leader Ned Ludd) who in the years around 1811–13 stormed the textile mills in the north of England and destroyed the new machines. The prevalent view among the upper classes of society was that the protests must be ascribed to lack of insight among the workers who did not understand their own best interests—

at least not their long-run interests. Not surprisingly therefore, Ricardo was sharply criticized, also by some other economists, but he considered his new view as being as securely founded as a proof in geometry!

Actually, Ricardo's point of view was not that the new technology *necessarily* went against the interests of the working class (note the word *frequently* in the last quotation). It could in fact come to benefit the workers, but this could only happen if the increased income of landowners and capitalists were so substantial that their increased demand for consumption goods succeeded in creating new employment for the workers that originally had been laid off. The possible harm to workers could also be less serious if technological change progressed gradually over time and not as suddenly as Ricardo's thought experiment might indicate.

The stir created by Ricardo's new view of this question says much about his standing as an economist during his lifetime, which continued to be high long after his death. His restatement and development of the labor theory of value, his theory of rent, and his analysis of foreign trade together constitute some of the high points of the economic theory of the classical school. The clarity and rigour of his exposition also contributed to making Ricardo's work an important reference for almost all further development of economic theory during the nineteenth century.

Further Reading

Malthus's *Essay on Population* is still a very enjoyable book to read, easily accessible to the modern reader. This is especially true of the first edition of 1798, which conveys the impression of having been written with great enthusiasm by a writer who feels that he has an epoch-making new message. There are several editions of the *First Essay*. The quotations in the text have been taken from the Pelican Classics edition from 1970. The *Second Essay* exists in an excellent edition by Cambridge University Press (1992) with an introduction by Donald Winch. It is based on the 1803 edition but with footnotes that refer to the changes made in the later editions.

Economists, demographers, and philosophers have all been interested in Malthus's work, and the literature about him is therefore very extensive. There are several articles about him and his work, including further references, in *The New Palgrave*. For a short biography, there is no better alternative than Keynes's (1933) brilliant article. The standard life of Malthus is by Patricia James (1979), who is also the editor of Malthus's travel diaries that were first discovered in the 1960s and published as Malthus (1966). It contains a number of interesting observations particularly of life in the Scandinavian countries with emphasis on economic and social conditions. Malthus also had more general interests; he notes, for instance, that Norwegian women are often very beautiful, while the men are rather below the average!

The Italian economist Piero Sraffa, who spent most of his academic life at Cambridge University, began to edit Ricardo's collected works, including his correspondence, newspaper articles and parliamentary speeches, in 1931. This work developed almost into a lifetime occupation, and the first volume did not appear in print until 1951. The edition as a whole is regarded as a truly major work of academic scholarship, and Sraffa's introductions and notes on the text form an important part of the literature on Ricardo. All quotations in the present chapter are taken from Sraffa's edition of *The Works and Correspondence of David Ricardo*.

Ricardo's contributions to economic theory have been described in all textbooks on the history of economic thought. The most extensive monograph treatment of his economics is by Samuel Hollander (1979). Stigler's article about Ricardo and the labor theory of value has been reprinted in a collection of essays (Stigler 1965) which also contains a number of other important articles on the history of economic thought. The friendship between Malthus and Ricardo has been beautifully described in an article by Robert Dorfman (1989).

Consolidation and Innovation:
John Stuart Mill

THE FAME OF JOHN STUART MILL (1806–73) rests mainly on his contributions to philosophy. He was the most prominent spokesman for the school of philosophical thinking known as utilitarianism, and he was also a prolific writer on economic and social questions, making him one of the most influential intellectuals in Victorian Britain. But he was also a very important theoretical economist. His work can be seen as the definitive statement of the classical tradition from Smith and Ricardo, but in some important respects it also foreshadows the great changes in economic theory that were to occur in the two decades following his death. He can therefore be regarded as the main figure in the period of transition between the classical economists and the neoclassical school, which came to dominate theoretical developments toward the end of the nineteenth century.

His father, James Mill, also a well-known economist in his time, had close contacts with famous contemporaries like David Ricardo and the philosopher Jeremy Bentham (1748–1832). He held strong ideas about how children should be raised, and the education he provided for his oldest son, John Stuart, has become famous—if not notorious. James Mill's view was that education was all-important for man's intellectual development, and that anyone could attain the highest level if only he was led in the right directions at an early age. John received hardly any formal education but was educated at home, where his father ran him through a tough program of classical languages (he began Greek when he was three), philosophy, history, and mathematics. At an early stage he was required to read the works of Adam Smith and Ricardo, and the latter, when he called on the family, apparently enjoyed discussing economic issues with the young Mill, who was seventeen at Ricardo's death. In his autobiography Mill acknowledges the value of what his father did to further his intellectual development. He says that no education could have been more thorough than the one that his father gave him, and that as a consequence he began his adult life with a quarter of a century's head start on his contemporaries. At the same time, however, his purely intellectual upbringing led to personal problems which, when he was twenty years old, developed into what he referred to as a mental crisis, from which he only managed to escape by cultivating a new set of interests in poetry and music.

Throughout his life Mill, like many of his contemporaries, carried out an extensive correspondence with other intellectuals, and the correspondence fills several volumes of his collected works which were published by University of Toronto Press between 1963 and 1985. Here is a letter to the philosopher Jeremy Bentham:

> July 18, 1812.
>
> My Dear Sir,
>
> Mr. Walker is a very intimate friend of mine, who lives at No. 31 in Berkeley Square. I have engaged him, as he is soon coming here, first to go to your house, and get for me the 3rd and 4th volumes of Hooke's Roman history. But I am recapitulating the 1st and 2nd volumes, having finished them all except a few pages of the 2nd. I will be glad if you will let him have the 3rd and 4th volumes.
>
> I am yours sincerely,
>
> John Stuart Mill
> (Mill 1963–85, vol. XII, p. 3)

At first glance the contents of this letter may seem unremarkable—until one looks at the date and discovers that the writer has just turned six! There can be little doubt that he had a truly unusual childhood.

At the age of seventeen Mill entered the services of the East India Company, the trading company that ruled India during the first period of the English colonial reign, and where his father also worked. His employment in the company lasted until 1858, when its privileges were withdrawn and the administration of India was taken over by the government. Accordingly, until he was fifty-two his writing and editorial activities were primarily carried out during his leisure time. His publications during this period include his two major books, *A System of Logic* (1843), a highly influential work in the philosophy of science, and his main work on economics, *Principles of Political Economy* (1848). This went through seven editions in Mill's lifetime and became the standard exposition of the whole field of economics in the English-speaking world until about 1890. However, Mill's most original contributions to economic theory were contained in his *Essays on Some Unsettled Questions of Political Economy* (1844).

After his retirement from the East India Company, Mill published a series of other important works on philosophy and social and political issues, among others *On Liberty* (1859), *Utilitarianism* (1863), and *On the Subjection of Women* (1869). His fascinating description of his own life, *Autobiography* (1873), was published after his death. He also wrote a large number of articles on philosophical, political, and economic topics in the leading intellectual periodicals of the time.[1]

An aspect of Mill's life that has fascinated many historians is his relationship with Harriet Taylor, whom he first met when he was twenty-four. Harriet Taylor was not especially happily married to a man who was considerably older, and she and Mill gradually became close friends and intellectual partners. Nineteen years after their first meeting Mr. Taylor died, and two years later Mill married Harriet. The account of her in Mill's *Autobiography* includes an appreciation of her intellectual gifts which posterity has found difficult to accept at face value; this concerns particularly his insistence that she should be given credit for a major share of what is original in his work. However, there can be no doubt that she was an important discussion partner and inspiring force in Mill's life, also for his work on economics. His collected works includes some of the letters that he wrote to Harriet while he worked on the *Principles*, and this is serious academic correspondence. Her own side of the correspondence has unfortunately not been preserved.

A common view of Mill's role in the history of economic thought was for a long time that he consolidated the teaching of the classical school without making any original contributions of his own. This view was to some extent encouraged by Mill

---

[1] O'Brien (2004, ch. 1) gives a survey of the leading reviews and their importance for the dissemination of the ideas of the classical economists.

himself, who was very much concerned with relating his own views to formulations in the work of Smith and Ricardo. He also revealed a fairly static view of the development of the subject in the following infamous statement:

> Happily, there is nothing in the laws of Value which remains for the present or any future writer to clear up; the theory of the subject is complete. (Mill 1848; 1965, p. 456)[2]

This was hardly a well-considered statement, and a century and a half later it is easy to see that the prediction was a complete miss. Of course, Mill did not say that the whole science of economics had found its final form. His judgment was limited to the theory of value or prices, but it has to be admitted that this does not make his lack of foresight much less remarkable.

The view of Mill as primarily a consolidator with little originality of his own has changed significantly in recent times. He is now regarded as an important predecessor of the marginalist revolution that occurred in the 1870s, and as one who contributed a number of new ideas and insight to economics. This revaluation began with an article by Stigler (1955; 1965) who begins by saying that he believes that as an economist Mill has not had any true admirer in the twentieth century but ends with the statement that Mill is the most undervalued of the great economists. The view of Mill has indeed changed radically since Stigler wrote this.

QUESTIONS OF METHOD

Mill's mental crisis and his reading of writers like Coleridge and Wordsworth also led him to revise his views on economics as a subject. The romantic poets were skeptical about the benefits of the modern industrial society, arguing that economic development created a new society that in important respects involved a lower quality of life. The economists were regarded not only as

---

[2] All page references are to the edition of Mills *Principles* in volumes II–III of his *Collected Works*, published by University of Toronto Press (1963–85). This is based on the 7th edition of the book, which came out in 1871.

the interpreters of this development but also as its ideologists. Mill pointed out that this view was erroneous; the effort to understand and predict actual social and economic developments did not involve any moral acceptance of them. On the other hand, he agreed that the critical voices deserved to be taken seriously, and he was a keen participant in the public debate about these issues.

Another important influence on Mill's thinking during the period of his mental crisis came from the French philosopher Auguste Comte (1789–1857). Comte maintained that all social phenomena must be studied in a broad context, and that all the social sciences, including economics and history, ought to be unified in a single science of man, which he called *sociology*.[3] He was skeptical about the direction that economics had taken under the influence of Ricardo, and which had led it to be dominated by abstract theory and deductive reasoning without, in his view, empirical support and historical perspectives. Mill was in some sympathy with these views, but it did not lead him to give up his own attachment to Ricardo's theories. In his opinion, economic and social phenomena were so complex that they could not be understood without a theoretical approach that made it possible to understand the interplay between them and to identify causes and effects. A fruitful theory had by necessity to abstract from many aspects of real life, and this was a strong argument for the continued existence of economics as a separate science, both theoretical and empirical. Nevertheless, one ought to keep in mind that in many cases economic problems had to be considered in a broader context of social science. In the preface to *Principles of Political Economy* he writes:

> For practical purposes, Political Economy is inseparably intertwined with many other branches of social philosophy. Except on matters of mere detail, there are perhaps no practical questions, even among those which approach nearest to the character of purely economical questions, which admit of being decided on economical premises alone. (Mill 1848; 1965, p. xci)

[3] Comte's sociology was clearly conceived as something different and broader than the modern field of sociology, which is a discipline in line with the other social sciences.

CHAPTER 5

PRICE THEORY

The modern reader of the works of Adam Smith and David Ricardo cannot avoid being struck by the fact that the supply side of the economy gets far more attention than the demand side. Their theory of price formation was primarily a cost theory with demand playing an almost invisible role. In the simplest version of the theory where the unit costs of production are constant, a modern economist would be able to admit the logic in the view that prices are determined by costs, while the role of demand is to determine the quantities produced and consumed. But in Ricardo's more complex theory of decreasing returns in agriculture, demand must also play a more active role in the determination of prices, and Ricardo did not manage to clarify his theory of price formation in this framework. Smith and Ricardo do make frequent references to demand, but mostly as a phenomenon that is determined by factors for which their theory does not offer any real explanation.

An important case of the neglect of the demand side is Ricardo's theory of comparative advantage, as described in chapter 4. In the absence of international trade, prices in England and Portugal will be determined by cost conditions—the ratio of labor requirements—in each of the two countries. However, when the countries engage in trade with each other, the international price ratio will deviate from each of the two national price ratios which ruled in the absence of trade. So what determines the international price ratio? From Ricardo's numerical examples we are led to understand that the international price ratio will be intermediate between the two price ratios that would exist in England and Portugal when there is no trade. But what exactly it is that determines the price ratio within this interval is left as an open question. Therefore we also lack an answer to the problem of how the gains from international trade are distributed between the trading countries.

The young John Stuart Mill realized that this was an important unsolved problem in economic theory. In 1829, when he was twenty-three, he wrote a paper on it, "Of the Laws of Interchange between Nations; and the Distribution of the Gains of Commerce among the Countries of the Commercial World." The paper remained unpublished for many years, but in 1844 it appeared in print together with several other articles in his book *Essays on Some Unsettled Questions of Political Economy*. Here, for the first time in the literature, we encounter the idea of demand and supply as *functions* of price, and market equilibrium as a situation where the price has adjusted to a level where there is equality between demand and supply. In Mill's account we may also see the beginnings of a theory of general economic equilibrium, since he realizes that in each country there is a connection between demand and supply in international trade. In the *Principles* the core of the theory is presented as follows:

> The produce of a country exchanges for the produce of other countries, at such values as are required in order that the whole of her exports may exactly pay for the whole of her imports. This law of International Values is but an extension of the more general law of Value, which we called the Equation of Supply and Demand ... the value of a commodity always so adjusts itself as to bring the demand to the exact level of the supply. But all trade, either between nations or individuals, is an interchange of commodities, in which the things that they respectively have to sell, constitute also their means of purchase: the supply brought by the one constitutes his demand for what is brought by the other. So that supply and demand are but another expression for reciprocal demand: and to say that value will adjust itself so as to equalize demand with supply, is in fact to say that it will adjust itself so as to equalize the demand on one side with the demand on the other. (Mill 1848; 1965, p. 604)

In this passage, which summarizes a long and detailed analysis, we may observe that Mill has made three important contributions to the theory of value or price theory.

First, we see that he solves Ricardo's unsettled problem of price formation in international trade. By bringing demand conditions into the analysis he finds that the solution is that prices—or, more accurately, the relative price of export and import goods—adjust to the level where the value of exports equals the value of imports. This is, of course, not a numerical solution. We cannot on the basis of Mill's theory say whether the equilibrium price ratio will be midway between the two national price ratios, or whether it will be closer to that of Portugal or that of England in the absence of trade. The solution takes the

95

form of a theoretical model which gives a logically consistent framework for the analysis of price formation. If we wish to arrive at a numerical solution, we will naturally also have to introduce numerical assumptions into the model, but in that case we have moved into applications and beyond the framework of general theoretical principles.

The second important contribution is Mill's insistence that this solution to the problem of international price formation is a special case of a more general theory, namely, that the price of a commodity tends to adjust to the level where supply equals demand. For this to make sense, one has to assume that both supply and demand are functions of the price, so that the equilibrium price can be inferred from "the equation of supply and demand." The use of the word *equation* is interesting. It could simply mean "equality," but it could also refer to the mathematical concept. It was clearly the second interpretation that Mill had in mind, for in the general discussion of price theory in the *Principles* he is very explicit about it. Price is determined by the mutual adjustment of demand and supply, and

> the proper mathematical analogy is that of an *equation*. Demand and supply, the quantity .demanded and the quantity supplied, will be made equal. If unequal at any moment, competition equalizes them, and the manner in which this is done is by an adjustment of the value. If the demand increases, the value rises; if the demand diminishes, the value falls; again, if the supply falls off, the value rises; and falls if the supply is increased. (Mill 1848; 1965, pp. 467–468)

The third important innovation that emerges in the first quotation has to do with the concept of "reciprocal demand," which shows that Mill had a perspective on price formation that went beyond the case of equality between supply and demand for a single commodity. From the equality of export and import values for each of the two countries it follows that supply becomes equal to demand for the export commodities of *both* countries, so there are the beginnings here of a general and not just partial equilibrium theory. "Reciprocal demand" remains a theoretical concept in international trade theory and is now associated with the geometrical construction called "offer curves," invented by Alfred Marshall several decades later. Mill did not draw any diagrams and used apparently no mathematics, but the degree of precision in his literary exposition is remarkably high. Here is an example that shows that the mathematical structure in his reasoning lies just below the surface; he analyzes international price formation with reference to a particular example:

> As the simplest and most convenient, let us suppose that in both countries any given increase of cheapness produces an exactly proportional increase of consumption: or, in other words, that the value expended in the commodity, the cost incurred for the sake of obtaining it, is always the same, whether that cost affords a greater or a smaller quantity of the commodity. (Mill 1848; 1965, p. 609)

Mill's wording differs from the language that we use today, but it is easy to restate his assumptions in modern terms.[4] The first sentence introduces the assumption that the relative decrease in the price equals the relative increase in consumption; in modern terminology he assumes that the price elasticity equals minus one. He then goes on to say that this is equivalent to assuming that the expenditure on the commodity in question is constant and independent of the price. In a certain sense this is of course an elementary insight, but how obvious is it to someone who has not seen a mathematical derivation of it? Mill had studied mathematics in his youth, and one may perhaps imagine that he had derived this implication mathematically without including it in the 1844 article or later in the *Principles of Political Economy*.[5]

In his survey of international trade theory, John Chipman (1965) emphasized that Mill's theory was much ahead of his time, both as regards economic content and analytical precision; he says that his theory of prices in international trade is "one of the great achievements of the human intellect." Judgments of this kind can always be debated, but no one who has read Mill's exposition can avoid the impression that, relative to Smith and Ricardo, it represents a very important step forward in terms of analytical rigor.

---

[4] As, for instance, when he writes "increase of cheapness" for a lowering of the price.
[5] The article by de Marchi (1972) presents evidence that Mill in his youth must have received a good training in pure mathematics, and that he continued to study mathematics in later years.

So in Mill's view the fundamental principle of price formation is the tendency of the market mechanism to establish equality between demand and supply. In other respects he drew the same line between the short and the long run as the earlier classical writers had done. In the long run, prices tend to converge to the "natural values" of commodities. For some commodities these may simply be reflections of scarcity, but for most commodities it will be true that their long-run exchange values reflect relative costs of production. In this respect Mill is in line with the analysis of Smith and Ricardo. But when we take a closer look at his formulations, we discover that there are some differences to show that he had modified the theory of the early classical economists. One of these emerges in his discussion of the concept of cost that is relevant for the determination of "the natural value" of a commodity. He says that the natural value corresponds to the unit cost of the most costly part of production. Here he comes close to the concept of marginal cost, but it is fair to say that he did not manage to integrate this perspective in his general discussion of price theory.

In Ricardo's work the relative costs of production were mainly identified with labor cost. He does modify the pure labor theory of value in the direction of the "93% theory" (see chapter 4), but remarks that labor cost alone is a fully acceptable simplification. Mill's discussion of the various elements of cost is held in more general terms:

> Of these elements, the quantity of labour required for the production is the most important: the effect of the others is smaller, though none of them are insignificant. (Mill 1848; 1965, p. 499)

This is clearly a significantly revised labor theory of value. Mill's exposition is more than a summary of the theories of the early classical writers; in several respects it is also a preview of the developments that were to come in the next couple of decades.

Labor and Wages

Principles of Political Economy is a work that in volume and scope can be compared to the *Wealth of Nations*. It covers many of the same topics, although it is somewhat differently organized.

Mill begins with a discussion of the prices of the factors of production, land, labor, and capital, and only a good deal later takes up the prices of commodities and the more general theory of price formation.

In his discussion of labor and wages Mill pays close attention to the contributions that different types of labor make to the economic activity in society. He puts great weight on a distinction that was introduced by Adam Smith and which played a central role in the classical theory: that between productive and unproductive labor. He admits that the distinction is difficult to define in a precise manner, but his point of departure is a definition of production as an activity that produces material wealth (*Principles*, p. 46). The part of the labor force that produces material wealth in the form of concrete objects is productive, while the part that does not is unproductive. As examples of what economists have meant by unproductive labor Mill mentions government employees, the military, doctors, teachers, musicians, dancers, actors, and domestic servants. He remarks that the distinction has been controversial, especially because many have felt the term *unproductive* to be disparaging (hardly surprising to a modern reader). He mentions in particular the view of Jean-Baptiste Say that all labor in a fundamental sense produces *utility*, and that it therefore should be natural to regard all labor as productive. However, Mill maintains that this argument is based on a confusion of the distinction between productive and unproductive with the distinction between labor that is useful and nonuseful. Unproductive labor is also as a rule useful, but the characteristic feature of productive labor is its positive contribution to material wealth and economic growth. Capital accumulation is associated with the production of material objects like machinery, and the labor employed in the production of machines is accordingly productive. To have a large share of the labor force employed in productive work is therefore important for economic growth.

The distinction between the two types of labor has long since been discarded in economics, and Mill's own discussion of it makes it easy to see why. He admits that the concept of productive labor really ought to be extended to comprise workers who are engaged in improving the quality of the labor that produces material wealth. But, he argues, the terminology in this area is so well established that he does not see any reason to change it. Having said this, however, he contributes to further confusion by the statement that he will interpret the concept of production in a broad sense, so that labor that is aimed at teaching others the skills necessary to produce material goods will be classified as productive. Government employees who help to create the security that is necessary for economic activity, should also, according to this broad definition, be seen as productive. But with such interpretations little remains of the whole distinction and the judgment of posterity has been that it is of little value as an element in the study of economic growth.[6]

In his analysis of the distinction between productive and unproductive labor Mill is accordingly loyal to the tradition from his classical predecessors. And even though he indicates that he can see reasons why this part of economic theory ought to be rewritten, his respect for tradition is so great that he refrains from doing so. In another area of labor economics, however, he broke significantly with earlier classical teaching. This concerned the idea of the wage fund.

The idea behind the wage fund as a theoretical construction was that the wages of workers are prepaid by the employers, or capitalists. Employers must therefore build up capital, what the classical economists called circulating capital, in order to fund the wage payments to workers. It is the size of this capital for the economy as a whole that constitutes total wage income in the economy, and this is called the wage fund. The demand for labor was assumed to be determined by the existing technology, so that at least in the relatively short run the wage fund would be constant. Wages would therefore be determined by technology. An implication of this view is that it is useless to try to push up wages through trade union activity.

In a book review that he wrote in 1869 Mill rejected the theory of the wage fund, which in the main he had accepted in the earlier editions of the *Principles*. The reason that he gave for his change of mind was that the hypothesis of the constancy of the wage fund—

[6] Even if it has been discarded by economic theorists, however, it lives on in more popular views of economic issues. There are still those who maintain that productive labor consists of those who produce concrete objects (preferably for export!), and that those who do not are therefore unproductive.

which in itself was not directly observable—had implications that were inconsistent with observations of the actual functioning of the economy. Of special significance was the implication that trade unions were unable to influence wages. Mill argued that actual experience strongly suggested that they could in fact do so, and that the theoretical hypothesis on which the conclusion was founded therefore had to be rejected. Neither in the review nor elsewhere did Mill offer an alternative theory of the demand for labor. In spite of this, however, his rejection of the wage fund theory was widely regarded as an important change in the existing theory. The fact that he thereby discarded a central element of the classical theory was clearly important for the reception of the new theory of wage formation that arrived with the breakthrough of the marginalist theories some years later.

CRISES AND UNEMPLOYMENT

The study of economic fluctuations and unemployment was not a central part of the theory of the classical economists. A common view of their interpretation of the alterations between good and bad times, between full employment and unemployment, was that these were frictional problems that were not in need of any deeper theoretical explanation. If the market mechanism were allowed to work without interference, these problems would be solved by the self-regulating adjustments of demand and supply in the labor market. The foremost proponent of this view was Jean-Baptiste Say, who was in close contact with the British classical economists. In his main work, *Traité d'économie politique*, which appeared in its first edition in 1803,[7] he formulated the conclusion later known as Say's Law, the short version of which is that "supply creates its own demand." Since total income in society must always be equal to its total expenditure on goods and services, it follows that a situation where aggregate supply exceeds aggregate demand simply cannot exist. There may indeed be situations where there is excess supply in a particular market, but this must always be balanced by excess de-

[7] The English translation of the book appeared as *A Treatise on Political Economy* (Say 1803; 1971).

mand in some other markets. Depressions—bad times—cannot therefore be explained by overproduction. This question was much discussed between Ricardo and Malthus. Ricardo supported Say, while Malthus thought that the conclusion went against common sense. It was the view of Say and Ricardo that became the dominant conviction among economists in the coming decades.

Mill discusses this issue in book III, chapter XIV, in his *Principles*, posing the question, "Can there be an oversupply of commodities generally?" He begins by declaring a strong support for Say's Law, saying that those who reject this conclusion, as for instance, Malthus, argue in such an illogical manner that it is difficult to present their views in a comprehensible way. The correct way to look at the problem, according to Mill, is the following:

> Is it ... possible that there should be a deficiency of demand for all commodities, for want of the means of payment? Those who think so cannot have considered what it is which constitutes the means of payment for commodities. It is simply commodities. Each person's means of paying for the productions of other people consists of those which he himself possesses. All sellers are inevitably ... buyers. Could we suddenly double the productive powers of the country, we should double the supply of commodities in every market; but we should, by the same stroke, double the purchasing power. (Mill 1848; 1965, p. 571)

This is just Say's Law. Since Mill believes that this insight is really elementary and fundamental for all who have concerned themselves with the study of economics, he asks himself how otherwise reasonable economists can hold on to the hypothesis of general overproduction as a cause of economic crises. A possible explanation, he says, is that they have drawn erroneous conclusions from what they have observed at times of crisis. But when he attempts to explain what it is that they have actually observed, he comes up with a new interpretation of Say's Law, which appears to be in conflict with the previous statement. After a description of the nature of a commercial crisis he states:

> At such times there is really an excess of all commodities above the money demand: in other words, there is an under-supply of money. (Mill 1848; 1965, p. 574)

For these two statements to be logically consistent, we have to interpret the "commodities" in the first quotation so as to include money. In this way one solves the logic of Say's Law, while accepting that that the aggregate supply of goods and services, in the ordinary sense of the word, may exceed aggregate demand. Accordingly, Mill admits that a crisis may emerge in the form of a gap between the supply and demand for commodities. There is too much production and too little money, but this holds, as he somewhat paradoxically puts it, "only while the crisis lasts." He does not discuss unemployment as such, but it seems to be implicit in his analysis that overproduction of goods will lead to production cutbacks and layoff of workers.

It appears then that Mill's stand on the question of overproduction as a cause of economic crises was ambivalent. On the one hand, he gives a strong theoretical defense of Say's Law. On the other hand, however, he suggests an interpretation of it that acknowledges the existence of crises and overproduction without making it necessary to reject the law. Relative to Smith and Ricardo he took a small step in the direction of making the explanation of crises and recessions an integrated part of economic theory, but this set of problems continued for a long time to occupy a position on the outskirts of the central part of economic theory.

LONG-RUN DEVELOPMENT AND THE STATIONARY STATE

Mill is an important figure in the history of economic theory, but a modern reader may find his work even more interesting for the number of new ideas and perspectives that he introduced into economics, which are often at the borderline between economics and the other social sciences. Examples of such ideas can be found in book IV of *Principles*, entitled "Influence of the Progress of Society on Production and Distribution." In the introductory chapter to this part of the work Mill discusses the driving forces behind economic growth—the progressive society, as he calls it. The previous parts of the book contains what he calls the static aspects of economics, but to understand the growth and development of society, the static theory has to be extended:

103

We have still to consider the economical condition of mankind as liable to change and indeed ... as at all times undergoing progressive changes. We have to consider what these changes are, what are their laws, and what their ultimate tendencies; thereby adding a theory of motion to our theory of equilibrium—the Dynamics of political economy to the Statics. (Mill 1848; 1965, p. 705)

The growth of material welfare is one of most characteristic features of modern society, and the causes of growth are in his view the developments in science, technology, and economic organization. Natural science has improved our insight about physical processes, while the distance in time between scientific breakthroughs and commercial exploitation becomes progressively shorter. At the same time, the social conditions for engaging in economic activity are getting steadily better. The reasons for this are, first, that society more than before is based on law and order, and that common people to a lesser degree are exposed to arbitrary decisions by those in power. Second, there has been a significant improvement in the conditions for organized economic cooperation, as in "establishments like those called by the technical name of joint-stock companies."[8] There is reason to believe that economic growth will turn out to benefit all classes of society, although Mill also suggests that the growth of population may prevent the working class from getting a share in it.

But the growth of material welfare cannot, Mill argues, go on indefinitely. As society continues to accumulate capital, the rate of return on new investment will fall. This process may be delayed through various forms of technical progress, but in the end the rate of return will become so low that the incentives for further accumulation will vanish. In the long run, therefore, society will approach the stationary state where there will be no further growth of national income, capital, or wages. This vision, which was in line with the view of the earlier classical economists, appeared to many people to paint a dismal picture of the future. But this was not the way that Mill saw it. A society that was stationary in an economic sense did not have to be stationary in an intellectual, social, or moral sense. One could even imagine

[8] Joint-stock companies had existed for centuries. But it was at the time when Mill wrote that they began to play a central role in business life.

increases in productivity in such a society, although not for the purpose of increasing material wealth, but in order to reduce the need to work. On this background he formulated a more optimistic view of the future:

> I cannot, therefore, regard the stationary state of capital and wealth with the unaffected aversion so generally manifested towards it by political economists of the old school. I am inclined to believe that it would be, on the whole, a very considerable improvement on our present condition. I confess I am not charmed with the ideal of life held out by those who think that the normal state of human beings is that of struggling to get on; that the trampling, crushing, elbowing, and treading on each other's heels, which form the existing type of social life, are the most desirable lot of human kind, or anything but the disagreeable symptoms of one of the phases of industrial progress. (Mill 1848; 1965, pp. 753–754)

Mill's ideal society was not one of steady material progress but rather of stronger emphasis of nonmaterial values. He reached out to the critics of modern society while at the same time clarifying the role of the economist: to understand social and economic development is not the same as approving of it.

New Issues: The Progress of Socialism and the Future of the Working Class

Even if there are points of similarity between *The Wealth of Nations* and the *Principles of Political Economy*, there are also obvious differences that stem from the fact that Mill wrote his book three quarters of a century after Smith. The times had changed, and the questions that a social and economic thinker had to confront were at least in part new ones. There was no longer a need for polemics against the mercantilists, although Mill was a strong believer in the market mechanism both nationally and in international trade. However, the socialist movement was on the move—1848, the year of publication of the *Principles*, was also one of the great revolutionary years in European history—and Mill was affected by many of the questions raised by the socialists. He has a clear understanding of the hardships of working-class life, and in a famous chapter of the *Principles*, "On the Probable

Futurity of the Labouring Classes," he discusses the possibility of relieving these problems within the framework of a basically liberal economic order. By way of introduction, he remarks that while he employs the concept of the "working class" according to common usage at the time, this does not mean that he accepts or sympathizes with a society in which some people do not work except when it is due too poor health or advanced age.

Mill was critical toward those who argued that a better life for the poor was to be achieved by the upper classes taking more responsibility for them, like parents for their children. In a modern society, all should be allowed to participate in society on terms of equality: the poor should not be dependent on the rich but should be enabled to make choices that would make them masters of their own lives. A key factor necessary to achieve this goal would be equal access to basic education for all. The present lack of equality between the social classes also creates strong psychological and social frictions, especially between workers and employers, and this is destructive for the spirit of cooperation in society:

> The relation is nearly as unsatisfactory to the payer of wages as to the receiver. If the rich regard the poor as . . . their servants and dependents, the rich in their turn are regarded as a mere prey and pasture for the poor. . . . The total absence and regard for justice or fairness in the relations between the two, is as marked on the side of the employed as on that of the employers. (Mill 1848; 1965, p. 767)

On this background Mill envisaged the gradual emergence of a society where the capitalist economic structure would be replaced by a system of firms that would be owned and managed by the workers themselves:

> The form of association ... which if mankind continue to improve, must be expected in the end to predominate, is not that which can exist between a capitalist as chief, and workpeople without a voice in the management, but the association of the labourers themselves on terms of equality, collectively owning the capital with which they carry on their operations, and working under managers elected and removable by themselves. (Mill 1848; 1965, p. 775)

Mill thought that a liberal economic order could be developed in a direction that would change the distribution of economic resources in favor of the working class. He was skeptical of a purely economic theory of the distribution of income. While he maintained that the "laws of production" were determined by economic relationships, he believed that the "laws of distribution"—the mechanisms determining the distribution of income between individuals and social classes—had to be understood in a political and social context. More than the other classical economists he was therefore also a social reformer, and he was not without sympathy for some of the socialist ideas. But on one fundamental issue he took a strong stand against the socialists: "I utterly dissent from the most conspicuous and vehement part of their teaching, their declamations against competition" (Mill 1848; 1965, p. 794).

In his opinion, the socialists had quite confused and erroneous views on the real effects of competition. They tended to forget that where there is no competition, there is monopoly, and this is definitely not in the interests of the working class.

In his strong emphasis on the benefits of competition and free markets Mill throughout his life remained a liberal, but his economic liberalism was joined with the conviction that a policy of economic reform was necessary for the promotion of social justice.

THE PUBLIC SECTOR

Book V in the *Principles* contains a broad discussion of the public sector, and Mill begins by considering the duties and limits of government. The state has some necessary tasks that are inseparable from the fundamental notion of government and some that are optional, where views may differ as to whether they belong in the sphere of the public sector or not. Having introduced this distinction, Mill goes on to define the necessary tasks of the state, arguing that they are far more extensive than many are inclined to admit. Some hold the view, Mill says, that the tasks of government should not extend beyond those of protecting the country against foreign enemies and creating a safe domestic environment for life and property. He points out, however, that there are a number of tasks that are easily overlooked but that can only be carried out satisfactorily by the state. The examples that he mentions include the operation of the laws of inheritance, the regulation of the right to issue money, and the standardization of weights and measures. One of his most interesting examples concerns the ownership of natural resources. The role of the state in protecting ownership rights can be interpreted narrowly as that of ensuring each individual the right to his own produce or to what he has legitimately obtained from other producers. But the state must also define the kind of resources that should be subject to property rights, and material goods are not simply those that man has produced: "Is there not the earth itself, its forests and waters, and all other natural riches, above and below the surface? These are the inheritance of the human race, and there must be regulations for the common enjoyment of it" (Mill 1848; 1965, p. 801).

The regulation of the limits to private property is part of the necessary task of government, and this is closely associated with the very idea of a civilized society. In this connection it is natural to interpret Mill as saying that the tasks of government are far more extensive than is commonly believed, especially by market liberalists. On the other hand he also remarks that there are social and political forces that encourage the expansion of the state beyond reasonable limits. The special interests of many citizens lead them to argue in favor of an understanding of the duties of government that is harmful for society as a whole. A good example of a poorly justified state activity is protectionism. The protection of some industries against foreign competition may yield short-run benefits for some groups, but for the country as a whole it will in the long run be a harmful policy. An example of an activity that does require government activity is a voyage of discovery; society may reap a huge benefit from such a voyage, but for a single person the gain can never be so large as to exceed the cost of the expedition. The lighthouse system is another example of justified government activity; the reason is that it is practically impossible to collect individual payment from the vessels that benefit from the signals of the lighthouses although the benefit to society is very large.[9] In such cases, it is pointless to argue against government activity with reference to the principle of laissez-faire. These are thoughts that we recognize from the

[9] However, modern technology has made it possible to do this, and the lighthouse example is therefore not as convincing as it was in Mill's time.

work of Adam Smith and which have a counterpart in the modern theory of public goods and externalities.

Thus, while the production and use of goods and services as a rule should be left to the market, there are a number of tasks that require state intervention because the market is unfit to solve them. But the area of state activity must in any case be limited out of regard for the individual's legitimate demand for freedom to act without interference within his private sphere: "There is a circle around every individual human being, which no government ... ought to be permitted to overstep" (Mill 1848; 1965, p. 938).

A further justification and elaboration of this principle is contained in Mill's famous book *On Liberty* (1859). In the present connection it is worth pointing out that this rejection of state intervention is of an entirely different kind than the critique of protectionism. In the latter case the counterargument is as close as one can come to a purely economic one: protectionism will lead to a less efficient use of the economy's resources. By contrast, the inviolability of the private sphere is a principle that has been derived from moral philosophy, and which could conceivably come into conflict with the requirement of efficiency.[10]

In line with the tradition from Smith and Ricardo, Mill also includes several chapters on tax policy. He takes his point of departure from Adam Smith's discussion of the principles of taxation with particular emphasis on the policy rule that Smith proposed, according to which citizens should contribute to the public revenue in accordance with their ability to pay. This principle requires, in Mill's opinion, a more careful justification: What does taxation according to ability to pay really mean? Some argue that it involves progressive taxation, so that the percentage of income paid in tax increases as income increases.[11] Mill is skeptical of this view and belives that the chief rule of taxation should be that

[10] There is an interesting connection between Mill's thinking and the ideas of the moral philosopher John Rawls (1972). Rawls proposes two fundamental principles of justice, where the principle of certain fundamental individual rights has priority over that of distributive justice. The possible conflict between efficiency and individual freedom has also been discussed in a famous article by Amartya Sen (1970).

[11] Mill has few references to the literature. Both here and elsewhere there are references to "some," "many," and "certain individuals" whose opinions Mill often disagrees with. But we rarely get to know who they are.

everyone should pay the same share of their income, i.e. proportional taxation. However, he also recommends that income below a certain lower limit (he suggests fifty pounds) should be exempt from taxes, while all income in excess of this amount should be taxed at a constant percentage. So he concludes after all in favor of a form of progression, since this system necessarily involves an average tax rate that increases with income.[12]

Mill also discusses the question of the proper base for the income tax. Here he comes out as spokesman for a system that makes all saving tax deductible.[13] The justification for the recommendation is that when the standard form of income tax levies tax on that part of the income which goes to saving and thereafter taxes the return on savings, this involves a "double taxation" of interest income that discriminates against saving and investment, and this is harmful for the economy as a whole. Although this particular form of the argument is no longer accepted by public finance economists, Mill was influential in starting a debate on the so-called expenditure tax as an alternative to the conventional form of income taxation. This has been a recurrent theme in modern discussions of tax reform.

UTILITARIANISM, FREEDOM, AND THE RIGHTS OF WOMEN

Mill's economic writings cannot be sharply separated from his work in philosophy. In the history of philosophy Mill is known both as a logician and philosopher of science, and as a representative of the utilitarian brand of moral philosophy where he continued the tradition from Jeremy Bentham. In his book *Utilitarianism* (1863) he maintains that the fundamental moral principle is the promotion of utility, which he also interprets as happiness.

---

[12] If the tax exempt income is 50 pounds and the tax rate on the excess income is 10 percent, a person with an income of 50 pounds or less will pay no tax, while an income of 100 pounds will be subject to a 5 percent average tax rate. A person with an income of 1000 pounds, will pay 9.5 percent of it in taxes.

[13] A reasonable interpretation of his view is that negative saving (as when one withdraws money from the bank to finance spending above one's current income) would count as an addition to current income for tax puposes. However, this interpretation is not obvious from the text.

Promoting the sum of utility or happiness in society ought to be the moral guideline both in the life of the single individual and for public policy. In modern language it might seem natural to say that Mill proposed a special form of social welfare function as the sum of individual utility functions, an idea that later came to play an important role in economic theory. But Mill did not formalize his argument along such lines, and his broad discussion takes up a number of issues that are usually considered to be outside the purview of economics, such as the moral principles of individual behavior. When modern economists refer to the maximization of the sum of individual utility functions as the utilitarian principle, this is clearly a highly simplified version of Mill's utilitarianism.[14]

One of Mill's most read and influential books is *On Liberty* (1859), which many have referred to as the bible of liberalism. This book, where the influence of Harriet Taylor may be particularly strong, is a powerful plea for individual freedom, not only in the form of freedom from political suppression, but also as freedom from the oppression of people who attempt to control the opinions or lifestyle of others.[15] The most radical aspects of Mill's social attitudes appeared in his support for the rights of women, particularly in his book *On the Subjection of Women* (1869). Also in the *Principles*—unusual for an economic treatise— he devotes some attention to this question. The views that he expressed were at that time unconventional, both among academics and more generally in society. Among other things, Mill expressed himself strongly in favor of women's right to freedom of occupational choice: "Let women who prefer that occupation [as a wife and mother], adopt it; but that there should be no option, no other *carrière* possible for the great majority of women, except in the humbler departments of life, is a flagrant social injustice" (Mill 1848; 1965, p. 765).

[14] That the modern formulation is a simplification should obviously not be read as a derogatory statement. Simplification and formalization has led to many new and important insights. See the discussion of Edgeworth's contributions to this area in chapter 11.

[15] The strong emphasis on interference in the private lives of other individuals has frequently been interpreted in the light of Mill's and Harriet Taylor's experience of the public's interest in their relationship at the time before they were married.

Both as a man and as a scientist Mill was a complex personality. He was market liberal and social reformer, elitist and spokesman for democracy and freedom.[16] To him, however, all these attitudes were consistent with each other. In the *Autobiography* he writes: "When I had taken in any new idea, I could not rest till I had adjusted its relation to my old opinions, and ascertained exactly how far its effect ought to extend in modifying or superseding them" (Mill 1873; 1969, p. 94).

The Last of the Classical Economists?

Mill's death in 1873 coincides more or less with the so-called marginalist revolution in economic theory (to be treated in chapters 8 and 9), and one might perhaps believe that the classical school died with him. But this is not quite correct. Mill's *Principles* continued for several years to hold its position as the leading textbook in the English-speaking world, and there were still economists who, unaffected by the new approach, held on to the theoretical framework of the leading members of the classical school. A prominent example of such an economist was the Irish-born John Elliot Cairnes (1823–75). He was only active as an academic economist in the last twenty years of his life, but during this period he became probably the best-known English economist after Mill. He wrote both on theoretical and applied topics, and it was primarily his books on current topics like agricultural reform in Ireland and slavery in the American South that made his name known to the general public. But it is his last book, *Some Leading Principles of Political Economy* (1874), which has secured him a name in the history of thought. This is an exposition of the main elements of economic theory as they appeared to a friend and admirer of John Stuart Mill. In the preface to the book he is careful to point out that he does not wish his exposition to be interpreted as a criticism of the theory that was created by Smith, Malthus, Ricardo, and Mill. It is also striking that the only point at which he is critical of one of his idols concerns Mill's rejection of the wage fund theory. This was a break with the classical tradition, and in Cairnes's opinion Mill should have stuck to the

[16] He was, e.g., in favor of graduated voting rights on the basis of education.

position that he took in the *Principles* and refrained from his later critique of the theory. Cairnes is also critical to Jevons's path-breaking *Theory of Political Economy*, which had been published three years earlier, arguing that it presents nothing new that is of any significance; the teaching of the classics was in no need of any essential revision. It is easy to regard Cairnes's attitudes as typical for one who does not manage to absorb the new developments in the subject, instead defending the theoretical system that he masters. But the case of Cairnes also shows that the theoretical framework of the classical economists could still provide a satisfactory foundation for a gifted and well-read economist whose main interest was in theory as the basis for analysis of practical problems.

FURTHER READING

To read the whole of the *Principles of Political Economy* is a major effort, but it is not really necessary to read it from beginning to end in order to form a good impression of Mill as an economist. The introduction by V. W. Bladen to the *Collected Works* edition is an excellent guide to the book. Of Mill's other books there are particularly two that have had a strong appeal to readers ever since they were first published. *On Liberty* is available in a number of editions. In addition to the edition in the *Collected Works* there is an edition in the Pelican Classics series with an interesting introduction by the American historian Gertrude Himmelfarb. *Autobiography* is a classic of English literature and is also available in many editions. It is highly recommended reading for anyone who wishes to form a picture of Mill as a person and thinker. Most of Mill's other books are also easily available in modern editions, testifying to modern readers' fascination with his life and work. His life and achievements have been described in a large number of books and articles; a recent biography is Capaldi (2004).

The view of Mill as one who consolidated classical economic theory without making any significant contributions of his own was sharply criticized in the 1955 article by George Stigler, "The Nature and Role of Originality in Scientific Progress," reprinted in Stigler (1965). O'Brien (2004) presents Mill's economics in the context of the classical school as a whole and gives extensive references to the secondary literature.

In earlier times it was a common view that the classical economists had a uniformly negative attitude toward the state and about the possibility of achieving improvements by public policy, and that they had a correspondingly strong and rather simplistic belief in the ability of the market to solve all economic and social problems. The example of Mill clearly shows this view to be incorrect. A book that played an important role for the creation of a new view of the classical economists was Robbins (1952), which is still very much worth reading and which includes an interesting chapter on Mill's attitudes to socialism. In his lectures Robbins (1998) provides a more personal perspective on Mill, including a discussion of his relationship with Harriet Taylor and Auguste Comte.

Karl Marx as an Economic Theorist

A MAIN PURPOSE of this account of the history of economic thought is to display the historical roots of the economic theories of the present time. Seen from this perspective, one may perhaps ask whether Karl Marx deserves a place among the most important economists of the past. Many people would no doubt feel this question to be both paradoxical and provocative, but it is a fact that a modern student of economics is unlikely to find even an indirect reference to Marx's work in his textbooks. Moreover, the attention paid to his thinking, at least by economists, would probably have been much less if it were not for the fact that so-cialists and communists have claimed his ideas as the theoretical foundation for their preferred political and economic system.

However, judgments about Marx's importance have varied considerably over time, even in the noncommunist part of the world.[1] A main reason why most of today's economists are so little concerned with him is obviously the poor economic performance of the countries whose leaders claimed to be inspired by his thoughts. But not long ago the attitude to Marx was rather different. In his well-known textbook on the history of economic thought, Mark Blaug, in the introduction to his chapter on Marx, writes that "Marx the economist is alive and relevant in a way that none of the other writers are that we have thus far considered" (Blaug 1962; 1997, p. 215). This statement was unsurprising when read in the early editions of the book from the 1960s and 1970s, but it is remarkable that it is still there in the fifth edition of 1997. The statement is interesting but also somewhat problematic. One reason for Blaug's claim may be that when economists,

---

[1] They have in fact varied not only with time but also between countries. While the internationally dominant form of economic science has an insignificant connection with Marx's theories, there are academic environments in countries like Italy and Japan and in Latin America which are still strongly inspired by Marxism. See, e.g., Negishi (1989, pp. 23–24) for a short description of the position of Marxist economics in Japan.

whether they are Marxist or "bourgeois," write about Marxian economics, it is to a large extent Marx's own texts that they write about. In non-Marxist economics, by contrast, very little attention is paid to the economists of the past. Modern writers of textbooks on subjects like price theory, international trade, and economic growth are of course aware that the modern theory in these fields originated in the writings of economists like Smith, Ricardo, and Cournot. But since their thoughts have been absorbed and developed in the more recent literature it is usually found to be superfluous to quote them or engage in any form of textual criticism of their work. "Bourgeois" economic theory can therefore be presented with a minimum of attention to the individuals who developed it. Marxian economic theory, on the other hand, is closely related to interpretations of Marx's own texts, and it must be in this sense that we—perhaps—may regard him as more alive today than Adam Smith and his successors.

There are many reasons, however why we cannot possibly neglect Marx. His indirect influence on the development of modern Western economics has doubtlessly been greater than one can measure by the number of references to his books and articles in the current literature. In addition, of course, Marx as an economic and political thinker has had an influence on the actual social development in many countries like few other intellectuals in history. For this reason alone, it is important to have some knowledge of his theories. Moreover, Marx was far more than an economist in the more narrow sense of the word, and to an even greater degree than in the cases of Adam Smith and John Stuart Mill, his thoughts about philosophy, history, and politics were intimately connected with his economics. A brief sketch of Marx's place in the history of economics must therefore by necessity be an incomplete account of the totality of his thought and its influence.

LIFE

Karl Marx (1818–83) was born in Trier in Germany. His family was Jewish, but his father converted to the Catholic faith the year before his son Karl was born. When Marx had finished his secondary education in Trier he began his university studies, first in

Bonn, where he studied law, and later in Berlin, where he took up philosophy. As a student he seems to have been somewhat disorganized; he read much but with little focus. He finished his studies by obtaining a doctorate in philosophy at the University of Jena with a dissertation on the history of philosophy in ancient Greece. He became strongly influenced by the thoughts of the philosopher Georg Friedrich Hegel (1770–1831) and began to move in radical circles in the university environment. Marx's ambitions for the future may at this time have been toward an academic career, but this soon proved to be unrealistic. This may in part have been due to the fact that his qualifications for a university position were unconvincing, but also to the Prussian government's suppression of the leftist opposition, which made it difficult for a man with his opinions to pursue a career within the public university system. Instead he began to work as a journalist, and in 1842 he became the editor of the newspaper *Rheinische Zeitung*, which politically expressed the views of the liberal left. In 1843 Marx married Jenny von Westphalen, the daughter of Freiherr Ludwig von Westphalen, a high-ranking official in the Prussian state administration. For Marx, this was obviously a step upward on the social ladder. The couple had seven children, only three of whom survived to adult age.

In 1843 publication of the *Rheinische Zeitung* was stopped by the government censorship. Marx no longer saw a future for himself in Germany, and the couple moved to Paris where they joined a circle of socialists and communists; it was there that Karl Marx became a convinced communist. At the time it may not have been completely clear what it meant to be a communist, since the term did not have the relatively well-defined meaning that it has today. But at any rate a communist was in opposition to the ruling political system and held that the market economy and the institution of private property were the roots of social injustice and poverty.

By all accounts, Marx was a difficult person who did not associate easily with other people. But during his time in Paris he made an acquaintance that became of decisive importance for himself, his writing, and the whole communist movement: he met Friedrich Engels. This meeting marked the beginning of a close personal friendship and intellectual partnership that lasted until Marx's death in 1883.

Friedrich Engels (1820–95) was the son of a German industrialist who as a young man was sent to Manchester to work for a company that was partly owned by his father. While he was still living in Germany Engels had acquired radical opinions, and they were strengthened by his impressions of the social destitution in the working-class areas of Manchester. These were described in his book *Die Lage der arbeitenden Klasse in England* (*The Condition of the Working Class in England*, 1845). In spite of his own social position he gradually came to regard himself as a communist, and he started to write about communist theories of society. The encounter with Marx strengthened his ambition to contribute to the development of communism both as an ideology and political force, and there is no doubt that their collaboration was highly stimulating to both of them.

As individuals they were very dissimilar. Marx was of a brooding disposition and had difficulties associating with people outside his own family, while Engels was an extrovert and good-humored person. Marx found it difficult to escape from his reading and his ever-increasing volume of notes in order to put his thoughts down on paper, while Engels's pen in comparison flowed easily. Marx was clearly the leading theorist and the deeper thinker, but Engels should be given a significant part of the credit for bringing Marx's manuscripts to the state where they could be published.

The first published result of the Marx-Engels collaboration appeared in the revolutionary year 1848 in the form of the small book *Manifest der kommunistischen Partei* (Manifest of the Communist Party, better known as *The Communist Manifesto*).[2] An organization called the Communist League had asked Marx and Engels to draw up a political program for the league. The result was probably the most influential political pamphlet that has ever been written. In addition to its inflammatory political slogans—"Working men of all countries, unite!"—the Manifesto also contains the beginnings of a more fundamental political and

---

[2] The 1848 revolutions in Europe started in Sicily and spread to France, the German states, and the Habsburg Empire. Their causes varied from the desire for national independence to demands for more political and economic freedom, but they also contained a large element of social unrest among the working classes.

economic analysis and critique of the capitalist system, which were later to be expanded and elaborated in Marx's main work *Das Kapital* (*Capital*).

As a result of intervention from the Prussian government Marx was expelled from France in 1845. He moved to Brussels and later to Cologne where he resumed his activities as a journalist, now as editor of the *Neue Rheinische Zeitung*. But in 1849 this newspaper was also forced to stop publication, and once again Marx was expelled. This time he moved with his family to London where he lived for the rest of his life. He earned his living chiefly by freelance journalism, in addition receiving financial support from Engels who was in much easier economic circumstances. But Marx and his family lived in rather poor conditions and at times in direct poverty.

Marx spent much of his time in the reading room of the British Museum where he read and took notes, which grew mountainous with time. Many of his early manuscripts he never managed to get ready for publication, and some of them were not published until many years after his death. His long-term plan was to write a large book that would lay the theoretical foundations for the more propagandistic approach of his popular writings, especially for the sketchy analysis in the *Manifesto*. But the work on this proceeded slowly with frequent interruptions for his journalism and activities in communist organizations, and it was not until 1867 that volume 1 of *Capital* was published. During the last sixteen years of his life he attempted desperately but unsuccessfully to bring his notes in order and to publish the rest of the work, but he died without having achieved it. The reason why today we know *Capital* as a book in three volumes is due to the work of Engels. After his retirement from business life in 1869, he undertook the task of creating order in the chaotic state in which Marx's manuscript had been left at the time of his death. Engels managed to publish volume 2 of *Capital* in 1885 and volume 3 in 1894 before his own death in 1895. A fourth part of the work, which is Marx's account of the history of economic thought, was later (1905–10) edited and published by Karl Kautsky under the title *Theorien über den Mehrwert* (*Theories of Surplus Value*).

For a modern economist it is not easy to penetrate the theories of Marx as they are presented in *Capital*. His economic analysis is sometimes embedded in complex philosophical discussions, and his terminology and conceptual apparatus are in part very different from that used by his classical predecessors as well as that of later generations of economists. Neither is it always easy to decide which of his ideas are the most significant and deserve to be remembered in the history of ideas. However, we have a relatively easily accessible introduction to at least some of his thought in *The Communist Manifesto*.

THE COMMUNIST MANIFESTO

According to Marx and Engels, the ruling class in society is the bourgeoisie. The bourgeoisie has come to occupy its position of power by means of an economic and social revolution that led to the ruin of the feudal society. Early in the book it is emphasized that the victory of the bourgeoisie has led to an unprecedented economic growth, but at the same time to man's *alienation* (a concept introduced in some of Marx's earlier writings); personal relations that used to be based on established tradition and social duty have been "torn asunder," and in its place the bourgeoisie has left "no other nexus between man and man than naked self-interest, than callous 'cash payment'" (Marx and Engels 1848; 1998, p. 53).[3] Alienation implies that "the work of the proletarians has lost all individual character, and, consequently, all charm for the workman. He becomes an appendage of the machine, and it is only the most simple, most monotonous, and most easily acquired knack, that is required of him" (Marx and Engels 1848; 1998, p. 58).

The enormous economic and social changes that have occurred during the rule of the bourgeoisie have their roots in feudal society. The basic cause of economic and social development is the growth of the *productive forces*. The productive forces are determined by technology and natural resources, and these are in part dependent on factors outside the economic system as such. However, they are also affected by human activities such as discoveries, inventions, and conquest and colonization. Any level of the productive forces requires a corresponding *mode of*

[3] All quotations from the *Manifesto* are from the Signet Classics edition of 1998 (Marx and Engels 1848; 1998).

production, a certain organization of production based on a set of property rights and institutions that in turn determine the distribution of income and power. The mode of production corresponds in other words to the modern concept of "the economic system." The mode of production is, in the interest of the rulers of society, in turn kept in place by an *ideological superstructure* that serves to add legitimacy to the mode of production. The ideological superstructure consists among other things of the structure of government, the legal system, literature, art, and science. The superstructure is not a purely external feature of society; it determines the single individual's consciousness regarding his own place in society and his general understanding of his social context. As the productive forces develop, a tension arises between the productive forces and the mode of production, since the ideological superstructure prevents a flexible adjustment between them. This leads sooner or later to a revolution that establishes a new mode of production and ideological superstructure, which with time will lead to new tensions.

This view reflects a way of thinking that Marx and Engels had absorbed from the teaching of Hegel and his theory of the dialectic development of history. Hegel had turned against the rationalism of the age of enlightenment and its ambition to create a social science that would analyze society in the same way that the natural sciences analyzed the physical environment, that is, by empirical observations and generalizations from these. According to Hegel, this was a sterile and wrong-headed approach because society could only be understood in a dynamic historical context. The present must be studied on the background of the past from which it has developed. Moreover, the present must also be regarded in relation to the future, for the present contains the contours of the ages to come. These are not relationships that can be verified directly through empirical observation, but they constitute an inescapable theoretical framework for the study of history and society. The dominating forces in society release counterforces and thereby social tensions that, with time, release new dominant forces, and so the process continues.[4]

[4] Hegel characterized the dynamics of these forces as thesis, antithesis, and synthesis.

In the view of Marx and Engels it was the tension or contradiction between the productive forces and the mode of production that about one hundred years previously had led to the fall of the feudal society and the rise of the bourgeoisie. Their analysis of the tensions of their own age was now that they were close to the point where a new revolution would occur, consisting in the revolt of the proletariat against the bourgeoisie. What would happen after the victory of the proletariat?

> The proletariat will use its political supremacy to wrest, by degrees, all capital from the bourgeoisie, to centralise all instruments of production in the hands of the state, i.e., of the proletariat organised as the ruling class; and to increase the total of productive forces as rapidly as possible. (Marx and Engels 1848; 1998, p. 75)

The increase of the productive forces will occur through a new organization of the mode of production which, at least in the early stages of the rule of the proletariat, can only come about through "despotic inroads on the rights of property, and on the conditions of bourgeois production." This stage is known as the dictatorship of the proletariat.

Regarding the more specific political features of the future rule of the proletariat and the communists, Marx and Engels wrote down a program consisting of ten points. They allow for the program to vary to some degree from one country to another, but for "the most advanced countries" the ten points would in general be applicable. The main elements in their ten points are government expropriation of all land; a strongly progressive tax system; the abolition of the rights of inheritance; and the nationalization of credit, transport, manufacturing, and agriculture. The program also calls for "equal obligation of all to work" and for free education for all children in public schools. Following the presentation of the program, Marx and Engels add a remarkable vision of the new society:

> When, in the course of development, class distinctions have disappeared, and all production has been concentrated in the hands of a vast association of the whole nation, the public power will lose its political character. Political power, properly so called, is merely the organised power of one class for oppressing another. If the proletariat during its contest with the bourgeoisie is compelled,

by the force of circumstances, to organise itself as a class ... and, as such, sweeps away by force the old conditions of production, then it will, along with these conditions, have swept away the conditions for the existence of class antagonisms and of classes generally, and will thereby have abolished its own supremacy as a class.

In place of the old bourgeois society, with its classes and class antagonisms, we shall have an association in which the free development of each is the condition for the free development of all. (Marx and Engels 1848; 1998, p. 76)

In other words, as the results of the proletarian revolution materialize the dynamic process that is driven by the tension between the productive forces and the mode of production comes to a halt. In its place, a new society will be established that is characterized by economic and social harmony—a rather astonishing hypothesis. It is a typical expression of utopian thinking, a vision of a future stable ideal society. On this background it may appear surprising that Marx and Engels later in the *Manifesto* heap scorn on the so-called utopian socialists (e.g. the Frenchman Charles Fourier and the Englishman Robert Owen) for their visions of a future society with socialist or communist features. The criticism of socialist and other utopian thinkers both in the *Manifesto* and elsewhere in Marx's work is founded on a conviction that the utopian socialists failed to base their visions of the future on a correct understanding of the driving forces of history; in other words, their visions were inconsistent with the course that history would actually take. The Marxist utopia, by contrast, was, according to its originators, based on a scientific analysis of the dialectics of history, showing how the proletariat's rise to power would inevitably lead to the ideal communist society.

A central idea in the *Manifesto* is the theory of the all-important role of the productive forces for the development of society, at least up to the time of the revolution of the proletariat. This idea is often referred to as historical materialism, and because it tends to be associated with Marx this view of history and society has often been characterized as Marxist. This language may be a little imprecise. It is not very difficult to find examples of modern economists who look upon the development of technology as being of decisive importance for social and economic development but who would nevertheless protest strongly if one were to call them Marxists. In this we may perhaps see some of Marx's indirect influence on modern social science and economics through his theory that the technological, organizational, political, and cultural development in society are interconnected, and that it is technology, in a wide sense, that is the most decisive among these forces.

A notable feature of the argument in the *Manifesto* is the tension between on the one hand the thesis of the victory of the proletariat over the bourgeoisie as a case of historical inevitability and on the other hand the authors' appeal to the same proletariat to form a political alliance on the basis of the program of the Communist Party. If victory is predetermined, is it not unnecessary to call for political action? A possible interpretation of Marx and Engels is that what the proletariat can achieve by political activism is first to hasten the development that will in any case occur, and second to prepare the transition to the communist society. But in any case a paradox remains. According to Marx and Engels it is the growth of the productive forces that is the basic cause of social development, while the role of ideology is only to lend legitimacy to the existing mode of production. As the English philosopher Isaiah Berlin writes in his classic biography of Marx, the enormous influence of Marxist ideology must in itself be an indication that the theory is wrong.

CAPITAL

Of all Marx's works, *The Communist Manifesto* is the one that has had the strongest popular appeal and probably also the strongest influence on politics and society. But his place in the history of economic ideas is due above all to his main work, *Das Kapital* (*Capital*). This book contains an analysis of the functioning of a market economy that is based on the institution of private property, and in fact the use of the term *capitalism* to describe such a system originated with Marx. The most important factual background for his theoretical analysis was the economic system in England as he observed it from his life in London, for he believed that it was in England that the capitalist system was most highly developed. Marx's ambition was to understand how the system worked with respect to price formation and income distribution, and to justify his prediction that, with historical necessity, it was moving toward its own destruction. The system which in turn would succeed capitalism was the communist society. But the analysis of the economy of the new society plays a subordinate role in Marx's analysis; he is first and foremost a theorist of capitalism, not of socialism or communism.

In more than one sense, *Capital* is a many-sided work. Like the *Wealth of Nations* it moves between theoretical analysis and detailed descriptions of real life, often in large historical sweeps. As in Ricardo's *Principles* theoretical relationships are developed in careful detail, often supplemented by elaborate numerical examples. Marx's wide reading shows up in the form of numerous references to the literature of economics, history, and politics, and he draws on examples from contemporary economic life in order to illustrate his theory of the functioning of the capitalist system; the journal *The Economist* was an important source of his factual descriptions. Stylized theoretical analysis is interspersed with highly emotional accounts of social degradation and poverty. Equally emotional are the references to many other writers, who are characterized as vulgar, sentimental, banal, and complacent. The French economist Frédéric Bastiat is a "dwarf economist" and the philosopher Jeremy Bentham is an "insipid, pedantic, leather-tongued oracle of the ordinary bourgeois intelligence." But this less attractive side of Marx the polemicist should not be allowed to overshadow his more serious attempts to understand the principles of the market economy.

Capitalism and Surplus Value

Marx attempted to describe the difference between capitalism and the economic system of the traditional feudal society in terms of two alternative representations of economic circulation. A representative agent of the traditional society is the artisan, who initially has a stock of finished goods, C. This he exchanges for money, M, which he uses to buy goods for his own consumption, C. The economic circulation of this society can therefore be written as C-M-C. In the capitalist society the capitalists start out with money that they use to purchase goods which they in turn sell for *more* money; the circulation then becomes M-C-M'. The difference $\Delta M = M' - M$ is profit or, as Marx calls it, the surplus value of the capitalist. The surplus value forms the basis for capital accumulation and economic growth.

The use of mathematical symbols should not be construed to mean that Marx actually developed a formalized theory in the modern sense of the term. It is more natural to interpret the expressions of economic circulation as a compact statement of the characteristic features of the capitalist system. Marx's vision of capitalism was that there were some agents, namely, the capitalists, whose activities were motivated not by a desire to satisfy human needs, but to make the surplus value as large as possible and accumulate capital. The contradiction between human needs and capitalist objectives created the built-in inconsistencies and tensions between the productive forces and the mode of production. This tension would in the end lead to the breakdown of the capitalist system.

This vision is as far from Adam Smith's theory of the invisible hand as it is possible to come. Marx has no sympathy or understanding for Smith's argument that the desire of the capitalists to maximize profits—or surplus value in the Marxian terminology—could conceivably be in the interests of the consumers or workers. In Marx's view of the world, the interests of workers and capitalists are directly opposed to each other.

It can hardly be denied that this is a somewhat problematic view of the relationship between producers and consumers or between capitalists and workers. How can the capitalists maximize profit without regard to demand and, therefore, at least to some extent, to the interests of consumers and workers? Other economists were—to the extent that they read him—unconvinced by this aspect of Marx's analysis of the market economy. On the other hand, however, there can be little doubt that his analysis had some significant indirect influence on the manner in which economists approached the study of economic systems. Ricardo's theories are presented in a way that is disconnected from actual historical processes. Reading his *Principles*, one may form the impression that the theory he presents has a universal historical validity (although that may not actually have been his intention). Marx, on the other hand, presented an interconnected analysis of the development of technology and the economic system that had a great influence on later economic and social thought.

Marx's Labor Theory of Value

The economists who exerted the greatest influence on Marx's own work as an economic theorist were the classical economists, above all Adam Smith and David Ricardo; in fact, it was Marx who first used the term *classical* to refer to the early British economists. He took the labor theory of value, especially in the form given it by Ricardo, as the point of departure for his own price theory. Like Ricardo, he also took account of the indirect use of labor through a kind of reasoning that shows—to use a modern notion—an input-output perspective on the economy as a whole: in order to calculate the labor content of a particular commodity, we must take into account not only the amount of work that goes to produce the commodity itself but also the work required to produce the other inputs in the production process. In the end we find that all commodities are produced by labor, and when we have found how much labor is required to produce an additional unit of a commodity, we have found the value of the commodity in terms of labor.

This may sound like a fairly direct presentation of Ricardo's arguments, and Marx did not in fact contribute anything original to the pure labor theory of value. However, his justification for the theory is a different one from that of his classical predecessors and shows the influence on his thought as much from German philosophy as from English classical economics:

> A use-value, or useful article, therefore, has value only because human labour in the abstract has been embodied or materialised in it. How, then, is the magnitude of this value to be measured? Plainly, by the quantity of the value-creating substance, the labour, contained in the article. (Marx 1867; 1995, p. 16)[5]

This is a much more abstract justification of the labor theory of value than the more practical cost of production approach that we find in the works of Smith and Ricardo. In more concrete terms, the use value is defined as the socially necessary time required for production, including the indirect time used for the

---

[5] All quotations from *Capital* are from the 1999 edition in the Oxford World Classics series. This is an abridged edition, containing selections from all three volumes of the book.

production of non-labor inputs. The indirect time use reflects the labor input of the past: "As values, all commodities are only definite masses of congealed labor time" (p. 16). The socially necessary labor is to be computed as an average for the commodity in question; there are no attempts at the analysis of marginal cost, of which we saw the beginning in the work of John Stuart Mill.

Marx now applied the same line of reasoning to labor itself: How much labor is necessary to produce a unit of labor? Workers need an input of labor in order to acquire the goods and services that are necessary to survive and reproduce themselves; this is the classical theory of the subsistence wage. The value of goods must now be compared to the value of labor. For production to be profitable, the labor value of production must be greater than the labor value of labor itself. The difference is the *surplus value* which in Marx's theoretical framework is the unpaid work or the capitalists' *exploitation* of the workers, corresponding to profit or surplus value. In other words, the values that the workers produce go only partly to support their own consumption and standard of living, while a large part of their labor time is spent in working for the capitalists.

In the literature on Marxian economics, a central problem is the connection between various central concepts in Marx's theory of value or prices; the discussion of this question also raises the issue of how best to model his system in mathematical form. This will not concern us here, and the discussion will be limited to a brief sketch of the relationship between Marx's theory and the classical labor theory of value. In the simplest version of the classical theory relative prices are determined by the relative labor costs of production. Their way of taking account of other costs of production was either to assume that such costs were proportional to labor costs, or by modifying the theory so that it only held as an approximation. At least in volume 1 of *Capital* Marx did in fact assume that there was such a proportionality, which he expressed as the assumption that surplus value was a constant fraction of labor costs, uniform across industries. This constant was a result of the competition between producers who always strove to maximize surplus value. In that case, relative commodity prices would be equal to relative labor costs, even if there were a component of surplus value in all prices.

Especially in volume 3 of *Capital*, however, Marx adopted a more subtle approach to price theory. A central concept in this approach is "the organic composition of capital." Assume that the total of capital used in production is $c+v$, where c is the cost of fixed capital and v is wages (so wages are treated as variable or circulating capital, as in the classical theory of the wage fund). The organic composition of capital is then defined as $q=c/(c+v)$. In modern terminology, q is a measure of the capital intensity of production that lies between zero and one and must be assumed to vary between industries. In this version of his theory, competition between the capitalists leads to a rate of surplus value that stands in a constant ratio to *capital*. This means that the relative prices or exchange values of the commodities are only equal to relative labor costs when the organic composition of capital (the capital intensity) is the same in all industries.[6] There are accordingly two versions of Marx's price theory and the question may be raised of how they fit together. This question is known as "the transformation problem," and modern mathematical economists have found that the clarification of this issue is perhaps the greatest challenge in arriving at a better understanding of Marx's economic theories.

A reasonable view is that Marx had two price theories that were constructed with different purposes in mind. His pure labor theory of value was based on a desire to derive the "right" prices when workers received their legitimate share of factor income, namely, the whole. The other theory, which was based on the assumption on unequal organic composition of capital, had a more descriptive purpose. From this point of view, it seems rather doubtful that the transformation problem ought to be regarded as the most significant part of Marx's economic theories. It is of some interest to note that later discussions of the transformation problem have mostly been concerned with what Marx really meant, not with whether the solution of the problem yields any important economic insights.

---

[6] This line of reasoning is closely related to Ricardo's theory of the time dimension of capital and its variation among industries which led to his modification of the pure labor theory of value; see chapter 4.

ECONOMIC GROWTH

Many economists have argued that one of the most interesting economic theories in *Capital* is the analysis of the economic
growth process in a capitalist economy. The theory can be considered as a sketch of a model of economic expansion in a society
with two sectors of production. At the time of Marx's death, the
theory existed only in the form of fragmentary notes in his manuscripts, and it was Engels who attempted to systematize them
when he edited volume 2 of *Capital*. On this background, modern
economists have succeeded in constructing mathematical models of economic growth that in several respects are similar to a
growth model that was developed in the 1940s and is known
after the originators as the Harrod-Domar model.[7]

One of the sectors produces consumption goods while the
other produces investment goods. Part of the total income in
the economy goes into saving. As regards the demand for consumer goods and the supply of saving Marx assumes that workers consume the whole of their income, while part of the profit or
surplus value in each of the two sectors is saved. In other words,
the income of the capitalists is the only source of saving in the
economy. Equilibrium now requires that saving is equal to the
value of the output of investment goods. These assumptions provide the elements of a theory of growth: investment leads to an
increase of the capital stock and thereby to increased production
and higher income for the capitalists, who then increase their
saving, making room for additional investment. On the basis of
the exposition of this analysis in *Capital*, modern economists have
worked out rigorous mathematical models that claim to represent Marx's hypotheses and assumptions, and this is therefore an
area where the study of Marx has clearly provided inspiration for
modern economic theory. But it is likely that Marx would have
been puzzled by—and protested firmly against—the main result
generated by the modern reformulation of his theory: this is that
the theory can be interpreted as a model of balanced growth in
which the long-run rate of growth in the economy is constant.

---

[7] However, the original version of this model in Harrod (1948) and Domar
(1946) has only one sector of production, while two-sector models were not
developed until the 1960s.

This was definitely not what Marx had in mind: on the contrary, a central feature of his theory of capitalist growth was that the market economy possessed inherent contradictions which, in the long run, would lead to its own destruction. This is a far cry from the outcome of balanced growth where the economy grows at a constant rate without any time limits on its progress.

The Falling Rate of Profit and the Breakdown of Capitalism

One of Marx's theories that has received particular attention in the later literature is what he referred to as *the law of the falling rate of profit*. Traces of such a theory can be found in the works of the classical economists. Earlier we have seen that Ricardo postulated a law of decreasing returns in agriculture, and he also believed that the rate of return on capital would decline with increasing capital accumulation. Later economists like John Stuart Mill supported the view that the accumulation of capital would cause the rate of return on new projects to become so low that further accumulation would cease and that the economy would reach a stationary state. But it was not the law of decreasing returns which was at the center of attention for Marx.

Instead Marx assumed that capital income or profit only depends on the input of labor. If there is an increase of capital relative to labor it follows almost by definition that profit per unit of capital will fall. Capitalists will respond to this by accumulating more capital, but this only reinforces the tendency to a falling rate of profit. An issue arises at this point concerning the capitalists' incentives for capital accumulation: Why will they accumulate more when the rate of return falls? Their motive for doing this seems to be based on an erroneous belief on their part that an increase of capital will result in increased profit, while the outcome instead will be a further fall in the rate of profit. This goes back to Marx's hypothesis that the capitalist producer is motivated by a desire for profit and accumulation as goals in themselves, not as sources of consumption and the satisfaction of needs:

> The capitalist process of production consists essentially of the production of surplus-value, represented in the surplus-product or

131

that aliquot portion of the produced commodities materialising unpaid labour. It must never be forgotten that the production of this surplus-value ... is the immediate purpose and compelling motive of capitalist production. It will never do, therefore, to represent capitalist production as something which it is not, namely as production whose immediate purpose is enjoyment or the manufacture of the means of enjoyment for the capitalist. This would be overlooking its specific character, which is revealed in all its inner essence. (Marx 1894; 1995, p. 449)

The consequences for workers of the accumulation of capital are, according to Marx, twofold. First, each worker now has more capital to work with; this makes the worker more productive, and wages go up. At the same time, however, there will be an increasing concentration in industry ("One capitalist always kills many"), and this concentration means a lower demand for labor. With an increasing population, the net result of this will be that even if the number of employed workers were to increase, the number of workers who find themselves without work—the industrial reserve army—will also increase, both in absolute and relative terms:

The greater the social wealth, the functioning capital, the extent and energy of its growth, and, therefore, also the absolute mass of the proletariat and the productiveness of its labour, the greater is the industrial reserve army. The same causes which develop the expansive power of capital, develop also the labour-power at its disposal. The relative mass of the reserve army increases therefore with the potential energy of wealth. (Marx 1885; 1995, pp. 360–361)

Marx's great emphasis on the nature and extent of unemployment is a novel feature of his work relative to the modest place that this topic occupies in the earlier literature. But a natural question to ask in the context of this analysis is the following: Why do not wages fall so much that the excess supply of labor—unemployment—is eliminated? Marx's answer to this question is to some extent in line with the theory of Malthus: in the long run, the wage rate will tend toward a level where it is just sufficient to ensure the reproduction of the working class. But this level will, according to Marx, not be low enough to secure full employment.

The existence of the industrial reserve army implies that a large part of the proletariat lives in extreme poverty and misery. In the passages where he describes this, which are filled with vivid examples of the conditions of life among the poor, Marx reveals his passionate concern for social justice. He also expresses his conviction that an important aspect of the system is that the industrial reserve army serves the interests of the capitalists. Because there are large fluctuations in economic activity that involve a changing demand for labor, the industrial reserve army serves as a depository of labor that the capitalists can draw on without having to bid up wages when the need for additional labor arises.

But the trend toward more accumulation of capital, a falling rate of profit, higher industrial concentration, and greater social misery will in the end lead to tensions between the productive forces and the mode of production that are so strong that the capitalist system will be unable to survive:

> The monopoly of capital becomes a fetter upon the mode of production, which has sprung up and flourished along with, and under it. Centralisation of the means of production and socialisation of labour at last reach a point where they become incompatible with their capitalist integument. Thus integument is burst asunder. The knell of capitalist private property sounds. The expropriators are expropriated. (Marx 1885; 1995, p. 380)[8]

Impressive as it is, it is hard to avoid the conclusion that Marx's analysis of the falling rate of profit and the breakdown of capitalism is a prophetic vision rather than a convincing economic theory. Each element in his chain of reasoning may be criticized. It is not clear why capital accumulation occurs to such an extent that the rate of profit falls and even less obvious why the investment behavior of the capitalists is such that it reinforces this tendency. Moreover, Marx does not offer any really convincing arguments why increased capital intensity in production should lead to higher industrial concentration, and why increased concentration involves more unemployment. His argument can be viewed partly as an attempt at formal economic model building,

---

[8] The term *socialisation of labor* must here be understood as referring to the social condition of labor.

which he did not master, partly as an empirical generalization on the basis of his observations of contemporary economic and social life in England. There is no doubt that his ambition was to construct a theory that demonstrated the inevitable breakdown of capitalism under the pressure of its inherent contradictions. His accounts of the social consequences of the system in his own time cannot fail to make an impression even on the modern reader. However, considered as a body of economic theory, with the demands that this implies on the logical structure of the reasoning as a whole, it has to be said that he did not manage to realize this ambition.

THE IMPORTANCE OF KARL MARX

The widespread view of Marx, at least among economists, as a rather unsuccessful model builder in the classical tradition, has doubtlessly been colored by the selective attention that later economists have given to his work. They have tended to focus on those parts of Marx's economics that are especially well suited for mathematical modeling, often showing that they have logical flaws or that their predictions have been wrong. But from a modern perspective there are other themes in Marx's work that may be more interesting than those that so far have received most attention among his modern interpreters. An example is his analysis of the interplay between economic and political decision making, where his discussion places economic theory in the context of a broad social theory and philosophy of history. Other elements are to be found in his analysis of competition as a dynamic process and of technology as a crucial determinant of the development of political and economic institutions. Considering the great attention that economic theorists have accorded to the transformation problem, it is obvious that economists have focused on quite different—and possibly less interesting—elements in his theory than those that have appealed to social reformers and revolutionaries.

Should Marx be counted among the greatest of economic thinkers? Opinions have been divided on this question. Paul Samuelson (1962) on one occasion condescendingly characterized him as "a minor post-Ricardian,"[9] while Negishi (1989) says that he is "one of the greatest economists in history." Who is right? As a forerunner of modern mainstream economic theory he is—as we have already remarked—of little direct importance, even if there still are economists who find inspiration in Marx's work and who seek challenges in converting his ideas to the language of modern economics. However, as a polemicist and critic of the capitalist economic system of his time he was clearly of great importance, and it is undeniable that his visions of the breakdown of capitalism and of a future society of free and equal human beings have inspired politicians and intellectuals all over the world. His ideas about exploitation, the falling rate of profit, and the breakdown of capitalism, considered as economic theories, suffer from obvious weaknesses; nevertheless, their power to influence ideology and politics has, during a long period of recent history, been enormous. It is not necessarily the most rigorous and logical economic theories that succeed in manning the barricades.

MARX AND FRIEDRICH ENGELS

The role of Friedrich Engels in the development of Marxist economic theory is an interesting and controversial question. His importance as a provider of moral and economic support for Marx is indisputable. But what was his importance as an independent thinker and contributor to Marxist thought? Given their lifelong collaboration and Engels's later work on *Capital*, it is natural to ask whether much of Marx's economic theories should possibly be thought of as being the work of Engels or at least as being inspired by him.

Engels's role in the collaboration between the two seems to have varied over time. Until the publication of *The Communist Manifesto* he was indeed an important source of inspiration for Marx, both as a coauthor (partly of works that were left unpublished for decades) and through his own early writings. When

---

[9] Later, however, as in Samuelson (1971), he expressed a more positive evaluation of Marx's economic theories.

later on Marx went to live in England, Engels's role was of a more practical nature. But after Marx's death Engels's literary and scientific contribution became of major importance, above all as the editor of the second and third volumes of *Capital*. This was a very demanding task, not only in terms of the ability to bring order to Marx's manuscripts and decipher his difficult handwriting, but also in the need to penetrate his thought processes and give literary form to them. Marx's manuscripts of volumes 2 and 3 were extremely voluminous, and Engels had by necessity to leave out some of the material in order to prevent the two books from swelling to unreasonable proportions. Accordingly, we only know this part of Marx's work via the filtering that Engels undertook; this must necessarily have been based on his own view of which parts of the manuscripts were the most central and which parts that were of less importance. Still, there are many who believe that Engels out of respect for Marx's work may have shortened the manuscript by less than Marx himself would have wished, and that *Capital* as a whole suffers from more unnecessary elaboration and repetition than the author had intended.[10] But, of course, we can never know with certainty Marx's own intentions with respect to publication of the finished work. Engels's situation as editor of Marx's posthumous works was a very difficult one. All things considered, there is little reason to believe that in his editorial work he came to present Marx's thoughts in a misleading manner.

FURTHER READING

There are a large number of editions of Marx's works. All his books were originally written in German and only later translated into English and other languages. In fact, Marx's works, particularly the *Manifesto* and *Capital*, must be the most widely translated among the books of the major economists of the past. This is not primarily due to his place in the history of economic thought but to his position as founder of the official political and economic ideology of communism and socialism. The editions

[10] The three volumes of *Capital* in unabridged form consist of more than 2,000 pages.

used for reference in the present chapter both have very valuable introductions by the editors. There are several books that contain useful anthologies of Marx's work; one of the best is by David McLellan (2002).

While the *Manifesto* provides an easily accessible introduction to Marx's thoughts on economy and society, the exposition of his economic theories in *Capital* is less easy to read. This is reflected in the modern literature on Marxian economics that attempts to provide short and coherent versions of his theoretical system. This is no simple task, but some texts on the history of economic thought do it very well. In addition to the texts referenced at the end of chapter 1, the book by Dome (1994) can be particularly recommended. The American economist John Roemer has published numerous books and articles that draw inspiration from Marx and relate Marxian analysis both to modern economic theory and current problems; see for instance, Roemer (1988) and some of the articles in Roemer (1994). The transformation problem is treated in depth by Samuelson (1971).

The more general literature on Marx and Marxism is overwhelmingly large, and it is impossible in this context to provide even the beginning of a survey of it. An outstanding biography is by Isaiah Berlin (1939 and later editions), who is especially instructive in relating Marx's ideas to the main currents of political and philosophical thought in the nineteenth century. A broad survey of Marx's thinking, which also discusses his contributions to economics, is the book by Jon Elster (1985).

The Forerunners of Marginalism

PARTITIONING THE HISTORY of economic thought into schools and periods helps to add theoretical structure to the subject and is accordingly an aid to learning and understanding. However, when we try to be more precise about the defining features of the various schools or the extent of the periods, we quickly run into problems. Looking back at the description of the economic theory of the classical economists in previous chapters,[1] it is nevertheless reasonable to conclude that one of their common characteristics was a concern with the functioning of the economic system as a whole. They studied the fundamental principles of price formation, the determinants of the distribution of the national income between social classes, and the causes of long-run growth and development. To a modern economist, however, it is a striking feature of their work that they paid so little attention to the choices and decisions made by the individuals and firms that make up the market economy. It is often implicit in the analysis that individual agents are motivated by self-interest, and in some cases this assumption is also clearly expressed, as in Adam Smith's remarks about the butcher, the brewer, and the baker. But we search in vain in this literature for a more precise analysis of individual decision making and the implications of such an analysis for observable market behavior. The four economists that will be presented in the present chapter started to fill this gap in the literature. They too were concerned with "the big questions." But their most pathbreaking work was done within the field that we now call microeconomic theory, which is concerned with the decisions made by individual firms and consumers as a basis for the analysis of price formation. It is common to refer to these economists as "forerunners" of the marginalist revolution which began in the 1870s. This term may suggest that their analysis was

---

[1] Marx regarded himself as being in opposition to the classical economists, but his basic approach to economic theory still had important points of similarity with theirs.

at a rudimentary stage compared to later developments, but this is actually quite misleading. In several respects their work was decades ahead of its time, and in some areas their new insights only became part of established economic theory well into the twentieth century.

Scientific progress in economics in the nineteenth century often occurred in very small environments—sometimes consisting only of a single person—and the knowledge of new ideas and analyses spread slowly between individuals and countries. The exception to this generalization was England, where, as we have seen, the most prominent economists were informed about each other's work and to some extent also had close personal contact with each other. There is a marked contrast between them and the four economists that will be discussed in this chapter, who for the most part lived and worked in isolation from other researchers with whom they might otherwise have been able to discuss their work. Thünen, Cournot, Dupuit, and Gossen had a distant relationship to the English classical school, both geographically and intellectually. Their selection of problems to be studied and their general approach to economic theory were different, and in many ways their work was a signal of an entirely new view of the scope and method of economic analysis.

Johann Heinrich von Thünen

Johann Heinrich von Thünen (1783–1850) was born in Oldenburg in Germany. He was a farmer's son and was educated as an agronomist at the school of agriculture in Celle. One of his teachers in Celle was a prominent spokesman for the adoption of modern methods of cultivation in farming, and this appealed to Thünen. At the same time, however, he took a critical view of his teacher's recommendation that methods of cultivation that had proved to work well in England should also be adopted in Germany. In Thünen's view, the choice of production technology ought to depend on the prices of commodities and factors of production, and this insight was one that became one of the main themes of his later contributions to economics. Having completed his education in Celle he continued his studies at the University of Göttingen, where among other things he read

Adam Smith's *Wealth of Nations*. The book made a great impression on him and fostered his ambition to make a contribution of his own to the science of economics. But he did not embark on an academic career; instead he bought the large estate of Tellow in Mecklenburg. When he took it over, the estate was in poor condition, but under Thünen's management it developed into a model of modern agriculture. The economy of the estate appeared to him as a mirror image of that of society as a whole, and so the practical experience that he accumulated into farming went hand in hand with increased theoretical insight into the working of the economy as a whole. Gradually he collected material for his main work in economics, *Der isolierte Staat in Beziehung auf Landwirthschaft und Nationalökonomie* (The Isolated State in Relation to the Agricultural and National Economy), the first volume of which appeared in 1826 and the second in 1850.

Methods of Cultivation and the Analysis of Location

Thünen's possibly best-known contribution to economic theory is his analysis of location, factor use, and rent in an agricultural economy. His analysis is based on a set of highly stylized theoretical assumption:

> Imagine a very large town, at the centre of a fertile plain which is crossed by no navigable river or canal. Throughout the plain the soil is capable of cultivation and of the same fertility. Far from the town, the plain turns into an uncultivated wilderness which cuts off all communication between this State and the outside world. (Thünen 1826; 1966, p. 7)

This is the basic structure of the model—to use to modern expression—of the isolated state, which is sketched in the introduction to the book. The reader is asked to imagine a theoretical abstraction, a land area which is fictitious, but which has a rough similarity to something that exists in real life. Starting from these simplified assumptions Thünen now asks the following question:

> What pattern of cultivation will take shape in these conditions?; and how will the farming system of the different districts be affected by their distance from the Town? We assume throughout that farming is conducted absolutely rationally. (Thünen 1826; 1966, p. 8)

These are evidently important practical issues, and Thünen is clearly convinced that the answers yielded by the fictitious model economy are of relevance for the more complicated world of reality. The last clause is particularly interesting. Thünen realizes that the analysis must be based on a theory of the objectives of those who make the decisions regarding the choice of products and methods of cultivation. These decision makers are the landowners, the class to which he belonged, so presumably he has some firsthand knowledge about their motivation. The behavioral hypothesis that he adopts is that they manage their estates as well as possible; in modern terms he assumes that the landowners optimize. More precisely, he assumes that the landowners maximize the surplus from the estate, that is, the difference between revenues and costs.

Production per unit of land is taken to depend on the input of labor, and Thünen assumes explicitly that the marginal productivity of labor—the increase of output that results from a small (or infinitesimal) increase in labor input—is positive and decreasing. The wage rate is the same throughout the isolated state, and the individual landowner is unable to influence it. When the landowner attempts to make the surplus as large as possible, he will use labor up to the point where the value of its marginal productivity is equal to the wage rate. This appears to be the first time that this central optimality condition has been derived in the literature, and this alone would have been sufficient to secure for Thünen a place in the history of economics. But he did not stop there.

Assume now that the single product of the estate, which is assumed to be corn, is sold in the large town at a given price (i.e., a price which the single landowner must take as given), and that there is a cost of transportation that is proportional to the distance from the town. The price that must be used to calculate the value of the marginal product is therefore the price in the town minus the cost of transportation, and Thünen remarks that an increased distance from the market has the same effect on production as a lower price. The optimal use of labor in the production of corn will therefore be determined by the condition that the net price—the price in the town minus the transport cost per unit—multiplied by the marginal productivity of labor is equal to the wage rate. More formally, we can state this condition as:

Net price × marginal productivity of labor = wage rate.

The transport cost component of the net price varies with the distance of the estate from the large town. Since the net price accordingly is lower the farther away the estate is from the town, the marginal productivity of labor must be higher on the more distant estates, for the product of the marginal productivity and the net price must be constant since the wage rate is the same. But because the marginal productivity is decreasing with the amount of labor employed, it follows that the use of labor per unit of land will be lower, the larger the distance between the estate and the market in the large town.

The theoretical reasoning is striking in its clarity and simplicity. It is also interesting by the fact that it can be understood in two different ways. On the one hand, it can obviously be read as a descriptive theoretical hypothesis, an economic theory about the structure of agriculture. On the other hand, it can also be interpreted as a decision rule for landowners: if you own an estate far from the town, it is not a good idea to imitate the technology of production that is used at the best-run farms that are close to the town; because of the cost of transportation it will be profitable to choose a less labor-intensive technology. Thünen himself was clearly interested in both aspects of the analysis, which confirmed the more intuitive insight that he had arrived at during the agricultural studies of his early years: the choice of a rational method of cultivation depends on the prices of products and factors of production.

Thünen's theory is the first example of a logically rigorous economic theory of location choice and location equilibrium, and it has had a strong influence on this area of economics. He generalized the theoretical framework to the case where landowners produce several commodities and concluded that the products with the highest transportation costs per unit will be produced close to the town, while the farms that are farther away will specialize in products that have low transportation costs relative to the market price. The working landowner at Tellow did not shy away from formulating the conclusions to be drawn from his theoretical model in fairly abstract terms. Around the large town, he says, there will be concentric circles such that inside each circle one or a few products will be the dominating outputs of the estates.

Factor Use and Wage Formation

With his analysis of the structure of agriculture Thünen must be considered the founder of the economic theory of location. An important element of his theory is the analysis of the optimal use of labor, where he derived the condition that surplus or profit maximization implies that the value of labor's marginal productivity must be equal to the wage rate. He also realized that this analysis was valid beyond the special example from agriculture and that it also could be generalized to the more realistic case where there are more than one variable factor of production (in the original example the variable factor was labor, while the amount of land was taken as given). In particular, he looked at the case where there are two variable factors of production, labor and capital, and where he gave a clear definition of the marginal productivity of the two factors:

> We measured the effectiveness of capital by the increment in the output per worker due to an increase in the capital he works with. In this context, labour is constant, but capital is a variable magnitude. Suppose now that this procedure is continued, but in the reverse sense of considering capital as constant and labour as growing. In this case ... the effectiveness of labour (the contribution of the worker to output) is recognized from the increment in total output due to the augmentation of workers by one. (1850; translated in Dempsey 1960)

Mathematically speaking, these are partial derivatives translated into ordinary language, and Thünen is clearly conscious of the fact that it is the theory of maximum of several variables that underlies his reasoning:

> Our method of determining the maximum net product [the surplus] is thus in accordance with the method which in mathematics has been proved correct for determining the maximum value of a function containing several variables. (1850; 1966, p. 232)

There is no doubt that Thünen actually knew this method, which he employs at several places in *The Isolated State*. It is worth noting, however, that the formulations in the previous quotation are not quite symmetrical with the respect to the treatment of labor and capital. As regards the effectiveness (the marginal produc-

143

tivity) of capital, this is related to *output per worker* while the effectiveness of labor is defined in terms of its effect on *total output*. Thünen's following analysis indicates that this inconsistency is a slip of the pen, for he later arrives at the conclusion that the effectiveness or marginal productivity of capital and labor must be equal to the interest rate and wage rate, respectively.[2] Thus, Thünen has a complete theory of the optimal utilization of the factors of production in a market with perfect competition. Perfect competition is a concept that Thünen did not use, but this interpretation of his theory is the natural one, because he does in fact assume that both commodity and factor prices are independent of the decisions of the individual producer.

Thünen also looked on his marginal productivity theory as a theory of income distribution. Even if this also was a novel and important theoretical perspective, this part of his work was not as far developed as his theories of production and location. As regards wage formation, he appears to have assumed that the supply of labor was a given magnitude. It follows that the wage rate is determined by the demand for labor, and demand is determined by the optimizing behavior of the producers or the marginal productivity theory. A feature of Thünen's theory of location was, as we have seen, that the wage rate was the same for all producers, and this must be based on the assumption that workers can move freely and without significant costs between employers at different locations.[3]

The Natural Wage

There can be no doubt that Thünen is an important character in the history of economic thought. He was a pioneer in location theory, in the theory of production and income distribution, and in the application of mathematics to economic theory. He also had a strong empirical orientation and used recorded data from his own estate in order to throw light on empirical regularities.

[2] This implies that it is the latter definition of effectiveness, or marginal productivity, relating it to the increase in total output, which is the correct one.

[3] Samuelson (1983) has provided a modern analytical version of Thünen's theory, where he discusses how sensitive his theory of income distribution is to changes in the assumptions on which it is based.

However, like several other economists, he become particularly famous for a statement that is a little on the bizarre side. He was a man of strong social conscience who was concerned not only with the study of what determined actual wages, but also with the more normative question of what the wage rate ought to be. He maintained that this wage rate could be found as that which maximized the income from capital in society. This he called "the natural wage," a somewhat misleading term, since he did not really establish that this wage rate follows from "natural" market processes. The point of departure for Thünen's normative analysis of wages is questionable.[4] What he probably had in mind was that maximization of capital income would lead to more capital accumulation and thereby also increased labor productivity and higher wages. In the long run this criterion would therefore also be consistent with the interests of the workers. The theoretical justification is unconvincing, but with this starting point and some other special assumptions, for instance, that the whole of saving comes from labor income beyond a certain minimum of existence (a), Thünen derived his famous formula for the natural wage, A:

$$A = \sqrt{pa}$$

where p is the average productivity of labor or output per worker. The natural wage that maximizes income from capital is equal to the square root of the product of the average productivity and the subsistence minimum. On the assumption that $p > a$, therefore, the natural wage is higher than the subsistence minimum but lower than the average productivity.

There has been much discussion in the literature about the foundations of this formula, and the question has been raised whether the right-hand side of the expression also represents the marginal productivity of labor. There is no reason in this context to discuss this issue in detail here; there does exist a set of assumptions that ensures that the formula is logically valid, but these assumptions are so special that they are of little economic interest.[5] There is still reason to give credit to Thünen for an early

---

[4] Samuelson (1983, p. 1483) says, with a characteristic formulation, that it is "a crime against normative economics."

[5] A mathematical derivation and discussion of Thünen's result can be found in an article by Dorfman (1986).

attempt at an analytical analysis of economic welfare, even if a majority of later commentators have considered his attempt to be something of a failure.

At any rate, Thünen himself believed that the formula for the natural wage was one of his most important and original discoveries. He decided therefore that it should be engraved on his tombstone, and his wish was carried out when he was buried in the graveyard in Belitz, a village near his Tellow estate. The tombstone is still there, while the Tellow estate is a museum in memory of Thünen both as an economist and as a pioneer of German agriculture.

ANTOINE AUGUSTINE COURNOT

Antoine Augustine Cournot (1801–77) was born in a small town in the east of France. He attended local schools until he was fifteen and then continued for some years with independent studies, especially within mathematics and law. In 1821 he went to Paris to study at the famous École Normale Supérieure, and in 1823 he took a license degree in mathematics at Sorbonne University. He then became the private secretary of a field marshal who required assistance in writing his memoirs. This position must have left Cournot with considerable time for his own pursuits, for in the course of his ten years in the field marshal's employment he took two doctoral degrees, one in mechanics and one in astronomy. In addition, he published a number of articles and even acquired a degree in law. Through the assistance of one of his teachers, the famous mathematician Poisson, he obtained in 1834 a position as professor of mathematics and mechanics at the University of Lyon. Shortly thereafter, he moved to the city of Grenoble as rector of its academy. This was the beginning of a long and distinguished career as a university administrator which lasted until 1862, when he had to resign because of his failing eyesight.

Cournot was a prolific writer in a number of fields. Apart from economics, he wrote extensively on mathematics, philosophy, and intellectual history. As a mathematician he had a reputation for being competent but not creative in the sense of producing original and important results. A common view of his literary output in other areas is similar: it is academically respectable but does not display a high degree of scientific originality. However, in his main contribution to economic theory he was without doubt competent, creative, and original.

This contribution appeared in his 1838 book *Recherches sur les principes mathématiques de la théorie des richesses* (*Researches into the Mathematical Principles of the Theory of Wealth*), written during his time as professor in Lyon. This book is one of the great milestones in the development of economics as an analytical and quantitative science. For the first time one sees here the use of mathematics as a tool of economic model building. The elements of the theoretical models are formulated mathematically from the start, they are assembled in a logically consistent manner, and the models are finally used to derive hypotheses about the functioning of the economy. Cournot also has some interesting general reflections on the use of mathematics in economics. He says first that general mathematical formulations possess a great advantage over Ricardo's numerical examples, for with a more abstract approach one sees immediately analytical points that would otherwise require long and tedious numerical calculations. But he also stresses that the main point of the use of mathematics is not to arrive at numerical answers. By using mathematics as a tool for theoretical reasoning we may arrive at useful conclusions without having to wait for the establishment of empirical laws. In addition to the first systematic application of the differential calculus to problems of economics, the most important contributions in the book were the formulation of what Cournot called the law of demand and the theory of price formation in markets with only one or a few suppliers.

The Law of Demand

The analysis of demand did not occupy a prominent place in the writings of the economists of the classical school, at least not during its early period. By contrast, in Cournot's work demand plays a key role. In chapter 4 of the *Recherches* he includes a careful discussion of the concept of demand and criticizes inaccurate formulations by earlier theorists. Some of them, he says, express themselves as if demand means the same as the quantity bought and sold, while others seem to imply that the demand for a commodity simply refers to the desire to possess it. But both these views lead to meaningless conclusions; demand must refer to the quantity that individuals in fact will purchase at some given price. The lower the price, the larger is the quantity that they wish to buy; this is the law of demand. This relationship between the quantity demanded and the price can be represented by a mathematical function that can be written as

$$D=F(p),$$

where D is the quantity demanded and p is price.

How can we arrive at conclusions about the form of such a function? Cournot says that we can make observations in the market of which quantities that are demanded at different prices; we can then plot these observations in a diagram and connect them by a curve.[6] But it is difficult to make such observations, and there are also reasons to believe that the precise form of the relationship is subject to continuous change. But the difficulties of establishing a purely empirical relationship is not a decisive argument against the use of demand functions in theoretical contexts. As a rule we know at least something about the shape of the function; for instance, we may safely assume that it is decreasing, reflecting the law of demand. For theoretical purposes there can also be no objection to assuming that the function is continuous, at least if the market that we consider is sufficiently large. Cournot illustrates this point by hypothetical data for the demand for sugar in France as the price changes in steps of ten centimes per kilo. He also emphasizes that the demand function is based on a hypothesis that all other factors that have an influence on demand, such as the demographic composition of the population and the tastes of the consumers, are unchanged as the price varies. However, he makes no attempt to derive the demand function from a "deeper" theory of consumer behavior, as the later economists of the marginalist school did; the concept of marginal utility is absent from Cournot's treatment. He also constructs a diagram

[6] Cournot does not discuss the difficult methodological issue that is raised by this suggestion: since each observation is both of the quantity bought and the quantity sold, how can we know that the picture that we get is of the demand function and not of a function reflecting the desire to sell? Almost a hundred years were to pass before economists started to take this empirical problem seriously; see chapter 16.

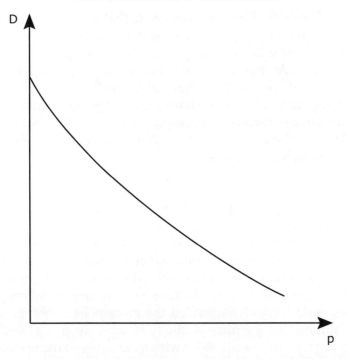

Figure 7.1. Cournot's demand curve with price (p) on the horizontal and quantity demanded (D) on the vertical axis.

that shows the quantity demanded as a function of price—interestingly with quantity measured along the vertical axis and price along the horizontal one.[7] This is probably the first time that this diagram was drawn, at least in published form.

Price Formation under Monopoly

Cournot formulates his monopoly model in a way that is quite similar to the one that we find in modern textbooks. The monopolist is assumed to maximize profit. To begin with Cournot pays special attention to the case where the variable cost of pro-

---

[7] This is the mathematically logical way to draw the diagram when price is considered to be the independent variable and quantity to be the dependent one. When in modern economics we use the reverse procedure, it is due to the influence of Alfred Marshall; see chapter 10.

duction is zero; the illustrative example that he uses is that of the owner of a mineral spring whose water has been discovered to have particularly healthy properties. The monopolist will then choose the price that maximizes income pD or $pF(p)$, which, in the absence of cost, will be identical to profit. This implies that the monopoly price can be characterized by the condition that the derivative of income with respect to price should be equal to zero. Writing the derivative of the demand function as $F'(p)$, the condition can be written as

$$F(p)+pF'(p)=0.$$

In modern usage this can also be expressed as the condition that at the optimum *marginal revenue* must be equal to zero. At this point, Cournot also comes very close to defining another concept that only emerged in the literature half a century later: by dividing the equation by $F(p)$ and defining the *price elasticity* as $pF'(p)/F(p)$, he could have become the father of this important concept, and he could have characterized the monopolist's optimum by the condition that the price elasticity be equal to -1. The fact that he did not take this small and—with hindsight—natural step is a good illustration of how apparently simple developments of the theory are difficult to discover at the stage where ideas are first formulated and concepts are defined.

Cournot continues by extending the analysis to the more general case of variable costs of production and arrives at a version of the condition that at the optimum—that is, at the maximum of profit for the monopolist—marginal revenue must be equal to marginal cost. As a mathematician, he is obviously aware that this equality may characterize both a maximum and minimum of profits. He accordingly calculates the second-order condition and shows that it is crucial for the derivation of hypotheses from the model that are of practical interest and that can be checked against empirical observations. He analyzes the effect of an increase in the unit cost on the monopoly price, and how a tax that is levied per unit of output will lead to changes in the price and the volume of production. In carrying out this type of analysis Cournot was far ahead of his time. As late as 1947, in his pathbreaking book *Foundations of Economic Analysis*, Paul Samuelson found it necessary to elaborate and emphasize the fundamental role of the second-order conditions for what we now refer to as comparative statics analysis. More than a hundred years later Cournot's contribution had not yet been absorbed in the common body of knowledge in the economics profession.

Competition among the Few: Duopoly

In a later chapter of his *Recherches*, Cournot considers the case where competition among producers is what he calls unlimited; what in modern terminology is called perfect competition. The producers are assumed to face a cost function with increasing marginal costs. When producers are unable to influence the market price, their marginal revenue will simply be equal to the price, so that profit maximization implies that marginal cost becomes equal to the price.[8] That he was the first to derive this condition in a rigorous manner is another of Cournot's great achievements. However, it has become overshadowed by the last and most famous of his theoretical innovations, which is the analysis of competition between a few producers, each of whom is large enough to influence the market price. Cournot's main emphasis is on the case of two producers, and this analysis is now known as the Cournot duopoly model. This model is a standard element in all modern textbooks on microeconomic theory, and the modern exposition of it is in fact not significantly different from the original presentation in the 1838 book.

Cournot begins with a discussion of the same example that he used in his monopoly theory, but now there are two producers (or proprietors, as he calls them), each with his own mineral spring, that compete with each other. The quality of the mineral water is exactly the same, so that for the consumers it is a matter of indifference which of the two producers they buy from. If both producers are to survive in the market, they must therefore sell their mineral water at the same price. If they do not, the one who charges the lowest price captures the whole of the sales volume. The question is now: How much will each of the firms produce, and what will the market price be?

It is easy to imagine that someone who started to study this problem from scratch could easily become frustrated by the ap-

---

[8] However, Cournot does not use the concepts of marginal cost and marginal revenue; he is content with letting the mathematical notation speak for itself.

parently insuperable difficulties that it raises. Each of the duopolists—which we now call the two producers—must be assumed
to realize that the profit he can obtain by choosing a particular
volume of output depends on the corresponding choice of the
other duopolist, and he must also realize that the other duopolist
thinks in the same way. What Cournot did was to cut through
this tangle of difficulties by going directly to the assumption that
we now know as the Cournot hypothesis: each of the duopolists
chooses his optimal output (D_1 or D_2) under the assumption that
the other's output is given.

> Proprietor (1) can have no direct influence on the determination of
> D_2: all that he can do, when D_2 has been determined by proprietor
> (2), is to choose for D_1 the value which is best for him. (Cournot
> 1838; 1960, p. 80)

Cournot showed that this assumption led to a determinate
theory of price formation, and that the duopoly price would lie
somewhere between the monopoly price and the price under
perfect competition. This is the result which is now known as
Cournot equilibrium and which is familiar to all students of
economics. Cournot also demonstrated that as the number of
competitors increased the equilibrium price would gradually
decline and approach the price under perfect competition. He
gave a geometric analysis of the duopoly case by means of the
construction now known as reaction functions, and he pointed
out that it was necessary to make an assumption about *market
stability* in order to be able to make predictions about the functioning of the market.

Cournot's theories of monopoly and duopoly introduced concepts and methods that were radically new for their time and
which did not gain general recognition in economic theory until
well into the twentieth century. Among French economists, to
Cournot's great disappointment, the *Recherches* caused little or
no interest. Economists were unfamiliar with the mathematical
exposition in the book, and to the extent that they took any notice
of it at all, it was mostly regarded as a purely formal exercise that
was of little economic interest. Cournot's later attempts to present his theories in nonmathematical form were also unsuccessful. But he lived long enough to observe that a new generation
of economists rediscovered his work and recognized his book as

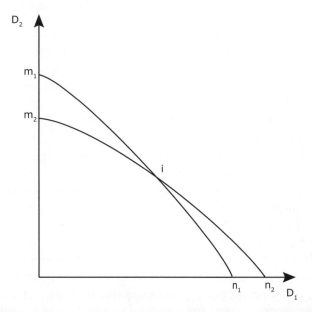

Figure 7.2. Equilibrium under duopoly illustrated by reaction functions. The curve m_1n_1 shows the quantity produced by duopolist 1 as a function of the quantity produced by duopolist 2, while the curve m_2n_2 shows the quantity of duopolist 2 as a function of the quantity produced by duopolist 1. The equilibrium is at the point of intersection i between the two curves.

one of the most original and pathbreaking contributions to this part of economic theory.

JULES DUPUIT

Jules Dupuit (1804–66) came from a family of civil servants in the south of France. Like Cournot, he received his education at one of the elite schools, *les grandes écoles,* in his case the famous École Polytechnique. In 1824 he obtained a position as engineer in the central government administration of roads and bridges, and he rose in his profession to become head of the municipal services in Paris. During most of his career he worked in the communications sector, where his administrative duties concerned roads and canals as well as water supply and sewage systems.

Much of what Dupuit wrote was within the field of engineering, but as he grew older he became gradually more interested in economic issues, mainly related to the practical problems that he had encountered in his work as engineer and administrator. Two issues in particular were central to his interests. First: How ought one to calculate the social profitability of a project like the construction of a road or a bridge? Second: What is the rational price to charge for public services—how much should be charged for the use of the road or bridge? Unlike most of his contemporary economists, Dupuit was primarily interested in deriving decision rules for the public sector, and his contributions to pure economic theory were motivated by his practical concerns. On the one hand, he can be regarded as the founder of a strong French tradition whereby prominent economists have been engaged with practical problems in the public sector while at the same time working on issues in basic research.[9] On the other hand, taking an international perspective, we may see him as one of the founders of normative economic theory or welfare economics, where the purpose of academic research is to arrive at recommendations regarding economic institutions or the use of policy instruments that are likely to promote social welfare.

Dupuit's reputation in the literature of economics rests primarily on two articles that were published in the journal *Annales des Ponts et Chaussées* (Annals of bridges and roads) in 1844 and 1849.[10] He mentions that the articles will in time be part of a larger work on the use of economic analysis in the public sector, but this book was unfortunately never written.

The Profitability of Public Projects

In his 1844 article Dupuit discusses how one can arrive at an estimate of the social profitability of a public project such as a bridge. He points out that it is often relatively easy to calculate

[9] Another of the traditions from Dupuit is that these economists have often had their first professional training in engineering.

[10] They have been translated into English as "On the Measurement of the Utility of Public Works" (1969) and "On Tolls and Transport Charges" (1962).

the cost of the project while there are great problems associated with the estimation of revenue. In fact, in many cases the project does not generate any direct money income, and one has instead to undertake an alternative assessment of the social gain or benefit from the project. Dupuit maintains that this must be calculated as the *utility* of the project. But how should this calculation be carried out? Dupuit refers to Jean-Baptiste Say who says that utility is the property that goods have in satisfying human needs. But this is too abstract to be of any practical value. Moreover, it goes against our intuition to postulate that utility is an objective characteristic of a good. Rather, Dupuit says, intuition suggests that utility is subjective, so that the evaluation of the utility of a good depends on the personal characteristics and circumstances of the person doing the evaluation. His own definition of the utility of a thing or object is therefore

> the maximum sacrifice which each consumer would be wiling to make in order to acquire the object. (Dupuit 1844; 1969, p. 262)

By this definition utility can obviously be measured in money and therefore becomes a practical tool of analysis for the evaluation of projects. How large this sacrifice or willingness to pay actually is, will obviously vary from one consumer to another and depend both on the individual consumer's tastes and needs and on his income or ability to pay. When we consider the utility that different individuals derive from the same object, we have to admit that the analysis may turn out to favor the rich because they have a higher ability to pay. But the objective science of economics cannot, according to Dupuit, be based on any other measure that the observable willingness to pay; it must be the task of others to decide how to care for those with little or no ability to pay.

Dupuit now goes on to apply his concept of utility to the analysis of the profitability of public projects, and he illustrates his theoretical approach by the example of the construction of a pedestrian bridge. It has been decided in advance that crossings of the bridge should be free of charge, so that there will be no money revenue that can be compared with the cost. How can we then decide whether the bridge is socially profitable or not? If the use of the bridge is free, it has been estimated that it will be crossed 2,080,000 times per year.[11] Dupuit now suggests that we make the following thought experiment: assume that we introduce the lowest possible price per crossing; this will be 1 centime or 0.01 francs. We now observe—exactly how we are supposed to do it is somewhat unclear—that the number of crossings goes down by 330,000. All of these persons must have had a willingness to pay of less than 0.01 francs; Dupuit rounds off by saying that it is "about 0.01 francs." The utility that these people would have enjoyed from crossing the bridge is accordingly 0.01 x 330,000 or 3,300 francs. Let us now increase the price to 0.02 francs; this leads to a further decline of an additional 294,000 crossings; using the same calculation as before this implies that these people have a utility of using the bridge of 5,880 francs. Dupuit continues his thought experiment with successive increases of the price up to 15 centimes, at which point the number of crossings has fallen to zero. He then takes the sum of all the utility numbers (3,300 + 5,880 + ...), which amounts to 102,000 francs. This is the estimate of society's total willingness to pay or the social benefit of the project. If the annual costs of maintenance plus the interest on capital are lower than this number, then—and only then—the bridge should be built. So what Dupuit does is to compare the costs with the area under the market demand curve for crossings, which is his measure of total benefits. This is the first example in the literature of an—obviously hypothetical—cost-benefit analysis of a public project that is based on a rigorous theoretical foundation.

[11] 2,080,000 is a very special number (although it corresponds to 40,000 crossings per week), but Dupuit does not tell us where this and the other (equally special) numbers in the example come from. In a modern pedagogical exposition one would in any case have used rounded and perhaps also smaller figures; the argument would be that it is the principle of calculation that counts and that the absolute size of the numbers is of little interest. Dupuit may have felt that his readers were unlikely to accept such stylized examples, and that to convince them he would have to use numbers with some appearance of realism. One may speculate on whether this shows that readers were less inclined to accept abstractions in 1844 than they are today, or whether Dupuit was perhaps a better expositor than modern textbook writers.

Demand and Optimal Pricing

In the previous example it had already been decided that use of the bridge should be free of charge. Both in the 1844 article and in the article published in 1849 Dupuit discusses more generally what prices ought to be charged for the use of publicly provided goods like a bridge or a canal. A private owner would wish to set the price that generated the maximum of revenue, but this should not be the objective of a public owner, who should aim at creating the maximum of utility. As long as there are no extra costs connected with the crossing of the bridge, the price ought to be zero, as in the example. If the public agency needs to collect a certain amount of revenue in order to cover the fixed costs, the best solution would be to let everyone pay a certain fraction of their willingness to pay. The reason for this is clearly that it would not deter anyone from using the bridge, since everyone's utility according to this principle would always be higher than the cost. But this form of price discrimination is rarely feasible, and in practice it may therefore be necessary to charge a price which is high enough to satisfy the revenue requirement, even if it leads to a lower number of crossings and lower total utility for the consumers.

Within pure economic theory Dupuit should be credited with one of the first formulations of the concept of marginal utility (even if he did not use this terminology) and its use as a basis for the analysis of demand. He derives a downward-sloping demand curve from the hypothesis of decreasing marginal utility, which is expressed in money terms in the form of marginal willingness to pay. As an example, the first hectolitre of water will be used for the needs that have the highest priority. The marginal utility of another hectolitre is accordingly lower, and how many hectolitres the consumer will demand depends on the price. As long as the marginal utility is higher than the price it is rational for the individual to buy more. The marginal utility curve, measured in terms of money, therefore becomes the consumer's demand curve.

Dupuit also produced an early version of the theory of monopoly, independently of Cournot (whom he did not know in spite of the fact that they were contemporaries and for a time both lived in Paris). In recent years it has also been pointed out that he showed

157

that as a private or public monopolist increases his price, sales revenue will first increase and then decrease, and the same is true for the relationship between a tax rate and tax revenue. In other words, Dupuit described the so-called Laffer curve, showing the relationship between tax revenue and the tax rate, more than a hundred years before the American economist Arthur B. Laffer popularized the concept in the 1970s.[12] Dupuit does not include a diagram showing the shape of the curve, but his description of it is crystal clear. He discusses this point in both of his famous articles, but the best statement is in the first of them:

> If a tax is gradually increased from zero up to the point where it becomes prohibitive, its yield is at first nil, then increases by small stages until it reaches a maximum, after which it gradually declines until it becomes zero again. It follows that when the state requires to raise a given sum by means of taxation, there are always two rates of tax which will fulfil the requirement, one above and one below that which would yield the maximum. There may be a very great difference between the amounts of utility lost through these two taxes which yield the same revenue. (Dupuit 1844; 1969, p. 278)

This description of the Laffer curve is as clear as can be desired. The implication of Dupuit's argument is obviously that in this situation the government should choose the lower of the two rates, since it yields the same revenue but with a lower loss of utility for the consumers.[13] Modern public finance economists will find it easy to support this conclusion.

It is regrettable that Dupuit did not manage to finish the book that he was working on and which would probably have established an even stronger case for considering him as one of the founding fathers of the field of public finance or public economics. A broader treatment is also likely to have contained more of

[12] There is a story that Laffer, who became a policy advisor to President Ronald Reagan, first drew this bell-shaped curve on a napkin in a Washington restaurant, but this story may not be true.

[13] Laffer's reasoning was of a similar nature, but in addition he maintained that taxes in the United States at the end of the 1970s were in fact so high that tax revenue could be increased through a lowering of the rates. When the Reagan administration decided to let its tax policy be influenced by this idea the result was a substantial increase in the government budget deficit.

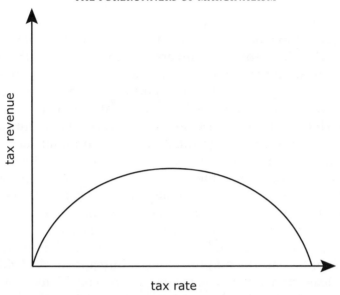

Figure 7.3. The "Laffer curve"—the relationship between tax rate and tax revenue—as described by Dupuit in 1844.

his thoughts about economic theory in general and about questions concerning research methods. Like Cournot, Dupuit was a firm believer in the benefits of using mathematics in economic analysis, and his remarks on this topic strongly convey his convictions and enthusiasm:

> No only do the symbols and drawings of mathematics give body and form to abstract ideas and thereby call the senses to the aid of man's intellectual power, but its formulae take hold of these ideas, modify them, and transform them, and bring to light everything that is true, right and precise in them.... They are machines which, at a certain stage, can think for us, and there is as much advantage in using them as there is in using those which, in industry, labour for us. (Dupuit 1844; 1969, p. 283)

HERMANN HEINRICH GOSSEN

Not very much is known about the background of the German economist Hermann Heinrich Gossen (1810–58). His father was a tax collector in the Prussian state administration who believed that his son ought also to seek employment in the public sector. During his school days, Gossen did especially well in mathematics, but when he went on to university studies he chose the fields of specialization that were assumed to be most useful for a bureaucratic career. He studied law and public administration in Bonn and Berlin and obtained a position at a court in Cologne. But he did not have a very successful career. He disliked his work, and his superiors gradually became so dissatisfied with him that he had to resign in 1847. At that time he had inherited some money from his father, and after a stay in Berlin he returned to Cologne as partner in an insurance company. During the last years of his life he used much of his time in the study of economics; perhaps his theoretical studies were a form of escape into a world where he could produce something of more importance than he had done in his life as a bureaucrat. And this he did, at least to his own satisfaction, for he considered his own importance for the development of economics to be comparable to that of Copernicus for astronomy. This was a view that was not shared by his contemporaries who mostly neglected him. His main work, which was also his only publication, was the book *Entwickelung der Gesetze des menschlichen Verkehrs, und der daraus fliessenden Regeln für menschliches Handeln* (*The Laws of Human Relations and the Rules of Human Action Derived Therefrom*), which was published in 1854. It did not receive much attention when it came out, and Gossen died without having received any recognition for his contribution. His book was rediscovered at the end of the 1870s by, among others, William Stanley Jevons who gave a very generous and laudatory appreciation of it as an important work on economic theory.[14] But a sad sign of the extent to which his life and work had been forgotten was that Jevons in 1879 wrote that he did not know whether Gossen was still alive—more than twenty years after his death.

Consumer Behavior

Gossen's *Entwickelung* is a pioneering work in the development of mathematical formulations of economic theory. Gossen was not a trained mathematician, and his use of mathematical meth-

---

[14] There is a further discussion of this in chapter 8 below.

ods testify to that. Still, there can be no doubt that he had a talent for mathematics, and that he had a good understanding of how economic theories could be formulated in mathematical language. How much he had read of the earlier literature of economics is very unclear. The *Entwickelung* contains no references to the literature, and speculations that he might have known and read Smith's *Wealth of Nations* either in the German translation or via German economic textbooks are uncertain.

The book's most important contribution to economics is its novel and original approach to the theory of consumer behavior. We have seen that Dupuit analyzed demand by postulating a decreasing marginal willingness to pay for each good, but he did not incorporate this analysis in a broader framework for the study of consumer behavior. This was to be Gossen's contribution. His approach was to assume that each individual maximizes a function that represents the total "enjoyment" of consumption. Gossen imagined that this function took the form of a sum of partial functions, so that there was a separate enjoyment connected with each good. A small increase in the consumption of a good gave rise to a positive pleasure (positive marginal utility) but to a decreasing degree (decreasing marginal utility). The latter assumption Gossen wrote as

> the magnitude of a given pleasure decreases continuously if we
> continue to satisfy this pleasure without interruption until satiety
> is ultimately reached. (Gossen 1854; 1983, p. 6)

Posterity has named this assumption "Gossen's first law," even if it can be argued that Gossen was not the first to formulate the principle.[15] This "law" forms the basis for the more specific theory of the consumer.

The maximization of enjoyment or utility takes place subject to the condition that the consumer must satisfy his needs within the constraint of his limited resources. In the first version of Gossen's theory this resource constraint takes the form of a restriction on

---

[15] The first appears to have been Daniel Bernoulli who in 1738 used the assumption of decreasing marginal utility of income to explain the existence of risk aversion; see the discussion of his work in chapter 2. But it should be noted that the context in which Bernoulli used the hypothesis is rather different from Gossen's consumer theory.

time use. The goods that appear in the utility function are the lengths of time used on different activities, and the resource constraint is that the total use of time must be equal to the amount of time available; this Gossen identified as the consumer's lifetime. He showed mathematically that the solution to this maximization problem implied that the marginal utility of time use must be the same for all activities. This is an interesting formulation of the consumer's problem,[16] but an obvious weakness of it is that it does not contain any *economic* constraint on the maximization of utility. Accordingly, it cannot be used to study the effects of changes in income and prices on consumer behavior. However, Gossen extended the analysis to a model with production and trade between individuals, so that all consumers can purchase goods at given market prices. He demonstrated that the consumers will then allocate their income such that "the last atom of income" will give the same pleasure for all goods, and this implies that marginal utility divided by price must be the same for all goods. This is known as "Gossen's second law" and is clearly his most original discovery. In modern times it is therefore often referred to simply as "Gossen's law," and in a more general form it is a core element in the modern theory of consumer demand.[17] There can be no doubt that this was a pathbreaking effort, both methodologically and in terms of new economic insights.

Other Contributions

Many years later Francis Y. Edgeworth said about Gossen that "he was a man of one idea; but that was an immortal one." It is the general theoretical framework and the second law that have left their marks on economics, but in the *Entwickelung* he also

[16] It reminds one of the modern theory of the optimal allocation of time, which is associated with the work of Gary Becker (1965). Becker does not refer to Gossen's book, which, however, had not been translated into English at the time when Becker wrote.

[17] In the case of two commodities we may write the marginal utilities as u_1 and u_2 and prices as p_1 and p_2. In the modern version of consumer theory the condition for utility maximization is that the marginal rate of substitution is equal to the ratio of prices, and this can be written as $u_1/u_2 = p_1/p_2$. By a simple rearrangement of this equation we obtain the expression $u_1/p_1 = u_2/p_2$, which is Gossen's second law.

developed his theory of consumer demand in a number of further directions. Among other things, he extended the framework for the study of the consumer to include variable labor supply, showing that (minus) the negative marginal utility of work must be equal to the positive marginal utility of the consumption that labor income made possible. This extension then enabled him to study a model with production where consumer goods are being produced with the input of labor. He went on to analyze an economy with exchange of goods between consumers, and where he also considered the problem of the socially optimal allocation of goods between consumers. He claimed that such an optimum would have to imply that the marginal utility of each commodity must be the same for all consumers, but he did not explain the concept of optimality on which these conditions were founded. In general, his discussion of these issues is unclear and has several weaknesses, but on the other hand his thinking was evidently moving in the direction of some important insights that during the coming decades were to be developed in the theories of general equilibrium and welfare economics.

The second part of Gossen's book is different from the first. Here he moves from formal theory to a presentation of his thoughts about economic systems. It turns out that he is not only interested in the theoretical analysis of the market mechanism; he is also firmly convinced that it is the best of all possible economic systems. This conviction is of an ideological nature, in the sense that it does not appear to be derived from economic theory. He is in favor of free trade, the protection of property rights, and free access to education for both sexes. But he also admits that the market mechanism may have some weaknesses, as when he expresses himself in favor of restrictions on child labor. He also maintains that markets do not function well when it comes to the allocation of land, and he proposes that the state should buy all land and then resell it to the public by auction. In this way the land would eventually be owned by those best fit to use it efficiently.

Gossen was an important pioneer of economic theory. The high recognition that his work gradually came to enjoy was in large part due to the fact that William Stanley Jevons and Léon Walras one generation later rediscovered his book and emphasized his role as an important forerunner of their own work. But his direct influence on his contemporaries was negligible; there were few people who bought his book and probably even fewer who read it. A likely explanation of the lack of interest and understanding is that the literary quality of the book was poor. It was not divided into chapters, and both the style of his language and his not especially elegant mathematics were such that the structure of his arguments was difficult to discover. The extensive use of mathematics also implied that the book was difficult to read for other economists, and especially in Germany the attitude to the use of mathematical methods in economics was quite hostile. A further reason for his lack of success was also that he worked entirely on his own without contact with others who might have been interested in similar problems and could have given him useful feedback both on the contents and style of his book.

FURTHER READING

Thünen's *Isolierte Staat* has been translated into English as *Thünen's Isolated State* (1966). This translation, which has an introduction by the geographer Peter Hall, contains most of the original first volume as well as selections from the second. Jürg Niehans gives an excellent summary of Thünen's central contributions in his article in *The New Palgrave Dictionary of Economics*. Samuelson (1983) and Dorfman (1986) provide formalized versions of Thünen's theories.

Cournot's *Recherches* was translated into English in 1897 under the title *Researches into the Mathematical Principles of the Theory of Wealth*. In 1927 a new edition appeared with an interesting preface by Irving Fisher, who also appended a bibliography of works in mathematical economics; this edition was reprinted in 1960. Even those who are not inclined to read the whole book may benefit from browsing in it to see how close Cournot's original exposition is to modern textbook treatments of the theories of monopoly and duopoly. In *The New Palgrave Dictionary of Economics* there is a good article about him by Martin Shubik. Ekelund and Hébert (1990) give an account of the reception given to Cournot's 1838 book by contemporary French economists, arguing that this was more positive than generally acknowledged by later economists.

Dupuit's two most famous articles have both been translated into English; the style is simple and clear and easy to follow for a modern reader. An extensive survey of Dupuit's contributions can be found in an article by Ekelund (2000), who covers much more of his work than the two articles that we have focused on here.

Gossen's *Entwickelung* appears in English translation as *The Laws of Human Relations and the Rules of Human Action Derived Therefrom* (1983). The English edition has been divided into chapters and is considerably more reader friendly than the German original. It also contains a long introduction by Nicholas Georgescu-Roegen, which is a brilliant presentation of Gossen's life and work. Georgescu-Roegen makes a special effort to explain why Gossen's work was so long overlooked and to tell the story of the rediscovery of the book.

The Marginalist Revolution I:
William Stanley Jevons and Carl Menger

$\mathbf{M}$ANY HISTORIANS of economic thought maintain that economic theory underwent a fundamental change during the decade of the 1870s. This change affected both the style and content of the theory, and the change was so sudden and dramatic that it has been referred to as a revolution. The revolution was not limited to England as the homeland of the classical school; it happened more or less simultaneously in the English-, German-, and French-speaking worlds. Conventionally, there are three individuals who are particularly closely associated with the revolution in the three areas: William Stanley Jevons in England, Carl Menger in Austria, and the Frenchman Léon Walras, whose academic base was Lausanne in Switzerland. Moreover, the common view has been that the revolution may be associated with three books by these authors: Jevons's *The Theory of Political Economy* from 1871, Menger's *Grundsätze der Volkswirtschaftslehre* which came out in the same year, and Walras's *Éléments d'Économie Politique Pure*, the first volume of which was published in 1874 and the second in 1877.

What was the nature of the marginalist revolution? On this, opinions differ, but one may at least point to three characteristic features of the new orientation in economic research:

1. A stronger emphasis on erecting economic analysis on the foundation of theories of behavior for individual economic agents, in other words, firms and consumers.
2. Increased focus on the demand side of consumer goods markets and on the supply side of factor markets, accompnied by a critique of the classical labor theory of value. Marginal utility became a new and central concept of economic theory.
3. More reliance on mathematical formalization, above all through the use of the differential calculus.

All of these features were brought together in what we may call the marginalist approach to economic analysis. Both producers (firms) and consumers were regarded as agents who attempted to achieve the best possible outcome for themselves in the form of the highest possible profit for firms and utility for consumers. In order to achieve this, they had to balance benefits and costs against each other such that on the margin there were no additional gains that could be obtained by any further actions. The marginalist principle, which could be formally characterized by the mathematical first-order conditions for a maximum, now emerged as the core of economic analysis, and this is the reason why the victory of the new theories has been characterized as the marginalist revolution.

Evidently, the triumvirate of Jevons, Menger, and Walras were not the first to introduce marginalist thinking in economics. We have already seen early traces of this line of thought in the work of the classical economists, as in Ricardo's theory of rent and Mill's theory of demand and price formation. And in the previous chapter we saw that the pioneers Thünen, Cournot, Dupuit and Gossen together did all that is said to be characteristic of the marginalist revolution: they focused on the decisions of individual agents, they saw the importance of the study of demand and its basis in the theory of utility maximization, and they began to formulate their theories in mathematical form. However, it may still be reasonable to look at the decade of the 1870s as the breakthrough for the new approach. To a larger extent than the pioneers, Jevons, Menger, and Walras incorporated the new theories into a unified system of thought. Moreover, in contrast to the early pioneers their ideas gained acceptance among other economists, gradually spreading to what one could now begin to regard as an economics profession.

Of the three central names during this period, we start by taking a closer look at Jevons and at Menger and his followers. Walras is sufficiently different from the other two to require a chapter of his own.

WILLIAM STANLEY JEVONS

William Stanley Jevons (1835–82) was born in Liverpool where his father was an ironmonger. He seems to have had a happy childhood with parents who had strong intellectual interests. But when Jevons was ten his mother died, and a couple of years later

167

his father's firm went bankrupt. Jevons's life situation became more difficult, but in spite of this he managed to begin to study at University College London in 1852, concentrating on natural science. After two years, however, he broke off his studies, probably for economic reasons, and immigrated to Australia where he found employment at The Royal Mint in Sydney. He spent altogether five years in Australia, where his working conditions were such that he could easily pursue his many and varied interests; he read meteorology and economics, collected statistical data and became a good amateur photographer. He was gradually filled by a desire to achieve something important in his life, and he wrote to his sister that what he wished was "to be good, not towards one or a dozen, or a hundred, but towards a nation or the world." His own contribution he saw as that of helping to establish a more fundamental understanding of human life—"to define the foundations of our knowledge of man." To reach such a goal was incompatible with his life in Australia, and in 1859 he returned to England to continue his studies, now with a focus on logic and economics, and he finished by obtaining an M.A. degree at University College with a thesis in economics. He was rewarded with a gold medal for the best candidate in his field, although he was dissatisfied both with his own achievements and with economics itself, which in his view ought to be reestablished on a more satisfactory theoretical foundation.

In the history of economics as a discipline Jevons is an interesting transitional character. Of the economists that we have so far encountered, he is the first with a formal university education in the subject. Many of the earlier economists also had an academic background but in a different field, such as theology, philosophy, law or engineering, and some of them, like Ricardo and Mill, had no formal academic qualifications at all. A common characteristic of them was that they had acquired their knowledge of economics through independent studies. Although the program of study in economics that Jevons attended at University College was hardly very comprehensive by modern standards, his experience is an important signal that we are approaching a new era with a higher academic status for the subject, and where economists gradually came to see themselves as members of a separate profession.

As early as 1862 Jevons presented a paper, "Notice of a General Mathematical Theory of Political Economy," to a meeting of a general academic forum, the British Association for the Advancement of Science. His presentation contained many of the ideas for which he later became famous, but at the time it did not meet with much interest. Disappointed at the reception of his paper, Jevons instead turned his attention toward applied problems, and he wrote a book that became a real best seller. *The Coal Question* (1865) caused a great stir by predicting England's demise as an industrial nation through the depletion of its coal reserves. He related the problem to Malthus's analysis of the population question. England's economic development was bound up with exponential growth in industries that were dependent on coal as a source of energy, but the coal itself could no longer be extracted at the speed that this growth required. The lack of coal would therefore act as a brake on the country's economic growth, and it was necessary to rethink its national strategy. The book received enormous attention; it was discussed in Parliament, and Jevons was invited to a personal conference with Prime Minister Gladstone. In the judgment of posterity, however, as a work on economics it was not a particularly impressive achievement.[1]

Jevons had now achieved a certain reputation as an economist and decided to make his career in academic life. He obtained his first position at a small college in Manchester, and it was largely there that he wrote *The Theory of Political Economy*, the book that has since been regarded as his main work. However, Jevons was not only a theoretical economist. He made important contributions to empirical economics through his work on the construction of price indices, and on business cycles and labor economics. He also worked on logic and the philosophy of science, where his main contribution was *The Principles of Science* (1874). In 1876 he moved to London as professor at University College. He died tragically in a drowning accident some weeks before his forty-seventh birthday.

---

[1] Keynes (1933) thought that the concern for resource depletion reflected a psychological trait of Jevons's character. He was, e.g., reported to have had the same kind of concern regarding brown wrapping paper, and his son had told Keynes that fifty years after Jevons's death the family had still not been able to use up the stock that Jevons had accumulated.

CHAPTER 8

The Mathematical Method

Was there really a marginalist revolution? Those who might be in doubt about its existence could easily become convinced that the answer must be yes after having read Jevons's *Theory of Political Economy,* as this is a book where the tone is unmistakably revolutionary from the very beginning.[2] Unlike Alfred Marshall twenty years later, Jevons feels no inclination to say that Ricardo and Mill had the right understanding of economic theory and that it was only their formulations that were sometimes unclear. Jevons is openly and strongly critical and turns especially sharply against Mill who was the most influential economist of the time and the great consolidator of the insights of the classical economists (sixty-five years later John Maynard Keynes was to employ the same tactics by using Pigou as the target of his attacks on those that *he* called the classical economists).

In the introductory chapter Jevons announces his program for making economics a mathematical and quantitative science:[3]

It is clear that if economics, if it is to be a science at all, must be a mathematical science. . . . To me it seems that *our science must be mathematical, simply because it deals with quantities.* Wherever the things treated are capable of being *greater or less,* there the laws and relations must be mathematical in nature. (1871; 1970, p. 78)

He accuses Mill of not having realized the need to employ mathematical methods in economics at a serious level. After having quoted Mill's statement that the equality between supply and demand can be represented by an equation (see the quotation in chapter 5), Jevons writes:

Mill here speaks of an equation as only a proper mathematical *analogy.* But if economics is to be a real science at all, it must not deal merely with analogies; it must reason by real equations, like all the other sciences which have reached at all a systematic character. (1871; 1970, p. 143.)[4]

[2] We shall return to the issue of the nature of the revolution at the end of chapter 9.

[3] All page references to the *The Theory of Political Economy* are to the 1970 Pelican Classics edition.

[4] In the continuation of this passage Jevons presents a critique of Mill's theory of price formation that seems to indicate a misinterpretation of the logic of Mill's reasoning.

Consequently, the science of economics must be reformulated by means of mathematics; the ideal model must be that of the natural sciences. Admittedly, there are those who maintain that an important difference between the natural and social sciences is that many social phenomena are difficult to quantify, but this objection is, in Jevons's view, of little significance. There are great possibilities for the application of mathematics to relationships that are not usually thought of as being measurable in the conventional sense of the word, and he mentions a number of such areas where we easily accept measurability either because we have become used to it or because measures have been developed that have turned out to work in practice. Examples that he mentions include probabilities as measures of belief and doubt, and various measures of energy and heat.

Jevons's enthusiasm for the mathematical approach to the study of economics is infectious, and much of what he says about the advantages of the use of mathematical methods is thoughtful and illuminating. However, his actual use of mathematical methods in *The Theory of Political Economy* is not very extensive or impressive. It shows that he had a limited mathematical training and that he found it difficult to translate his economic insights into the formal language of mathematics. In fact, some of the fascination of reading the book today is that it is so easy to follow the author's struggle with the formulation of theoretical ideas and models that many modern readers tend to regard as elementary.

Marginal Utility Theory

Jevons uses a large part of his main work to develop the theory of utility, and he begins his chapter on "Theory of Utility" with a discussion of the concept itself. In the first part of his discussion he seems to indicate that utility is a property that commodities possess, and he quotes statements by Jean-Baptiste Say and Jeremy Bentham that support this view. But he then rounds off the discussion by saying that even if these quotations "perfectly" express the meaning of the word as it is used in economics, one has to keep in mind that it is the judgment and attitudes of the individual person that is the real criterion of "what is or is not useful." The conclusion, therefore, is that utility is subjective and not an intrinsic quality of commodities.

171

Jevons then turns to the distinction between total utility and marginal utility, which he calls "the final degree of utility." He has a careful discussion of the hypothesis that marginal utility is a decreasing function of the quantity consumed, taking his departure from the following thought experiment:

> Let us imagine the whole quantity of food which a person consumes on an average during twenty-four hours to be divided into ten equal parts. If his food be reduced by the last part, he will suffer but little; if a second tenth part be deficient, he will feel the want distinctly; the subtraction of the third tenth part will be decidedly injurious; with every subsequent subtraction of a tenth part his sufferings will be more and more serious, until at length he will be on the verge of starvation. Now, if we call each of the tenth parts *an increment*, the meaning of these facts is that each increment of food is less necessary, or possesses less utility, than the previous one. (1871; 1970, p. 106)

This is a line of thought that we recognize from the work of Gossen and Dupuit. Jevons's diagrammatic illustration of the hypothesis is shown in figure 8.1 (1871; 1970, p. 107). The height of each of the ten columns shows the utility attached to successive increments of consumption, so that the sum of all the columns represents total utility. Beginning from the right, the utility of the last tenth of consumption is very small, while as we move toward the left the utility of successive tenths of consumption increases. Looking at the relationship from the left the successive increments of consumption generate steadily decreasing additions to total utility. Jevons goes on to remark that since the law of decreasing marginal utility in principle must hold however small the increases are, we can draw the relationship in the form of a continuous function (which he does on the following page). It is interesting to note that Jevons takes it to be obvious that the marginal utility of a particular commodity only depends on the quantity consumed of that commodity, although he has stressed earlier in the chapter that utility is not an intrinsic quality of commodities.

We recognize this as Gossen's first law. What about his second law, characterizing the consumer's optimum? This is not to be found in *The Theory of Political Economy*. The closest we come to it is in a paragraph where Jevons discusses the problem of al-

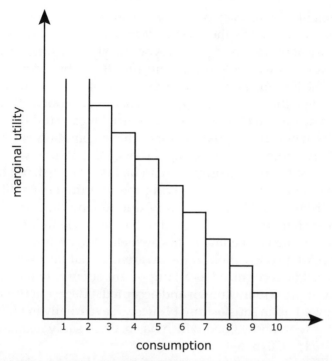

Figure 8.1. Jevons's illustration of the "Law of the variation of utility." Each additional tenth of consumption involves a smaller addition to utility than the previous one.

locating a given quantity of a commodity between two alternative uses, and where he shows that utility maximization implies that marginal utility must be the same for both uses. This is a special case of Gossen's second law, but since the price of the commodity is the same in both uses, prices do not appear in the optimality condition. As a theoretical contribution it is therefore of far less interest than the original Gossen version. Without the economic insight provided by the general version of the second law it becomes difficult to realize that utility theory can form the basis for a theory of consumer demand, and Jevons did not manage to construct such a theory.

The declared aim of Jevons's utility theory is to explain the determination of prices, and when one reads his exposition of the theory, there is no doubt that the author has achieved a significant improvement with respect to the role of consumer behavior in the formation of prices. His theory is a clear improvement over that of the classical writers, and Jevons is obviously very much aware of it. However, it was only some time after the publication of the book that he became familiar with the work of Dupuit and Gossen, and when the second edition of his book came out in 1879 he added a new introductory chapter in which he gave full recognition to the work of his predecessors. This recognition is mixed with his disappointment at having discovered that his own work had turned out to be less original than he first believed, but he is nevertheless very generous in giving the forerunners credit for their contributions: "Much is clearly due to Dupuit, and of the rest a great share must be assigned to Gossen." He fights off his frustration at the weakening of his own claim to an original discovery, seeking consolation in the awareness that his own effort must at least be recognized as an important attempt to make the new ideas more widely known and accepted: "Regret may easily be swallowed up in satisfaction if I succeed eventually in making that understood and valued which has been so sadly neglected" (Jevons 1871; 1970, p. 63).

It is difficult not to feel compassion for Jevons when one reads this, and to wish to tell him that this is modesty carried too far. The downgrading of the *Theory of Political Economy* to a sort of popularization of Dupuit and Gossen is after all a gross underestimate of the originality of the book. Fortunately, he did not do much to alter the main substance of the book from the first to the second edition; the revolutionary fire of the first edition is still there.

Demand and Prices

With the work of Jevons the consumer side of markets comes to occupy a much more prominent place in price theory. The theory of the demand for consumer goods—although somewhat incompletely developed—is related to a theory of consumer decisions, and Jevons emphasizes strongly the importance of marginal utility for the understanding of prices. At the same time there are aspects of his statement of the theory that are likely to confuse the reader. His ambition was clearly to develop a general price theory, but whether he achieved it remains at best an open question. In a central passage he writes as follows about the interrelationship between cost of production, supply, marginal utility, and price:

> In order that there may be no possible mistake about this all-important series of relations, I will restate it in tabular form as follows:
>
> *Cost of production determines supply;*
> *Supply determines final degree of utility;*
> *Final degree of utility determines value.*
> (Jevons 1871; 1970, p. 187)

Reading this "tabular form" straight through, it is hard to escape the conclusion that in the end it really is cost of production that determines price or value. It seems as if Jevons may also have felt that the passage could convey this impression, for shortly afterward he distances himself from Ricardo's labor theory of value by saying that in his view the value of labor is determined by the value of the product, not the other way round. Then it becomes even more difficult to interpret the last quotation, for it then follows that the value or price of the product determines the cost of production. The result is an apparently circular statement that at least demands a further explanation (which, in the light of later insights into general equilibrium systems, it would have been easy to supply). Jevons's ambition was clearly to arrive at a general price theory where cost of production as well as consumer demand was to play equivalent roles. However, he had no clear understanding of how to formulate a general equilibrium theory in which supply and demand are determined by prices, while prices in turn are determined by the condition that supply must equal demand in all markets. Therefore, Jevons cannot be said to have been successful in constructing a general equilibrium model in the modern sense.

Jevons's most ambitious attempt at mathematical economic model building is his model of market equilibrium in an exchange economy, where there are two consumers—or, as he calls them, "trading bodies"—who trade in two commodities, corn and beef, and where the total supply of each of the two commodities is given (Jevons 1871; 1970, pp. 141–143). Jevons shows, although without giving the details of the mathematical derivation, that the rate of exchange in quantity terms—the ratio between the number of units of corn and beef exchanged in the market—must be equal to the ratio of marginal utilities for consumer A, and also to the corresponding ratio for consumer B. We then have two equations in the two unknowns, namely, the traded quantity of corn and the traded quantity of beef. The analysis is impressive and the result is formally correct, but when we take account of Jevons's strong programmatic statement about the purpose of utility theory, it also contains some paradoxical features.

One is that the formal model has no prices in it, although the purpose of the theory is said to be the explanation of prices; it determines quantities but not prices. The further step required to arrive at the equilibrium prices is so small that it is curious that Jevons does not include it in the paragraph where he presents the model. After a further sixty pages he actually does so, but in a different context and without referring back to the first model. The point is the following: in the first model (pp. 141–143) Jevons shows that in equilibrium the ratio between the marginal utilities for both consumers must be equal to the ratio y/x, where y is the traded quantity of beef and x is the traded quantity of corn. Then comes the further reasoning on p. 204: let p_1 be the price of corn and p_2 the price of beef. Because the value of the two traded quantities must be the same (for both corn and beef, sales value must be equal to the cost of purchase), we have that $p_1 x = p_2 y$ or $y/x = p_1/p_2$. So the model does determine prices or—more precisely—the relative price, the price of corn in terms of units of beef. But this ought, of course, to be the main result of the exercise, and the fact that we find it placed so far from the model itself does not make it easy for the reader to grasp the essence of the analysis.

Another notable feature of the model is that it is limited to a situation of pure exchange where there is no production. Consequently, it cannot tell us anything about the role of production costs in the explanation of prices. Jevons does say that the analysis is fully consistent with the theory of supply and demand, but since the supplies of beef and corn are given the role of costs remains unclear. At this point, he makes life easy for himself in relation to his criticism of the classical economists, for when the costs of production are not included in the model their importance for the formation of prices is obviously zero.[5] Nevertheless, the model is of great historical interest since it is the first example in the history of economics of a formal mathematical model of general equilibrium in an exchange economy.

The shortcomings of Jevons's theoretical models force us to conclude that he was rather far from the realization of his ambition to construct a complete theory of the formation of prices. But he went a good part of the way, and the weaker parts of his analysis were so easy to identify that later economists were able to use them as a basis for further improvement. This illustrates a more general point: with the introduction of mathematical methods in economics the subject made a great step toward becoming a cumulative science, where every new researcher could build on the insights of previous generations, and where older theories could more easily be put aside if somebody succeeded in developing a new theory that was either more general or had greater explanatory power. Jevons has a large share of the honor of having started this process.

The Sunspot Theory

Jevons was also a pioneer of empirical economics. One of his achievements in this area was a study of the long-run development of the price level that is remarkable both for the systematic and thorough collection of data and for the originality of the design of price indices. But among the large number of his empirical studies there is one that is particularly well known and that brought him fame of a more dubious sort. This is his contribution to business cycle theory in the article "The Solar Period and the Price of Corn" (1875, published in Jevons 1884).

Like many other economists Jevons had observed the changes between good and bad times, between rises and falls of the business cycle. He arrived at the conclusion that the causes of these fluctuations must be sought in factors outside the economic

---

[5] In this sense Jevons's model is more closely related to Ricardo's brief sketch of the formation of prices for goods with fixed supplies, such as rare old coins, where prices are said to be determined by scarcity. The model can therefore be viewed as a formal analysis of this type of market, although this is clearly a more limited application than the one that Jevons had in mind.

system as such—exogenous factors, as we would say today. He combined his interests in economics, statistical analysis, and meteorology to formulate and test the hypothesis that the periodic changes of economic activity could be traced to the periodicity of the sunspots. Sunspots are areas of the sun with especially strong magnetic fields; the more numerous and larger the sunspots are, the colder is the earth's climate. The periodicity of the sunspots is about 11.1 years, but in the 1870s there were scientists who claimed that the periodicity was in fact shorter than previously believed, approximately 10.44 years. Jevons grasped at the new hypothesis, for it fitted much better to his statistical data for the business cycle. His idea was that the fluctuations in the temperature would first affect agricultural crops, especially in India, and from there would spread to other sectors of the economy and to other countries, for instance, to British industry. But both his theory of the transmission of the business cycle and his statistical work was unconvincing, and in addition astronomers soon returned to the original estimate of a periodicity of 11.1 years. Unfortunately for Jevons, his work on this problem ended up by becoming "the most ridiculed idea of his life," as Ekelund and Hébert (1997) put it.

But the view of the sunspot theory as a ridiculous one is too harsh. The idea of seeking the causes of the business cycle in exogenous factors is obviously an interesting one from a theoretical point of view, and the systematic—although imperfect—statistical test was clearly an innovative contribution to empirical economics.

CARL MENGER

Carl Menger (1840–1921) was born in a part of Austria that now belongs to Poland. The son of a lawyer, he studied law in Vienna and Prague and obtained a doctorate in law at the University of Krakow.[6] As an economist he was mainly self-taught, but after completion of his studies he began to work as an economic journalist and later as an economic analyst in the prime minister's

---

[6] At present, the three cities are located in three different countries, but at that time they were all part of the Habsburg Empire.

office. Part of his task in this position was to follow and analyze price movements in particular commodity markets, and he was struck with how little help he had in this work from established price theory that was founded on the labor theory of value. His attempt to work out an alternative theory resulted in his most famous book, *Grundsätze der Volkswirtschaftslehre* (*Principles of Economics*, 1871; 1950). This was also his dissertation for the *Habilitation*, the degree that is required for a top academic position in the German-speaking world. After this, he obtained a position at the University of Vienna, where he became a professor in 1879.

Menger's plan was to extend the *Grundsätze* by several volumes that together would represent an integrated view of the whole field of economics, but he never managed to achieve this goal. He was extremely well read, and the *Grundsätze* is full of references to the literature in several languages, both classical and modern, and far from limited to economic topics. A testimony to his pleasure in reading was his collection of books, which over the years became extremely voluminous, but his desire to achieve a complete knowledge of the existing literature gradually became an obstruction to his own writing. In 1903 he retired from his chair in order to work undisturbed on the continuation of his main work. He worked himself deeper and deeper into the literature, but he never managed to come up with a finished manuscript.

The Theory of Value

Menger's ambition in the *Grundsätze* is to develop a general theory of value that is capable of explaining all prices, both commodity and factor prices, on the basis of the same principle. He finds this principle in something that is similar but not quite the same as the hypothesis of diminishing marginal utility. If a limited number of units of a commodity can be used for different purposes, they will be allocated among these in such a way that every need that is satisfied is more important than any need that is not satisfied. The value of a satisfied need can be measured by the loss it would entail if a unit of the commodity had been removed. The concept of marginal utility lies just under the surface, but it does not quite emerge, and Menger did not introduce a particular term to denote marginal utility. He put forward the hypothesis that the subjective value of a unit of a good decreases the more one consumes of it. This corresponds to Gossen's first law, but the formal analysis is limited to a numerical example (Menger 1871; 1950, p. 127). Menger obviously did not think along mathematical lines, and he did not realize that the analysis would be much simplified if he had assumed that there was a continuous relationship between marginal utility and the quantity consumed, which could be drawn as a smooth curve.

While Menger can be said to have rediscovered Gossen's first law, he did not manage to formulate the second law, describing the consumer's optimal allocation of his income between alternative uses. But he does realize the importance of this problem, and it is interesting to see how he approaches it. We recall that the closest that Jevons came to Gossen's second law was in the analysis of the optimal allocation of the same good to the satisfaction of several needs. It notable that Menger considers exactly the same problem:

> If a good can be used for the satisfaction of several different kinds of needs, and if, with respect to each kind of need, successive single acts of satisfaction each have diminishing importance ... the end result of this procedure is that the most important of the satisfactions that cannot be achieved have the same importance for every kind of need, and hence that all needs are being satisfied up to an equal degree of importance of the separate acts of satisfaction. (Menger 1871; 1950, p. 131)

In other words, marginal utility is the same in all uses of the good. There is no reference to prices for the obvious reason that the good is bought at the same price, whatever the use to which it is put. But Menger, like Jevons, failed to solve the more general problem of the allocation of different goods with the objective of obtaining maximum utility or satisfaction of needs.

Menger applied his price theory not only to consumer goods, which he called goods of the first order, but also to the factors of production or goods of a higher order. He emphasized that the prices of the factors of production were derived from the prices of the goods of the first order that they helped to produce. The value or price of a factor of production is determined by the reduction in the value of the finished good that would result if the supply of the factor of production were to be reduced by one unit, given that the other factors of production were optimally reallocated. This result is an early version of the marginal productivity theory of the prices of factors of production. It was clearly an original contribution, although Thünen had formulated a similar theory some decades earlier, which was both clearer and more rigorous.[7] He illustrates the theory by a number of well-chosen examples that show him to have a good grasp of practical applications. In one of the examples he discusses the consequences of changes in tastes that lead to the disappearance of the need for tobacco. The most immediate effect of this is that existing stocks of tobacco lose their value.[8] Next, the value of the stocks of tobacco leaves in the factories, the specialized machines, and the services of the workers employed in tobacco production will all fall to zero. Moreover, the services supplied by the tobacco agents in Manila and Havana and by those who work in distribution and sales in Europe and elsewhere will all become worthless.

The Methodenstreit

As a theorist, Menger is not of the same stature as the other leading figures in the marginalist breakthrough, Jevons and Walras. There are, however, several reasons why he is still frequently mentioned as being on a par with them. First, he was seen as the pioneer in launching the new theories in the German-speaking world—although both Thünen and Gossen had previously presented German versions of the marginalist approach that in some respects were more advanced than that of Menger. Second, after his death his claim to be considered one of the founders of the new theory was strongly advanced by one of his prominent successors in Austrian economics, Eugen Böhm-Bawerk. Third, there emerged in the German-speaking academic world a major controversy about the right approach to economics, and in this controversy Menger came to appear as more of a pure theorist than he really was.

[7] Perhaps it is more correct to say that Menger was "subjectively original" at this point. His thinking was clearly original and independent, but in another sense his originality was due—curiously for one who was so well read — to a lack of knowledge of what Thünen and others had done before him.

[8] In Menger's language this is expressed by saying that since tobacco no longer satisfies a human need, the tobacco stocks lose their "goods-character."

Menger's opponents in the so-called *Methodenstreit* (the controversy about method) were adherents of what is known as the German historical school. The founder of this school was Wilhelm Roscher (1817–94), who was professor at the University of Leipzig. In his main work, *System der Volkswirtschaft* (The System of Economics), he maintained that the study of economic laws must be carried out on the foundation of historical studies and careful investigations of empirical relationships; economics had to become more of an *inductive* and less of a *deductive* science. He appreciated abstract theory as exemplified by Ricardo's work, but he warned against the applications of theory to a reality that was infinitely more complex than the picture that the theorists gave of it. There can be no doubt that Roscher was an important scientist, although he can hardly be said to have realized his program of erecting economic laws on the basis of historical studies. Menger was actually an admirer of Roscher, and the *Grundsätze* is even dedicated to him "with respectful esteem." This must imply that Menger from the beginning did not consider his own theoretical approach as a competing research program. But this was not the way the matter was seen in the historical camp, which was now headed by a younger researcher, Gustav Schmoller (1838–1917). While Roscher's view was that the position of empirical and historical studies ought to be strengthened, although without theory being thrown overboard, Schmoller took a less positive view of the role of theory. According to him, formalized and abstract theory had become of too much importance in economic research. All historical episodes, in fact every set of empirical data, had to be studied in detail and interpreted with a view to their unique and particular circumstances.[9] Generalizations about economic "laws" had to be derived from these detailed studies and with great caution. The historical school dominated teaching and research in Germany at this time, and its members gave Menger's *Grundsätze* a rather chilly reception.

[9] Schumpeter (1954, p. 810) suggests that the character of Jørgen Tesman in Henrik Ibsen's 1890 play *Hedda Gabler*, who is pictured as a narrow-minded researcher who is obsessed with detail (he has just written a dissertation on the textile industry in Brabant in the 16th century), can be interpreted as an exponent of the German historical school. But there is no evidence that Ibsen knew about the *Methodenstreit* or would have taken any interest in it if he did.

This provoked Menger into writing a new book, *Untersuchungen über die Methode der Sozialwissenschaften und der politischen Ökonomie insbesondere* (Investigations into the Method of the Social Sciences with Special Reference to Economics, 1883). In this book he argued that a crucial weakness of the research strategy of the historical school was that, in contrast to his own approach, it did not base its analysis on individual behavior. Schmoller replied to Menger in the form of a very critical review of his book, which in turn provoked Menger into a further attack. The end result of the *Methodenstreit*, which became very heated and personal in tone, was that both parties in the debate felt forced to take up positions that were more extreme than they may first have intended. At the same time it led to a long-lasting conflict concerning research methods between German and Austrian economists who supported Schmoller and Menger, respectively. In a later perspective the controversy may easily appear rather sterile, since it is obviously difficult to argue that economics as a science should *either* be theoretical and deductive or empirical and inductive. Rather than a question of either-or, the central issue must be the fruitful balance between the two approaches, and it must clearly be possible to discuss it at an objective and unemotional level.

ERNST ENGEL

A researcher whom it may be natural to classify under the historical school, but who took no part in the *Methodenstreit*, is Ernst Engel (1821–96). Engel was mainly a statistician and was for many years head of the statistical office of Prussia. His place in the history of economic thought is due to his empirical studies, especially his discovery of what later became known as Engel's Law. In the 1850s, the Belgian statistician Edouard Ducpetiaux had carried out a detailed investigation of the household budgets of Belgian working-class families, and after he had studied these data, Engel in 1857 put forward the hypothesis that there existed an empirical law regarding the composition of consumption, both at the individual and national level: the expenditure on food as a percentage of income falls as income increases. An alternative formulation of the law is that the income or Engel elasticity of food is less than one.[10] This law has actually been confirmed in a long series of budget studies for different countries and time periods. It is a common misunderstanding that Engel derived his law from his own studies of working families in Prussia, which is not the case. What he did was to present some numerical illustrations of the possible implications of Ducpetiaux's results for Prussia, and other statisticians believed these illustrations to be the results of original empirical research by Engel.[11]

In another paper Engel presented empirical estimates of what he referred to as the value of man. For different socioeconomic groups he calculated the expenditure of training a boy to practice his father's profession, demonstrating that this expenditure increased with the father's income and decreased with family size. This contribution is not as well known as his budget studies, but it is an interesting forerunner of the modern research on human capital that began in the 1960s.

In a historical perspective Engel's work is a good example of the fact that the interplay between theoretical and empirical research may develop in ways that were unforeseen at the time. Today, Engel elasticities and Engel curves are central and fruitful concepts in the theory of consumer behavior that has been founded on the work of the marginalist theorists. In this case, therefore, the history of thought confirms the conclusion that economics as a science must be both theoretical and empirical.

THE AUSTRIAN SCHOOL: EUGEN VON BÖHM-BAWERK AND FRIEDRICH VON WIESER

Partly as a result of the *Methodenstreit*, Menger and his supporters among Austrian economists came to appear as a particular school of economic research. When one's viewpoint is limited to that of the German-speaking world, this may have been a reason-

[10] The elasticity is defined as the percentage increase in food expenditure following a 1 percent increase in income.

[11] The history of this misunderstanding is described in a brilliant survey article by Stigler (1954), which also provides detailed references to Engel's most important publications.

able view, but in an international perspective it is more natural to regard the most prominent Austrian economists as part of the general development that, during the last decades of the nineteenth century, gradually changed the character of the subject. Whether or not it is reasonable to refer to this group of economists as a separate school, it is at any rate clear that Menger's two best-known followers, Böhm-Bawerk and Wieser, related their own work so closely to that of Menger that it is natural to consider them in the same context.[12]

Eugen von Böhm-Bawerk (1851–1914) was educated in law and political science, but under the influence of Menger he became gradually more interested in economics. His active years as an academic researcher were before 1889 and after 1904, while in the intervening period he was associated with the Austrian ministry of finance, serving as minister of finance at three different times. It was during the first period of his academic life, while he taught at the University of Innsbruck, that he made his most important contributions to economic theory.

Böhm-Bawerk's name is chiefly associated with his theory of capital and interest as it was laid out in his book *Kapital und Kapitalzins*, which was published in two parts in the years 1884 and 1889 (it has been translated into English as *Capital and Interest*, 1959). One of the questions that he raised in this book was why the rate of interest is positive. The answer that he gave became famous and is known as "Böhm-Bawerk's three reasons." The first is that individuals in general expect that more resources will be available for consumption in the future. The second is people's systematic tendency to underestimate future needs, which Böhm-Bawerk claimed to be an undisputable psychological fact. Both the first and the second reason imply that consumers must be compensated for transferring resources to the future, since they expect resources to be greater and needs to be less. His third reason was the advantages of "roundabout production": as trees produce more timber when one lets them grow longer, so other methods of production will be more productive when extended in time. But if production per worker increases with the length of

[12] Wieser and Böhm-Bawerk went to school together and later became brothers-in-law when Böhm-Bawerk married Wieser's sister. There were accordingly close ties between them, both at the academic and personal level.

the period of production,[13] there must be some factor that causes producers to stop the process of time extension, or in other words to choose a period of production of finite length. This factor is just the positive rate of interest. One sees immediately that the lower the rate of interest is, the longer is the period of production that will be chosen by producers, and the more resources will be tied up in the production process. The sum of these resources constitutes Böhm-Bawerk's concept of capital, so that his theory implies a negative relationship between the rate of interest and the capital intensity in production.

Böhm-Bawerk further developed his theory in the direction of a general equilibrium perspective, so that the rate of interest was determined as one of the prices in the economy. In this perspective, the discount rate—which is defined as $1/(1+r)$, where r is the rate of interest—is the equilibrium price of consumption one period from now expressed in units of present consumption. However, a weak point of his theory is that it was not formulated as a mathematical model, so that it was difficult to understand how the elements of its rather complicated structure fitted together. In spite of this, Böhm-Bawerk's theory became very important as a source of inspiration for a number of later economists who took up the study of this set of problems.

Böhm-Bawerk was a very prominent person in the Austrian society of his time, both as a politician, academic, and contributor to public debate. As a polemicist he showed considerable talent in his ability to express himself clearly and to the point, especially perhaps regarding the shortcomings of other people's efforts. He was the author of one of the classic critiques of Karl Marx's economic theories in the book *Zum Abschluss des Marxschen Systems* (*Karl Marx and the Close of His System*, 1896; 1949). On the other hand, he was considerably less willing to admit to shortcomings in his own theories, and during the last years of his life he was mainly occupied with refuting the critical comments of other economists. These came in particular from theorists who were more mathematically orientated, and as a kind of

[13] The definition of the length of the production process is no easy matter. Böhm-Bawerk defined it as the weighted sum of the time distance between inputs and outputs, taking into consideration that different inputs entered the production process at different moments in time.

shield against this criticism Böhm-Bawerk coined the expression "causal analysis" to characterize the distinguishing features of Austrian economics. But the exact meaning of this concept is difficult to define, and the attempt to single out Austrian economics as something fundamentally different from other kinds of economics had the unfortunate consequence that it tended to isolate economic research in Austria from the leading academic centers in other countries.

Like his friend Böhm-Bawerk, Friedrich von Wieser (1851–1926) studied law but was captured by economics from his reading of Menger's *Grundsätze*. After having been for some time a professor in Prague, he succeeded Menger in his chair at the University of Vienna. This position he held until 1922, only interrupted for a short interval as minister of trade in 1917. At the university he distinguished himself as an outstanding teacher with broad interests also outside his own field. His most original contribution is contained in his book *Der natürliche Werth* (*Natural Value*, 1889), while his *Grundriss der Sozialökonomik* (*Social Economics*, 1914; 1928) was a textbook exposition of the principles of economics as seen by the Austrian school.

As a theorist Wieser is chiefly remembered for two reasons. One of them is that he was the inventor of the term *marginal utility*—"Grenznutzen" in German. It was probably an attempt to translate Jevons's "final degree of utility," but it is both from a linguistic and mathematical point of view a much better expression, and it was translated back into English as "marginal utility." The invention of a word is obviously a smaller achievement than it is to invent the theory from which the word is derived. However, one should not underestimate the value and importance of having suggestive and precise expressions for the underlying theoretical concepts.

Wieser's other important contribution to economics was his theory of the relationship between commodity and factor prices. Menger had suggested that the value of a factor of production in principle could be computed as the decrease in the value of a commodity that would follow from a small decrease in the input of the factor. Wieser realized that the principle might imply that the total value of the factors of production might exceed the value of the commodity, an implication that made little sense for commodities that were in fact produced. He therefore proposed an alternative method for the imputation ("Zurechnung") of values to the factors of production that took account of the constraint that for each commodity the value of the inputs must be equal to the value of output.

A notable aspect of Wieser as a theorist was his interest in the study of alternative economic systems, especially in the comparison of the existing market system with an imaginary ideal socialist society. In a market economy the price of a commodity will reflect the utility of the marginal unit to all consumers, but the magnitude of the common marginal utility as well as the aggregate volume of demand will depend on the distribution of income. In an alternative economic system with a more even distribution of income (and without the deviations from perfect competition that stem from monopoly and similar imperfections), both the volume of demand as well as the price will be different. At the same time, however, a system like this will not be able to allocate resources in an efficient manner without use of the market mechanism, for without markets there will be no equalization of the marginal valuation between individuals. The issue of which type of social system and economic organization that is best suited for combining the concerns for social justice and economic efficiency would come to occupy the attention of many economists in the decades following Wieser's death.

FURTHER READING

Jevons's *Theory of Political Economy* is a book that is easy to read and conveys the enthusiasm of a pioneer in the field. It exists in several editions; the quotations in the text are taken from the paperback version of the second (1879) edition that was published in the *Pelican Classics* series in 1970. The 1879 edition is especially valuable because of the long introductory chapter that Jevons added to the first edition, and in which he relates his own work to that of Gossen and other earlier authors. The Pelican edition also has an excellent introduction by R. D. Collison Black, who both presents a sketch of Jevons's life and places the book in its historical context. Those who would like to know more about the man will get a memorable and enjoyable experience from reading Keynes's article about him in *Essays in Biography* (1933). Black

(1972) presents an interesting perspective on Jevons's work as a whole and emphasizes the importance of his training in the natural sciences.

Carl Menger's *Grundsätze* has been translated into English as *Principles of Economics* with an introduction by Friedrich Hayek. Hayek focuses on Menger's life and his role in the emergence of the Austrian school, including only a summary although very positive treatment of Menger's economics. Menger's opponents in the *Methodenstreit* have been neglected in most modern histories of thought, but Hutchison (1953), who also has good chapters on Jevons and on Menger and his successors, gives a positive presentation of the German historical school. Schumpeter (1954), himself a student of the famous Austrian economists of this period, gives a detailed presentation of their achievements, but the reader needs some patience and frequent use of the index to pick his way through the text.

The book by Stigler (1941; 1994) is an excellent and highly readable account of the marginalist breakthrough, which contains chapters on all the main characters in the present chapter as well as Walras and the later marginalists.

The Marginalist Revolution II:
Léon Walras

JEVONS, MENGER, AND WALRAS are the three names that are particularly associated with the breakthrough of the marginalist approach to economic theory. Of the three, Léon Walras is the one who has had the greatest direct influence on the later development of economics. Jevons and Menger made an important pioneering effort by directing attention to the consumer side of markets to a greater extent than the classical economists had done, and by introducing marginal utility as a central concept for theoretical analysis. By focusing more strongly on the decisions made by consumers, they succeeded in basing economic theory more directly on hypotheses about individual behavior, and this new orientation would prove to be of fundamental importance for the future of economics. But in their eagerness to promote the new perspective on the functioning of the market economy, they came to neglect some important elements of the classical theory, especially the role of cost of production for the formation of prices. Another aspect that was lost was the broad view of the economic system as a whole that was characteristic of all the great classical economists, such as Smith, Ricardo and Mill. With Walras's theoretical contributions the marginalist perspective was embedded in an economic world view that was comparable to that of the classics. But even in his work one should note that there are aspects of the classical theory that have been pushed to the background; this is particularly the case with regard to the central role of population growth for the classical theory of wages and economic development.

Léon Walras (1834–1910) was born in Normandy in the north of France. His father, Auguste Walras (1801–1866), was himself an economist who wrote on theoretical problems although without making any important contributions of his own. But the many long conversations that he had with his son became very important for Léon Walras's development, and he always held his father in the highest regard. Walras was admitted as an engineering student at the prestigious school of geology, École des Mines, but he never passed the final exams, nor did he ever practice the profession for which he had been trained. Instead he tried his luck as a railway employee, journalist, banker, and novelist, but without particular success. Then, during a stroll one summer evening in 1858, his father convinced him that he ought to devote his life to the study of economics. Auguste Walras argued that there were two tasks that remained for intellectuals to achieve during the nineteenth century. One was to establish history on a scientific footing; the other was to lay the foundations for a science of society, especially of its economy. This last task was for his son to take on, he said, and Léon Walras has related how their conversation on this occasion convinced him that this was his true calling. At this point, we find ourselves in the romantic age of European history, and there is indeed a romantic atmosphere surrounding the story of Léon Walras's life that took a new direction as a consequence of this talk with his father. In an autobiographical sketch he was later to refer to it as "the most decisive moment of my life."

As part of his activities in his new field of interest, Walras participated in a taxation congress in Lausanne in Switzerland in 1860. There he appears to have made a very good impression, but otherwise the decade of the 1860s was a disappointing one for a man with his ambitions. He published some articles on economic questions, but his attempts to obtain a position in the French university system were unsuccessful, mainly because of his lack of formal academic qualifications. Instead he went to work for a bank and began to think about abandoning his dreams of a life devoted to teaching and research. However, in 1870 the faculty of law at the University of Lausanne created a new chair in economics, and Walras was encouraged to apply. The faculty appointed a committee to evaluate the qualifications of the applicants consisting of four local politicians and three professors of economics. Walras was ranked first with four votes against three. Those who voted in his favor were three of the politicians and one of the professors. The two professors who voted against him were skeptical about what they saw as Walras's socialist leanings, while interestingly there were no socialists among the politicians who supported him.[1] In this case, therefore, it was the politicians and not the academics that showed themselves capable of drawing a distinction between academic merits and political convictions.

The appoinment to the chair in Lausanne gave a push to Walras's career while it also enabled him to realize his plans for the foundation of a science of economics. It was also during his time at the university that he wrote his most important works. Foremost among these is the *Éléments d'économie politique pure (Elements of Pure Economics)*,[2] which was published in two parts in 1874 and 1877. He had planned a further two volumes about applied and "social" economics, but this plan never came to fruition. However, he did publish a book about monetary theory, *Théorie de la monnaie* (Theory of Money, 1886), and two collections of articles about applied economics and economic policy. These show that Walras was more than a pure theorist, but it is the *Éléments* that has secured his prominent place in the history of economic thought.

Walras resigned from his professorship in 1892. He continued to be active in research and writing, but his most creative period was over. Much of his time in his later years was spent in trying to make sure that his earlier work received the attention that he thought it deserved. He seems to have been a rather difficult person who easily felt that he was underrated and misunderstood. However, from his extensive correspondence it is obvious that a number of the most prominent economists of his time had the highest respect for him, and he also received many honors (for instance, he was elected an honorary member of the American Economic Association in 1892).

---

[1] Walras's socialism was not of the Marxist variety. The part of his economic and political thinking to which the skeptics reacted were above all his recommendations concerning the nationalization of land and his positive attitude to the cooperative movement.

[2] What Walras meant by the concept of "pure" economics was evidently economic theory detached from practical applications, a terminology related to mathematicians' use of the term "pure mathematics."

Questions of Method

From his earliest days as an economist, Walras had an almost fanatical belief in the advantages of the mathematical method of economic analysis, and he believed that proving the superiority of this method was the most important goal of his life. But his background in mathematics was not particularly strong, and when he began his work in Lausanne he sought the help of mathematicians in order to acquire the insights that were necessary to realize his plans of a mathematical reformulation of economic theory. It is interesting to note what he writes in the *Éléments* about the use of mathematics and the relationship between pure and applied economics:[3]

> The mathematical method is not an *experimental* method; it is a *rational* method ... the pure theory of economics ought to take over from experience certain type concepts, like those of exchange, supply, demand, market, capital, income, productive services and products. From these real-type concepts the pure science of economics should then abstract and define ideal-type concepts in terms of which it carries out its reasoning. The return to reality should not take place until the science is completed and then only with the view to practical applications. (Walras 1874–77; 1954, p. 71)

He illustrates the importance of these ideal-types with reference to geometry. It is only in the case of the ideal triangle that the sum of the angles is equal to 180 degrees. When in practice one measures the angles of a triangle, one will find that their sum is only approximately equal to the ideal. The same truth holds for economic theory, where ideal prices are determined by ideal supply and ideal demand. But just as theoretical geometry is of essential importance for technological applications, theoretical economics provides the foundation for the use of scientific economic thinking in understanding real-world economic problems.

The last sentence of the quotation sounds a little problematic. Applications should wait until theory is fully developed, but

---

[3] All quotations from the *Éléments* are taken from William Jaffé's English translation, which came out in 1954.

how do we know when that is the case? One possible interpretation is that Walras believed that science—meaning theory—was fully developed with his own *Éléments*, and that it was at this stage that scientific applications, such as he had planned for volumes 2 and 3 of his projected main work, had become feasible. But another and perhaps more reasonable interpretation of his statement is that there ought to be a theoretical foundation for any economic analysis of a practical problem.[4]

As regards the employment of mathematical methods, Walras's view is that the right use of mathematics makes it easier to follow a piece of theoretical reasoning, while at the same time it protects us against logical mistakes:

> Why should we persist in using everyday language to explain things in the most cumbrous and incorrect way, as Ricardo has often done and as John Stuart Mill does repeatedly in his *Principles of Political Economy*, when these same things can be stated far more succinctly, precisely and clearly in the language of mathematics? (Walras 1874–77; 1954, p. 72)

Here Walras expresses a point of view that with time became the dominant conviction among academic economists, and it is obvious that the scientific progress that has taken place in economics would have been inconceivable without the use of mathematical and statistical methods. But the change in the character of the subject that began in earnest with the breakthrough of marginalism also had other consequences. Well-educated people with an interest in economic and social affairs were able to read the works of Smith, Ricardo and Mill without encountering major barriers to understanding. By contrast, they could not read the writings of Jevons, Walras, and their followers without knowledge of mathematics that went considerably beyond the elementary level. Accordingly, a divide was opened between the scientific literature of economics and the type of exposition that could be read by the enlightened public, and this divide was to grow

[4] We recall John Stuart Mill's remark (see chapter 5) about price theory being fully developed with no questions requiring further clarification. We know from Walras's published correspondence (Jaffé 1965) that he had read Mill, and it is impossible to imagine that he had not reacted negatively to this pronouncement. On this background it appears highly unlikely that he should have fallen into the same trap.

considerably broader in the twentieth century. The beginning of this development is not the least important result of the breakthrough of marginalism.

THE ANALYSIS OF EXCHANGE

Walras begins the analytical part of the *Éléments* by analyzing a problem similar to the one that had been studied by Jevons: he imagines a situation with two persons and two goods whose supply is fixed. How can one characterize the equilibrium of such an economy? He goes into this problem in great detail: the discussion of the two-by-two case fills more than sixty pages in the book (Walras 1874–77; 1954, pp. 83–149).

He starts by drawing demand curves for the two goods (like Cournot, with the price on the horizontal axis), and shows how an analysis based on these curves determines the quantities that will be exchanged between the two individuals in a situation of equilibrium. After a careful statement of the utility maximization problem of the consumer he goes on to the analysis of equilibrium. At this point he is much clearer than Jevons was in his discussion of a similar model. Walras shows (like Jevons) that the model determines the ratio between the quantities traded of the two goods. Then he points out that since the value of the quantity sold by one individual must be equal to the value of the quantity purchased by the other individual, the ratio of prices must be equal to the inverse ratio of the quantities. So the model determines prices, but only the *relative* price: the price of commodity 1 expressed in units of commodity 2 or the other way around. This means that to express the prices—moving for the moment beyond the two-commodity case—we may choose one of the commodities as a unit of account and state all other prices in units of this commodity, which Walras calls the *numéraire*.[5] The price of this commodity can therefore be set equal to one. The *absolute* price level is a concept that is only meaningful once we have decided on the choice of a unit of account, either in the form

[5] The term *numéraire*, meaning unit of account, has become part of the international vocabulary of economics; for many economists this may be the only French word that they know.

of a regular good or one which has as its primary purpose to serve as means of payment, that is, money.

Walras's discussion of the consumer as a utility maximizing agent is far clearer than those of Jevons and Menger. Like Jevons, he assumes that utility is a magnitude that is attached to the consumption of each commodity separately, so that total utility is the sum of all commodity-specific "utilities." He then shows that to obtain maximum utility the consumer must compose his consumption in such a way that marginal utility—or *rareté*, as he calls it—divided by price must be the same for all commodities.[6] In other words, he rediscovered Gossen's second law. It follows that it is the consumers' marginal utilities of the different goods—the structure of their preferences—that determine prices in an exchange economy. Walras summarizes the core results of his theoretical model as follows:

> The exchange of two commodities for each other in a perfectly competitive market is an operation by which all holders of either one, or of both, of the two commodities can obtain the greatest possible satisfaction of their wants consistent with the condition that the two commodities are bought and sold at one and the same rate of exchange throughout the market. (Walras 1874–77; 1954, p. 143)

If we were to take a critical view of this formulation we might object that the condition that the price ratio is the same throughout the market strictly speaking ought to be part of the definition of perfect competition. A better formulation might therefore have been "... consistent with the condition that supply is equal to demand for both commodities." However, when one reads the statement in the context of the discussion as a whole, there is no doubt that this is what Walras has in mind.

The two-by-two model is evidently to be considered as a simplified introduction to the more general version of the theory. The generalization implies an extension to the case of many consumers and commodities, also moving beyond the simple case of pure exchange to incorporate the production side of the economy. It was in the analysis of this more general case that Walras made his most important contributions to economic theory.

[6] *Rareté* means rarity or scarcity and was a term that Walras had inherited from his father.

GENERAL EQUILIBRIUM

Walras was careful to specify the structure of the interrelationships between markets, or the *economic circulation* in society. Firms supply finished goods that are demanded by the consumers. In order to produce consumer goods, firms demand factors of production, labor in particular, that are supplied by consumers. Consumers maximize utility and firms maximize profit, and both consumers and firms take market prices as given. General equilibrium exists when (1) the consumers' demand is equal to firms' supply for all consumer goods and (2) the firms' demand is equal to the consumers' supply for all factors of production.

Now let us assume that there is an arbitrary number m of commodities and a corresponding number of prices. We can then write the conditions for general equilibrium as a set of equations, one for each commodity, which says that demand, which is a function of all prices in the economy, is equal to supply, which is also a function of all prices. Because we have m markets altogether, we have m such equations. We have therefore as many equations as there are unknowns (i.e., prices), and this should normally ensure that in the mathematical sense the prices are determined by the system of equations. It appears then that we have succeeded in constructing a mathematical model of the economy that determines all prices as the result of decentralized decisions about consumption and production by a large number of firms and consumers.

However, there is one problem that is raised by this conclusion. An important insight from the analysis of the two-by-two case was that the theory only determines relative prices, so that the price of one of the commodities, the *numéraire* good, can be set equal to 1. But if we transfer this insight to the more general model we are left with m equations and $m-1$ relative prices. So it looks like we have one equation too many and that we have an overdeterminate system. However, Walras showed that one of the m equilibrium conditions could be derived from the others, so that in fact there were only $m-1$ independent equations, just sufficient to determine the $m-1$ relative prices; relative, that is, to the *numéraire*. The way in which he did this is most easy to explain if we go back to the case of an exchange economy, but now with an arbitrary number of consumers and commodities.

For the individual consumer it must be the case that the value of what he consumes is equal to the value of his stock of goods, or, equivalently, the value of what he sells must equal the value of what he buys. But since this must be true for all consumers, it must also be true in the aggregate: the value of total sales must equal the value of total purchases. Suppose now that demand is equal to supply in *m-1* markets, say, in the markets for the goods 2 to *m*. This means that the value of sales must equal the value of purchases for these *m-1* markets. But if that is the case, the value of sales must be equal to the value of purchases— supply must be equal to demand—for the first market as well, so all markets must be in equilibrium. In other words: if *m-1* of the *m* markets are in equilibrium, the last market must also be in equilibrium. This result is known as *Walras's law*. Since one of the equilibrium equations can be derived from the others, we are left with *m-1* equations in the *m-1* relative prices. Walras's model of general competitive equilibrium for the economy as a whole is one that determines all relative prices, expressed in units of the *numéraire* good.[7]

Walras went on to extend the theory to an economy with production. He started, following the lead of the classical economists, by assuming that there were fixed coefficients in production, and then generalized the analysis to the case where the marginal productivity of the factors of production varied with the amount of input, and where factor substitution was possible. He derived the conditions for cost minimization and concluded that "free [perfect] competition brings the cost of production down to a minimum" (Walras 1874–77; 1954, p. 385).

The *nominal* price level cannot be determined until one brings monetary factors into the picture. As regards this part of his theory, Walras was basically a quantity theorist, although his theory of the demand for money was a sophisticated one. This theory started from the assumption that the agents of the economy faced

[7] The condition that the value of total sales must be equal to the value of total purchases can be written as $\Sigma p_j x_j = \Sigma p_j y_j$, where x_j is the consumption of commodity j, and y_j is the initial stock. This can be rewritten as $\Sigma p_j(x_j-y_j) = 0$. Suppose now that the last *m-1* elements in this sum are equal to zero, so that these *m-1* markets are in equilibrium. Since the sum taken over all *m* goods must be zero, it follows that the first element must equal zero as well: if demand equals supply in *m-1* of *m* markets, the same must be true for the remaining market.

a lack of synchronization of income and expenditure payments. The function of money was to bridge the liquidity problems that this entailed. Walras showed that the theory led to the conclusion familiar from the earlier and simpler quantity theory: money is neutral with respect to the real economy. A doubling of the quantity of money would lead to a doubling of all nominal prices and therefore leave relative prices and real decisions unaffected. This distinction between the real and the monetary economy places Walras in a tradition that goes back to David Hume (see chapter 2), and which is often referred to as *the classical dichotomy.*

Walras's theory of general equilibrium was a major step forward for the theory of price formation in competitive markets. But it was a model at a level of mathematical abstraction beyond anything that had appeared in the literature so far, and few of his contemporary colleagues were able to follow the details of Walras's analysis. Among those who could, there was also considerable doubt whether this construction could ever come to be of any practical significance. However, much of the skepticism and critical comments were based on a misunderstanding of what Walras actually tried to achieve. Some people interpreted his theory as an attempt to calculate the actual prices that would cause markets to be in equilibrium, which clearly was not Walras's intention.[8] His ambition and great achievement was to show that theories of individual market behavior could be fitted together to an integrated whole, to a model of general equilibrium that gave a logically consistent description of the functioning of a competitive economy. The very general version that Walras developed in the *Éléments* did not in itself provide much opportunity for application to practical problems, but with the passage of time other economists gradually came to accept it as the standard competitive model that would serve as a general reference for future de-

---

[8] This type of misunderstanding is not limited to Walras's contemporaries. In a popular book about the history of economic thought, Robert L. Heilbroner devotes altogether 8 lines to Walras. Heilbroner uses these to make fun of him because "one could deduce by mathematics the exact prices that would just exactly clear the market ... never mind the difficulties; theoretically the problem could be done" (Heilbroner 1999, pp. 177–178). It should be added that Heilbroner does not reserve his irony for Walras: other mathematically orientated economists like Thünen and Jevons receive a similar treatment, while Cournot and Gossen are not mentioned at all.

velopments of the theory. Walras's own analysis has been further developed by a number of later economists, but his own influence is still easy to trace both in pure theory and in applications to fields like international trade and public economics.

The Road to Equilibrium: The Theory of *Tâtonnement*

Walras was not satisfied with having demonstrated the internal consistency of his theory. The system of equations described the nature of the equilibrium, but a model that claimed to say something about the real world—about the real-type concepts versus the ideal-type concepts—would also have to explain how the market mechanism arrived at the equilibrium. The theory that underlies the system of equations that determines equilibrium prices cannot in itself explain how the markets arrive at them. If general equilibrium theory aims to explain the actual formation of prices, it must be able to argue that the market always has a tendency to approach the equilibrium. This implies that the description of equilibrium must be extended by a dynamic theory of the movement towards equilibrium. Walras attempted to do this with his famous theory of *tâtonnement*. The term is not easy to translate. "Groping" has been suggested as a term that communicates some of the essence of the concept, but most economists tend to prefer the French term.

Walras's theory of market adjustment must also be seen on the background of his methodological argument about the necessity of reasoning by means of idealized concepts. He imagines a market where there is an administrator or auctioneer. The auctioneer begins by crying out prices at random for all commodities that are subject to trade. At these prices consumers and firms write down the quantities that they wish to buy and sell. The auctioneer then collects this information, summing the planned quantities of supply and demand for each individual market. If he finds that for some or all commodities the planned demand is not equal to the planned supply, he cries out a new set of prices. He increases the prices for the commodities where the planned demand exceeds the planned supply and decreases them in markets in which the reverse is true. At the new set of prices, consumers and firms

200

again write down the quantities that they wish to buy and sell and the process continues. In other words, prices increase where there is excess demand and fall where there is excess supply. This mechanism, Walras claims, will lead the economy to a situation of general equilibrium. The market mechanism is *stable*.

Most economists, both at Walras's time and later, have in fact subscribed to the view that excess demand in a market causes prices to rise and that excess supply leads them to fall. Opinions have differed, however, on whether the *tâtonnement* process provides a convincing theoretical picture of the path towards equilibrium. The most crucial objection to Walras's construction concerns the role of the auctioneer, for in most markets there exists no administrator of this kind. Therefore, it must be the agents themselves—the consumers and firms—who see to the adjustment of prices. But then we run up against the paradox that these agents are assumed to take prices as given. It is obviously contradictory to assume both that the agents assume prices to be given and that they play an active role in changing them. This suggests that it is only in equilibrium that it can be strictly true that all agents regard prices as given in the market and beyond their control. Another aspect of Walras's market metaphor that is open to criticism is the assumption that no transactions take place while the prices that the auctioneer cries out are different from the equilibrium prices. In this area, modern theorists are still groping for convincing theoretical descriptions of how the market mechanism functions.

THE PROBLEM OF EXISTENCE

One issue that Walras did not take up is the so-called existence problem. As we have seen, he concluded that his general equilibrium model was logically consistent because it contained the same number of equations as unknowns—as many equilibrium conditions as relative prices. But can we really from the equality of the number of equations and unknowns conclude that the equation system has a solution? The answer is no, and this is easy to see by considering a simple example. Suppose that there are three goods in the economy, labeled 1, 2, and 3. We select good 1 as the *numéraire*, so that its price $p_1=1$. We can then follow Walras's method and represent the equilibrium by two equations, one for good 2 and one for good 3. Each of these can be written on the form "demand = supply." We assume now that the demand and supply functions have a particularly simple form, so that in the case of good 2 we can write

$$10-p_2-p_3=4+p_2.$$

The left hand side of the equation is the demand function, which says that the demand for commodity 2 falls when the price p_2 goes up, and that it also falls when p_3 increases; the two goods are complementary in demand. The right hand side is the supply function, showing that the supply of commodity 2 increases when its price goes up. For commodity 3 we have correspondingly

$$5-p_2-(1/4)p_3=3+(1/4)p_3.$$

In this case also demand is a decreasing function of both prices, while the supply function is increasing in p_3.

Even if these demand and supply functions look reasonable enough, it is not difficult to see that there exists no pair of prices that solves the equation system; the model does not have an equilibrium solution.[9] A related problem is the following: even if the system of equations was found to have a solution, not all solutions would be meaningful from an economic point of view; prices must by definition be positive—or at least not negative. But it is easy to construct cases which, like the present example, look innocuous and do have a solution, but where the solution does not satisfy the condition that prices must be nonnegative.[10]

What do examples like these tell us? They illuminate the fact that equality between the number of equlibrium equations and the number of relative prices provides no guarantee that the equation system has a solution that makes economic sense. The

---

[9] By simple manipulation, we can rewrite the two equations as $2p_2+p_3=6$ and $p_2+(1/2)p_3=2$. If we now multiply the second equation by 2, we see that the left-hand sides of the two equations become identical, while the constants on the right are different from each other. The equations are therefore mutually contradictory and no solution exists.

[10] A simple example are the equations $6-p_2+p_3=3+p_2$ and $7-p_2-p_3=6+p_3$. By solving the system of equations one finds that p_3 is negative.

uncertainty that this raised about the internal consistency of Walras's model was to receive much attention toward the middle of the twentieth century, when a number of prominent economists attempted to identify the conditions under which the general equilibrium model had a solution involving nonnegative prices. This became known as the existence problem in general equilibrium theory; we shall return to a further discussion of it in chapter 17.

MARKET EQUILIBRIUM AND WELFARE

A somewhat disputed issue in the literature on Walras is how he looked at the ethical aspects of the market equilibrium that he analyzed. Some interpreters have maintained that Walras erroneously regarded his general equilibrium theory not only as a good analytical description of the actual functioning of markets, but also as describing an ethically just outcome. His statement about the satisfaction of wants under perfect competition, as quoted above, has by some been read as meaning that individual transactions under perfect competition maximize utility not only for the individual consumer but for society as a whole.[11] Is this a reasonable interpretation? It clearly depends on one's understanding of the words "all ... can obtain the greatest possible satisfaction of their wants." The interpretation really hinges on the word *all:* Does it refer to (1) each individual for himself or (2) all individuals together? According to (1) it means that the individual consumer who maximizes utility cannot do better for himself, given the equilibrium prices that he faces in the market. In the case (2) the interpretation is that the equilibrium in some sense corresponds to a maximum of social utility or welfare. With our modern insight we know that interpretation (1) is the correct one, but Walras's critics believed that he subscribed to interpretation (2). Should we draw the conclusion that Walras misinterpreted his own theory?

---

[11] Jaffé (1983) refers to several such interpretations, among others by Knut Wicksell, John Hicks, and William Baumol, and argues strongly that they do not give the right impression of Walras's view of the relationship between market equilibrium and social welfare.

There are several reasons why we should be convinced that Walras was not guilty of such a misinterpretation. First, only a few pages later he emphasizes (Walras 1874–77; 1954, p. 146) that utility and marginal utility are subjective concepts and can only be defined in relation to the preferences of the single individual. Therefore, it makes no sense to take the sum of the utilities of different individuals. Second, in a later chapter he says the following:

> Though our description of free competition emphasizes the problem of utility, it leaves the question of justice entirely to one side. (Walras 1874–77; 1954, p. 257)

Third, we have his own answer to the criticism that had been raised against him in a letter to the German economist Wilhelm Launhardt, dated in May 1885. In this letter Walras writes:

> I have maintained that free competition leads to the maximum of utility, *given the condition of the uniformity of price,* in other words a relative, not an absolute maximum. In is quite clear that if one imagines that commodities were sold at a high price to the rich and a low price to the poor, the former would only have to give up superfluous goods while the latter would be able to afford necessities. Consequently, there would be a large increase in utility. (Jaffé 1965, Vol. II, p. 50)

These quotations should make it quite clear that Walras did not regard the competitive market system as something that necessarily leads to an ethically good result. On the other hand, it is fair to say that his formulations are not exactly crystal clear. The argument that price discrimination in favor of the poor would lead to "a large increase in utility" is difficult to understand in the light of his own emphasis on the view that utility is a subjective concept. For the large increase in utility that he refers to must evidently be understood as an increase in utility *for society,* or at least as an assertion that the increase in utility for the poor is greater than the decrease in utility for the rich. The problem is that if utility is completely subjective, a sum or comparison of the utilities of different individuals becomes logically impossible. But in spite of these obscurities we may conclude that Walras did not subscribe to the naive view of the relationship between markets and welfare of which his critics accused him.

Walras's conviction seems to have been that free or perfect competition would lead to a rational or efficient use of society's resources. However, his work does not contain a more precise and general definition of the meaning of efficiency for society as a whole. It is possible that he had begun to think along the lines of the formulation that was introduced by his successor, Vilfredo Pareto, a few years later, but this remains speculative. It is more realistic to assume that he believed that rational use of resources followed more or less directly from utility and profit maximization, and that a further elaboration of the reasoning was unnecessary. At the same time Walras was aware that the efficiency of the market mechanism had its limitations and that there were important social problems that had to be solved by other means. On this issue he felt that other economists sometimes had been guilty of facile policy recommendations:

> The principle of free competition, which is applicable to the production of things for private demand, is not applicable to the production of things where public interest is involved. Are there not economists, however, who have fallen into the error of advocating that public services be brought within the fold of free competition by turning these services over to private industry? (Walras 1874–77; 1954, p. 257)

We must conclude that the interpretation of Walras as a market liberalist of the more naive kind receives little support from what he actually wrote, and it is difficult to understand why so many prominent economists have chosen to read him in this way.

A CURIOUS EPISODE

A rather strange but interesting episode in the life of Léon Walras is his attempt to be awarded the Nobel Peace Prize.[12] His efforts in this regard have been documented in a series of letters in his published correspondence (Jaffée 1965, volume 3). The first is a short letter of April 13, 1905, from Walras to one of his colleagues, Ernest Roguin, who was professor of international law in Lausanne; Walras writes that he needs some advice and would

---

[12] More details about this episode are given in Sandmo (2007).

like to see him. From the further correspondence between them it is clear that the advice concerned the Nobel Prize, for on May 4 he writes again to thank Roguin for having taken account of his comments on the letter that Roguin and two other colleagues eventually sent to the Nobel Committee of the Norwegian Parliament on July 20, proposing Walras as a candidate for the 1906 prize.

The proposal from the three professors emphasizes Walras's exceptional scientific merits and his irreproachable moral attitude. It is true, they write, that the immediate results of Walras's work may not be apparent, but theoretical research is in certain respects more important than practical activities: its perspectives are longer and its results are more durable and certain. As an enclosure to the letter they send an extensive memorandum that sets out a more detailed argument in support of the proposal; a draft of this memorandum has been preserved in Walras's handwriting, so that he has clearly written it himself. The main point in it is that peace and fraternity between nations presupposes international free trade, and the most important obstacle to free trade is the lack of theoretical understanding. Moreover, free trade is hampered by tariffs, taxes, and charges, which therefore ought to be removed. Instead, the state ought to raise its revenue through the nationalization of land, which would enable it to collect the rent. With these reforms free trade will be able to work in the interests of world peace and for the brotherhood of individuals and nations. In setting out these arguments, Walras refers implicitly both to the results of his own theoretical research and to the reformist views that he had inherited from his father.

What are we to think of this initiative that at first glance seems both pathetic and unrealistic? It is important to keep in mind that in 1905 the Nobel Peace Prize had been awarded only four times. It is therefore unlikely that a common understanding of the criteria for the award existed, and the prize was obviously also far less well known than it is today. On the other hand, some of the first prizes had been awarded to people like Henri Dunant, the founder of the Red Cross, and Bertha von Suttner, the German peace activist, so that it cannot have been very natural to believe that the Peace Prize Committee would be inclined to give the prize to an economic theorist. However, the Nobel Committee asked one of its consultants, V. K. Hammer, to write a report on Walras's qualifications. Hammer gave a very positive account of Walras's contributions to economic theory but paradoxically did not even mention its possible relevance for world peace. The negotiations of the Nobel Committee are secret, so that we will never know its view of the proposal and of Hammer's report. We only know that the committee decided to award the 1906 prize to the American president, Theodore Roosevelt.

Today, the episode is perhaps mainly of interest because of the light it throws on Walras's personality and his desire for recognition and honors. It may still be of relevance, however, to ask how good or bad the argument in support of his candidacy really was. The idea that free trade is conducive to peace is one that must be taken seriously, and more people than Walras have maintained that international trade gives all countries a stake in the maintenance of a peaceful world order. On the other hand, although the benefits of free competition is a central topic in Walras's *Éléments*, the more specific issue of international trade receives little attention. In addition, there may be good reasons to be skeptical to the claim that the cause of peace would benefit from government ownership of all land, which could conceivably provide some nations with stronger incentives to start wars of conquest. All taken together, it was not an unreasonable decision of the Nobel Committee not to award the Peace Prize to Léon Walras.[13]

Perspectives on Léon Walras

Walras was the first to work out a theory of general economic equilibrium in the form of an explicit mathematical model. With this he created a framework of analysis that has been of tremen-

---

[13] But was it reasonable to give it to Theodore Roosevelt? The account of Roosevelt's qualifications that was submitted to the committee was written by a young Norwegian historian, Halvdan Koht, who was later to rise to eminence in his profession. His report is very negative, and when one reads the reports on Walras and Roosevelt together, one could easily come to conclude that if the choice had only been between these two (but there were actually 27 more candidates), the best would have been to award the prize to Walras, who at least had done nothing to harm the cause of peace. The decision of the Committee must be seen in the context of the political situation at the time, when Norway was in strong need of international political goodwill. From that point of view, the award to the American president was a wise move.

dous importance for the further development of the science, and his place in the history of economic thought is indisputable. In fact, Schumpeter (1954, p. 827) writes that Walras in his opinion is the greatest of all economists. His justification for this claim is that the development of general equilibrium theory is the only achievement by an economist that is comparable to the results of theoretical physics. But one may of course doubt whether the comparison with theoretical physics ought to be decisive for an economist's place on the global ranking list, and in any case it is an open question whether lists of this kind provide much insight in the history of economic thought beyond their entertainment value.

Walras was himself in no doubt that through his general equilibrium model he had grasped the essence of the complexity and internal structure of economic life like no other economist before him. This conviction emerges clearly in the following grand vision that concludes Walras's analysis of general equilibrium and that also lays great emphasis on the aesthetic appeal of the theory:

> The law of supply and demand regulates all these exchanges of commodities just as the law of universal gravitation regulates the movements of all celestial bodies. Thus the system of the economic universe reveals itself, at last, in all its grandeur and complexity: a system at once vast and simple, which, for sheer beauty, resembles the astronomical universe. (Walras 1874–77; 1954, p. 374)

On the background of this statement it is natural to ask whether Walras actually believed that the theory of perfect competition gave a realistic picture of the functioning of the real-world market economy. Clearly, he realized that in practice there were undoubtedly some deviations from the ideal picture drawn in his own model. In the *Éléments* he does include a discussion of the monopoly case, but this is limited to a rather brief account of Cournot's theory, and he does not appear to regard monopoly and imperfect competition as topics of central theoretical interest. Other passages also indicate that Walras considered perfect competition as the system toward which a market economy would necessarily converge and that it therefore was the case on which a general theory ought to focus.

Was There Really a Marginalist Revolution?

What characterizes a scientific revolution, according to the American historian of science Thomas Kuhn (1962), is what he calls a paradigm shift. The revolution stems from a perception that the science finds itself in a crisis, where the dominating theories are unable to explain—in the case of economics—important observations of the functioning of the economy. Within the existing theoretical framework researchers carry on "normal science." A revolution or paradigm shift means that the framework for normal science is changed. Was the marginalist revolution such a paradigm shift, and was it perceived as such in the contemporary world of economists?

It is a difficult question to answer. Many historians of thought believe that there can be no doubt that there was indeed a revolution in Kuhn's sense. An important argument in support of this view is that the emphasis on demand conditions, the introduction of marginal utility theory, and the increased use of mathematical methods represented a radically new approach to economic theory. Another argument is that the younger generation of economists believed that the economic and social development in their own time proved that important parts of the theory of the classical economists were untenable. This was true above all of their theory of population, which implied that wages were determined by the minimum level necessary for the survival of the working class.[14] The increase in real wages and the decline of population growth that were notable features of economic development in the late nineteenth century were strong indications that the classical theory was incorrect, and there arose a need for a new theory that could provide a better explanation of economic progress.[15]

---

[14] Walras criticizes Malthus's description of the increase in food production in terms of an arithmetic series and says that it lacks both logical and empirical foundations (Walras, 1874–77; 1954, pp. 387–88). More generally, he argues that a basic weakness of Malthus's theory is that it fails to take sufficient account of technological progress. In an article published in a book about the World Exhibition in Paris in 1867 he emphasizes the benefits that technological progress has implied for the working class and confronts them with the "ridiculous theory" of Malthus about their eternal poverty and misery.

[15] Hutchison (1953, ch. 1) is one among several writers who have stressed this point.

Even if the new theory was not at first able to provide such explanations, it had at least rid itself of some elements in the older way of thinking that were now regarded as highly misleading.

Others have been more skeptical about the revolutionary hypothesis. First of all, they have argued that there were no strong indications of a feeling of crisis among practitioners of economics at the time; thus the increase in real wages could be explained by pointing out that the minimum level was determined not only by biological requirements but also by acceptable social standards that were rising over time. Second, historians like Blaug (1972) maintain that the fact that Jevons, Menger, and Walras published their main works at about the same time is simply a coincidence in time and cannot be taken as a sign that the field was in a crisis and only waited for a new paradigm to be established. They were three individuals of very different personalities who worked independently of each other and in very different intellectual climates in their respective countries. In particular, Blaug points out that Jevons as an Englishman may have felt a strong need to liberate himself from the dominating classical tradition, while Menger and Walras, who were more distant from the English classical economists, felt no such urge. Blaug concludes that the marginalist revolution was a process rather than a unique historical incident, and that the characterization of it as a revolution is mainly due to intellectual historians' sense of drama.

Another objection toward looking at the 1870s as a period of revolution is that many of the central ideas and theories of Jevons, Menger, and Walras had already been formulated by writers like Thünen, Cournot, Dupuit, and Gossen several decades earlier. Even John Stuart Mill, whom at least Jevons regarded as the major defender of the classical view, may be regarded as one of the forerunners of the new developments. Nevertheless, it was not until the decade of the seventies that the new approach grew into something more than the isolated efforts of a few economists in the early part of the century. Following the three leaders of that period, another generation of economists who had incorporated the new ideas rose to prominence with contributions that extended and refined the marginalist theories. This was in sharp contrast to the fate of the early pioneers who were mostly neglected by their contemporaries and who had to wait for decades for their work to be rediscovered.

Were the new ways of thinking about economic theory that came to the forefront in the 1870s a scientific revolution in the sense that the concept has been used by Thomas Kuhn? As we have seen, there are arguments both for and against this view. It must also be emphasized that even if Kuhn's concept of scientific revolution has caused much interest among students of intellectual history, it is still somewhat vague: it is difficult in a concrete case to decide whether a revolution has occured or not. But we may still conclude that the developments during this decade were significant enough to be counted as a *breakthrough* for the marginalist approach.

FURTHER READING

Walras's *Éléments* has been translated into English as *Elements of Pure Economics*; the translator, William Jaffé, has also supplied the book with an extensive set of explanatory notes that clarify the interpretation of the text and relate it to the literature. It is not an easy book to read, but it is not necessary to read it from beginning to end in order to benefit from it. We no longer study it in order to learn general equilibrium theory; for that purpose, modern textbooks are better suited. But the book gives a fascinating impression of the author's efforts to give shape to a complex material of which there was no prototype in the previous literature. As readers, we may therefore participate as witnesses to the foundation of a central part of economic theory.

Jaffé was also the editor of a large three-volume edition of Walras's correspondence (Jaffé 1965). Walras's letters are all written in French, while many of his correspondents write in their own language. There are, for instance, a number of letters written between Walras and Jevons that show clearly, at least to begin with, that the two economists see themselves as fighters for the same cause—which, as Jevons says, is the truth. (With time, Walras's relationship with Jevons became more strained since he felt that his English colleague did not give him the recognition that he deserved.) William Jaffé, who devoted his life to the study of Walras, has also written a number of articles about various aspects of his writings; many of these have been collected in Jaffé (1983).

211

Donald A. Walker (2006) discusses Walras's philosophical and methodological approaches to economics and traces his influence on the work of later economists. This book also contains a complete bibliography of Walras's books and articles. A shorter presentation of his life and work is contained in Walker's article in *The New Palgrave*. The reader who would like to have more details about the mathematical aspects of Walras's general equilibrium model, especially issues related to the existence and stability of equilibrium, may read the excellent account in Negishi (1989, ch. 7).

The question of whether a marginalist revolution really occurred in the 1870s has been discussed by Blaug (1972), which is one of several articles on this topic in a special issue of the journal *History of Political Economy* (fall 1972).

Alfred Marshall and
Partial Equilibrium Theory

Wითн ALFRED MARSHALL (1842–1924) we come to the group of economists that many have called the second generation of marginalists. There is little doubt, however, that Marshall himself would have preferred to be classified as belonging to the first. He liked to point out that he had come far in working out the new approach as early as the 1860s, but the fact is that he did not publish his version of it until 1890. But even if he was later to publish than Jevons, Menger, and Walras, Marshall gave the new theories a form that made them more accessible both to professional economists and others, and more useful as practical tools for applied economic analysis.

Alfred Marshall's father was a cashier in the Bank of England, but there is little indication that the central bank connection kindled the son's interest in economics. His father wished him to study theology in Oxford, but Marshall wanted to study mathematics and physics, and with the assistance of a wealthy uncle he began his studies at the University of Cambridge in 1861. He gradually turned more toward philosophy and economics, and according to his own account, his interest in economics stemmed from a desire to do something to improve the standard of living of the poorest in society. He began his economic studies by reading Ricardo and Mill, using his mathematical skills to give their theoretical analyses a more precise mathematical form.

After the completion of his studies in 1865 Marshall obtained a fellowship at St. John's College in Cambridge, and he also began to teach economics. In 1877 he married Mary Paley who had been his student and who was also an economist. The couple moved to Bristol, where they both lectured at the newly established University College, and they also collaborated on a book, *The Economics of Industry*, which was published in 1879. Among specialists on Marshall there has been some disagree-

213

ment about the respective shares of the two authors in the work that went into this book. There can be no doubt that from the beginning it was Mary's book, while her husband gradually came to play a more important role as coauthor. With this book, which Marshall later tended to speak about in rather patronizing tones, Mary Marshall's career as an economics writer was over, and she devoted the rest of her life to support her husband's work.

From Bristol, Marshall moved to the University of Oxford, but after two years he returned to Cambridge as professor of economics, a position that he occupied for twenty-three years. That Marshall should have been the obvious choice for the only chair in economics at his old university is a little surprising. At that point in his career he had published little. He had plans about a book on international trade theory, but what he wrote on this topic remained unpublished in his lifetime and was only read by a small circle of colleagues and students.[1] He had begun work on the book that was destined to become his major achievement, but nothing of this material had so far been published. Nevertheless, he had achieved a position and reputation that made him the undisputed leader of academic economists in the English-speaking world. This position was strengthened when the *Principles of Economics* was finally published in 1890. The book appeared in eight editions, and a large part of Marshall's time was spent in revising and extending it, particularly by adding an increasing number of appendices. Originally, Marshall had planned this as the first volume of a multivolume work, but he never completed the other volumes (we recall that Menger and Walras had similar plans that did not succeed). However, in his later years he managed in spite of poor health to realize at least part of the plan with the two books *Industry and Trade* (1919) and *Money, Credit, and Commerce* (1923). They were based on material that he had been working on for decades and seemed at least in part to be dated already at the time of publication. They therefore became far less influential than the *Principles*.

---

[1] His best-known and most highly regarded work in this field is the chapter draft "The Pure Theory of Domestic Values" (reprinted in Whitaker 1975). It was there that Marshall introduced his so-called "offer curves," which he used in a geometric version of John Stuart Mill's analysis of price formation in international trade (see chapter 5).

Style and Ambitions

Many have wondered why Marshall needed such a long time to publish his ideas. Keynes (1933) thought that one explanation was Marshall's high demands on the standard of his published work. Another explanation lies in his sensitivity to criticism; he was especially keen not to publish anything that could hurt or provoke others. In this connection it is interesting to note the review that he wrote in 1872 of Jevons's *Theory of Political Economy*, which had appeared a year earlier. The review is on the whole positive, although the tone is rather chilly. If is true that Marshall had already arrived at many of the same results, it is easy to imagine his frustration at reading an author whom he felt had overtaken him in terms of time of publication. Some of his criticism of the style and contents of Jevons's book also reveals something about Marshall's attitudes toward theoretical innovation in economics, as when he writes:

> The main value of the book, however, does not lie in its more prominent theories, but in its original treatment of a number of minor points, its suggestive remarks and careful analyses. We continually meet with old friends in new dresses. ... Thus it is a familiar truth that the total utility of any commodity is not proportional to "its final degree of utility."... But Professor Jevons has made this the leading idea of the costume in which he has displayed a large number of economic facts. (Marshall 1872; Pigou, ed. 1925, p. 95)

The remark on utility theory does not testify to a clear understanding of the theoretical novelty of Jevons's book. Clearly, Marshall had also reacted negatively to Jevons's revolutionary tone and his tendency to downgrade earlier writers;[2] maybe there is also an element of jealousy in the picture. He is also critical to Jevons's use of mathematics. He says that the recent application

---

[2] Marshall frequently stressed the historical continuity of economic thought and the close connection between his own theoretical framework and that of the classical economists, especially Ricardo and Mill. By contrast, he was disinclined to refer to and give credit to the work of his contemporaries, and in his later years he seems to have lost interest in the new theoretical developments that took place.

of mathematics to economics by several writers both in England and on the Continent has led to several "valuable suggestions." However,

> all that has been important in their reasonings and results has, with scarcely an exception, been capable of being described in ordinary language.... The book before us would be improved if the mathematics were omitted, but the diagrams retained. (Marshall 1872; Pigou, ed. 1925, p. 99)

It is remarkable that someone with a solid mathematical background should have this attitude to the use of mathematics in economics. Marshall admitted that mathematics could indeed be helpful, but only for the theorist's private use. If his mathematical analysis led to new economic insights he should be able to express them in "plain English," and when that had been achieved the mathematics could be "burned." If, on the other hand, it turned out to be impossible to express the results of the mathematical analysis in plain language, it was necessarily of little interest and value to the public to which it was addressed. When writing the *Principles*, Marshall followed up this view by relegating all formal analysis to footnotes and a separate mathematical appendix.

What was the nature of the public that Marshall tried to reach? His *Principles* was clearly intended as a textbook for students, and as such it was very successful. But it was also a scientific treatise directed toward other economists, and it became very influential as an authoritative statement of the state of the subject in 1890 and the following decades. In addition, another of Marshall's ambitions was that the book should be read by practical men of business. It is more doubtful to what extent this aim was achieved, but it exerted a significant influence on the structure and style of the book.

The *Principles* are divided into six main parts, or "books." Of these it is book 5 that has received most attention by later economists, because it is there that Marshall establishes the theoretical framework for partial equilibrium analysis that was to have such an important influence on the development of economics. But the other books are also of great interest, not least because they demonstrate Marshall's broad perspective on economy and society.

Supply and Demand

It is likely that the modern reader of the older literature of economics will first recognize the theoretical framework of modern textbooks (at least in microeconomics) in Marshall's *Principles*. Partial equilibrium theory—the analysis of price formation in a single market—is forged into an operational tool of analysis that can be used to analyze a range of theoretical and applied problems. An important aspect of his price theory was also that it provided an integrated view of the relationship between the classical approach and the new view that was associated with the marginalist breakthrough.

The price theory of the classical economists was a cost-of-production theory; the unit cost of production determined the price. However, they made an exception for goods that existed in fixed quantities, such as rare coins or works of art. In such cases price would be determined by scarcity. This dichotomy was unsatisfactory because it did not establish a *general* theory of price formation. One of Marshall's most important contributions was that he developed an analysis that effectively buried the controversy surrounding the respective roles of demand and supply in the determination of prices. The essence of that contribution was the now well-known supply and demand diagram, where an upward-sloping supply curve and a downward-sloping demand curve were drawn in the same diagram and where equilibrium is represented by the point of intersection between the two curves—the "Marshallian cross," as it has been called.[3] Keynes writes that "after Marshall's analysis there was nothing more to be said" (Keynes 1933, p. 182). Even if this is an exaggera-

---

[3] Actually, it was Marshall who introduced the convention of drawing this diagram with price on the vertical and quantity on the horizontal axis, the reverse of what Cournot had done in 1838. This was motivated by his conception of the "supply price" as a function of the quantity produced; the supply price is accordingly the price that the producer must receive in order to supply a specific quantity. With the demand curve similarly defined in terms of the demand price it therefore became natural to think of supply and demand prices as the dependent variables and quantity as the independent variable for firms and consumers, and of equilibrium as defined by the equality of supply and demand prices. In modern theory we have long ago reverted to Cournot's way of thinking, while sticking to the geometrical convention established by Marshall.

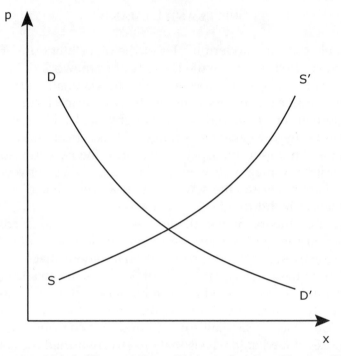

Figure 10.1. Marshall's partial equilibrium diagram. The equilibrium price (*p*) and quantity (*x*) are determined by the intersection between the demand curve *DD'* and the supply curve SS'. Note that Marshall, in contrast to Cournot, measures price on the vertical and quantity on the horizontal axis.

tion, there can be no doubt that the diagram clarified the logic of competitive price theory and was a major improvement over the treatment in Jevons (1871; 1970). Marshall gives supply and demand equivalent roles in the process of price formation and emphasizes with a famous metaphor that none of them can have priority over the other:[4] "We might as reasonably dispute whether it is the upper or the under blade of a pair of scissors that cuts a piece of paper, as whether value is governed by utility or cost of

[4] However, the metaphor can also be found in Mill's *Principles* as an illustration of the futility of ascribing to one of two causal factors a decisive role for the outcome. But Marshall's use of it is obviously especially striking because the image of the pair of scissors reminds us of the supply and demand diagram.

production" (Marshall 1890; 1920, p. 348).[5] With Marshall's clarification the two versions of price theory that can be found in the work of the classical economists become just special cases of a more general theory: price is determined by the cost of production in the case where the supply curve is horizontal, while in the case of fixed supply, represented by a vertical supply curve, it is determined by demand. But between these two extreme cases there is a continuum of possibilities.

How pathbreaking was this insight? Historians of thought have disagreed about this. Keynes (1933) maintains that it was one of Marshall's most important innovations, while Stigler's (1990) attitude is that Walras in the general equilibrium theory of his *Éléments* had already clarified this issue. Even if we accept Stigler's view as correct in principle, however, there can be no doubt that Marshall gave the theory a much simpler and more comprehensible form, and his formulation was quickly accepted as the correct way to regard the problem of price formation in competitive markets.

A central and important implication of Marshall's approach is that the relative importance of supply and demand as determinants of prices depends on the time perspective of the analysis and not only, as the classics had maintained, on the nature of the commodity (manufactured goods versus rare coins). He illustrates his discussion of the general theoretical point by an example taken from the fishing industry (Marshall 1890; 1920, pp. 369–371). From day to day there will be fluctuations around a normal price level for fish, which is mainly determined by the cost of capital and labor input in the fisheries. This input, which determines production capacity, must in a day-to-day perspective be considered as fixed. In the short run, which in the example could amount to a couple of years, changes in demand will cause production capacity to change also. As an example of what might cause a change in demand Marshall mentions a change in preferences from meat to fish as a consequence of an animal disease that makes it dangerous to eat meat. This type of shift in demand might be imagined to last for a couple of years before the pattern of demand returns to its original state. Obviously, even

---

[5] All quotations and page references to the *Principles* relate to the eighth edition from 1920, which is identical to volume 1 of the 1961 *Variorum Edition*.

in this time perspective the population of fishermen and part of the capital stock must be considered as fixed; however, part of the population which otherwise would have gone to work in the commercial fleet would now become engaged in the fisheries, and vessels that had been laid up or used for other purposes would be reequipped for fishing. But this can only happen if the producers receive a price that makes the restructuring profitable. The conclusion is therefore that in the short run a change in demand will lead to an increase in the price of fish.

In the long run the conclusion may be a different one. If the shift in demand in favor of fish becomes permanent, there will be an increased inflow of capital and labor to the fisheries. In a number of cases this could come about without any increase in the unit cost of production, so that in the long run an increase of demand would leave the price unaffected. One could even imagine that the price would fall; the increased activities in the fisheries might lead supporting industries like shipbuilding and tools production to organize themselves more efficiently and exploit economies of scale to such an extent that the unit cost in the fisheries would fall.

The distinction between short-run and long-run analysis may perhaps appear to be a rather trivial one, but Marshall made it into an important theoretical distinction by linking it to the scope for capacity adjustment. This actually became of great importance for economic theory. The best-known application of it is due to Marshall's most famous student, John Maynard Keynes, who in his *General Theory* (1936) made this distinction play a central analytical role in his macroeconomic theory.

PARTIAL AND GENERAL EQUILIBRIUM

Marshall's analysis of the workings of the market economy laid the foundations for what we now call partial equilibrium theory. "Partial" should be understood in contrast to the general equilibrium theory that had been pioneered by Walras, and it is natural to ask whether Marshall's analysis did not represent a step backward relative to that of his French predecessor. Is it not necessarily the case that the partial approach must be less general and therefore of less scientific value? The answer to this question is not quite as obvious as it may seem. We may note as a fact that after more than a century has passed since the time of Walras and Marshall, economists as a whole have not wished to discard any of the two approaches. Each of them has their strong and weak sides, some areas where its application is fruitful and others where it is less suitable.

Marshall was aware that a weakness of partial equilibrium theory was that it might neglect causal factors that were important for the solution of a concrete problem. His main defense of the approach was that the human intellect had "limited powers," so that it was necessary to simplify complex problems in order to understand and be able to solve them. But it was essential to be conscious of the simplifications that one made; one had to be aware of the factors that were disregarded during the analysis but which ought ideally to have been included. This technique of analysis he characterized by means of the Latin term *ceteris paribus*—everything else equal. One area where this technique was especially fruitful and valuable, in Marshall's view, was related to the time dimension of economic problems, but the following presentation of the approach is actually quite general:

> The element of time is a chief cause of those difficulties in economic investigations which make it necessary for man with his limited powers to go step by step; breaking up a complex question, studying one bit at a time, and at last combining his partial solutions into a more or less complete solution of the whole riddle. In breaking it up, he segregates those disturbing causes, whose wanderings happen to be inconvenient, for the time in a pound called *Cæteris Paribus*. The study of some group of tendencies is isolated by the assumption *other things being equal*: the existence of other tendencies is not denied, but their disturbing effect is neglected for a time. The more the issue is thus narrowed, the more exactly can it be handled: but also the less closely does it correspond to real life. Each exact and firm handling of a narrow issue, however, helps towards treating broader issues, in which that narrow issue is contained, more exactly than would otherwise have been possible. With each step more things can be let out of the pound; exact discussions can be made less abstract, realistic discussions can be made less inexact than was possible at an earlier stage. (Marshall 1890; 1920, p. 366)

By the intelligent use of this approach the analytical economist would gradually move from a partial to a general perspective, and most modern practitioners believe that partial equilibrium theory has turned out to be so useful that Marshall deserves all the praise that he has received as a pioneer in the field. However, some of his admirers are not satisfied by this. They believe that Marshall in fact *was* a general equilibrium theorist; it is just that this is obscured by the mode of exposition in the *Principles* that was designed in order to reach the broadest possible audience. There are some points that can be made in favor of such a view: in his early unpublished work on international trade theory Marshall used a general equilibrium framework that he had taken from Mill, and in the *Principles* he frequently emphasizes the mutual interdependencies of economic life. In a certain sense, therefore, he can be said to have a *perspective* on the subject that corresponds to that of general equilibrium. Lionel Robbins says in his lectures on the history of economic thought that it is simply "Nonsense!" to argue that Marshall was not a general equilibrium theorist (Robbins 1998, p. 306).

However, to have a certain perspective on the economic system is one thing; formulating one's perspective in the shape of a formal theory is something else. We have in fact a very reliable source of Marshall's thinking in his own Note XXI in the mathematical appendix of the *Principles*. Here he writes down a set of equilibrium conditions for an economy consisting of n commodity markets and m factor markets and argues that this model determines the $n+m$ prices in the economy. This is clearly in the Walrasian spirit, but there is a paradox involved in the procedure that he does not appear to realize. Marshall's model determines not only relative prices but—in spite of the fact that there is no money or unit of account in the model—also the absolute price level. As we saw in the previous chapter this fundamental problem had been solved by Walras several years before, but Marshall seems not to have known it or to have misunderstood Walras's analysis.[6] On this point, therefore, we have to conclude that although Marshall may have had a general equilibrium

---

[6] Robbins (1998) says that the mathematical appendix shows that Marshall understood Walras's contribution "perfectly well." But this is unconvincing in view of his misunderstanding of this crucial point.

perspective on economic theory, he had not developed a general equilibrium *model.*

Utility, Demand, and Welfare

Marshall's theory of consumer demand is based on marginal utility considerations, even if he shows little interest in utility theory as such. His critique of Jevons that was cited above is repeated in the *Principles*: Jevons "exaggerates"—one of Marshall's favorite words of criticism—the importance of marginal utility. However, Marshall makes good use of the concept, although with a modest degree of formalization. He assumes that the marginal utility of each good is decreasing and that the consumer will choose his demand so that the marginal utility of consumption, measured in terms of money, is equal to the price. Because marginal utility is decreasing, an increase in price must lead to a point of adjustment where marginal utility is higher than before and the amount of consumption is lower. The demand curve is accordingly a decreasing function of the price.[7]

Marshall realized that this line of reasoning was based on a simplifying assumption. Marginal utility as measured in money must reflect not only the marginal utility of the good as such but also the amount of income that the consumer has. When the price of a commodity falls, the purchasing power of money and therefore the real income of the consumer goes up, and this leads to a more complex relationship between price and demand. However, Marshall considered this complication to be of less importance, and he assumed it away with the formulation that the marginal utility of income is constant. He believed that this was a justifiable assumption as long as the commodity in question only made up a small share of the consumer's budget.[8]

---

[7] This reasoning presumes that the marginal utility of a good depends only on the quantity consumed of that good and not on the consumption of other goods. This is the assumption also made by Gossen, Jevons, and Walras, and Marshall obviously saw no need to generalize it.

[8] Since what is important for demand is the change in *real* income, we may find the effect of a price change on real income by deflating nominal income by a price index where the individual prices are weighed together by means of the budget shares of the commodities. If we now consider a situation where only

Later experts on Marshall have spent much effort in trying to reformulate this assumption in more rigorous terms, but it seems clear that Marshall was on the track of the modern distinction between income and substitution effects of a price change. The assumption of constant marginal utility of income implies in economic terms approximately the same as the disregard for income effects.

The main reason why Marshall made this somewhat artificial assumption was probably that he wanted to use his consumer theory not only as the foundation of the analysis of demand, but also for welfare considerations. When we can neglect the effect of price changes on the marginal utility of income, this means that the individual consumer's demand curve will correspond to his marginal utility of the commodity in question, or to his demand price, to use Marshall's own concept. Suppose that the price of a commodity falls. We can now ask the question: What is the utility or welfare gain to the consumer of this fall in price? The answer can be shown by considering figure 10.2. Marshall defined the *consumer surplus* as the difference between the maximum amount that the consumer would have been willing to pay for some given quantity *OH*, and what he actually pays. It is easy to see that the maximum amount that he would have been willing to pay is the area below the demand or marginal utility curve to the left of *H* while the amount paid is the quantity *OH* times the price *HA* which is the rectangle *OHAC*. In other words, the consumer surplus is the area between the demand curve and the price line,[9] and the value of a decrease in price becomes equal to the increase of consumer surplus.

In practice, it is virtually impossible to observe individual demand curves. If the concept of consumer surplus is to be of any practical use, it must therefore be possible to apply it to the demand curve for the market as a whole. At the conceptual level, we arrive at the market demand curve by taking the horizontal sum of the individual demand curves, and we can now use a similar geometric construction to calculate the consumers' sur-

---

one of the prices changes and this commodity has a very small budget share, Marshall's argument is that the effect on real income can be neglected.

[9] Marshall does not refer to Dupuit's analysis, which is closely related to his own (see chapter 7).

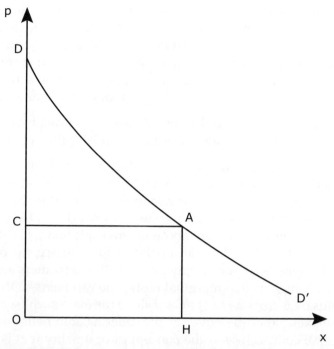

Figure 10.2. The consumer surplus corresponding to the quantity consumed *OH* and the price *OC* or *HA*. The consumers would at the maximum be willing to pay the area *OHAD* for this quantity, while they in fact pay the amount *OHAC*. The difference between the two areas is the consumer surplus, *CAD*.

plus for the market as a whole. One problem with this procedure is that we take the sum of marginal utility curves for consumers with very different incomes. We cannot decide from the change in the aggregate consumer surplus whether a price decrease mainly benefits the rich or the poor. If one is concerned with the redistributive aspects of a price change or a tax reform, one must therefore go behind the consumer surplus analysis and study the effects on particular individuals or groups.

The aggregate social surplus of a certain volume of production cannot be measured only by the consumer surplus. In addition one has to take account of the producer surplus, which is revenue minus the cost of production. Adding the consumer and producer surplus together, we obtain the total social surplus, which is the area between the demand and supply curves. If this area is to be as large as possible, consumption and production must be at the point of intersection between the demand and supply curves (see figure 10.1), in other words, at the point corresponding to the competitive equilibrium. This is Marshall's interpretation of what he regards as the "general doctrine," namely, that

> a position of (stable) equilibrium of demand and supply is a position also of *maximum satisfaction*. (Marshall 1890; 1920, p. 470)

In this context, "maximum satisfaction" evidently refers to market agents as a group or even to the group of all economic agents in the economy. This is a central and important conclusion, which Marshall might, although he does not do so, have related to Adam Smith's argument about the invisible hand. He also provides an interesting elaboration of it: if, for instance, the demand price is higher than the supply price—if the consumers' marginal benefit is higher than marginal cost—one can increase the social surplus by increasing output and share the extra surplus in a way that makes either the buyer or the seller or both better off. Here Marshall comes close to the concept of optimality that is associated with Pareto, which will be discussed in the next chapter.

However, if we are to acquire a deeper understanding of the meaning of maximum satisfaction we must take account of the problems with the summary measure of social surplus that are associated with the distributive effects of economic reforms. Marshall is very much aware of this: he argues, for example, that in the case where the producers are significantly poorer than the consumers, aggregate satisfaction can be increased by restraining production so that the price goes up and some of the social surplus is transferred from consumers to producers. This clearly involves the value judgment that a shilling is worth more to the poor than to the rich. Still, the assumption of the simple surplus analysis that the worth of a shilling is the same for all is, according to Marshall, a legitimate simplification; we only have to keep in mind the nature of the simplifying assumptions that we have made.

The concept of consumer surplus—or, more generally, the social surplus—turned out to have a number of possible applications, especially in the analysis of economic policy. It could be used to analyze problems as diverse as the efficiency of alternative forms of taxation, price setting in public firms, the effects of protectionist trade policies, and several other issues. However, it also had its clear limitations. It was unsuited for studying the effects of public policy on the distribution of income and welfare, and it could not be used to analyze the interplay between markets. But social surplus analysis has survived to this day as part of the economist's tool kit, even if later theorists have developed more sophisticated measures of welfare and economic efficiency. It must therefore be counted among one of Marshall's most important contributions to economic policy.

The Concept of Elasticity

One of Marshall's innovations that from a purely theoretical viewpoint may be considered as almost trivial, but which has been of great practical importance, is the concept of price elasticity. He introduces the price elasticity of demand (Marshall 1890; 1920, p. 102) by pointing out the usefulness of having a measure of the sensitivity of demand to a change in the price. In the main text of the *Principles* the definition of the elasticity is not very precise; he says that the price elasticity in a market is great or small depending on whether the quantity demanded increases by much or little as the price falls, or diminishes much or little when the price goes up. But in a footnote he provides a graphical interpretation, and in an appendix he presents a mathematical definition in terms of the relative change in demand divided by the relative change in price. This measure of price sensitivity is important because it is independent of the units that we use in measuring quantity and price, thereby making it possible to compare the price sensitivity of demand across markets.[10]

Corresponding to the definition of the elasticity of demand one may also define the elasticity of supply, but in the discussion of this concept Marshall is a bit more guarded (Marshall 1890;

[10] Marshall could conceivably have got the idea for his elasticity concept from his early reading of Mill's *Principles*. As shown in chapter 5, Mill used a similar concept in an example illustrating his price theory for international trade, and Marshall may have developed his own concept while trying to put Mill's theory into mathematical form.

1920, p. 456). The reason for his caution is that the price elasticity of supply must be assumed to be very different in the short and the long run, a complication that in Marshall's opinion was of much less relevance for the elasticity of demand.

In his overview of Marshall's most important contributions, Keynes (1933) puts great emphasis on the introduction of elasticities. He says that with regard to the development of terminology and theoretical concepts, this was Marshall's greatest service to economics. This may be putting it too strongly, even if it obviously is difficult to distinguish clearly between terminology and conceptual issues on the one hand and more substantial theoretical progress on the other. George Stigler has a quite different view of this part of Marshall's work; elasticities, he says, often give an elegant form to theoretical results and give rise to an unlimited number of examination questions—and that is all (Stigler 1990, p. 3). This, although amusing, is too negative. The use of elasticities enables economists to compare the price sensitivity of demand or supply by a single number that is comparable between different goods, time periods, and countries, and the invention of this concept must therefore be regarded as a significant achievement.

External Effects

Marshall is often credited with being the originator of the concept of external effects or externalities. In a certain sense this is clearly true, but in comparison to the modern use of it Marshall's focus is rather special. He was primarily interested in an explanation of why the long-run supply curve under perfect competition could be decreasing. His view that this possibility was of practical relevance was based on a conviction that an increase in demand frequently led to a lower price, and this could only be true if the supply curve was declining. But this result raised a difficult problem for theory: under perfect competition the supply curve of the individual firm must be equal to its marginal cost curve, and decreasing marginal cost is inconsistent with the assumption of perfect competition. His solution to the problem was to introduce the concept of "external economies" as a term describing factors beyond the control of the individual producer, which led to lower costs for the firm. These factors are external to the firm, but internal to the branch or industry. The individual firm will always confront increasing marginal costs, but an increase in demand that has as its immediate effect a higher price will lead all firms in the industry to increase their output, and this expansion of the industry could possibly lead to lower costs at the level of the individual firm.

The concept of external economies has been specially designed to describe a relationship of this kind, and Marshall also introduced "external diseconomies" to represent the opposite case where the long-run supply curve is increasing because industry expansion leads to increased costs for the individual firm. In the following, we shall use the terms positive and negative external effects, even if they are currently used to describe a much wider class of phenomena than those that Marshall was interested in. In Marshall's sense, both positive and negative external effects imply that the market does not function efficiently, because each single firm does not take account of the fact that changes in its own volume of output will have an effect—positive or negative—on the costs of other firms.

What are the causes of these external effects? As regards the positive effects, Marshall argues that industry expansion within a limited geographical area may lead to improved information and technological progress within the single firm. It may also imply improved access to highly qualified labor and to more exploitation of economies of scale through the emergence of specialized support activities.[11] In the case of negative external effects he refers to the example of the fisheries, where a decline in the stock of fish as a consequence of excess fishing can in the long run lead to increasing marginal and average costs, even if the individual firm experiences constant returns to scale. With less access to fish, fishermen must travel further and use longer time to catch a given quantity, so that unit costs go up. In this discussion, Marshall expresses himself with characteristic caution concerning the underlying reality of the example, which was a controversial issue in the contemporary debate about fisheries policy.

[11] This way of thinking has a descendant in the modern theory of "clusters" and the so-called new economic geography.

Having shown that both positive and negative external effects lead to market inefficiencies, Marshall suggests that one ought to tax increasing cost industries and use the revenue to subsidize industries with decreasing costs (Marshall 1890; 1920, p. 472–473). The point is that when there are positive external effects and therefore decreasing unit costs for the industry, the single firm will not take account of the lower costs that its own activity entails for the other firms in the industry. By subsidizing the firms, thereby stimulating them to increase output, one is able to compensate for this lack of incentives. On the other hand, with negative external effects and increasing unit costs for the industry, firms will expand too much, and a tax will provide an incentive to reduce output and thereby the costs of the other firms in the industry. This is a "simple plan," he says, although he immediately turns to a number of qualifications as regards its practical implementation. The costs of collecting the taxes and distributing the subsidies may be considerable and could also involve attempts at fraud and corruption. He also points out that the desire to benefit from the subsidies could lead businessmen to transfer their attention away from the management of their firms and toward attempts to influence the public authorities in charge of the subsidies.

FACTOR MARKETS AND INCOME DISTRIBUTION

Book 6 in the *Principles* is concerned with problems of income distribution. Marshall begins with a review of the classical economists' theory of income distribution, especially their theories of the determination of wages and rent. Ricardo and Mill tended to assume that both the wage rate and the return to capital were given magnitudes; the wage rate, according to Malthus's theory of population, would be equal to the subsistence minimum, while capital owners were assumed to require a rate of return on investment that determined the interest rate. According to Marshall, this is not in line with factual observations, and he goes on to develop his own theory. The point of departure for his theory of wages is the analysis of the decisions of the profit maximizing producer: How many workers should he hire? Given the assumption of decreasing marginal productivity of labor, Marshall (1890; 1920, pp. 516–517) shows, using a numerical example, that it is profitable to hire more workers as long as the value of the marginal productivity exceeds the wage rate, which the producer takes as determined in the market. This, Marshall argues, is an example of a general principle: for all types of labor it will be the case that the wage rate is equal to the value of its marginal productivity. He warns, however, about regarding this as a complete theory of wages. Even if he does not clearly say why, it is reasonable to interpret him as implying that marginal productivity represents only the demand for labor, and that a complete theory must also include a theory of labor supply. In a later chapter he presents a theory of the supply of labor that is based on marginal utility analysis. Bringing demand and supply together, wages are determined by demand and supply in the labor market, and the "iron law of wages" of the classical economists is no longer valid in modern society.

In a corresponding manner, Marshall presents a theory of the demand for capital, where profit maximization implies that the marginal productivity of capital will be equal to the rate of interest. In this way he establishes a theory of the demand for the factors of production that in its fundamental structure is symmetrical between labor, capital, and other inputs in production. Elements of this theory of the rewards to the factors of production can be found in the earlier literature (e.g., in the work of Thünen), but Marshall's version of it was illuminating and became of great importance for the further work on this topic.

However, Marshall's theory of wages and the labor market is in fact far more complex than his discussion of the marginal productivity perspective might lead us to believe. Thus, in his criticism of the classical theory of wages, he points out that earlier writers tended to underestimate the positive effects of higher wages on productivity, and he suggests that this may be an important part of the explanation of the historical increase in real wages. There may also be other reasons why the productivity of labor increases over time. Parents are motivated to save for their children but perhaps even more motivated to *invest* in them (Marshall 1890; 1920, p. 562). They can do this above all by paying for a good education for the children,[12] but also by ensuring that they grow up in a good home and family environment. In

---

[12] Actually, Marshall writes in this connection not about children but about sons. In his view of women's rights and their role in the labor market, Marshall was a far less progressive thinker than John Stuart Mill.

his discussion of these issues Marshall appears as an important forerunner of the modern theory of human capital.

While parents will invest in their children without regard for their own gain, the case of human capital investment in the labor market is more problematic. An employer who trains his workers to master skills that are valuable also outside of his own firm has no property rights in the capital that he has helped to create. This is the property of the worker who can take it with him to his next employer. But Marshall does not draw the natural conclusion that the labor market will offer too little training and education. He accepts the possibility that employers can be motivated by more than their own profits, and when he describes this motivation he moves a good distance away from his own marginal productivity theory of wages:

> In paying his workpeople high wages and in caring for their happiness and culture, the liberal employer confers benefits which do not end with his own generation. For the children of his workpeople share in them, and grow up stronger in body and in character than otherwise they would have done. The price which he has paid for labour will have borne the expenses of production of an increased supply of high industrial faculties in the next generation: but these faculties will be the property of others ... neither he nor even his heirs can reckon on reaping much material reward for this part of the good that he has done. (Marshall 1890; 1920, p. 566)

To the extent that this is intended as a descriptive theory of the behavior of employers (and not as an encouragement to employers to adopt an idealistic view of their profession), it becomes natural to ask what perspective Marshall really had on economic behavior. In his more formal derivation of the marginal productivity theory, the employer is a coolly calculating person whose actions are driven by comparisons between wages and productivity. In the quotation above he is an altruist who spends money for the good of society with little or no compensation for his own effort. It is not easy to see how the two perspectives can be reconciled. In fact, however, Marshall considers this problem at a more general level in one of the introductory chapters of the *Principles*, where he also presents his famous definition of economics as a field of study:

> Economics is a study of men as they live and move and think in the ordinary business of life. But it concerns itself chiefly with those motives which affect ... man's conduct in the business part of his life. Everyone who is worth anything carries his higher nature with him into business; and, there as elsewhere, he is influenced by his personal affections, by his conceptions of duty and his reverence for high ideals. (Marshall 1890; 1920, p. 14)

The reconciliation of the two views is not easy. A reasonable interpretation of what Marshall had in mind could be that although the actions that people take in the business part of their lives can at some level be explained by rather narrow theories like profit maximization, their actions are also constrained by moral and social concerns. In order to fully understand the way in which the economy and society functions, one must also take these considerations into account.

ECONOMY AND SOCIETY

Above all, it is Marshall the analytical economist, the author of book 5 in the *Principles*, who has received most attention by historians of thought. Modern readers have tended to shrug their shoulders at the more philosophical side of Marshall's work, of which we have already seen some examples. They have problems with accepting his somewhat patronizing attitude to "the lower classes" and his moralist view of the higher and lower parts of human nature. Nevertheless, Marshall's reflections contain a number of interesting points that deserve the attention of the modern reader, especially because the problems that he raises to a large extent have been neglected in contemporary economics

As we have seen, Marshall kept an open mind about the motivation of economic agents: it could be quite complex, going beyond the single-minded goal of profit maximization or the desire to obtain the highest possible individual standard of living. A minor modification of the maximization hypotheses was the great emphasis that he put on family considerations, as in his discussion of parents' investment in their children. But in addition he maintains that managers and other men of business are also driven by motives that are socially conditioned. Foremost

233

among these are social responsibility and the desire for recognition by others. Social responsibility, or a sense of duty, may induce monopolists to charge a lower price than called for by pure profit maximization because they take account of the burden that a high price will impose on the customers. Similarly, trade union leaders may moderate their wage claims in order that their members may not be too much out of step with the wage level of other workers. The desire for recognition may lead to behavior that is in particular favor with public opinion, thereby encouraging social conformity. But it could also result in a strengthening of the competitive spirit, as when recognition is won not simply by doing well but by being the best.

Marshall was a strong adherent of free markets. Part of his justification of this attitude was the conventional one: freedom of industry and free competition led to an efficient use of resources. But in addition he emphasized the view that such a system was good for the building of character; it made men become hardworking, conscientious, and prudent. This would have a long-run effect on economic development and growth, for these characteristics would be inherited—socially if not genetically—by later generations. We do not necessarily need to agree with Marshall about the details of his argument in order to feel that these are interesting and important issues.[13]

MARSHALL'S IMPORTANCE

Marshall's standing as an economist varies a good deal among those who have studied him carefully. Some believe that he is one of the most important economists in the history of the subject, while others regard him chiefly as one who consolidated the knowledge of his time, but who himself possessed only a small degree of originality.

Scientific originality is not easy to define. Some cases are simple: there can be no doubt that Cournot was a highly original scientist. He gave a rigorous formulation of new theories in an area

---

[13] Marshall's thoughts on the relationship between the economic system and the general development of society have been further described by Whitaker (1977).

that, at least in part, was completely unexplored before his time, and the originality of his work is easy to see. By way of contrast, John Stuart Mill is an economist that for a long time occupied a modest place on the scale of originality (not least because of his tendency to gloss over his own innovations), while during the last forty to fifty years his star has been rising. We should probably realize that a scientist can be original in terms of his ability to integrate and consolidate the existing knowledge in his field. In this respect Marshall is similar to Mill: he wrapped up his original contributions in a way that made them difficult to see, and his exposition of the field as a whole was so well rounded that the conflicts and disagreements that are the roots of progress did not come to the surface. A balanced evaluation must be that Marshall was an original economist both by virtue of his own extensions of economic theory and his ability to integrate old and new contributions to the development of the field.

Marshall is also one of the first among the important economists who exerted an important part of his influence through his teaching, even if his lectures appear to have been almost chaotic. His wife told John Maynard Keynes that Marshall's teaching philosophy was that, by never presenting his topics in a well-ordered and systematic way, he would encourage the students to think for themselves. Keynes, who followed his lectures at a relatively late point in Marshall's teaching career, clearly felt this to be in line with his own experience: "I think that the informality of his lectures may have increased as time went on. Certainly in 1906, when I attended them, it was impossible to bring away coherent notes" (Keynes 1933, p. 196).

In addition to his teaching and tutorial activities, Marshall also did much to establish economics as a central field of study in Cambridge. His students—among whom were Pigou, Keynes, and many other great names of English economics—were strongly influenced both by his teaching and personality. Pigou's development of the theory of external effects and Keynes's distinction between the short and the long run in macroeconomics were both strongly inspired by Marshall's teaching and writings. However, there are also those that have wondered whether this strong influence—both the personal one and the status of the *Principles* as the Bible of economics—was all to the good for English economics. There emerged a belief among English economists that all theoretical insights of any importance could be found in Marshall, and this attitude may in the long run have contributed to the relative decline of economics in England.

Many textbooks on the history of thought pay more attention to Marshall's work than to that of any other of the great economists. The most important reason for this may be that his *Principles* forms the bridge between the old and the new, between the literature that—with some exceptions—now seems remote and that which is closer to the economics of our own time. It says much about the book that it has managed to hold this position for so long.

Further Reading

Marshall's *Principles* is not a difficult book to read for modern economists. The theoretical chapters give a good impression of the state of the subject at the end of the nineteenth century, and the mixture of theory with institutional and empirical facts may still be inspiring reading. The last revised edition to appear in Marshall's lifetime is the eighth edition from 1920. It has been reproduced in a so-called *Variorum Edition* (sometimes misleadingly referred to as the ninth edition) that was published in two volumes in 1961. The first volume is a reproduction of the 1920 edition, while the second volume presents an account of the changes that were made between the various editions of the book. It also contains extracts from Marshall's other publications and correspondence, which throw light both on the origin of the book and on Marshall's scientific development.

The major biography of Marshall, covering his life, work, and intellectual environment, is the book by Peter Groenewegen (1995). Shorter surveys of Marshall's contributions to economics with emphasis on the *Principles of Economics* can be found in a number of books in addition to the standard texts, for instance, Hutchison (1953) and Stigler (1941; 1994). Frisch (1950) is a classic exposition of the main features of Marshall's price theory. A collection of articles edited by John Whitaker surveys his research and professional activities in a number of different areas (Whitaker 1990). Whitaker (1975) is also the editor of a selection of

Marshall's early works—from the end of the 1860s to 1890—where he has written an extensive introduction that describes Marshall's life and thought in this period of his life. Keynes's (1933) elegant and interesting essay on Marshall testifies to the student's respect for a treasured teacher but also contains some critical reflections on Marshall as an economist.

Equilibrium and Welfare:
Edgeworth, Pareto, and Pigou

As EARLY as in Adam Smith's statement about the invisible hand we encountered the idea that the market mechanism is not only a system for the allocation of resources, but also that it works in the public interest. Smith's formulation was lacking in precision in two important respects. First, it did not clarify which forms of competition would lead to a result that was in the interests of society. Second, it contained no convincing definition of the real meaning of the public interest. Among later economists, John Stuart Mill maintained that the right measure of social welfare was the sum of utilities, but he did not formulate this objective in such a way that it could be of practical use for issues like the evaluation of different market forms or the relationship between government and markets. We have also seen that similar problems emerged in the writings of several other authors. Thus, while Alfred Marshall argued that market equilibrium implied "maximum satisfaction" for society as a whole, he was also willing to accept that social concerns could justify government action that led to distortions of market equilibrium. Obviously, this conclusion raises the question of the real meaning of the concept of maximum satisfaction.

The three main characters of this chapter all attempted to tackle this problem, although they approached it in rather different ways. Their work has had significant effects on modern economics, both in terms of pure theory and the analysis of important problems of economic policy.

FRANCIS Y. EDGEWORTH

Francis Ysidro Edgeworth (1845–1926) was born in Ireland but lived in England from the age of twenty-two. He travelled a long and winding road toward his eventual position as one of the leading economists of the age. He received his university education in Dublin and Oxford, specializing in classical languages and literature. Having finished his studies he moved to London to be trained as a lawyer, but he never came to practice this profession. Instead he began to study mathematics and philosophy on his own, until under the influence of Jevons he began to develop an interest in economics. In 1880 he obtained his first academic position, teaching logic at University College, London, and in 1891 he was appointed professor of economics at Oxford University, a position he had until his retirement in 1922 at the age of seventy-seven. He was the editor of the *Economic Journal*, at that time the most prestigious scientific journal in economics, for an impressive period of thirty-five years, partly alone, partly together with John Maynard Keynes. At present he is regarded as one of the foremost theorists of his time and especially as a pioneer in the development of mathematical economics. One reason why he never attained a professional status comparable to that of Marshall may have been that he did not attempt to reach a wide readership by publishing a broad treatise. His extensive output of monographs and articles was aimed exclusively at academic readers, and he had no ambition to write for students or for practical men of business. But even for academic economists his works were not easy reading. He was a highly trained mathematician who used his mathematics to an extent that was difficult to understand for the great majority of the economists of his time. Moreover, as an expert on classical literature he sprinkled his texts with quotations in Latin and Greek—without translation!

Edgeworth published three books, the most important of which are *New and Old Methods of Ethics* (1877) and *Mathematical Psychics* (1881).[1] In addition he wrote a large number of journal articles, both about pure theory and more applied topics, such as the economics of banking, the economics of war and peace, and equality of wages for men and women. As editor of the *Economic Journal* he wrote numerous book reviews, many of which are of great interest from the point of view of the history of thought. He also contributed more than 130 articles to *Palgrave's Dictionary of*

---

[1] The third book is *Meretrike or the Method of Measuring Probabilities and Utilities*, which was published in 1887.

Political Economy, an important reference work whose first edition was published during the years 1894–1899. He was also the author of several important papers within the area of mathematical statistics.

Exact Utilitarianism

Edgeworth was a utilitarian: he maintained that total welfare in society should be measured by the sum of individual utilities. The individual person's utility was identified with the satisfaction that resulted from his consumption and activities. Can utility be measured? Not, according to Edgeworth, in a literal sense but still to a sufficient degree to make utility a meaningful concept. This view he expresses in a characteristically colorful way:

> We cannot *count* the golden sands of life; we cannot *number* the "innumerable smile" of seas of love; but we seem to be capable of observing that there is here a *greater*, there a *less*, multitude of pleasure-units, mass of happiness; and that is enough. (Edgeworth 1881; 2003, pp. 8–9)

In spite of his utilitarian convictions Edgeworth believed that the earlier utilitarian thinkers like Bentham and Mill had not defined their welfare objective in a way that led to any practical conclusions. He granted that the principle of "the greatest happiness for the greatest number" could be used to argue intuitively for the desirability of social reform, but the earlier authors were unable to present a logical proof that their conclusions followed from their utilitarian assumptions. As a contrast to their more intuitive form of reasoning Edgeworth suggested the approach that he called "exact utilitarianism," which was based on a rigorous mathematical formulation.

In *New and Old Methods of Ethics* he applied the theory of exact utilitarianism to the following problem: Which distribution of income will create the greatest possible happiness (or welfare) for society as a whole? He first considered the question of how individual utility depended on income, building on an analogy with the empirical insights that originated from the research of the German psychologist Gustav Fechner (1801–87). Fechner's central result was that the perception of a sensual stimulus increases less than proportionally with the strength of the stimulus.[2] If, for example, in a dark room one lights more and more lamps of the same strength, the increase of light will be experienced as less and less noticeable. From this result Edgeworth concluded that a similar result must hold for the utility of income: the marginal utility of income must be decreasing. In other words, the higher income one has, the less is the addition to utility from a given addition to income. Suppose now that a given amount of income is to be distributed between a number of persons in society. If all of them have the same utility function—if the relationship between income and utility is the same for all—the optimal distribution of income consists in giving the same amount to everybody. For if we try to modify this distribution by transferring some small amount of income from person A to person B, we will find that the increase in utility for B is smaller than the loss of utility for A; this follows directly from the assumption of decreasing marginal utility of income. So the sum of utility in society will diminish, and we may conclude that an equal distribution of income is best for society. In his *Mathematical Psychics,* Edgeworth had also analyzed the case where individuals either have different capacities for work or differ in their ability to create utility from income. For the case of inequality in working capacity he shows that the utilitarian principle under certain assumptions implies that those with the greatest capacity should do the most work.

This theoretical approach obviously raises a challenging question: How do we know that utility is comparable between individuals? Comparability is an assumption that we need to make whether we assume that the relationship between utility and income is the same for different individuals or that it varies in some systematic way with their work capacity or psychological makeup. Edgeworth (1881; 2003, p. 59) actually takes it as an axiom that happiness or utility is measurable and comparable between individuals and defends the assumption by reference to the results of psychological research.[3] As Paul Samuelson

[2] The so-called Weber-Fechner law is actually more specific than this in that it implies that the perception is proportional to the logarithm of the stimulus.

[3] In other words, as a self-evident truth that is not in need of any further proof.

241

(1947, p. 206) has put it, for Edgeworth utility was as real as his morning jam.

It is easy to be convinced that Edgeworth's exact utilitarianism in analytical terms was a step forward in comparison to the more intuitive use of the utilitarian principle that had been prevalent in the earlier literature. With the mathematical formulation of social welfare as the sum of individual utility functions it became far easier to realize which conclusions could be drawn from this normative assumption, which assumptions were necessary for the conclusions to hold, and—not least important—which conclusions could *not* be drawn. Thereby it also became easier, assuming that one understood the mathematics and Edgeworth's sometimes peculiar style of writing, to form an opinion about the utilitarian principle as representing a special set of ethical values. It also helped to make it clear that it was quite possible to be concerned with the social issues of the time *without* being a utilitarian.[4]

The Equilibrium of Exchange

The theoretical contribution for which Edgeworth is best known is his analysis of market equilibrium in an exchange economy. The framework of the analysis is an economy with two consumers and two goods that are in fixed supply, and where the two consumers own given shares of the supply. The problem is to characterize the equilibrium that will emerge when the two consumers are free to trade with each other. In order to solve this problem it is first of all necessary to make some assumptions about the consumers' preferences for the two goods. Following the tradition from Gossen, Jevons, and Walras, Edgeworth let preferences be represented by utility functions, but he made two important new contributions to utility theory.

The earlier writers had assumed that an individual's total utility could be written as a sum of "utilities" associated with the

---

[4] It needs, however, to be kept in mind that Edgeworth's approach inevitably narrowed down the issues to which utilitarian reasoning could be applied. One of the main issues that concerned Jeremy Bentham, the father of utilitarianism, was the question of prison reform, which would be hard to analyze in a meaningful way using Edgeworth's analytical framework.

consumption of each good. In the case of two goods that are consumed in quantities x and y, this total utility, U, could therefore be written as the sum of the utility of x, $u(x)$, plus the utility of y, $v(y)$, so that

$$U=u(x)+v(y).$$

Utility functions of this kind are said to be *additive*. Edgeworth introduced a more general formulation where total utility is a function of the two quantities, but without any presumption that it could be written as a sum. Instead of using the additive form we can therefore write the utility function as

$$U=U(x,y).$$

From a mathematical point of view this is more general, but Edgeworth did not explain why the generalization was of *economic* interest. The difference between the two formulations is that in the latter version the marginal utility of each good will depend not only on the quantity consumed of that good, but also on the quantity consumed of the other good. Edgeworth assumed that the relationship was such that an increase in y would reduce the marginal utility of x (and vice versa). More generally one could easily imagine that the relationship could also go the other way, but Edgeworth did not take up this question. This was done, however, by the two Austrian economists Rudolf Auspitz and Richard Lieben (1889), who defined two goods as being *substitutes* or *complements* according to whether an increase in the consumption of one of the goods reduced (coffee and tea) or increased (sugar and tea) the marginal utility of the other. This definition of substitutes and complements has later tended to be associated with Edgeworth, but historically this is incorrect; the honor should go to Auspitz and Lieben.[5]

[5] The definition is now mostly of historical interest, since the modern classification of substitutes and complements is based on properties of demand functions, not utility functions; the definition in terms of marginal utility is only meaningful under assumptions that can hardly be said to have empirical content. Rudolf Auspitz (1837–1906) and Richard Lieben (1842–1919), who were cousins, were bankers by profession and partners in a bank in Vienna, and in their leisure time they were also economic theorists. Their 1889 book, *Untersuchungen über die Theorie des Preises* (Investigations in Price Theory), was based on a mathematical approach and received critical comments from Menger and

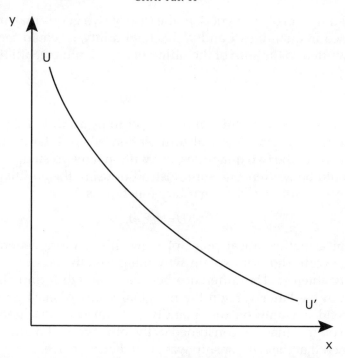

Figure 11.1. Along an indifference curve like *UU'* utility is constant: the consumer considers all combinations of the goods *x* and *y* on this curve as being equally preferable.

Edgeworth's other important contribution to utility theory was the concept of *indifference curves.* When we construct a diagram with the quantity *x* on the horizontal axis and *y* on the vertical axis, we may draw curves in the diagram along which utility is constant: the consumer is indifferent between all combinations of the two goods represented by a given curve. Edgeworth drew these curves in the shape that is familiar to us today and showed that the convexity of the curves followed from the assumptions that he made about the marginal utilities, namely, that the marginal utility of each good was a decreasing function both of the quantity consumed of that good and the quantity consumed of the other.

Böhm-Bawerk, who were both hostile toward the use of mathematical methods in economics (see chapter 8).

Equipped with his indifference curves, Edgeworth now turned to the analysis of equilibrium in an exchange economy. Assuming that there are no constraints on the transactions between the two consumers, none of them—let us call them A and B—will accept an outcome which is worse than that which they could have achieved on their own by simply consuming their initial stocks of goods. Moreover, Edgeworth argued, the final agreement between the two would have the property that it would not be possible to suggest a further exchange that would be to the advantage of both parties. But there would be a number of contracts with this property, and without detailed information about preferences and negotiating power it would be impossible to be more precise about the nature of the equilibrium. Suppose now, however, that there are not only two consumers, but four—two of the A type and two of type B, where each of the A types are exactly equal in terms of preferences and initial ownership, and similarly for the B types. This leads to a smaller set of possible contracts that involves all four parties. For one of the individuals of type A has now not only the choice between the alternatives of trading with one of the Bs and consuming his initial resources: he has several alternatives of trading contracts that involve two or three parties. He is therefore able to achieve a better result for himself in the four-party negotiation than he would be able to obtain on his own. By pursuing this line of reasoning through further increases of the number of consumers of type A and B, Edgeworth showed that the equilibrium of exchange would in the end approach that of perfect competition. The importance of this theoretical result is that it shows that it is in an economy with a large number of agents that the assumption of perfect competition can be given a rigorous justification. As shown in chapter 7, Cournot had arrived at a similar conclusion on the basis of partial equilibrium theory, but Edgeworth's formulation was more general and theoretically deeper. As he says, the mathematical analysis of the perfect market had been developed by "Messrs. Jevons, Marshall, Walras," but his own theory characterizes the equilibrium in a more fundamental way.

Many will be familiar with at least part of this theory through the famous geometrical construction known as the Edgeworth box diagram. However, one will search in vain for it in Edgeworth's collected works, for in spite of the name he was not in

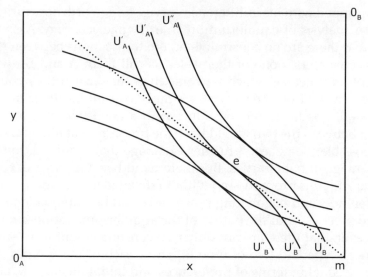

Figure 11.2. "Edgeworth's box diagram," as drawn by Pareto. The length and height of the box represent the fixed supply of the two commodities x and y. To begin with, consumer A owns the whole stock of commodity x, while consumer B owns the total supply of y; this is represented by the point m. A's indifference curves are drawn from the origin O_A while those of B are related to O_B. The price ratio corresponding to equilibrium of supply and demand is given by the slope of the straight line through m. The equilibrium point e is also a Pareto optimum; it yields a maximum of utility for A (U'_A), given that B has the utility level U'_B.

fact the first to draw it. Although there are two related diagrams in the *Mathematical Psychics*, it takes a benevolent reading to recognize the modern box diagram in any of these. On the other hand, Edgeworth introduced so many of the elements required for its construction (in addition to indifference curves he also introduced the concept of the contract curve) that it is not unreasonable that the diagram carries his name. But the first to draw the diagram as we know it today was Vilfredo Pareto.

It is obviously a paradox that Edgeworth's fame is so closely associated with a diagram that was invented by someone else. Nevertheless, he was clearly among the most important economists at the end of the nineteenth century. His contributions to normative economic theory through "exact utilitarianism," his innovations in consumer theory, and—not least—his analysis of perfect competition are more than sufficient to secure this position.

VILFREDO PARETO

Vilfredo Pareto (1848–1923) was born in Paris to a French mother and an Italian father. When he was six the family moved to Italy where he received his university training in science and engineering. Having finished his education he began to work as an engineer for a railway company and later became director of an iron works in Florence. However, his main interest was in economic and social questions. In his leisure time he studied economics and sociology and gradually embarked on a career as an extremely active writer in these areas. His political views were somewhat unusual: he combined a conviction of the social benefits of free competition and free trade with support for pacifist, anti-imperialist, and republican movements. Through his acquaintanceship with the prominent Italian economist Maffeo Pantaleoni (1857–1924) he became familiar with the work of Walras and became convinced that general equilibrium theory was the most fruitful framework for the analysis of economic and social problems. After Pareto had published a series of articles on various topics in economic theory he became, on Pantaleoni's recommendation, appointed as Walras's successor to the chair of economics at the University of Lausanne in 1893. Unlike Walras, Pareto was a skilled and popular lecturer, but after having inherited a large fortune from an uncle in 1898 he cut down on his teaching and retired from his professorship in 1907. Toward the end of his life his political convictions became more conservative, and he expressed himself in a way that showed his contempt for parliamentary democracy. Mussolini and the Italian fascists claimed him as an adherent of their ideology, but Pareto was not himself politically active and never expressed any direct support for Mussolini and his party.

He was an extremely productive writer. An American expert on Pareto, John Chipman (1976), has estimated that his total literary output is larger than the collected works of Ricardo, Mill, and Keynes taken together; and these are authors that by any reasonable standard must also be considered as having been very

247

productive. Pareto published over an extremely wide field that also included sociology, statistics, economic history, and political science, and his position in the history of sociology is as strong as it is in economics. His main works in economics are the two books, *Cours d'économie politique* (A Course of Political Economy, 1896–97) and *Manuel d'économie politique* (*Manual of Political Economy*, 1909; 1971).[6] The first of these books is based on his lectures in Lausanne and contains both a pedagogical exposition of Walras's theories and a broad scholarly review of the social sciences that shows an impressive knowledge of a wide range of subjects. But it is the second book that contains most of his original contributions to economic theory, and it is to this that he owes his position in the history of thought. There is no sharp division between his work in sociology and economics, and his main work in sociology, *Trattato di Sociologia Generale* (1916; translated as *The Mind and Society*, 1963), also contains a good deal of material on topics in economics.

Pareto was Walras's successor in more than a formal sense. Like his predecessor he was a strong believer in the benefits of the mathematical method of economic analysis, and he saw it as one of his central tasks to generalize and further develop Walras's ideas. At the same time, however, the exclusive focus that historians of thought have had on his formal theoretical work may have tended to present a biased view of an economist who had an unusually broad approach to the study of his science.

Utility and Demand

In earlier chapters we have encountered the concept of utility in two different contexts. First, it appears as an important element in the normative analysis of economic issues, as, for instance, in Edgeworth's discussion of the optimal distribution of income. Second, utility is central in the marginalist economists' theories of consumer behavior and general equilibrium, which are not normative but descriptive or positive. "Utility" is there-

---

[6] An earlier edition of the latter book appeared in Italian in 1906 under the title *Manuale di economia politica*. Pareto was bilingual and wrote partly in Italian, partly in French. However, the French edition of the *Manuale* was produced by a French translator.

fore used in quite different ways in the two types of theory, and there may be reasons to ask whether we really are dealing with the same concept.

This was one of the questions that Pareto asked himself as he penetrated more deeply into the general equilibrium theory of Walras, and he set himself the task of arriving at a version of the theory of consumer behavior that was as general as possible in the treatment of individual preferences. In this area, his work to a large extent ran parallel to that of Edgeworth. But Pareto managed to reach a deeper understanding of the real connection between the utility function and the indifference curves. What economists should be chiefly interested in as regards the behavior of consumers is their demand; utility theory should therefore be seen as a tool for a better understanding of demand. But what is needed for this task is an understanding of consumers' *preferences*, and these are fundamentally speaking best described by the indifference curves.[7] If we know the consumer's indifference curves, we can attach numbers to them, so that indifference curves that lie up and to the right have higher numbers than those that are down and to the left. This connection between consumption and the utility numbers may be referred to as the utility function, but the function is just a representation of the preferences; the basic information about the structure of preferences lies in the system of indifference curves—the indifference map. This view was in marked contrast to Edgeworth's way of looking at the problem, and Pareto gave a clear formulation of the contrast between the two approaches:

> [Edgeworth] assumed the existence of *utility* (ophelimity) and deduced the indifference curves from it. On the other hand, I consider the indifference curves as given, and deduce from them all that is necessary for the theory of equilibrium, without resorting to ophelimity. (Pareto 1909; 1971, p. 119)

In fact, Pareto did not completely discard the utility functions. He continued to use them as a convenient mathematical method of representing preferences, but his own concept of utility was

---

[7] Indifference curves can, of course, only be used in the case of two goods, but there are mathematically more abstract ways to represent preferences in the more general case.

something far less concrete than the jam on Edgeworth's break-fast table. For the numbering of the indifference curves from the lowest to the highest is in reality arbitrary as long as the numbers are increasing. One increasing series of numbers can be substituted for another, provided only that the two series rank the indifference curves in the same order. Pareto's concept of utility is *ordinal* in contrast to that of Edgeworth which is *cardinal*.[8] An assumption like that of decreasing marginal utility has no place in Pareto's system, because such an assumption depends on which numbers we apply to the indifference curves. What replaces the assumption of decreasing marginal utility is the requirement that the indifference curves are convex toward the origin. Pareto believed that his own concept of utility was so different from that which Edgeworth and others had taken from the utilitarian tradition that he invented a new name for it, namely, ophelimity (*ophélimité*) as in the quotation above. But ophelimity never became a part of the standard vocabulary of economics, and economists have continued to use the concepts of utility and utility functions, even when they use them in exactly the same sense as Pareto's ophelimity.

Pareto realized that the value of utility theory was that it could be used to derive hypotheses about demand: What were the properties of demand functions (the functions relating demand to prices and income) that followed from the hypothesis of utility maximization? His mathematically ambitious attempt to derive these properties shows Pareto as a highly skilled analytical economist who pioneered the technique that in modern jargon is called comparative statics analysis (Pareto 1909; 1971, pp. 421–31). He derived the conditions for utility maximization for an individual consumer and carried out a mathematical analysis of what happened to the optimal choice of consumption goods when one of the prices changed while the remaining prices and

[8] Let us imagine that a consumer ranks three different combinations of consumer goods as *a, b, c*, where *a* is the best and *c* is the worst alternative. An ordinal utility function will imply a higher value for *a* than for *b* and a higher value for *b* than for *c*. However, it will not be meaningful to ask whether the transition from *c* to *b* gives a greater increase in utility than the transition from *b* to *a*. A cardinal utility function will on the other hand imply that this question can be answered; in other words, a cardinal utility function will provide a ranking of *differences* in utility.

income remained constant. But he had problems with the economic interpretation of his own results and did not manage to present them in a form that appealed to the reader's economic intuition. However, Pareto's analysis laid the foundation for the development of demand theory that was to come some years later and which is particularly associated with the Russian economist Eugen Slutsky.[9]

Market Equilibrium and Optimality

More than anything else, Pareto's fame rests on his role as the originator of the modern theory of welfare economics. In an article from 1894 he stated that the Walrasian equilibrium satisfied the conditions for maximum welfare; in support of this statement he referred to Walras's own analysis, even if this must be considered less than clear (see chapter 9). But as he went more deeply into the study of the foundations of utility, he rejected this conclusion, for the comparison of utility between different individuals that the analysis requires can in Pareto's opinion not be justified:[10]

> The utility, or its index, for one individual, and the utility, or its index, for another individual, are heterogeneous quantities. We can neither add them together nor compare them. … A sum of utility enjoyed by different individuals does not exist; it is an expression which has no meaning. (Pareto 1909; 1971, p. 192)

So is the conclusion that there cannot exist any measure of the total utility or welfare in society that corresponds to Marshall's "maximum satisfaction"? Pareto's answer is yes, but only in a

---

[9] Eugen Slutsky (1880–1948) showed in a famous 1915 article that the effect on the demand for a consumer good of an increase in its price can be expressed as the sum of two partial effects. First, the price increase implies that this good becomes relatively more expensive than other goods. For a constant level of utility this causes individuals to move their consumption demand from this good to other goods. This is called the substitution effect. Second, a price increase in a situation where nominal income is constant means that the consumer's real income falls. This so-called income effect implies reduced demand for normal goods and increased demand for inferior goods. Thus for all normal goods demand is a decreasing function of the price.

[10] In these quotations I have substituted "utility" for Pareto's "ophelimity."

certain and limited sense, for in a later chapter of the *Manual* he formulates the criterion of social efficiency, or welfare, that we now call Pareto optimality:

> We will say that the members of a collectivity enjoy *maximum utility* in a certain position when it is impossible to find a way of moving from that position very slightly in such a manner that the utility enjoyed by each of the individuals of that collectivity increases. (Pareto 1909; 1971, p. 261)[11]

In modern textbooks, the definition of Pareto optimality is usually written as the condition that it is impossible to increase the utility for one individual without decreasing the utility for somebody else. But it is easy to see that this is equivalent to Pareto's own definition under the assumption that goods are perfectly divisible. For if we can make one individual better off without anyone else being worse off, we could take the increase in the consumption of the first individual and divide it up among all individuals (including the first) and thereby make everyone better off.

The expression *maximum utility* is a rather misleading term for the criterion that Pareto had established. First, it leads one to think along the lines of a social or aggregate sum of utilities, which Pareto himself had said to be a meaningless concept. Second, the "position" that Pareto describes is not uniquely determined. Even in the simple case of an exchange economy with two consumers and two goods there will be many such positions, corresponding to different distributions of resources between the two individuals. In other words, there will be several positions that satisfy the conditions for optimality, and it makes little sense to say that they all lead to "maximum utility." This unfortunate formulation has led some later economists to question whether Pareto really understood his own concept of optimality. However, when one reads the quotation in its context, there is little

---

[11] At the end of this sentence Pareto actually writes "increases *or decreases*" (my italics). This is obviously wrong, and the incorrectness of the statement also appears from his own more detailed analysis in the form of diagrams and mathematics. I have therefore chosen to present the quotation without this slip of Pareto's.

reason to doubt that he did. In any case, his attempt to arrive at a concept of optimal resource allocation for society as a whole was innovative and pathbreaking, and like many other pioneers he found it difficult to arrive at an illuminating terminology that would set his findings in the right perspective. We shall have to excuse him for not realizing that "Pareto optimality" would have been a much better term than "maximum utility"!

Pareto states clearly that this definition of an optimal use of resources could be used to characterize market equilibrium under perfect competition, and he discusses this property of the equilibrium very carefully. He begins with the case of pure exchange, introducing "Edgeworth's box diagram," and goes on to generalize the analysis to an economy with production. He also argues that his definition of optimality is of interest for the analysis of alternative economic systems: in a socialist state that is concerned with the welfare of its citizens the ministry of production ought to organize production and factor use in accordance with the rules for optimal resource allocation implied by his analysis. Such a society would probably also rely on the market mechanism as an instrument for the allocation of resources, although only to a limited extent. However, in its planning activities for the nonmarket sector the ministry of production would have to rely on calculation prices, for without prices the ministry would grope in the dark as regards the planning of production. After having discussed a number of issues pertaining to the choice between markets and socialism, he concludes soberly that

> the pure theory of economics does not give us a truly decisive criterion for choosing between an organization of society based on private property and a socialist organization. This problem can be solved only by taking other characteristics of the phenomena into account. (Pareto 1909; 1971, p. 269)

In this context Pareto does not provide a systematic discussion of what these other characteristics of social systems really were. But at various points both in the *Manual* and in his other works we find passages that show him to have a clear understanding of the fact that real life markets had several imperfections that were assumed away in the idealized world of the competitive model. He was also aware of the problems that would arise in a socialist economy, in particular the weakening of incentives that would result when the individual's income was allowed to become independent of his own effort. Moreover, he stressed the need for looking at the interconnections between economic and political institutions, arguing that the two systems involved different political incentives that in both cases would be of major importance for the determination of the equilibrium of the economy.

Pareto's Law of Income Distribution

Pareto also took a strong interest in applied economics and empirical research. Among his achievements in these areas, there is one contribution for which he is particularly remembered. This is his hypothesis about the distribution of income, which was founded on empirical regularities rather than theoretical considerations and which he presented in his book *Cours d'économie politique*.

The classical economists had chiefly been concerned about the *functional* distribution of income, that is, the distribution of income between the social classes—landowners, capitalists, and workers—who owned the main categories of the factors of production. Pareto, on the other hand, studied the *personal* distribution of income between the individuals in society, independent of the factor markets from which their incomes were derived. On the basis of statistical data from many countries, Pareto believed that one could establish the following generalization: let us draw up a list of all incomes in society from the lowest to the highest. We first focus on the income that is exactly in the middle of the list and which is defined as the median income. By definition, 50 percent of the incomes are higher and 50 percent are lower than the median income. We now move up to the level of income which is 1 percent higher than the median income. It is obvious that the number of individuals who have an income above this level is less than for the median income—but how much less? Pareto found that his data showed that the answer was 1.5 percent and that this number was constant, whatever level of income one started from. So when income goes up by 1 percent the number of income earners who have at least this income falls by 1.5 percent. Mathematically, the general form of this relationship can be represented by the equation

$$logN = logA - a \cdot logy.$$

Here N is the number of persons that have an income which is greater than or equal to y, A is a constant representing the size of the population, and a is the constant that Pareto believed to be equal to 1.5. This distribution has the interesting property that the average income of those whose income is greater than y, always is equal to $a/(a-1)$ times y. With $a=1.5$, the average income of those who, for instance, have an income above 100,000, will accordingly be 300,000. In many cases this function has turned out to be a good approximation to actual data for income distribution,[12] but the notion of "Pareto's law" is still misleading; there is no justification for the view that the "law" provides a universally valid description of the distribution of income. The "law" led to an increased interest in the study of income distribution, but it was also controversial. First of all, critics pointed out that it had no foundation in economic theory, since it was not derived from an analysis of the functioning of factor markets. Second, it was argued that the law could be used to support a socially reactionary viewpoint by which the distribution of income between rich and poor acquired the status of a natural law.[13] But even if one does not interpret the relationship as a law in the strict empirical sense—and even Pareto himself warned against this interpretation—there is no doubt that his work in this area became of great importance for later research on distributional issues.

Today Pareto is above all remembered for his innovations in demand theory and welfare economics, but in a broad view of his place in the history of economic thought one should also include his general efforts to promote more rigorous use of mathematical methods in economics as well as his repeated reminders that economics is only one of the social sciences and that a broader approach is needed for a deeper understanding of the social system.

[12] With the modification that it describes the upper part of the income distribution significantly better than the lower part.

[13] Both of these points are, e.g., contained in the strong criticism by Pigou (1920: 1952, pp. 647–55).

ARTHUR C. PIGOU

Arthur Cecil Pigou (1877–1959) was educated first at Harrow, one of the most famous public schools in England, and then at Cambridge University. In Cambridge he first studied history and literature, but after he had attended lectures by Alfred Marshall his interests began to turn in the direction of economics. Marshall had managed to establish economics as a central university discipline in Cambridge, and in 1904 Pigou began to lecture on the subject. In 1908 he succeeded Marshall as the only professor of economics at the university, a chair that he occupied until his retirement in 1943.

Pigou was a prolific writer: he wrote more than twenty books and a large number of articles, and his research spanned an impressive series of different topics. His general approach to economics was strongly influenced by Marshall, and in much of his work he continued the tradition from his old teacher. He has often been quoted as saying, when students or others brought up some theoretical problem, that "it is all in Marshall"; according to him, the answer could always be found by sufficiently careful study of the *Principles of Economics*. This is an indication both of scientific conservatism and a certain English provincialism, and it seems to be the case that Pigou did not keep in touch with the theoretical developments that took place in other countries. Since he was one of the pioneers of modern welfare economics one might expect that in his main book in the area, *Economics of Welfare* (1920), he had referred to the work of Pareto. However, the few references that can be found concern—apart from Pareto's law of income distribution, which gets a chapter of its own—rather peripheral topics like the treatment of medical services in estimates of national income and the competition between different types of shops in retail trade.

But it is easy to underestimate Pigou. Within the Marshallian partial equilibrium framework he contributed a number of extensions and applications of the theory that showed more convincingly than Marshall had done how it could be used to analyze important problems of economic policy. His general approach to welfare economics and economic policy was in some sense much simpler than that of Pareto. At the same time, however, the contrast between the two is interesting and informative when one studies the history of this particular field of economic theory.

Pigou's career was to some extent interrupted by the First World War when he served as an ambulance driver at the front in France. His experiences there are said to have changed his personality from being lively and outgoing to become reserved and shy. But it had no visible effects on his productivity. In fact, he made some of his most original contributions during the later part of his life, and from being in his early years practical and applied he also—somewhat unusually—became gradually more theoretical and abstract.

Utilitarianism and Material Welfare

It has been argued by several writers that Pareto's innovations in utility theory and welfare economics were unknown in the English-speaking world until the 1930s. This cannot be quite right, for as we have seen Pigou did in fact refer to Pareto's *Manual*—it is only that he showed no interest in the theoretical parts of the book. In contrast to Pareto, Pigou felt no urge to immerse himself in the foundations of utility theory, and he definitely did not share Pareto's view that interpersonal comparisons of utility lacked scientific foundations. Pigou was a convinced utilitarian who thought it was obvious that redistribution in favor of low income groups would increase the sum of utility in society:

> It is evident that any transference of income from a relatively rich man to a relatively poor man of similar temperament, since it enables more intense wants to be satisfied at the expense of less intense wants, must increase the aggregate sum of satisfaction. The old law of "diminishing [marginal] utility" thus leads securely to the proposition: Any cause which increases the absolute share of real income in the hands of the poor, provided that it does not lead to a contraction in the size of the national dividend from any point of view, will, in general, increase economic welfare. (Pigou 1920; 1952, p. 89)

The contrast to Pareto's analysis could not have been greater. According to Pareto's line of thinking, utility is ordinal, which implies that the hypothesis of decreasing marginal utility has no meaning; Pigou, on the other hand refers to this hypothesis as

257

a "law." Pareto maintained that it was meaningless to compare the utility of different individuals, while Pigou argues that such a comparison leads to "evident" results. But we see also that he makes an important reservation about the social benefits of the redistribution of income: a transfer of income between the rich and the poor could conceivably reduce the total income of society and thereby weaken the economic basis for redistribution. What Pigou had in mind was, for instance, that high marginal rates of income tax might reduce work effort, so that a trade-off must be made between the concerns for economic efficiency and distributive justice.[14]

How are we to evaluate Pigou's—as well as Edgeworth's—employment of utility theory to argue in favor of an egalitarian society? Gradually, as Pareto's concept of ordinal utility became more generally known, especially in the 1930s, many became convinced that normative arguments of this kind were simply subjective and unscientific. Within the ordinal theory of utility the law of decreasing marginal utility lost its meaning, and even if there was no simple connection between ordinality and cardinality on the one hand and noncomparability and comparability on the other, it seemed clear that when utility became reduced to being only ordinally measurable, it could certainly not be comparable between individuals. A strong attack on Pigou's utilitarian approach was contained in a book by Lionel Robbins, *An Essay on the Nature and Significance of Economic Science* (1932), which became very influential for the development of welfare economics during the coming decades.

However, it is far from obvious that one ought to take such a negative view of Pigou's approach. What Pareto had shown was that the utilitarian concept of utility—cardinally measurable and comparable between individuals—was unnecessary for a logically consistent theory of consumer demand. It does not follow from this that measurable and comparable utility could not be a useful tool of analysis for problems like poverty and inequality.

[14] This trade-off became a main theme in normative public economics in the later part of the twentieth century, and it plays a central role in the theory of justice of the American philosopher John Rawls (1972).

This controversy about the use of the concept of utility in welfare economics can be regarded as based on methodological differences.[15] There is actually no contradiction between utility as used by Pareto and by Pigou; at least, there is no reason to read them in that light. They developed two different concepts that were intended to be used for different purposes. Pareto's main interest lay in a concept that—under a minimum of restrictive assumptions—could serve as a basis for the theory of consumer demand. Once having arrived at his minimalist definition he was interested in studying its implications for the optimality properties of competitive markets. Pigou, on the other hand, was interested in utility in the sense that the concept had been used by the older utilitarian philosophers and which he used to denote material standard of living. The law of decreasing marginal utility is therefore not primarily related to the shape of indifference curves but to a proposition about the relationship between income and the standard of living, which Pigou believed could be empirically justified. According to this interpretation the law implies that as income increases it becomes gradually less efficient in its ability to "produce" standard of living.

Efficiency and Market Failure

In the *Economics of Welfare* Pigou introduces a distinction between what he calls the social and private marginal net product. The marginal net product refers to the value of an extra unit of resources—such as labor or capital—that is made available for production. This is a rather complex notion, and Pigou (1920; 1952, p. 132) explains carefully how we ought to think about it. We should imagine that resources initially are used in a rational or efficient manner: in Pigou's words, that the economy is "appropriately organised." We should further imagine a small increase in resource input, which is used in such a way that after the increase the economy is also "appropriately organised." The net product is the increase in the total value of production that follows from the resource increase. A rational use of society's resources implies that for each resource—every factor of produc-

[15] Cooter and Rappoport (1984) argue convincingly in favor of this view.

tion—its marginal net product should be the same in all uses. This is a criterion of economic efficiency, and Pigou emphasizes that the desirability of efficiency must be considered together with the issue of income distribution. An increase of the national product, he says, is a good thing, at least as long as the increase does not involve a worse situation for the poor.

If all the costs and benefits that follow from such an increase of resource use are taken into account by firms and consumers, private and social marginal net products are the same. In this case, therefore, the market mechanism operates efficiently and there is no need for public intervention to improve it. But in many cases there are deviations between the two measures, and these can go both ways. If in some industry there is a monopoly, the market equilibrium will involve a marginal willingness to pay on the part of consumers that is higher than marginal cost. There is therefore a social gain involved in the increase of production; the social marginal net product is higher than the private one. If a subsidy were to be applied either to production or consumption it would increase the resource use in this market and contribute to an increase of the national product. An example that tends in the opposite direction is that of production activities that cause environmental pollution. These impose costs on consumers that are not charged to the firms that cause the pollution. In this case, too much is produced so that resource use can be improved by imposing a tax on the producers corresponding to the additional costs that they inflict on society. To the firms the tax is like an increase in private costs, and it therefore induces them to act as if they took the environmental pollution into account. This proposal to use taxation as an instrument of environmental policy is perhaps Pigou's best-known contribution to economics, and in his honor they are often referred to as Pigouvian taxes.

Pigou's distinction between social and private marginal net product was based on a minimum of formalized theory, but in his many applications he showed that it was very useful for the analysis of practical problems of economic policy. Pareto had shown that the competitive equilibrium under certain assumptions led to an efficient use of resources. Pigou's analysis yielded the same conclusion, while the strength of his approach was his ability to analyze deviations from the assumption of perfect competition and demonstrate which kind of public intervention was best suited to restore efficiency. While Pareto laid the foundations for theoretical welfare economics, Pigou showed how it could be used to derive guidelines for economic policy.

Public Economics

The Economics of Welfare was to a large extent a book about the justification for political interventions in economic life, but it did not provide a systematic discussion of the instruments of economic policy. This was done in another of Pigou's most important books, *A Study in Public Finance* (1928; 1947). This is a pioneering effort within public economics and contains a number of ideas that were to become central issues in the later development of this area.

The book contains analyses both of public expenditure and taxation. With regard to expenditure Pigou emphasizes the general principle that the social gain from a marginal increase in resource use should be the same everywhere. This principle ensures an efficient balance between resource use in the private and public sectors and also between resources used in different parts of the public sector. He illustrates the last point by the following tongue-in-cheek example:

> Expenditure should be distributed between battleships and Poor Relief in such wise that the last shilling devoted to each of them yields the same return of satisfaction. (Pigou 1928; 1947, p. 31)

This is obviously an extremely general principle, and Pigou does not offer much in the form of practical guidelines for its use. Nevertheless, it is not a trivial statement. It leads the reader to think about public expenditure in a way that focuses on the best use of society's resources and the optimal distribution of tax revenue among the various branches of government.

Imagine now that the public sector has to finance an increase of expenditure by taxes that are socially harmful in that they reduce the efficiency with which the market economy operates. Then one has to think differently about the balance between the public and private sectors, for the efficiency loss of the tax increase has to be counted as part of the cost of public expenditure. In addition to the direct resource cost associated with the use of labor, capital, and other factors of production comes the indirect tax cost, which will act as a brake on the use of resources in the public sector. In the recent literature this tax cost is known as the marginal cost of public funds, or *MCF*.[16] Let *MB* be the marginal benefit of public expenditure and *MC* its resource cost. If taxes had no adverse effects, optimal public expenditure should be characterized by the condition *MB=MC*. But with harmful or distortionary taxation this rule would have to be rewritten as *MB=MCF x MC*, where *MCF* is the marginal cost of public funds. According to Pigou's line of thought, it should be the case that *MCF>1*, and most empirical studies of this issue do indeed confirm the result.

Another of Pigou's important contributions to public economics is the idea of *the optimal tax system.* Disregarding the special case of environmental taxes, all feasible taxes involve harmful effects for the economy. In Pigou's terminology, they lead to differences between the social and private net marginal product; taxes have incentive effects on labor supply, consumption, and saving that are costly to society.[17] In spite of this, taxes are needed to finance public expenditure. This raises the following question: if all taxes cause damage to the economy, how should the tax system be designed in order to make this damage as small as possible?[18] Pigou's attempts to throw light on this question were both direct and indirect. The first thing he did was to set out a clear formulation of the problem. Next, he presented the problem to the young philosopher and economist Frank Ramsey and encouraged him to analyze it by means of a mathematical model. This Ramsey did in a famous article (Ramsey 1927), which today is regarded as an important forerunner of the modern theory of optimal taxation.[19] Ramsey showed that in order to make the total damage, or

---

[16] The first modern analysis of this problem is the article by A. B. Atkinson and N. Stern (1974).

[17] Pigou used the term *announcement effects* for what we today would refer to as incentive effects.

[18] We may recall Ricardo's statement that taxation is a choice between evils.

[19] Frank Ramsey (1903–30) was primarily a philosopher, but he also wrote two very important articles on economic topics. The second article analyzed the problem of "optimal saving": How much of its national income is it rational for a country to save (Ramsey 1928)? While the taxation article was inspired by Pigou, the article on saving benefited from suggestions by Keynes. Both articles use relatively advanced mathematical methods, and it was not until the 1970s that they began to leave their marks on the research in their respective fields.

the efficiency loss, from taxation as low as possible, the percentage reduction in consumption (and production) ought to be the same for all goods. This result can be achieved by imposing the highest taxes on goods that are inelastic in demand or supply. In the later editions of *A Study in Public Finance* Pigou showed in an insightful way how a simplified version of Ramsey's results could be derived from partial equilibrium analysis.

Unemployment and Public Policy

The causes of unemployment and the question of what should be done to secure full employment were issues that concerned Pigou throughout his career. He wrote several books in this area, the most famous of which is *Theory of Unemployment*, which was published in 1933. Perhaps the main cause of its fame is the use that Keynes made of it in his *General Theory* (1936), where he took the book and its author as representative of what he called the classical view of unemployment. This view Pigou had expressed as follows:

> With perfectly free competition among workpeople and labour perfectly mobile, the nature of the relation will be very simple. There will always be at work a strong tendency for wage-rates to be so related to demand that everybody is employed. Hence, in stable conditions every one will actually be employed. The implication is that such unemployment as exists at any time is due wholly to the fact that changes in demand conditions are continually taking place and that frictional resistances prevent the appropriate wage adjustments from being made instantaneously. (Pigou 1933, p. 252)

According to this view, therefore, the fundamental causes of unemployment are to be found in imperfections of the market mechanism, particularly in the market for labor, that delay the adjustment of supply and demand. Keynes's view, on the other hand, was that unemployment was an equilibrium phenomenon, and he severely criticized Pigou's views (see chapter 15 below). However, Pigou felt that Keynes's presentation both of his theoretical analysis and his policy views were simplified and unfair and in turn strongly criticized Keynes's theories. Later on he modified his views, and in *Employment and Equilibrium* (1941;

1949) and elsewhere he went far toward accepting, at least for the short run, the possibility of equilibrium with unemployment. The controversy with Keynes had as a consequence that Pigou's reputation during the 1950s and 1960s very undeservedly was determined by his initially skeptical attitude to Keynes's analysis. But later economists have had a higher appreciation both of Pigou's macroeconomic theories and—not least—of his important work in welfare economics and public finance.

Why Study Economics?

Pigou's standing in the history of economics does not rest—as in the cases of Edgeworth and Pareto—on his contributions to pure economic theory but on his uses of the theory to illuminate social issues. His strength lay in the identification of important problems and the adaptation of existing theory to illuminate the need for economic policy and institutional reform. An interesting expression of his scientific convictions can be found in the preface to the third edition of *The Economics of Welfare*, where Pigou addresses some words to "the beginning student of economics" that make clear what he sees as the true purpose of economics:

> The complicated analyses which economists endeavour to carry through are not mere gymnastic. They are instruments for the bettering of human life. The misery and squalor that surround us, the injurious luxury of some wealthy families, the terrible uncertainty overshadowing many families of the poor—these are evils too plain to be ignored. By the knowledge that our science seeks it is possible that they may be restrained. Out of the darkness light! To search for it is the task, to find it perhaps the prize, which the "dismal science of Political Economy" offers to those who face its discipline. (Pigou 1920; 1952, p. vii)

To modern readers, this forceful expression of emotional and moral views may seem old-fashioned. But it is important to realize that Pigou does not imply that it is moral indignation that should guide economic analysis. It is natural to interpret him as saying that scientific priorities should be determined by what one conceives as being important social problems. But at the same time he makes it clear that the economist cannot do any good for society by disregarding the scientific standards of the subject. In this respect he was in line with Marshall, who said that economists should have cool heads but warm hearts.

FURTHER READING

Edgeworth's style of writing does not make for easy reading, but a good place to begin is a recent one-volume selection (Edgeworth 2003) that contains his two most important books and a number of articles and book reviews. The editor, Peter Newman, has written an excellent introductory essay on Edgeworth's life and his place in the history of thought; this is identical to his article in *The New Palgrave*. Keynes (1933) paints a lively picture of Edgeworth as a person but does not go into any detail concerning his contributions to economic theory.

Pareto's *Manuel* has been translated into English as *Manual of Political Economy* (1971). Even if one does not read the whole book it is interesting to browse it to form an impression of Pareto as a scientist and writer. Formal derivations of theoretical relationships are interspersed with passages on classical and modern literature and sharply formulated comments on current political and economic affairs. Jaffé's (1972) extremely critical review of the English translation and the translator's response to it (Schwier and Schwier 1974) raise interesting questions about the presentation of classical texts for modern readers. Thus, Jaffé criticizes the translator for the lack of explanatory notes, while Schwier defends herself by arguing that Pareto's original text ought to be easily accessible to the modern reader. There is little doubt that the common view is that the translation does not hold the same standard as Jaffé's own translation of Walras (a view clearly shared by Jaffé). An article by Chipman (1976) provides an extensive survey of Pareto's contributions to mathematical economics and relates them to modern research. In *The New Palgrave* there are two good articles about him: Giovani Busino writes about his life and surveys his literary output, while Alan Kirman describes Pareto's contributions to economic theory.

Of Pigou's books, both the *Economics of Welfare* and *A Study in Public Finance* are still very well worth reading. For specialists in public finance the latter is particularly interesting in showing how many of the modern developments in the area were actually anticipated by Pigou. Jan de V. Graaf has a well-written article about him in *The New Palgrave*, but otherwise the biographical literature is modest. However, Graaf refers to several obituaries, including one published in the *Alpine Journal* that celebrates Pigou's achievements as a mountain climber.

Interest and Prices:
Knut Wicksell and Irving Fisher

I N THEIR EFFORTS to understand the workings of the market mechanism, the early marginalist economists focused primarily on the markets for consumption goods. Some qualifications of this statement are obviously in order: we have seen that Alfred Marshall emphasized the distinction between price formation in the short and the long run, so that in a sense he had developed an analysis of how capital investment depended on changes in the demand for consumption goods. However, he did not have a more formal theory of capital, investment, and the rate of interest. Walras developed the elements of a general equilibrium theory for a growing economy, which also contained a theory of capital accumulation, but this is not the part of his work that has had the greatest influence on later theorists. Another characteristic of the early marginalist period was the focus on relative prices, with less attention being paid to the determination of the general price level and the rate of inflation or deflation. To the later generation of marginalists, who did their most important work at the end of the nineteenth and the beginning of the twentieth century, these issues became of greater interest, and the Swedish economist Knut Wicksell and the American Irving Fisher gave important contributions to the theory as we know it today. But their work in the fields of capital and money is only part of the reason why they are remembered in the history of thought. They also contributed to the more general development of what gradually became known as the neoclassical theory, and they did important work in the theory of public finance. In addition, they both took an active part in the economic and social debate in their respective countries, where they acquired a visibility in public life that was very different from that of economists like Marshall and Walras who led the quiet life of the scholar.

CHAPTER 12

Knut Wicksell

Knut Wicksell (1851–1926) was born in Stockholm where his father ran a grocery store. He attended the gymnasium (secondary school) in Stockholm, and in 1869 he was enrolled at the University of Uppsala with the aim, according to Gårdlund (1956; 1958), of becoming a doctor of philosophy and eventually professor of mathematics. During his first years at Uppsala he was a hardworking student who made good progress. By January 1872 he had obtained the degree of fil.kand.—corresponding roughly to a B.A.—and continued his studies toward a licentiate degree in mathematics.[1] All seemed set for a promising academic career.

At this time, however, things happened to Wicksell that gradually made him think along very different lines. He abandoned his Christian faith which until that time had been one of the mainstays of his existence. At the same time he began to lead a more active social life and take a stronger interest in social and political questions. One of the results of his new outlook on life was a lecture that he gave in February 1880 on the temperance movement where he surveyed the causes of drunkenness; these he found to be poverty, hunger, poor housing, and prostitution. In Wicksell's opinion, the most important remedy for poverty and social distress was birth control. In this analysis he was indirectly influenced by the thought of Malthus via the so-called Neo-Malthusian movement which was very influential in the public debate at the time. He advanced the view that doctors ought to help people with advice about prevention of pregnancy, since this would lead to a reduction in the number of children and raise the standard of living among the poorest families. At this point, he was not in agreement with Malthus, who had classified prevention as sin (see chapter 4).

This clear talk about issues like prostitution and prevention created a great stir in Swedish society, and in many circles it caused Wicksell to be regarded as a dangerous radical who attempted to undermine the basic institutions of established society. It also led to further detraction from his academic studies. For many years he lived as a freelance journalist and lecturer, and he did not obtain his licentiate degree in mathematics until

[1] The licentiate degree marked a step on the road toward a doctorate.

1885, at which time he had long been regarded as an "eternal student." Having passed his examinations he obtained a scholarship for further studies, and it was during a stay in London that he began to study economics in earnest. His social concerns had awakened in him a desire to view the economic problems of society in a wider and more theoretical perspective. Malthus's ideas he knew already, but he now broadened his knowledge by reading Smith and Ricardo, Cournot and Mill, Jevons and Walras. He was attracted by the theoretical approach of the marginalists, although he remained skeptical of those who thought that the unregulated market economy was in the best interest of society. Wicksell also took a long sojourn in Germany, where he made the acquaintance of many of the leading German economists of the time.

On his return to Sweden in 1889 he applied for permission to give lectures in economics at the institution known as Stockholms Högskola—the forerunner of Stockholm University—but the application was turned down. The background for this decision was that the school felt that its relationship to the government authorities could be endangered if it supported someone with Wicksell's convictions. Instead he gave his lectures to the Stockholm working men's association under the title "Value, Capital, and Rent According to Modern Economic Theories." To begin with, the lectures attracted a large audience—perhaps they expected a new scandal—but it diminished as the lectures went on. His lecture notes later grew into his first major book, *Über Wert, Kapital und Rente* (*Value, Capital, and Rent*), which was published in 1893.[2]

1889 was also in other respects a memorable year in Wicksell's life. He met a Norwegian woman, Anna Bugge, who became his lifelong companion although they never married. His radicalism had led him, as a matter of principle, to a rejection of the institution of marriage, and Wicksell was a firm adherent to the view

---

[2] It is of interest to note that Wicksell, whose native language was Swedish, published his most important scientific work in German, not English, which was also a language that he mastered well. One reason for this appears to have been that his first book was strongly inspired by Böhm-Bawerk's capital theory, which made it natural to write in German. But another important and more general reason was that in Wicksell's time both Swedish and other Nordic academics had much closer intellectual contacts with the German universities than with those of the English-speaking world.

that one's convictions ought to guide one's personal life. He became a controversial person in the public life of Sweden, and his tendency to issue provocative statements led to a number of disputes and controversies throughout his life.[3] But the decade of the 1890s was also his most productive scientific period. He obtained his doctorate at Uppsala University in 1895 on the basis of a dissertation on the economics of taxation that was later turned into the book *Finanztheoretische Untersuchungen* (Investigations in Fiscal Theory, 1896). His third major theoretical treatise, *Geldzins und Güterpreise* (*Interest and Prices*), was published in 1898. His last book was *Föreläsningar i nationalekonomi* (*Lectures on Political Economy*), which came out in two volumes in 1901 and 1906. After his retirement he remained active and continued to publish academic articles until the time of his death.

Wicksell's attempts to build an academic career met with a number of difficulties. Having obtained his doctorate, he applied for several university positions in economics, but his applications were turned down on formal grounds. Economics was part of the faculty of law, but as Wicksell did not have a law degree the university regulations did not allow him to be appointed to a professorship in this faculty. When he was at the end of his forties he therefore began to study law and obtained his degree after three terms of study. This removed the formal obstacles to his university career, and in 1899 he was appointed to the chair of economics at Lund University.

Wicksell exerted a great influence on Swedish economists. It was perhaps not so strong during his time in Lund, where he was mostly occupied with undergraduate teaching, but when after his retirement in 1916 he moved to Stockholm he was in close contact with the younger generation of Swedish econo-

---

[3] Here is a couple of examples: In a talk that he gave in 1892 he argued that the economic resources used on Swedish defense was a complete waste, since the country would in any case not be able to withstand an attack from one of the great powers; at the time it was Russia that was thought to be a threat to Swedish independence. Wicksell proposed that the resources used on defense should rather be used on social spending, and that Sweden ought to seek military protection as part of the Russian Empire, where the country would function as a civilizing force. In 1908 he was sentenced to two months' imprisonment for blasphemy, following a lecture where he had ridiculed the relationship between the Virgin Mary and the Holy Spirit.

mists. Among them were Bertil Ohlin, Gunnar Myrdal, and Erik Lindahl, who were central participants in what was to become known as the Stockholm School in macroeconomic theory, and who also made other important contributions in many different areas of economics.

Production and Distribution

The intellectual basis for Wicksell's interest in economics was the issue of population growth and the social problems that he considered to be directly related to it. It was therefore natural for him to emphasize the central place that the population problem ought to occupy in the science of economics. Thus in the first volume of his *Lectures* he writes:

> In actual fact, it is impossible to consider economic problems profitably, whether they are of a practical or theoretical kind, unless we constantly keep population and its changes in view. (Wicksell 1901; 1934, p. 6)

This is clearly an overstatement, and in Wicksell's writings there are many examples of analyses that have no special connection with the problem of population. The quotation should therefore be interpreted as a testimony to Wicksell's deep concern about the problem rather than a statement of research priorities. As a matter of fact, Wicksell's standing in the history of economic thought bears little relationship to his work on population.

One of the key features of the breakthrough of marginalism was the increased interest in the study of consumption demand in contrast to the classical economists' focus on the costs of production as determinants of prices. With the work of Gossen and the later marginalists the analysis of demand was derived from the theory of utility maximization. Gradually, there also emerged a theory of producers as profit maximizing agents, but this part of the theory lagged behind that of the consumer. One of Wicksell's major contributions was to generalize and develop the theory of production and firm behavior, and this also led him to the study of the pricing of the factors of production and the distribution of income in a market economy.

Wicksell's innovations in the theory of production and distribution were first presented in *Value, Capital, and Rent*, and it was

CHAPTER 12

further elaborated in his later work, both in articles and in volume 1 of his *Lectures*. He was among the first to formulate the concept that we now know as the production function: the mathematical representation of the connection between the volume of output and the input of factors of production. Wicksell assumed that this relationship was such that a small decrease in the input of one factor of production could always be compensated by a small increase in the input of another factor so as to hold production constant; in more technical language, he assumed that there was continuous substitution between the factors of production. Taking this as his point of departure, he showed that profit maximization under perfect competition, where the firm takes both commodity and factor prices as given in the market, would imply that the value of the marginal productivity of each factor of production is equal to its price. The assumption of continuous substitution implies that the firm's demand for factors of production will change with even small changes in factor prices, and this perspective on production decisions became established as an important characteristic of marginalist theory. Because both Wicksell and other representatives of this approach emphasized its connection with the economic theory of the classical economists, it became common to refer to the theoretical framework that was worked out around the turn of the nineteenth century as *neoclassical economics*. This framework continues to form the basis of much of modern economic theory.

The condition that the value of the marginal productivity at the optimum of the firm must be equal to the price of the factor of production was also interpreted as a hypothesis about the determinants of factor prices. In particular, it can be read as saying that wage rates for different types of labor are determined by their respective marginal productivities, and in this interpretation it became known as the marginal productivity theory of income distribution. However, it is not a complete theory. The condition can be used to show how firms' demand for labor depends on commodity prices, wages, and the prices of other factors of production, but in order to arrive at a complete theory of wage formation we must also have a theory of the supply of labor—and more generally of the supply of factors of production. As regards the supply side, Wicksell's analysis was less systematic, but there is little doubt that he was aware of the limitations of the

272

marginal productivity theory. Thus, in his *Lectures* he discusses how technical progress must be assumed to increase the marginal productivity of labor and therefore tend to raise wages. However, he believed that it was doubtful whether there really had been a significant increase in wages over the last two hundred years, and the main reason for this was the growth of population:

> Such an increase [in population] must, other things being equal, continually reduce the marginal productivity of labour and force down wages; or—what comes to the same thing, though the connection is easily overlooked on a superficial view—*prevent* the otherwise inevitable *rise* in wages due to technical progress. (Wicksell 1901; 1934, p. 143)

This argument shows a clear understanding of the interaction between demand and supply in the determination of wages and income distribution. The increase in the marginal productivity of the laborers has led to an increase in the demand for labor, but this has wholly or partly been offset by an increase of labor supply.

Nevertheless, there is no doubt that marginal productivity theory is a central element in the theory of income distribution. Once wages have been determined, the firms' supply of commodities and demand for labor will determine the share of the total value of output in society that will accrue to the various categories of labor and other owners of factors of production such as capital and land. An interesting question is now whether the sum of these shares will be equal to one. In other words, will the total income of factor owners be equal to the value of output, or will some of the value remain in the form of pure profits? The latter alternative is not a very attractive one in the theory of income distribution, for even pure profits must in the final instance be due to some factor of production that should therefore be included in a theory of price formation for the factors of production.

Wicksell pointed out that the sum of factor shares would be equal to one on the assumption that there were constant returns to scale,[4] such that, for example, a doubling of all inputs leads to

---

[4] With constant returns to scale, the production function must in mathematical terms be a linear homogeneous function. Wicksell (1901; 1934, p. 128) takes as an example ("among the infinite number") of such functions $P=a^\alpha b^\beta$, where

a doubling of output.[5] In this case the average cost will be constant, and then marginal cost will have to be constant also. But if this is the case there is no well-defined optimum for the individual firm; optimal output is either zero, infinite, or indeterminate according to whether the market price of the product is less than, greater than, or equal to the marginal cost. This raises the question of how one can reconcile the requirements for a logical theory of income distribution with the theory of profit maximization at the level of the individual firm.

Wicksell presented an elegant solution to this problem. He assumed that the average cost curve of the individual firm was U-shaped, first decreasing and then increasing. Along the falling part of the curve there will be increasing returns to scale, while along the rising part returns to scale will be decreasing. At the minimum of this curve the average cost is at its lowest level, and *at this point* there are constant returns to scale. But this point is also the one to which competition will force firms to produce, for as long as the price is higher than the minimum of average cost, there will exist pure profits that will encourage new firms to enter the market, causing the price to fall. Therefore, for the industry as a whole, assuming that it consists of firms with identical cost structures, there will in the long run be constant returns to scale, even if the individual firms have U-shaped cost curves.

The equality between wage and marginal productivity is an important element in the theory of wages in a competitive economy. But to *explain* wage formation and income distribution is obviously not the same as *defending* it as a principle of just distribution of resources in society, and Wicksell never used the mar-

---

P is the volume of production, a and b are the inputs of two factors of production, and α and β are positive constants so that $\alpha+\beta=1$. This is the well-known Cobb-Douglas function, named after two Americans who used it as the basis for an empirical study of productivity as late as 1928. Its name may therefore be considered a historical injustice, but it should be kept in mind that volume 1 of Wicksell's *Lectures* was not translated into English until 1934.

[5] This had also been shown by the English economist Philip Wicksteed (1844–1927), who pointed out that the conclusion could be derived from the mathematical result known as Euler's theorem for homogeneous functions. Stigler (1941; 1994, chapters 3 and 12) surveys Wicksteed's work as well as the discussion between some of the leading economists of the time about the relevance of Euler's theorem in this context.

ginal productivity theory as an ethical justification for the market determination of income distribution. However, the American economist John Bates Clark (1847–1938) actually argued in favor of this view. His contention was that a just distribution of income ought to give to each the fruits of his own labor, and wages that reflect marginal productivity were, he argued, consistent with this principle. Whatever one may think about the ethical premise of Clark's argument, it has some obviously weak points in terms of economics. One problematic aspect is that a person's marginal productivity depends not only on his own labor but also on that of others and on the input of nonhuman factors of production. Does he have the right to the fruits of these inputs as well? In the history of thought, what Clark achieved in terms of original contributions to economic theory has tended to be overshadowed by this confusion of descriptive and normative analysis. He also became a target for those critics of economics who were convinced that economic theory was simply an apology for the institutions of the market economy and the existing distribution of income. These critics would have been led to think differently if they had read Wicksell instead of Clark.

Capital and Interest

When during his visits abroad in the 1880s Wicksell began his systematic studies of economic theory, Böhm-Bawerk's work on capital theory (see chapter 8) made a strong impression on him. However, he was no uncritical admirer of the Austrian economist. He was convinced that the problems that Böhm-Bawerk raised could only be satisfactorily solved by a mathematical approach to the theory. More particularly, he was critical to Böhm-Bawerk's attempts to measure the capital stock of society by calculating the average period of production. Wicksell worked out an alternative theory of capital and investment that laid a more solid foundation for an assessment of the aggregate capital stock of the economy.

In volume 1 of his *Lectures* Wicksell presented the essence of this theory in the form of an example concerning the storage of wine. We are asked to imagine a vineyard where the grapes have just been harvested; through storage a barrel of grape juice will gradually develop into wine. The quality of the wine and therefore its price will increase with storage, at least until a certain point in time. The store of wine is accordingly the capital of the vineyard. Let us for the sake of the argument suppose that the owner of the vineyard has financed the cost of the barrel of juice (the purchase of the barrel, the wages of the harvesters etc.) by borrowing the necessary amount of money at a given rate of interest, r. The present value of a barrel of wine that has been stored for T years is the value of the wine at time T, discounted to the present by r. The question now is: How long is the optimum storage time? In other words, what is the most profitable time to sell the wine? Suppose that the percentage rate of price increase is largest in the beginning of the storage period and that it gradually declines. Wicksell showed that the optimal sales time occurs when the percentage increase in value equals the rate of interest. The economic intuition behind this result is obvious: the percentage rate of price increase is the rate of return associated with an extension of the storage process, while the rate of interest represents the cost. The equality between the two can be interpreted as a special case of the equality between the marginal productivity and the factor price.[6] The higher is the rate of interest, the shorter is the period of storage, and the lower is the price of the wine supplied to the market.

The total stock of real capital is the amount of wine that is tied up in the production process. Because the storage time of the wine is determined by the rate of interest, the value of the capital stock also depends on the interest rate: the lower is the rate of interest, the higher is the value of the capital stock.

As a theory of capital and interest, the theory is incomplete. It explains the accumulation of capital in the individual firm— assuming that we may take the wine-growing example as representative of the more general case—but the rate of interest is taken as given outside the model. Wicksell extended the analysis by assuming that the supply of capital for society as a whole was constant. Then the rate of interest will be determined by the con-

---

[6] The assumption of loan finance is not important for this line of reasoning, since the rate of interest in any case represents the alternative cost of the wine grower. At any point in the production process he will have the option of selling the wine and using the proceeds to buy an interest-bearing asset such as a bank deposit.

dition that in equilibrium the demand for capital must be equal to its supply; if demand is greater than supply the interest rate will go up. But the assumption of a given capital stock is a rather special one. In order to explain the size of the stock we have to consider the supply of capital, and this makes it necessary to work out a theory of saving.[7] To do this was one of the main contributions of Irving Fisher, as we shall see below.

Macroeconomic Theories

Wicksell's analysis of the theories of production, income distribution, and capital formation is closely associated with the core of the marginalist theories that emerged at the end of the nineteenth century. More than most of his contemporaries, however, he was also interested in issues that we would now classify as macroeconomic. One of these was the problem of the general price level. The most generally accepted theory of the price level, both among the classical and the neoclassical economists, had since the time of David Hume been the quantity theory. According to this theory the price level was determined by the money supply. The quantity theory also contained a theory of inflation. If the velocity of money is constant the percentage change in the price level will be equal to the difference between the rates of growth of money supply and the national product. For a given rate of growth in the real economy the rate of inflation will accordingly be determined by the rate of growth of money supply.

In his *Interest and Prices* Wicksell proposed an alternative theory of the determination of the rate of change of the price level. In this theory the rate of interest is the main determinant of the price level, and the central element in the theory is the distinction between the natural and the market rate of interest. The natural rate is determined by the real rate of return on capital, which is assumed to be independent of monetary relationships. The market rate, on the other hand, is determined by the banking system.

[7] Moreover, the model does not explain the development of the price of wine over time; the nature of the time path is simply assumed. In order to explain this, the model would have to be further extended to include preferences for wine relative to other consumption goods.

If the banks set the market rate equal to the natural rate the price level will be stable and the rate of inflation will be zero. If the market rate of interest is set lower than the natural rate this will induce increased demand for new capital, and this will lead to a positive rate of inflation. This "cumulative process" will continue as long as the market rate is lower than the natural rate of interest. The process will come to a halt if banks increase the market interest rate or—in the long run—if the natural rate falls as a result of a decreasing rate of return on capital.

In *Interest and Prices* Wicksell also discusses the issue of the most favorable rate of inflation for the economy as a whole. He says that there are many who hold the view that the best state of affairs is a slowly increasing price level, because this eases the burden for all those who struggle with a heavy debt that they have incurred because of lack of foresight. However, he points out, if such a low rate of price increase could be predicted with certainty it would be taken into account in all sorts of contractual relationships, and the result would be that it would have no real effects:

> Those people who prefer a continually upward moving to a stationary price level forcibly remind one of those who purposely keep their watches a little fast so as to be more certain of catching their trains. But to achieve their purpose they must not be conscious or remain conscious of the fact that their watches are fast; otherwise they become accustomed to take the few minutes into account and so after all, in spite of their artfulness, arrive too late. (Wicksell 1898; 1936, p. 3)

Wicksell's view was that if it were possible to completely control the development of the price level, the best would be to have a zero rate of inflation, so that changes in relative prices would take place within the framework of a constant price level. His main argument was that the adjustment of contracts to changes in the price level takes time and leads to unintended redistribution of income between groups in society. Price stability would accordingly be in the interest of the great majority of the population, and it ought therefore to be a natural objective of public policy.

His firm belief in price stability as a goal of economic policy led him to lend his support to the politicians who aimed to neutralize the effects of the inflation during the First World War by bringing the price level back to its prewar level through a period of deflation. In newspaper and journal articles Wicksell emphasized the injustice involved in the wartime inflation: persons who before the war had lent money or taken out life insurance to secure the future of their children were forced to realize that their savings had been reduced by more than a half of its original value. This unintended redistribution of wealth ought in his opinion to be reversed, even if the resulting deflation were to lead to new gains and losses that could not be said to be reversals of past injustices. The norm of a stable price level was a central one in his thinking about monetary questions, and it says much about Wicksell's independent and original mind that this "dangerous radical" should put such great weight on the desirability of a stable value of money.

Just Taxation

One part of Wicksell's contribution that in recent decades has received renewed attention is his normative approach to the study of public economics and to the issue of justice in taxation. In his 1896 book *Finanztheoretische Untersuchungen* he took as his point of departure the distinction in the current literature between two approaches to just taxation, known as the benefit principle and the principle of ability to pay. The benefit principle implies that an individual's tax payment ought to reflect his benefits from the provision of public services; taxes were in other words to be considered as payment for services rendered to them by the government. The alternative was to levy taxes on the basis of the taxpayer's ability to pay. Even if this principle was rarely defined in very precise terms it was often interpreted as lending support to the system of progressive income taxation.

Wicksell's main concern was that the public sector should be organized so that expenditure and tax policies were in the citizens' interest. As a basic principle of budgetary policy he maintained that for a public project to be worthwhile its value, as measured by society's aggregate willingness to pay, should be at least as large as its cost. Given that this requirement was satisfied, it ought in principle to be possible to distribute the increased taxes that the project required in such a way that everyone gained from it; each citizen would then feel that his gain from having the project carried out was at least as large as his loss from the increase in taxation. This corresponds to the benefit principle, and Wicksell argued that if one abstracts from distributional concerns, it must be clear that it is the benefit principle which is the fundamental criterion for justice in taxation:

> At this point the distribution of taxes cannot and need not be influenced by any other notions of justice. No-one can complain if he secures a benefit which he himself considers to be (greater or at least) as great as the price he has to pay. But when individuals or groups find or believe they find that for them the marginal utility of a given public service does not equal the marginal utility of the private goods they have to contribute, then these individuals or groups will, without fail, feel overburdened. It will be no consolation to them to be assured that the utility of public services as a whole far exceeds the total value of the individual sacrifices. (Wicksell 1896; 1958, p. 79)

How is it possible to ensure that just taxation in this sense becomes a reality? According to Wicksell, there is only one solution to this problem. The public projects and their tax finance requirements—in the form of a concrete plan for the distribution of the tax burden—must be approved by democratic institutions on the basis of unanimity. The requirement of unanimity will ensure that the government is forced to find a distribution of tax payments that gives everyone a share in society's gain. Therefore, when a project has been approved we can be sure that all citizens have gained a net benefit from it. The relationship with Pareto's optimality criterion is easy to see, and Wicksell's thoughts were further developed by Erik Lindahl (1919) who in a more formalized way showed theoretically how the supply of collective goods could be combined with taxes that reflected the individual benefits from public expenditure.[8]

The requirement of unanimity may seem surprising, coming from someone with Wicksell's radical leanings. Will not such a

---

[8] This book by Erik Lindahl (1891–1960) is today regarded as a classic in the theory of public economics; a modern exposition of it was provided by Leif Johansen (1965).

rule prevent all attempts at redistribution between social classes via the public budgets? It is important to realize that Wicksell explicitly says that the principle does not take distributional issues into account, and the concept of "just taxation" must therefore be seen as having a special and rather narrow meaning. It follows also that the principle cannot be used to decide on projects that have a purely redistributive purpose. But Wicksell's view was also that the implementation of this view would give the Swedish working class a much-needed protection against paying an unreasonably high share of public expenditure.

In a later chapter of the *Finanztheoretische Untersuchungen* Wicksell comes back to the question of justice in taxation. He points out that the Swedish tax system contains a number of provisions that are difficult to justify, such as tax relief for capital gains on fixed property, and argues that these should be eliminated (although he does not say how the reforms should be implemented). In other respects, however, he is reluctant to recommend radical redistribution of income via the tax system, and once more he comes back to the benefit principle as the fundamental rule for justice in taxation:

> The propertied classes undeniably include a significant share of a nation's intelligence and economic initiative, and in many a case their preferred position is due at least in part to their own efforts. These classes should not be forced by the ill-considered claims of a precipitant democracy to assume the whole burden of the community's tax load. But neither should the members of the poorer classes ... be called upon to pay for expenditures of whose utility and necessity they cannot be convinced, perhaps for very valid reasons. (Wicksell 1896; 1958, pp. 117–118)

As regards his views on economic policy in general, Wicksell is not an easy person to categorize. His blatant and partly provocative radicalism went together with ideas that are more naturally associated with conservative attitudes. This may explain why it is that his writings have also appealed to some later economists who have had quite different philosophical and political convictions. This is true, for example, of the American economist James Buchanan, whose work will be discussed in chapter 17 below.

IRVING FISHER

Irving Fisher (1867–1947) is the first great name in American economics. Although his family background was a difficult one—his father died of tuberculosis when Irving was seventeen—he managed to complete his education at Yale University where he started by studying mathematics. But he soon became convinced that the life of a mathematician would be one of too much isolation from social and economic affairs. He therefore decided to take advantage of his mathematical training in the study of economics, and he obtained his doctorate with a dissertation that built on the insights of the new marginalist theories; in this he was inspired particularly by Jevons (1871; 1970) and Auspitz and Lieben (1889). When his dissertation was published, Fisher was immediately recognized as a promising economist of the new analytical school. At about the same time he married a young lady who came from a very rich family. Her father's wedding present to the young couple consisted of a year's stay in Europe in addition to a large house in New Haven; Fisher had obtained a position at Yale, where he was appointed professor of economics in 1898.

Like Wicksell, Fisher became an intellectual celebrity of his time. This was not because of any political radicalism, but because he had strong views on a number of different questions like teetotalism, eugenics,[9] health food,[10] and environmental protection. In these areas he wrote a large number of articles and books (one was called *How to Live*) which, although not of great academic interest, testify to his strong social concerns and his

[9] Fisher shared his positive view of eugenics with many of his contemporaries, including other economists both in the United States and elsewhere. The condescending attitude to what he conceived as inferior groups and races was part of his intellectual arrogance that was displayed in statements like the following: "The world consists of two classes—the educated and the ignorant—and it is essential for progress that the former should be allowed to dominate the latter." Leonard (2005) provides an interesting account of how attitudes like this influenced the stand that many American economists took on issues like immigration policy and the minimum wage.

[10] His concern with questions of health may be explained by his personal history. He was infected by tuberculosis toward the end of the 1890s, and the doctors' prognosis was to begin with very pessimistic, but over a period of six years Fisher managed to achieve a full recovery.

inexhaustible energy. His activities in some of these areas also materialized in a series of more or less original inventions such as a new type of sundial and a thermostat heated hospital bed. He was also an active investor in the stock market both on his own account and as an advisor through a financial column that he published in a number of American newspapers. During the course of the 1920s his successful speculations made him a multimillionaire, but he lost everything after the great crash in 1929. The same fate was suffered by a number of people (including members of his own family) who had followed the advice that he gave in his column and that turned out to be much too optimistic in relation to what actually happened on the stock exchange. As he became older his private economic adventures and his propaganda for the various causes that were close to his heart took more and more of his time with the result that his academic activities suffered.

Like Walras and Pareto, Fisher was firmly convinced that in the future economic science would have to be based on increased use of mathematical and statistical methods. In 1930, together with a group of economists with similar convictions (among them Joseph Schumpeter and Ragnar Frisch) Fisher founded the *Econometric Society*, an organization whose purpose was to advance the use of mathematical and statistical methods in economics, and he also became its first president.

Fisher was a prolific writer who often published a book per year as well as numerous articles. Many of these were of a popular nature, but his more serious scientific publications are both in terms of quantity and quality more than sufficient to secure him a prominent place in the history of economics.

Consumer and Producer Theory

The history of the marginalist breakthrough contains many examples of theoretical innovations that were achieved at about the same time by several theorists, and Fisher's doctoral dissertation *Mathematical Investigations into the Theory of Value and Prices* (1892) must clearly be regarded as one of the pioneering works of the period. He was one of the first to use indifference curves in economic theory, although Edgeworth was even earlier in introducing this important concept. However, Fisher was the first to draw the now well-known diagram where the indifference curves are combined with the budget line of the consumer, and where the optimum is located at the point of tangency between the budget line and an indifference curve. He also made a similar construction for the production side where he showed that profit maximization implied that the marginal rate of transformation between two goods—the ratio of their respective marginal costs—must be equal to the ratio of their respective prices. Thereby he had in place two central building blocks for a general equilibrium model, and he brought them together using relations that showed the flows of commodities and factors of production in the economy.[11] In some ways, however, the model was incomplete; thus, it did not really take account of price formation in the factor markets, and in this respect it was less satisfactory than the general equilibrium model of Walras.

The model in Fisher's dissertation was set in the framework of a single period. Accordingly, it could not be used to analyze questions regarding the allocation of resources over time, although these are obviously very important for the understanding of the functioning of a market economy. Jevons and Walras had both analyzed such problems; however, Jevons's treatment was very sketchy while that of Walras, on the other hand, was so general that the fundamental ideas were difficult to understand. It was in this field of economic theory that Fisher was to make his most important contribution.

Saving and Investment

Fisher's theory of capital and investment became an important element both in economics in general and more particularly in the field of finance. The theory was developed in three books. In *The Nature of Capital and Income* (1906) he presented the basic theoretical concepts, including the accounting relationship between concepts like capital and investment, current income,

[11] He also designed a mechanical construction in the form of a model that was built of glass and filled with water of different colors, intended to show the equilibrium of the economy. By experimenting with shifts of the demand or supply functions one could demonstrate how this led to changes in relative prices and the distribution of income. The model was located in the basement of his house in New Haven where it was displayed to students and colleagues.

and present value. The formal theory of saving and investment decisions and equilibrium in the capital market was contained in *The Rate of Interest* (1907) and *The Theory of Interest* (1930). It is in the latter book that the theory appears in its fully developed form with diagrams and mathematics, detailed interpretations and empirical examples.

Fisher wished to build his theory of saving and investment decisions on the assumption of rational behavior. He therefore started from the analysis of a consumer who has preferences over consumption in different periods of time. He simplifies by assuming that there is only one consumption good, to be considered as an aggregate of all goods that the consumer is interested in, and two time periods. In the simplest version of the theory, there is a given amount of labor income in each of the two periods, while the consumer faces a "perfect" capital market in which he can borrow and lend at the same rate of interest. Fisher shows that these assumptions imply a budget constraint for the consumer, in which the present or discounted value of consumption must be equal to the present value of labor income. The consumer's decision problem is to choose the point on the budget line that maximizes utility, which turns out to be the point of tangency between the budget line and an indifference curve—similar to the general analysis in his *Mathematical Investigations*. At this point the consumer's marginal rate of substitution between present and future goods—his rate of time preference—is equal to the rate of discount, defined as $1/(1+r)$, where r is the rate of interest. The rate of discount can be understood as the present price of a dollar's worth of consumption goods one year from now: if the interest rate is 5 percent and we wish to save for the purpose of buying a commodity that next year will cost 1,000 dollars, we have to save $1,000/1.05$ which is roughly equal to 950 dollars. The present price of a dollar's worth of consumption next year is therefore approximately 0.95 dollars.

The indifference curves between present and future consumption depict what Fisher called the consumer's rate of time preference, and which he sometimes also referred to as impatience. Previously, Böhm-Bawerk had maintained that human nature was characterized by systematic underestimation of future needs, but Fisher did not take a stand on this issue. He does not exclude that there may be such a tendency, but in his own analysis the

285

rate of time preference will depend on the time profile of consumption. If one initially finds oneself in a state of high present consumption and low future consumption, one will value an increase in future consumption more highly than if one had been in the reverse situation. As he puts it: "Impatience may be and sometimes is negative!" (Fisher 1930, p. 67). He also offered some speculations about the more fundamental causes that determine people's time preferences. He concluded that

> the rate of interest is dependent upon very unstable influences many of which have their origin deep down in the social fabric and involve considerations not strictly economic. Any causes tending to affect intelligence, foresight, self-control, habits, the longevity of man, family affection, and fashion will have their influence upon the rate of interest. (Fisher 1930, p. 505)

In Fisher's formal analysis the basic motive for saving is to reallocate the income available in the two periods so as to bring them in line with the time preferences. Thus suppose that one has a preference for an even level of consumption over time while one has a high present labor income that is expected to fall in the future. Then it is optimal to save some of one's present labor income because the reduction of present consumption will be more than compensated by the increase of consumption in the future. With this analysis Fisher laid the foundation for modern theories of life-cycle saving and permanent income; current consumption is determined not by income in the same period but by *lifetime* income.

The model can be further extended to include an analysis of investment, and Fisher assumes that the representative consumer can now also invest in real capital. The capital produces consumption goods for the future with a positive but decreasing rate of return. How much is it rational to invest in real capital? Fisher shows that the rational amount of investment—the amount that maximizes consumer utility—is that which maximizes the present value of the investment, which corresponds to the point where the marginal productivity of capital is equal to the rate of interest.[12] An interesting feature of this conclusion is

---

[12] In Wicksell's analysis this corresponds to the case where the percentage increase in the value of wine is equal to the rate of interest.

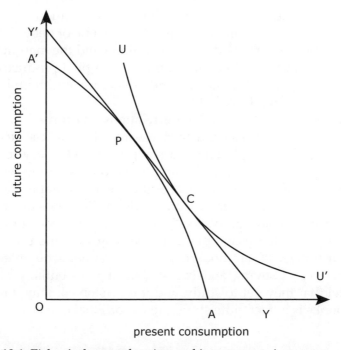

Figure 12.1. Fisher's theory of saving and investment. A consumer with an initial income corresponding to *OA* can carry out real investment along the curve *AA'*. When the market rate of interest is given by the slope of the straight line *YY'*, it will be profitable to invest until the point *P*, where the marginal productivity of capital is equal to the rate of interest. The present value of the consumer's income now and in the future then becomes equal to *Y*. However, this time profile of income does not yield an optimal time profile of consumption. To achieve this, the consumer will take up a loan, thus moving along the line *YY'* from *P* to *C*, which is the consumption profile that maximizes utility.

that the optimal amount of investment is independent of the consumer's time preferences. If the real investments in the economy are decided by private firms, these will act in the interests of the consumers or owners as long as the objective of the firm is to maximize the present value of its investment; this is the policy that maximizes the individual consumer's lifetime income and thereby his utility.

Fisher completed his analysis by showing that it could also be used to study equilibrium in the capital market. In a closed economy where there are no financial transactions with foreigners the value of total claims must be equal to the value of debts. The rate of interest is determined by this condition and the marginal productivity of capital. In equilibrium the marginal productivity of capital is equal to the rate of time preference, and both become equal to the rate of interest.

Fisher's formulation of these relationships turned out to be very fruitful in terms of further research. The basic structure of the theory is a simple one and has proven to be easy to adjust to incorporate alternative assumptions to those underlying the original version. In its analysis of the role of capital in the economy it avoids the special features of Böhm-Bawerk's average period of production or Wicksell's wine example, and it does not rest on particular assumptions concerning the time preferences of consumers. When modern students first get acquainted with the theory of saving and investment, it is essentially Fisher's model that they get to study, and the version contained in their textbooks is in fact quite similar to the original one.

The Quantity Theory of Money

The question of the role of money in the economy was one of Fisher's main research interests. With respect to the basic theoretical approach he was an adherent of the quantity theory. This theory found a compact expression in the so-called quantity equation,

$$MV=PY,$$

where M is the quantity of money, P is the price level, and Y is the real value of the national product. V is the velocity of money, the ratio between nominal national income and the amount of money, measured in such a way that it fits with data for the three other factors in the equation. From this point of view the equation is therefore an identity, but it becomes a meaningful theory when one begins to make assumptions about the determinants of the various elements in it.[13] Fisher believed that Y was given by

---

[13] It is a common belief that Fisher was the first to write down the quantity equation, but the person who should receive the honor for having done this is apparently the American astronomer and economist Simon Newcomb (1835–1909).

the "real" side of the economy, that is, by the production, investment, and consumption decisions of private and public agents.
He also thought that V was determined by institutional arrangements like the banking structure and the payments technology,
which in his view were likely to stay approximately constant over
long periods of time. With these assumptions it followed that the
price level was determined by the quantity of money. The adoption of this theory is the natural choice for an economist with
a background in general equilibrium theory, since Walras and
later Fisher himself had shown that relative prices were determined in an economic model where there was no role for money.
The amount of money determined the *absolute* price level, but the
price level did not affect the real side of the economy, which was
guided by *relative* prices.

For Fisher, however, the simple version of the quantity theory
represented only a first approximation to the problem. Fluctuations of the general price level had in his opinion a series of unfortunate consequences for the economy, not least because it led
to arbitrary and undesired redistributions of income. Like Wicksell, he believed that a central task for monetary policy should
be to hold the price level constant, and with the slogan of "the
compensated dollar" he was a keen propagandist for this view.

Fisher also attached great importance to monetary policy for
the stabilization of the economy in the face of business cycle fluctuations. With regard to this issue the core concept in his thinking was *the real rate of interest*, which was a measure of the real
rate of return on financial assets. This was defined as

real rate of interest = nominal rate of interest - rate of inflation.

The definition could be interpreted in two ways, one backward
and one forward looking. The *realized* real rate could be estimated
statistically on the background of data for nominal interest rates
and the rate of inflation. However, for current decisions about
saving and investment the relevant magnitude would be the *expected* real rate, and since this was based on firms' and consumers' views about the future it was not directly observable. On the
basis of his studies of historical statistics, Fisher concluded that
the realized real rate tended to increase during upturns and decline during downturns of the business cycle. Ideally, one could
imagine that the nominal rate quickly adjusted to changes in the

rate of inflation, so that the real rate would stay constant. But Fisher's view was that this process in fact tended to take considerable time, and he maintained that an important reason why the crisis in the 1930s lasted so long was that the real rate of interest continued to stay at a very high level, acting as a brake on the investment activity in the economy.

Fisher's interest in monetary economics also led him to concern himself with the measurement problems that arise when one works with highly aggregated magnitudes for the economy as a whole, and problems of this kind emerged in particular in the attempts that were made to verify the quantity theory of money. How are we to measure the real value of the national product, Y, and the price level, P, when there are thousands of goods and services in the economy? The only possible answer is that the aggregates must be computed with the aid of price and quantity indices, and Fisher therefore became deeply engaged in the theory of index construction. "Fisher's ideal index" is still a concept that is currently used in the literature in this area.[14]

Income and Taxes

In *The Nature of Capital and Income* Fisher discussed the real content of the concept of income and arrived at the conclusion that the correct definition of income during a given period, such as a year, was the value of consumption. "True income" is equal to money income as we conventionally think of it (with the addition of the current consumption value of durable goods) minus saving. Going even more deeply into the problem, Fisher argues, income is at bottom our standard of living according to our subjective experience ("enjoyment income"), but this is impossible to measure. On the other hand, we are in fact able to measure the cost of our living standard, and this is just our consumption expenditure. To include saving in the concept of income was in Fisher's opinion double counting, for saving leads to an increase in the real capital of society, which in turn generates new income.

[14] Fisher's ideal index is the geometric average of the better-known indices of Laspeyre and Paasche.

This definition may seem paradoxical. Modern economists are used to thinking of income as being by definition equal to consumption plus saving, and to define income as being equal to consumption is therefore likely to create serious confusion. Even if there was less agreement about the precise content of the concept of income at the beginning of the twentieth century, most economists even at that time found it difficult to accept Fisher's definition. However, Fisher stuck to his definition, and in the 1930s and 1940s he used it as justification for his proposal of a tax reform that would abolish the income tax (as conventionally defined), instead introducing a tax on consumption or expenditure, i.e. "true income." His main argument in support of the proposal, which he described in a number of articles and in a book that he wrote together with his brother (Fisher and Fisher 1942), was that the existing income tax involved double taxation of saving. This led to a weakening of the incentives to save, so that the introduction of a tax on expenditure (which is really an income tax with deductibility for saving) would provide better incentives for saving and capital accumulation.[15]

The advantages of such a tax reform have been much discussed in the more recent literature of public economics, and there is no doubt that Fisher's discussion contained a number of good points. There may have been several reasons why he did not gain the support of his contemporary colleagues, but one of them must certainly have been his insistence on the definition of income as consumption. This led to detraction from the main point of the proposal, and there is now general agreement that the argument for allowing deductibility of saving is completely independent of the definition of income. Those economists who have agreed with Fisher in recommending the adoption of an expenditure tax have therefore not joined him in his proposal for a redefinition of income.[16]

Irving Fisher died in the same year as Paul Samuelson published his pathbreaking *Foundations of Economic Analysis* (1947).

[15] We recall that a similar proposal had been made by John Stuart Mill.

[16] This does not imply that the conventional concept of income is uncomplicated and easy to define. Especially in the literature on income taxation the question of the correct definition of income has been the subject of extensive debate. A historical survey of this debate can be found in Wildasin (1990).

It was the end of an extremely active life as an economist that began with his 1892 dissertation, which was published two years after the first edition of Marshall's *Principles of Economics*. This is a long period in the history of economic thought, whether we measure it in years or in the scientific development that lies between the *Principles* and the *Foundations*.

FURTHER READING

Knut Wicksell's *Lectures on Political Economy* are well worth at least a selective reading for modern economists. Obviously, one reads the two volumes today mostly for their historical interest, but the theoretical exposition is so thoughtful and deep that it is unavoidable that one also gets a better understanding of modern economics. One can form a good impression of the wide scope of Wicksell's writings from the selection of his articles that have been translated into English and edited by Erik Lindahl (Wicksell 1958). The most important theoretical parts of *Finanztheoretische Untersuchungen* can be found in English translation in the book by Musgrave and Peacock (1958).

Wicksell's life and academic activities have been described in an outstanding book by Torsten Gårdlund (1956), one of the best biographies of an economist ever written. Gårdlund tells the story of Wicksell's life and work on the background of the social, political, and cultural life in Sweden, but without going into the details of his scientific achievements. A shorter but also very readable biography is Lindahl's introductory chapter in Wicksell (1958).

The Theory of Interest (1930) is Irving Fisher's definitive statement of his capital theory and the best source of forming an impression of his general approach to economics. It builds on his earlier book, *The Rate of Interest* (1907), and also contains a summary of *The Nature of Capital and Income* (1906). It has been written by an author with a great deal of experience in didactic and popular writing: he treats every major problem using a variety of different approaches and often includes summaries that repeat the main points of the foregoing chapters. From a pedagogical point of view, *The Theory of Interest* is a model of good economic writing.

Robert Loring Allen (1993) has written an interesting biography that covers all aspects of Fisher's many-sided activities, and James Tobin has a very good article about him in *The New Palgrave*. An article by Samuelson (1967) presents a personal evaluation of Fisher as an economist, combined with an elegant exposition of his capital theory. Fisher's and other American economists' attitudes to eugenics are described in the fascinating and rather disturbing article by Leonard (2005).

New Perspectives on
Markets and Competition

FROM THE TIME OF Adam Smith's analysis of competition as a "system of perfect liberty," in their studies of markets economists had mainly focused on the case of free or perfect competition. With the increasing formalization of economic theory that began during the last third of the nineteenth century the assumptions underlying this particular case became increasingly clearer. Agents both on the demand and supply side of the market would have to take prices as given, and there must be free entry for new firms. The consumers were rational utility maximizers, and firms were equally rational in their desire to maximize profit. There also grew up a consensus that the market in some sense—which was not always made precise—worked for the common good or the public interest.

Actually, perfect competition was not the only market form that was studied in the theoretical literature. Adam Smith had discussed monopoly as a contrast to free competition and showed that it was not necessarily in the interests of the market agents to sustain the conditions for perfect competition. Cournot made a detailed study of price formation under monopoly and oligopoly, and Edgeworth argued that the assumptions of perfect competition only made sense with a very large number of agents. Nevertheless, the model of perfect competition had a dominating place in the theoretical literature, and for an outsider to the field it must have seemed obvious that it was this model that reflected the world view of most economists. But within economics there began to emerge a feeling that this theory did not present a realistic picture of the actual functioning of a market economy.

The criticism of the dominant worldview took several forms. One type of reaction was to place the responsibility for the lack of realism on the increasing theoretical formalization and the theorists' lack of contact with historical and institutional realities. This was the view of, among others, the American institutional school, a somewhat loose grouping of economists who tended to regard Thorstein Veblen as its founder and most prominent spokesman. Another type of reaction consisted in developing new theoretical models that could fill the holes in the existing theory. This led to a number of new theories of imperfect competition, associated with the names of Edward Chamberlin and Harold Hotelling in the United States, Joan Robinson in England, Heinrich von Stackelberg in Germany, and Frederik Zeuthen in Denmark. This chapter surveys some of the main features in the new theories of imperfect competition.

Thorstein Veblen

Thorstein Veblen (1857–1929) was born into a family of Norwegian immigrants in Wisconsin, and he grew up with Norwegian as his first language. He was the first of his family to receive a university education: he obtained a Ph.D. in philosophy from Yale University in 1884, and his studies also included a good deal of economics. At the personal level he was an unconventional and eccentric person who both through his lifestyle and opinions seemed provocative to the attitudes of established society. After graduation he found it difficult to obtain a position at a university, and it was only after several years of unemployment that he managed to secure an appointment at Cornell University in 1891. A year later he got a position at the University of Chicago, which became his academic base for more than a decade. At the end of this period he was forced to resign; his disregard for academic rules and conventions and his unconventional methods of teaching as well as his womanizing became increasingly unacceptable to the university authorities. Later on he taught at several other universities, but in spite of his extensive output of academic articles and books he never succeeded in becoming a full professor.

Veblen's writings have often been classified as "economic sociology," but they are in fact hard to place in terms of standard academic classifications. He clearly felt an intellectual affinity to economics, but elements of sociology, philosophy, political science, and history also played a considerable role. The characterization of his work as multidisciplinary may nevertheless be misleading for Veblen did not consider himself as bound by scientific standards and methodological principles. The form of his books and articles is satirical and polemical. They contain no attempts at formal analysis; neither are his theories formulated in a way that makes it possible to subject them to empirical tests. In general, his use of empirical data and observations is casual and impressionistic. When in spite of this he remains an important figure in the history of economic thought, it is due to the fact that he expressed—sometimes in a very persuasive and elegant form—a type of criticism to which the mainstream of economic theory has always been exposed: the picture that it paints both of individual behavior and of the functioning of markets is too simple and stylized to capture the complex realities of economic life.[1]

The American institutional economists have often been characterized as being antitheoretical. This term does not actually fit very well in Veblen's case, for he was not really an opponent of economic theory as such. On the other hand, however, he felt that the economic theory of his time was moving along a wrong track. According to him, it was based on an unrealistic view of man, which in turn led to misleading conclusions about the nature of the economy as a whole. Man was seen as a rational and calculating agent, solely concerned with a narrow conception of self-interest. In reality, Veblen argued, human behavior is to a large extent determined by instincts and habits. Instincts and habits are formed by the social interaction between individuals and by the material basis of society, which is determined by the state of technology. As a result of technological progress these factors undergo continuous change. An economic theory that focuses on states of equilibrium makes it impossible to understand the development of society as dynamic and evolutionary. In sum, Veblen's criticism of economic theory consists in questioning the use of the two central theoretical concepts of rationality and equilibrium.

What was Veblen's alternative to conventional economic theory?[2] In this respect he is far more difficult to interpret. In his

---

[1] It is elegant in a literary sense, but it is not always easy to realize who or what is the target of the criticism. In this connection it is remarkable that *The Theory of the Leisure Class* does not contain a single reference to the literature.

[2] The term *conventional theory* may be misleading. At this time the study of economics at American universities was not based on formalized theories of utility and profit maximization and general equilibrium. Much of the teach-

best-known book, *The Theory of the Leisure Class* (1899), he offers a description of individual behavior as motivated mainly by the desire for social recognition and prestige. These goals may be achieved first by demonstrating that one belongs to a class that does not depend for its living on practical work; historically, this had been the situation of warriors and priests. But recognition may also be gained by adopting a prestigious pattern of consumption. Veblen coined the term *conspicuous consumption* to describe what he saw as the fact that preferences originate in a wish to demonstrate to the rest of society that one commands significant economic resources. An implication of this idea is obviously that the more expensive a commodity is, the better suited it is to emphasize one's economic status. An increase in the price of a commodity can therefore make it more suitable for being part of an individual's conspicuous consumption and an implication of this is that demand may be an increasing rather than decreasing function of price.[3] Another consequence of Veblen's line of thinking is that it raises doubts about the ability of markets and competition to allocate society's resources in an efficient manner: if resources are used to a considerable extent to promote one's own status relative to others, there will be a large element of waste in the way that markets function. However, it is not easy to reformulate Veblen's general views so as to generate more precise and testable theories. Thus he emphasizes that different types of consumption goods cannot easily be classified as either useful (i.e., as functional for practical purposes) or conspicuous. They will typically have elements of both characteristics and careful research is required to establish the weights to be assigned to each of them, but it is not indicated what kind of research that will be required to settle this issue. This vagueness in Veblen's thought is an important explanation of why it has not had more influence on economic theory, even if it continues to be a source of inspiration to modern researchers in the area of consumer behavior.

---

ing used an institutional or historical approach, while Veblen's criticism was chiefly directed against the new marginalist school. At the time that he wrote, this was still considered to be at the frontier of research in economics and had not yet reached the textbooks or the more popular literature.

[3] This so-called Veblen effect was first pointed out in an article by Harvey Leibenstein (1950).

Another area where Veblen's work was very influential was in the importance assigned to private industry for the economy as a whole. His views on this issue were presented in another famous book, *The Theory of Business Enterprise* (1904). Veblen was deeply skeptical about modern business leadership. The people who really understood the nature of production processes were the engineers and the production workers, but the positions of power in modern companies had passed to shareholders and financial specialists who had lost touch with basic production activities; they had, in another of Veblen's famous formulations, become "absentee owners." Their strategy for maximizing profits for their companies consisted mainly in efforts to limit competition in order to be able to charge higher prices, while on the other hand they were less concerned with the lowering of costs. This was a very different perspective on private industry from the usual one in the economics literature, and when considered together with Veblen's analysis of consumer behavior it implied a rather pessimistic view of the ability of the market economy to solve the basic economic problems of society.

Although Veblen is commonly considered to be the founder of the American institutional school he had no direct descendants among academic economists; for that, his approach was too idiosyncratic and too closely connected with his literary role as a satirical commentator on social developments. Two other economists who are considered to be prominent members of this school are John R. Commons (1862–1945) and Wesley C. Mitchell (1874–1948), but their research does not have many features in common either with Veblen or each other. Commons specialized in the study of the interrelationships between the economy and the legal system, while Mitchell concentrated on building a reliable data base for the American economy, which he later used for detailed studies of the business cycle. The case for referring to this group of economists as a separate school can only to a limited degree be based on the unity of their research program. Rather, it must be justified by their common skepticism to the fruitfulness of formalized economic theory and to the view that markets could be seen as functioning according to the model of perfect competition.[4]

---

[4] A more modern economist who may also be classified as an institutionalist is the Canadian-born John Kenneth Galbraith (1908–2006), who for many

EDWARD CHAMBERLIN

As we saw in chapter 10, Alfred Marshall was convinced that many industries were characterized by the presence of increasing returns to scale or—equivalently—declining average costs. However, this assumption, if applied to the level of the individual firm, was inconsistent with the assumption of perfect competition. In order to "save" this assumption, Marshall introduced the hypothesis of positive external effects, which ensured that the average cost in an industry as a whole could be declining in spite of the fact that it was increasing for each single firm.

However, there was another way out of this dilemma. This consisted in the rejection of the assumption of price-taking behavior on the part of the firm, assuming instead that the firm sees the price as a decreasing function of its output. If that is the case, the volume of production and the size of the firm will be determined by the condition of equality between marginal revenue and marginal cost, even if average cost is decreasing. In other words, the behavior of the firm is the same as described in the theoretical model of monopoly: each firm in the industry behaves like a monopolist. According to Adam Smith's perspective on monopoly as the opposite of competition, this change of assumptions may seem extreme. But in a world of differentiated products it may also be seen as a movement toward increased realism. This change of perspective lay behind two books that were both published in 1933: Edward Chamberlin's *Theory of Monopolistic Competition* and Joan Robinson's *Economics of Imperfect Competition*.

Edward Chamberlin (1899–1967) was educated at three American universities. He received his B.A. at the University of Iowa and went on to study for an M.A. at the University of Michigan. Finally, he obtained his doctorate at Harvard University in 1927. Some years later, his Harvard dissertation became the book whose full title was *The Theory of Monopolistic Competition: A Re-*

---

years was a professor at Harvard University. His many books, of which *The Affluent Society* (1958) and *The New Industrial State* (1967) are the best known, are strongly critical both of contemporary economics and of modern social and economic developments, and they are written in a popular form that appealed to a wide readership. Like Veblen, Galbraith is a satirist, and he makes no use of modern analytical methods, but his work is more anchored in empirical facts than is that of Veblen.

orientation of the Theory of Value. The title is an ambitious one, and Chamberlin was firmly convinced that the book was a contribution of fundamental importance to economic theory. Practically the whole of his later career came to revolve around this book; he elaborated the various arguments in more detail, and he was an ardent defender of his theory toward all who criticized it or wished to improve it. In particular, he was concerned with the differentiation of his product in relation to that of the economist that he saw as his most serious competitor, Joan Robinson. Posterity has not had very high thoughts about this part of his activities, but at the same time it has recognized that the work of his youth was indeed a significant contribution to economic theory.

The term *monopolistic competition* suggests that the market form that Chamberlin analyzed was something in between monopoly and perfect competition, in fact a case of competition between monopolies. Chamberlin imagines that a typical industry or branch consists of firms that do not produce identical goods, but products that are different although they are close substitutes for each other. The closeness of the substitution relationship may be due to similarity of their technical properties; roughly speaking, they satisfy the same type of consumer needs while still appearing to have a producer-specific profile. Cars from different producers, furniture, clothing, and food are all commodity groups that contain a number of examples of this kind of substitutes. This implies that each producer is a monopolist with respect to the sale of his own commodity, but his monopoly position is relatively weak, since he must pay attention to the competition from those who produce commodities that are closely related to his own. The demand curve faced by the single producer is therefore not horizontal, as under perfect competition, but in comparison to the monopoly case it is relatively flat; if the firm raises its price, it will lose many customers who will switch to the commodities offered by its competitors.

In Chamberlin's opinion, the new theory provided a picture of the market mechanism that was more consistent with the common understanding of the concept of competition. Thus he argues that under perfect competition there is in fact no competition in the everyday sense of the word. The terms that are in common use to describe real competition, like "underselling," "price cutting," and "securing a market" have no meaning under the market form of perfect competition, whose principles

> are based on the supposition that each seller accepts the market price and can dispose of his entire supply without materially affecting it. Thus there is no problem of choosing a price policy, no problem of adapting the product more exactly to the buyers' (real or fancied) wants, no problem of advertising in order to change their wants. The theory of pure competition could hardly be expected to fit facts so far different from its assumptions. But there is no reason why a theory of value cannot be formulated which will fit them—a theory concerning itself specifically with goods which are not homogeneous. (Chamberlin 1933; 1948, p. 10)

Chamberlin also assumed that there was free entry in the industry, so that new producers would enter if the existing producers earned an abnormally high profit. This would put a downward pressure on the price until it became equal to average cost. In the long-run equilibrium of the industry, profits would therefore be zero, just as under perfect competition. However, the price would remain higher than marginal cost, and for this reason there would be an efficiency loss of the same type as under monopoly. The nature of the equilibrium is shown in figure 13.1.

A part of Chamberlin's analysis that came to be of special importance for later research was his emphasis on the incentives that the producer had to differentiate his product as much as possible from those of his competitors, since the degree of product differentiation would determine the strength of his monopoly position. This he could do in two ways; either by using resources on product development and differentiation or through the use of advertising and other forms of sales promotion for the purpose of impressing consumers with the unique character of his product. Even if Chamberlin did not carry this part of his analysis very far in theoretical terms, his general discussion of these issues became very influential. It demonstrated that there were forms of economic activity in firms that were of great economic importance but which so far had been neglected by theorists. Over time, these became central themes of research in the branch of economics now known as industrial organization.

301

JOAN ROBINSON

Joan Robinson (1903–83) has been characterized as the only woman among the great economists. It is true that in earlier chapters we have encountered women who have played a role in the development of economics, but Harriet Taylor and Mary Marshall are not known for their own contributions to the subject but for their role in inspiring and supporting their husbands' work. In this respect economics is not very different from other fields of academic research. It is only during the past couple of decades that female economists have risen to prominence in the international research community.

Joan Robinson studied economics at the University of Cambridge, but in contrast to Chamberlin's program of study towards a doctorate, she finished her formal education with a B.A. degree at the age of twenty-two. In the academic environment at the old English universities the general opinion was that formalized research training was superfluous; a lower degree provided the necessary foundation for independent research, at least if the degree had been obtained in Oxford or Cambridge. This attitude may have been one reason why the geographical center of economic research gradually moved from England to the United States, but in the case of Joan Robinson it seems clear that her ability to do independent work and establish fruitful interaction with other economists in Cambridge more than compensated for her lack of formal research training. During the whole of her university career she was associated with Cambridge, where she obtained her first position as a lecturer in 1931. However, she was not appointed a professor until 1965, and to an outsider it may seem strange that such a prominent and productive researcher had not been appointed to a top position much earlier. There may have been several reasons for this. Being a woman in academia was more difficult in those days, and her situation may not have been made easier by the fact that her husband, Austin Robinson, was a professor in the same faculty; she did in fact receive her appointment in the year that he retired. In addition, her research and writing after about 1950 were highly controversial and may have contributed to her late promotion.

Joan Robinson made a name for herself by her first book, *The Economics of Imperfect Competition* (1933). In spite of the linguistic difference between "monopolistic" and "imperfect" competition, the two books have a number of features in common. Like Chamberlin, Robinson modeled the individual firm as if it had a monopoly of its own product, although such that it was exposed to competition from other firms that produced close substitutes:

> The demand curve for the output of the individual firm will normally be falling. Its elasticity will depend upon many factors, of which the chief are the number of other firms selling the same commodity and the degree to which substitution is possible, from the point of view of buyers, between the output of other firms and the output of the firm in question. (Robinson 1933; 1969, p. 50)

Like Chamberlin, she also assumed that free entry would put downward pressure on the price until pure profits were eliminated, so that the equilibrium could be characterized as a mixture of monopoly and perfect competition:

> Full equilibrium thus requires a double condition, that marginal revenue is equal to marginal cost, and that average revenue (or price) is equal to average cost. (Robinson 1933; 1969, p. 94)

Like Chamberlin's theory, equilibrium under imperfect competition can be illustrated by means of figure 13.1.

In contrast to Chamberlin, however, Joan Robinson put little emphasis on the discussion of advertising and product development. The Cambridge environment was strongly influenced by the tradition from Marshall and Pigou (who at this time was still active), and these themes were rather far from the type of questions that had concerned the older generation of economists.[5] On the other hand, she paid more attention than Chamberlin had done to the consequences of imperfect competition for price formation in the factor markets. Among other things, she showed how monopsony (the case of a market with a single buyer) implied that workers were paid less than the value of their marginal product. Another of the original contributions of her book was the analysis of price discrimination, where her discussion followed the analysis founded by Pigou (1920). Robinson

---

[5] It is notable that *The Economics of Imperfect Competition* contains virtually no references to the work of other economists except Marshall, Pigou, and Robinson's contemporaries in Cambridge.

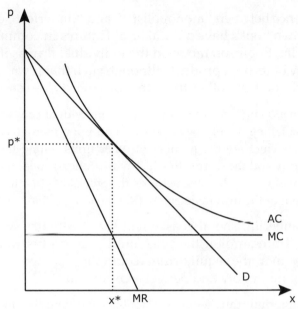

Figure 13.1. Equilibrium under monopolistic or imperfect competition. Profit maximization leads the firm to set marginal revenue (*MR*) equal to marginal cost (*MC*). At the same time, free entry pushes the demand curve inward to the point of tangency between the demand curve (*D*) and the average cost curve (*AC*), at which price is equal to average cost and profit is zero. The equilibrium price and quantity are *p** and *x**.

showed that if a monopolist could sell the same commodity in two separate markets, he would set prices such that the percentage difference between price and marginal cost in each market would be equal to the inverse of the price elasticity of demand. Consequently, the price would be higher in that of the two market segments where demand was most inelastic.

Although it is clear that there were some differences between Chamberlin's and Robinson's contributions to the theory of imperfect competition, when one takes a broader view there is little doubt that it is the parallels that are the more striking. How did it happen that two so similar theoretical analyses could come to be written practically simultaneously, on each side of the Atlantic and by two authors who hardly knew about each other? One important explanation is that these ideas were "in the air." Many economists who were interested in theoretical models of the market mechanism must have been conscious of the fact that there were a large number of cases where none of the two standard models—perfect competition and monopoly—provided a good description of real life markets. Moreover, the building blocks that were required for the construction of a new theory had already been produced in the form of a theory of monopoly and of long-run equilibrium under perfect competition. It remained for creative and skilled theorists to put them together. That two theorists of this kind were to emerge in different places and at about the same time is therefore hardly surprising, but that the year of publication turned out to be the same must obviously be seen as a coincidence.

Robinson did not long pursue the success that she experienced with her first book. Instead, she became an active member of the group of young and talented economists who functioned as a discussion and advisory group for John Maynard Keynes while he was writing his *General Theory*, and she also wrote books and articles of her own about the new macroeconomic theory. Gradually, her interests turned toward the study of economic growth and long-run development problems.[6] Her main work in this area was *The Accumulation of Capital* (1956), which is strongly critical of the views of many leading economists, particularly of what she considered to be their uncritical use of concepts like production functions and aggregate capital. This led to an extended debate that from a later perspective appears to be of little significance, and there are few traces of it in the modern literature. Even if Joan Robinson's productivity and her wide range of interests are impressive, it is her early contribution to the theory of imperfect competition that secures her a prominent place in the history of economics.

HAROLD HOTELLING

Harold Hotelling (1895–1973) began his university training in journalism, and as part of his studies at the University of Wash-

---

[6] She also developed an affinity for Marxian economics and sometimes expressed a rather undisguised and uncritical admiration for communist dictatorships like the Soviet Union, China, and North Korea.

ington he wrote a thesis that used statistical regression analysis to study the influence of the Seattle newspapers on the outcome of the local elections. This impressed a mathematics professor at the university so much that he convinced Hotelling to change his field of study, and he obtained his Ph.D. in mathematics at Princeton University in 1924. His special field of interest was mathematical statistics, and most of his scientific publications were actually in this area. But he also took a strong interest in economics, and during the period that he taught at Columbia University in New York (1931–46), he had also a position in economics. The volume of his writings in economics is relatively modest, but of the ten articles that he published at least four have attained the status of classics in economic theory. The most famous of these is his analysis of oligopolistic competition "Stability in Competition" (Hotelling 1929), which takes its point of departure from a problem of business location.

Hotelling's article is among other things distinguished by the weight that the author attaches to showing the relationship of his analysis to the earlier literature, for example, by references to the work of Cournot, Dupuit, Walras, and Edgeworth. By way of introduction, he remarks modestly: "After the work of the late Professor F. Y. Edgeworth one may doubt that anything further can be said on the theory of competition among a small number of entrepreneurs" (Hotelling 1929, p. 41).

Fortunately, Hotelling overcame this doubt! The simple mathematical model that he designed illuminates the interplay between two producers who produce the same commodity, but where there are factors that may cause their customers to have a preference for buying from one of the duopolists rather than the other. The reason for such a preference on which Hotelling focuses in his formal model is difference in transportation cost, but he also mentions several other explanations that may lead to similar results. Some of these are very concrete, like differences in product quality or the degree of service provision, while others are of a more psychological nature, as when one of the producers is a member of the same Masonic lodge as the customer.

Hotelling's model can briefly be described as follows. A city consists of one long street with the population uniformly distributed between its endpoints. The sales outlets of the two producers are located at two different points along the street for reasons that are given by unexplained historical circumstances. Each consumer buys one unit of the commodity per unit of time and transports it to his home at a given cost per unit of distance. The problem is now what prices the two producers will set and how they will divide the market between them. At which store the consumers will buy is determined by the price that the producer charges with the addition of transportation costs. If, as an example, the producers set the same price they will share the part of the market that lies between them equally, while in addition each of them will serve that part of the market that lies on their outside, relative to their competitor. But will it be profitable for them to set the same price, as they would have done in a Cournot-type duopoly without transportation costs? Hotelling showed that the answer is no; the duopolist who has the larger market on his outside will charge the higher price, get the higher profit and capture the larger share of the market. The result is therefore that the duopolist who has the more favorable location will exploit this by charging a higher price, and Hotelling argues that the result carries over to other cases that one can imagine where one of the duopolists has some kind of competitive advantage.

Later in the article Hotelling extends his theory by assuming that it is only one of the producers whose location is fixed while the other is free to choose his own location. On the basis of the foregoing analysis it is fairly obvious that what the other producer will do is to locate as close as possible to the first producer on that side where the market is larger. But while this is the most profitable choice for the producer, it is not a favorable outcome for society, for it implies that the average distance from consumer to producer becomes longer than it would have been if the second producer had chosen a location closer to the endpoint of this side of the market. The same analysis would be valid for other product differences as, for example, the degree of sweetness of drinks. Hotelling drew very general conclusions from this observation. When a new producer enters a market where there already exist firms that produce a good or service of the same type,

> there is an incentive to make the new product very much like the
> old, applying some slight change which will seem an improve-

ment to as many buyers as possible without ever going far in this direction. The tremendous standardisation of our furniture, our houses, our clothing, our automobiles and our education are due in part to the economies of large-scale production, in part to fashion and imitation. But over and above these forces is the effect we have been discussing, the tendency to make only slight deviations in order to have for the new commodity as many buyers of the old as possible, to get, so to speak, *between* one's competitors and a mass of customers. (Hotelling 1929, p. 54)

At the close of the article he draws the conclusion even further in the following witty observation on the tendency to excessive similarity:

It leads some factories to make cheap shoes for the poor and others to make expensive shoes for the rich, but all the shoes are too much alike. Our cities become uneconomically large and the business districts within them are too concentrated. Methodist and Presbyterian churches are too much alike; cider is too homogeneous. (Hotelling 1929, p. 57)

Hotelling's article broke new ground in several ways; first as an extension of Cournot's analysis of duopoly, second as a contribution to the theory of location, and third as pointing out that economic models of interaction between independent agents could be applicable to the analysis of wider problems in the social sciences.

In his article, "The General Welfare in Relation to Problems of Taxation and of Railway and Utility Rates" (1938), Hotelling studied two problems in public economics that are closely related to each other. First, should taxation be direct or indirect from the point of view of social welfare maximization? Second, what prices should a public utility, for instance, a railway company, charge for its services? Hotelling showed that if an individual is to pay a given amount of tax, it is better for him to pay the amount directly than paying it indirectly via taxes on the consumer goods that he purchases. For a social optimum (Hotelling does not use the concept of Pareto optimality) demands that consumer prices are equal to marginal costs, and indirect taxes cause the prices to deviate from marginal costs; taxes lead to price distortions. In Hotelling's view, on the other hand, a tax on income causes no such distortion. The analysis is rigorous and elegant, although from a modern point of view it has an obvious weakness: it neglects the fact that a tax on income prevents the wage that the individual receives from corresponding to the value of his marginal product, so that the income tax leads to a distortion in the labor market. As regards the price policy of public utilities his conclusion is that all prices should be set equal to the marginal cost of the commodity in question. If there are significant fixed costs of production, it would be wrong to try to cover these by higher prices. Instead, the fixed costs should be financed by transfers from the general government budget with the income tax as the main source of revenue. This conclusion is vulnerable to the same criticism, for if the income tax leads to a distortion in the labor market Hotelling's principle simply transfers the price distortions from one set of markets to another.

Yet another of Hotelling's articles that has been very influential is "The Economics of Exhaustible Resources" (1931). Here he raises the question of the socially optimal exploitation of an exhaustible or finite natural resource. His best-known result is that in order to achieve an optimal rate of utilization over time, one should aim at a rate of price increase for the resource that is equal to the real rate of interest as determined in the market; this is often referred to as "Hotelling's rule." He also showed that this condition would be satisfied under perfect competition, and that monopoly would lead to a rate of utilization that was too low. The article did not receive much attention when it came out but became a central reference in the flourishing of research in the economics of exhaustible resources that followed in the wake of the so-called oil crisis in the middle of the 1970s.

Harold Hotelling was a pioneer of mathematical economics, but he combined his mathematical knowledge with a sharp eye for interesting and relevant economic problems and he never used more advanced mathematical methods than were necessary to illuminate the real economic content of his theoretical models. Thus his duopoly article uses only elementary mathematics, and the simple and elegant exposition is an obvious explanation why the model has become so popular among writers of undergraduate textbooks.

HEINRICH VON STACKELBERG

Heinrich von Stackelberg (1905–1946) was born in Russia, but after the revolution of 1917 his German-Argentinean parents fled to Estonia, where his father's family had deep roots in the German minority community. In 1918, after the Russian annexation of Estonia, they were again forced to escape and they now settled in Germany. Stackelberg studied economics at the University of Cologne, where he received his doctorate in 1930. Later he taught at the universities of Berlin and Bonn, and at the time of his death he was a visiting professor at the University of Madrid. Stackelberg's posthumous reputation has been colored by the fact that he was a member of Hitler's national socialist party and for a period even of the SS. The depth of his political convictions has been a matter of some dispute, and so has their possible influence on his scientific work. As regards the first point, there can be little doubt that Stackelberg, at least during the first part of his career, displayed antidemocratic and antiliberal attitudes, and in some of his writings he expresses his support for a fascist economic ideology. But toward the end of the 1930s he began to revise his views and to get in contact with groups that were in opposition to the Nazi regime. At any rate, there is no doubt that he was an important economist, and his main contributions to economic theory can hardly be read as reflections of his political views.

Today, Stackelberg's name is mostly associated with his theory of duopoly, which was presented in his book *Marktform und Gleichgewicht* (Market Structure and Equilibrium, 1934). According to Cournot's theory each of the duopolists would choose the volume of output that would maximize profit, taking the other duopolist's output as given. In contrast to this, Stackelberg treated the two duopolists in an asymmetric manner. He assumed that each of the producers can choose to act as "leader" or "follower."[7] The follower behaves like a Cournot duopolist; he maximizes profit

[7] These are the standard terms that are used in modern expositions, but it was not Stackelberg who introduced them. In *Marktform und Gleichgewicht* he describes the two alternative roles as independence and dependence. The leader-follower terminology was introduced by the American economist William Fellner (1949) in his account of Stackelberg's theory. Speculations that this terminology could be inspired by Stackelberg's political views are therefore without foundation.

taking the other producer's *output* as given. The leader takes *the follower's adjustment to the leader's output* as given and maximizes profit under this assumption. If both producers choose the role of follower, the resulting equilibrium is that of Cournot. If one of them chooses to be a leader and the other a follower, we have the case of what modern textbooks refer to as Stackelberg equilibrium, where the typical outcome is that the leader produces the larger output and receives the highest profit. If, as a third possibility, both producers choose the role of the leader, there will not exist any equilibrium in the Stackelberg model. In fact, Stackelberg considered the third case as the most likely outcome, even if his more general view of oligopolistic markets was that the theory led to no clear predictions of which roles the producers would adopt. He was therefore of the opinion that duopoly and oligopoly could not be analyzed by means of equilibrium models. However, the later literature in the area has tended to identified Stackelberg only with the case where one of the producers has chosen the role of leader and the other that of the follower, and the notion of Stackelberg equilibrium therefore refers to this case.

What are the factors behind producers' choice among the roles of leader and follower? In Stackelberg's perspective, it is partly due to conventions, partly to a lack of information that causes many markets to function according to the model of perfect competition and many oligopolists to choose the role of follower. Many producers do not understand that they have the ability to influence market conditions, and it is as a result of improved information and accumulated experience from their own activities that they come to realize that they do indeed have market power and that it is possible for them to choose the role of leader. The market system has accordingly a built-in dynamics that makes it move toward a state of increasing instability and gradually also a higher degree of concentration. This diagnosis of the market economy as an unstable system raises perspectives that clearly transcend the simple textbook version of Stackelberg's analysis.

It appears, therefore, that Stackelberg took a pessimistic view of the ability of the market to function in a way that allocates resources rationally, and this view led him to support fascist proposals for the establishment of government-supported cartels and a corporative state. The corporative state would organize and regulate the private sector, including the labor market, according to what was seen as the needs of the state or nation. Even this would fall short of being the perfect economic system, but it would have greater possibilities for approximating the ideal than the unregulated market economy,[8] because

> the corporative market leads in principle to the same result as perfect competition. The actual deviations of the corporative-state equilibrium from its ideal should not after all be assessed any differently from the actual deviations in the past of the approximately competitive markets of the free capitalist economy from their theoretical ideal. (Stackelberg 1934, p. 105)

In the early phase of Stackelberg's career, therefore, there was clearly a connection between his theoretical analysis and his view of what constituted the best economic system. Later on, he modified his views, ascribing more importance to perfect competition as a practically relevant norm of efficiency. Nevertheless, he continued to regard his oligopoly theory as important for the understanding of how at least part of the market economy functioned.

Stackelberg was a productive researcher who also wrote articles and books in areas like cost theory, interest and capital, and the theory of exchange rates. His use of mathematical models was of great importance for German economics which, in the wake of the *Methodenstreit* of the 1880s, had lagged behind the development in other countries.

FREDERIK ZEUTHEN

Frederik Zeuthen (1888–1959) is the great name in Danish economics. He was born into an academic family where his father was a well-known professor of mathematics at the University of Copenhagen. Zeuthen studied economics and obtained the equivalent of a master's degree in 1912. He then entered the civil service, working first in the administration of the social

[8] In the next chapter we shall see that Oskar Lange, starting from a similar diagnosis of the shortcomings of the market economy, was led to recommend socialist planning as the best approximation to the ideal system.

security system and later in the Ministry of Social Affairs. He had a strong interest in questions related to income distribution and social security and published a number of articles and reports in these areas. Simultaneously with these activities he also found time for academic work, and in 1928 he defended his doctoral thesis on the basis of his book *Den økonomiske fordeling* (The Economic Distribution), which is a broad theoretical and empirical study of the distribution of income in Denmark. The book also contains his arguably most important theoretical contribution, which was the analysis of bilateral bargaining with special reference to the labor market. A few years later, the theory was presented in English in his best-known book, *Problems of Monopoly and Economic Warfare* (1930). Right up to the time of his death he continued to publish articles on economic theory, and it is as a theorist that he achieved international fame. However, through all these years he also carried on his writing in the field that he referred to as social policy and which was based on his extensive factual knowledge including the legal and institutional framework. From 1930 to 1958 he was professor of economics at the University of Copenhagen.

Zeuthen's theory of bargaining starts from the case of bilateral monopoly (one buyer and one seller) where a trade union and an employers' organization negotiate about wages. For the case of simplicity it is assumed that none of the parties has any alternative use of their resources: workers have no other employment opportunities, and the capital of the employers is tied up in this particular industry. The alternative to arriving at an agreement is strike or lockout, which after a certain time must be expected to end in a new agreement. Can anything be said about the likely outcome of the negotiations? Zeuthen assumes that both parties have a common expectation about the cost of a conflict and about the wage that will be established once the period of conflict has come to an end. Suppose now that a wage has been proposed that is above the expected wage. In that case the workers' negotiators will wish to aim at a low risk of conflict, since they have a lot to lose by it. The employers, on the other hand, will be inclined to act so as to create a high risk of conflict because they have little to lose from this outcome. In the continuation of the negotiations the wage will therefore be pushed downward. If, on the other hand, the first proposal had been below the expected postconflict level, the union would have been the aggressive party while the employers would have liked to settle for an agreement, so that there would have been an upward pressure on the wage. At some point between these two wage levels there will exist a wage which is such that both parties consider the risk of pushing for a better alternative (higher for the union, lower for the employers) to be equally large, and this will be the equilibrium wage that is the outcome of the bargaining. Zeuthen's theory was an important contribution to better understanding of the role of bargaining and labor conflicts in modern industrial society. From a purely theoretical point of view it was an important forerunner of the game theoretic approach to bargaining that is particularly associated with the work of John Nash (see chapter 17).[9]

Zeuthen was also interested in other aspects of the theory of imperfect competition, and in *Problems of Monopoly and Economic Warfare* he constructed a model that can be seen as a generalization of Cournot's theory of duopoly. The difference from the framework of Cournot is that the two firms are not assumed to produce identical commodities. Although in equilibrium the two duopolists will charge the same price, through product development and advertising one of the duopolists will be able to capture a higher market share than his competitor. In this area, Zeuthen's discussion leads in important respects to results that are similar to those of Chamberlin (1933). However, Zeuthen's theory never received a similar attention, probably because the structure of Chamberlin's theory was simpler and more transparent and his literary exposition much more appealing to a wide readership.

Yet another area where Zeuthen did original work was in the theory of general equilibrium for a competitive economy. The general equilibrium theory of Walras had succeeded in determining the prices of all commodities and factors of production, but Walras had assumed that all equilibrium prices were positive. Zeuthen pointed out, with special reference to factor markets, that this assumption was unsatisfactory. If, for example, the equi-

---

[9] The similarity of the theories of Zeuthen and Nash was pointed out by Harsanyi (1955). The Hungarian born John C. Harsanyi (1920–2000) was a prominent contributor to the theory of games and bargaining, and together with John Nash and the German economist Reinhard Selten he was awarded the Nobel Prize in 1994.

librium demand for a factor of production was less than its supply, part of the supply would not be utilized. In that case there would be no scarcity with respect to this factor, and its equilibrium price would therefore be zero. Walras's way of writing the equilibrium equation—requiring that demand must be *equal to* supply—had therefore to be changed to an inequality: demand must be *less than or equal to* supply, and it is in the case where *less than* holds that the equilibrium price is zero. It is the market itself that determines which goods will be free and which will be scarce; this distinction cannot be taken as given in advance. This was an important insight that pointed ahead to the postwar interest in a deeper mathematical analysis of general equilibrium models. We shall return to this theme in chapter 17.

PERSPECTIVES

The thread running through this chapter has been the development of theoretical models of imperfect competition in the sense of market structures that lie between the two extremes of monopoly and perfect competition. Apart from the more critical writings of Veblen, the economists whose work we have discussed in this chapter approached the subject by different versions of partial equilibrium models that aimed to describe competition between a small number of economic agents. For many economists who followed the literature in this area, the diversity of approaches seemed fundamentally unsatisfactory. The concept of perfect competition had after all a simple and precise definition. Why could not the same be true with regard to imperfect competition? A possibly superficial answer might be that there is only one way to be perfect while there are many alternatives in regard to imperfection. As a matter of fact, however, this is an important point for the understanding of the apparently divergent literature of imperfect competition. There are so many different assumptions that one can make about the strategic interplay between the market agents and about the relationship between the different products or variants of products that the number of alternative theories must by necessity become large. One might argue that some of the models could be eliminated as completely unrealistic, but there are also limits to how far one can go in this direction. The imperfect markets of the real economy display so much variation that there will probably remain a need for a relatively large arsenal of theoretical models to capture it. It is in this perspective that we must consider the diversity in the theoretical literature on imperfect competition.

FURTHER READING

Thorstein Veblen is not an easy economist to read. This is not because the pages of his books are filled with equations and diagrams—they are not—but because his literary style makes rather heavy demands on the reader. Still, *The Theory of the Leisure Class* offers inspiring and amusing reading that economists ought to be acquainted with.

In many of the best-known texts on the history of economic thought Veblen's name cannot even be found in the index. From one point of view it is not difficult to understand why. He did not formulate any new analytical theories, nor did he contribute to the generation of systematic empirical knowledge. Still, some authors take him seriously enough to devote some space to the presentation of his ideas. A good treatment of Veblen and the American institutional school can be found in Ekelund and Hébert (1997, ch. 16); a more popular and very entertaining exposition is that of Heilbroner (1999, ch. 8). In *The New Palgrave*, Thomas Sowell has written a balanced article about his life and work.

Edward Chamberlin's *Theory of Monopolistic Competition* is well worth reading, at least in part. The structure of the theory is easier to grasp by studying a modern textbook, but once one has done that, there is much to be gained by reading the more general chapters of the original work. Kuenne (1967) has edited a collection of articles where several authors consider the importance of Chamberlin's work, and Kuenne has also written about him in *The New Palgrave*.

The Economics of Imperfect Competition by Joan Robinson remains a book from which the reader can learn a good deal, especially if he or she has a liking for geometric analysis. George Feiwel (1989a, b) is the editor of two collections of essays where a number of modern economists write about topics that concerned her. Although some of the articles make little reference to Robinson's own research, others are of more direct interest from the viewpoint of the history of thought. Thus the books contain several interesting interviews where economists like Frank Hahn, Robert Solow, and James Tobin reflect on their personal relationship with her. In *The New Palgrave* Luigi Pasinetti gives an enthusiastic account of her life and work.

Quite apart from their historical interest, Harold Hotelling's classic articles can still be read with profit by modern economists. The small volume of his work in economics is reflected in the scarcity of biographical literature. Kenneth Arrow's article in *The New Palgrave* makes one want to read more about him.

Heinrich von Stackelberg's theory of oligopoly is discussed in most textbooks in microeconomics, while texts on the history of thought mostly pay little attention to him. His own textbook *Grundlagen der theoretischen Volkswirtschaftslehre* (1948) has been translated into English as *The Theory of the Market Economy* (1952). James Konow (1994) gives an interesting account of his scientific contribution and his political sympathies.

Frederik Zeuthen's *Problems of Monopoly and Economic Warfare* gives the best impression of him as an original economic theorist. For those who read Danish, there are obituaries by Hans Brems and Henning Friis in the journal *Nationaløkonomisk Tidsskrift* in 1959, including a complete bibliography of his books and articles from 1915 to 1958. Brems has also written a much shorter article about Zeuthen as a mathematical economist in *The New Palgrave*.

The Great Systems Debate

A ROUND 1920 it had become a common view among economists that equilibrium in an economy with perfect competition implied an efficient use of society's resources. Although Pareto's welfare theory was not yet widely known, the proposition could claim support from Marshall's conclusion that market equilibrium represented a maximum of the social surplus, as well as from similar formulations elsewhere in the literature. At the same time, however, many were doubtful whether the real market economy, with its increasing degree of concentration and other imperfections, could be said to bear any close resemblance to its theoretical ideal. The socialist alternative to an economy with free markets became increasingly prominent in public discourse, and many economists began to feel that current economic theory did not really provide the defenders of the market system with much support. As pointed out in chapter 11, Pareto had concluded that "pure economics" was unable to decide whether a market or socialist economy was the best system; in principle, an ideal planning system could also lead to satisfaction of the conditions for efficient resource allocation. This point was further elaborated by the Italian economist Enrico Barone (1908; 1935). Barone interpreted the Paretian efficiency conditions as a recipe for how "the ministry of production" in a socialist state could achieve an efficient allocation of resources. The theory of optimal resource use included, among other elements, a set of rules for the best allocation of the factors of production among alternative uses; for each factor of production, the value of its marginal productivity ought to be the same in all units of production. Rules like these ought to guide the decisions of the ministry of production. If it followed them, the result for society as a whole would be just as good as under perfect competition.

THE CHALLENGE OF LUDWIG VON MISES

To begin with, Pareto's and Barone's thoughts about the choice between alternative economic systems received little attention

318

from other economists. However, in 1920 the Austrian economist Ludwig von Mises (1881–1973) published an article that was destined to become of major importance for the debate about this question. Mises was a student of Menger and Böhm-Bawerk and an enthusiastic spokesman for free markets as the system best suited for achieving both economic efficiency and individual freedom. He never obtained a top academic position in his home country, but from 1934 to 1940 he was professor of economics in Switzerland. In 1940 he emigrated to the United States, where he lived for the rest of his life.

In his famous article Mises maintained that in a socialist economy based on central planning, rational economic calculation is impossible. The reason for this is the absence of market-determined prices. Without prices that reflect scarcity and individual valuation, the planners will be unable to guide society's resources to their most productive uses. Without prices it will not be possible to compare the value of factor inputs with the value of output; therefore it will not be possible to carry out rational project evaluation. From this conclusion he derived far-reaching consequences:

> Without economic calculation there can be no economy. Hence, in a socialist state wherein the pursuit of economic calculation is impossible, there can be—in our sense of the term—no economy whatsoever. In trivial and secondary matters rational conduct might still be possible, but in general it would be impossible to speak of rational production any more. There would be no means of determining what was rational, and hence it is obvious that production could never be directed by economic considerations. . . . Would there, in fact, be any such thing as rational conduct at all, or, indeed, such a thing as rationality and logic in thought itself? Historically, human rationality is a development of economic life. Could it then obtain when divorced therefrom? (Mises 1920; 1935, p. 105)

These thoughts are not formulated with a high degree of theoretical precision, and Mises's inclination toward metaphysical vagueness did not make it easier for him to gain the attention of the international research community. However, he is much clearer in his practical illustrations, for instance, when he discusses the calculations that are necessary for the planning of a new railroad:

Should it be built at all, and if so, which out of a number of conceivable roads should be built? In a competitive and monetary economy, this question would be answered by monetary calculation. The new road will render less expensive the transport of some goods, and it may be possible to calculate whether this reduction of expense transcends that involved in the building and upkeep of the next line. That can only be calculated in money. It is not possible to attain the desired end merely by counterbalancing the various physical expenses and physical savings. (Mises 1920; 1935, p. 108)

Without a price system that enables one to compare costs and revenues, rational economic calculation is accordingly impossible.

Mises's article was translated into English in 1935, and it was then that the international debate in the academic community really started. In this connection, "international" means "English language"; at this stage, we are at the beginning of a development that would make English the universal language of scientific communication, also in economics. But in this case it is interesting to note that the main participants in the debate were not of English or American origin. They were Central Europeans who had come to view the socialist system as something far more than an intellectually fascinating theoretical model; they saw it as a very real political possibility for their respective home countries. Their hopes or fears for what this might imply explain much of the intensity and high temperature of the ensuing debate.

Oskar Lange and Abba Lerner

Mises himself was not to become a central participant in this debate; his article was the spark that started the debate, with other writers taking the center stage.[1] The first to take up the challenge from Mises was the Polish economist Oskar Lange (1904–1965). Lange began his university studies in Poland. After further studies at universities in Britain and the United States he returned to

[1] Mises's further work on socialism versus markets had less influence on the systems debate, and his other economic writings were mostly about monetary theory and policy.

his home country to teach economics at the University of Krakow. In 1938 he left Poland to take up a position as professor of economics at the University of Chicago, where he remained until the end of the Second World War. After the war he once again returned to Poland where he combined academic work with a seat in the parliament; for some time he was also a member of the government.

Lange was a highly skilled economist with a broad range of interests, and the analysis of alternative economic systems was one that had occupied him from his early years. In a 1934 study, published together with another Polish economist, Marek Breit, he presented a plan for a socialist economy that implied the socialization of all production apart from that which took place in small enterprises. The socialized production in the individual plants was to be coordinated by trusts, one for each branch of industry. The trusts were to be supervised by a public bank, which would play the role of a central planning board.[2] However, it was only after he had read Mises's article that Lange was led to formulate the model of a socialist economy for which he became famous. It was first presented to the economics profession in two journal articles in 1936 and 1937, which were later republished in book form (Lange and Taylor 1938).

Lange begins by saying that socialists ought to feel gratitude toward Professor Mises, who plays the role of devil's advocate for their cause,

> for it was his powerful challenge that forced the socialists to recognize the importance of an adequate system of economic accounting to guide the allocation of resources in a socialist economy. ... Both as an expression of recognition for the great service rendered by him and as a memento of the prime importance of sound economic accounting, a statue of Professor Mises ought to occupy an honorable place in the great hall of the Ministry of Socialization

[2] See Kowalik (1987) for a more detailed description of the Lange-Breit model. The organization of industry by means of branchwise trusts bears a striking resemblance to Stackelberg's ideas about rational organization of a corporative fascist economy; see chapter 13. This is hardly a coincidence. It is not surprising that economists who shared a skeptical attitude to the free market economy, a belief in the power of central planning, and little regard for the dangers of a powerful state should arrive at similar conclusions.

or of the Central Planning Board of the socialist state. (Lange and Taylor 1938; 1964, p. 57)

Lange's response to Mises's challenge was to develop the theory of decentralized or market socialism. He was familiar with the work of Walras and Pareto, but he had doubts whether the actual market economy could function in such a way as to satisfy the conditions for an optimal allocation of resources. In particular, he emphasized the trend that he perceived in the modern economy toward an ever increasing concentration of market power, with large companies working to limit competition by forming cartels or monopolies.[3] This development implied violations of the conditions for optimal resource use; through the concentration of industry and the use of monopoly power the free market system would lay the basis for its own decline. Lange also claimed that political attempts to gain control of monopolies and cartels were doomed to failure, since the large and powerful companies would easily come to have more political influence than the supervisory institutions that were set up to control them. He concluded his diagnosis of the market economy as follows:

> The most important part of modern economic life is just as far removed from free competition as it is from socialism; it is choked up with restrictionism of all sorts. When this state of things will have become unbearable, when its incompatibility with economic progress will have become obvious, and when it will be recognized that it is impossible to return to free competition, or to have successful public control of enterprise and of investment without taking them out of private hands, then socialism will remain as the only solution available. (Lange and Taylor 1938; 1964, pp. 120–121)

At the same time Lange recognized that the theoretical model of perfect competition had demonstrated how resources ought

---

[3] The problem had also been discussed by Mises, but his view of the causes behind this development was a completely different one. In Mises's view it was government policy, not the market itself, which was responsible for the trend toward increasing concentration. If only the government would keep away from attempts to regulate private competition, the market mechanism itself would work to eliminate the power of monopolies. Without government support no private monopoly would in the long run be able to protect itself against the forces of competition.

ideally to be allocated in the interests of society. The question was therefore whether the ideal model could be implemented in some other way than through a conventional market system.

Under Lange's system of market socialism firms would be owned by the state, and they would be instructed by their owner to maximize profit, just like firms in a market economy with private ownership. However, the prices of consumer goods and factors of production would not be determined by market forces but by the central planning bureau. In order for prices to lead the economy to an efficient allocation, they would have to be set so as to create equality between supply and demand in all markets. How was the planning bureau to identify these prices? It would, of course, have to collect data about costs and demand, but Lange's central idea was that the setting of prices would have to be based on an experimental process of trial and error which bore a strong similarity to Walras's *tâtonnement* process (see chapter 9). If the planning bureau initially had set the prices of some goods and factors too high, there would be excess supply, and in the next round the bureau would lower the prices. For other goods and factors the prices might have been set too low, leading to excess demand, and the rules guiding the decisions of the planning bureau would lead it to raise the prices. Through this process the bureau would gradually approach a general equilibrium of supply and demand, implying an efficient use of resources. In other words, the functioning of the planning bureau would imitate the ideal version of the market as described in the theories of Walras and Pareto.

The fundamental difference between market socialism and the system of free markets is that Lange's system requires all firms to take prices as given; it is impossible for any firm to exercise market power. Paradoxically, it is under socialism that the ideal version of the market system can be made to function! Lange also believed that the trend toward increasing concentration in modern industry was a major cause of the instability that was characteristic of contemporary capitalism, and that market socialism would be a system better designed to cope with the effects of the business cycle.

Lange admitted that market socialism, like other economic systems, could have some imperfections. In particular, he stressed the danger associated with an increasing bureaucracy that could follow from detailed state regulation of industry. However, he pointed out that this was a danger that would also be present in a private ownership economy dominated by large companies. At least, he argued, it was better to have public servants who were subject to democratic control than business managers who in his view were subject to no control whatsoever.

Many economists had argued that one of the most important points in favor of a private market economy was the incentives that it created to promote innovation and technical progress. It was Lange's belief that the trend toward increasing concentration and power of monopolies had already weakened the dynamic forces of the market system, but he also realized that the lack of incentives could become a problem when managers were no longer guided in their decisions by a concern for private profit. However, the issue of how the democratic control of managers could be exercised so as to encourage efficiency and innovation was a subject that he had little to say about, and he expressed the view that this was a type of question that ought to be studied by sociologists, not economists.

In the course of the first decade following the publication of his vision of the new economic system, Lange appears to have modified his view of the desirable extent of public ownership under market socialism. In the first version of his plan it seems as if he thought that public ownership would gradually come to extend to the whole of private industry, but in a letter to his critic Friedrich Hayek in 1940 he wrote:

> Practically, I should, of course, recommend the determination of prices by a thorough market process whenever this is feasible, i.e. whenever the number of selling and purchasing units is sufficiently large. Only where the number of these units is so small that a situation of oligopoly, oligopsony, or bilateral monopoly would obtain, would I advocate price fixing by a public agency. (Kowalik 1987, 127)

In an article that he wrote during the Second World War about the prospects for democracy in Poland, Lange went even a bit further in this direction by recommending that public ownership and the control of prices be limited to a few key industries like banking and transport. What he thought about these issues as he gradually came to occupy important positions in the Polish communist state is less clear. Both his official status and the general lack of freedom of expression in the country make it difficult to know whether the content of his writings about alternative economic systems represents his own thinking or the official views of the Communist Party.

Oskar Lange also made a number of influential contributions to other areas of economics. In the 1930s and 1940s he wrote some important articles both about Keynesian macroeconomic theory and the foundations of welfare economics. After his postwar return to Poland his interests appear to have turned more in the direction of technical analysis; he published a textbook of econometrics and wrote a number of studies of cybernetics (systems analysis). Maybe these were interests that were easier to cultivate in a political environment that did not tolerate very much in the way of deviations from official ideology.

Lange was not the only economist who took an interest in the theory of market socialism in this period. His chief ally in the scientific discussions that took place was Abba P. Lerner (1905–82). Born in Rumania, Lerner's academic career took him to several countries and universities. While he was a student at the London School of Economics, he wrote innovative papers about international trade theory that were published in the leading academic journals, and these were followed by contributions to macroeconomics and public economics. His political convictions were—especially for his time—a peculiar mixture of socialism and belief in the efficiency of the market mechanism. He was also firmly convinced of the importance of private firms for ensuring the individual's freedom regarding the choice of occupation. He published articles that elaborated the analysis of Lange's system, and it is Lerner's clarifications of the price adjustment mechanism under market socialism that has made it widely known as the Lange-Lerner mechanism.

Lerner also wrote the first modern textbook of welfare economics. *The Economics of Control* (1944) presented the first systematic exposition, of the type that we find in modern texts, of the conditions for efficient, or Pareto optimal, resource allocation. He pointed out that there were three sets of conditions that would have to be satisfied for the allocation to be Pareto optimal:

1. Efficiency in consumption: for given total quantities of consumer goods, it must not be possible to make one consumer better off without making one or more others worse off.
2. Efficiency in production: it must not be possible to increase the output of one commodity without reducing the output of one or more other commodities.
3. Efficiency in the product mix: it must not be possible to alter the composition of production so as to make one consumer better off without making one or more others worse off.

Lerner showed that these conditions would be satisfied both under perfect competition and under market socialism; the crucial condition was that all consumers and firms faced the same prices. He emphasized strongly a more practical interpretation of the abstract efficiency conditions: consumer prices should be equal to the marginal costs of production. Like Lange, Lerner's perspective on the main results of the theory of welfare economics was they could be read as a handbook of optimal decisions under central planning. However, he paid little attention to the problems that would have to be overcome for their practical implementation.

FRIEDRICH VON HAYEK

Friedrich von Hayek (1899–1992) was born in Vienna, where his university studies were concluded with doctoral degrees both in economics and political science; during his studies he also had close contacts with Mises. In 1931 he came to England as professor at the London School of Economics, and in 1950 he moved to the United States, where he was associated with a research institute at the University of Chicago. In 1962 he returned to Europe as professor at the University of Freiburg in Germany. Together with the Swedish economist Gunnar Myrdal he received the Nobel Prize in economics for 1974.

Hayek began his career with studies of monetary theory and the business cycle, and in the 1930s he became a prominent critic of the macroeconomic theories of John Maynard Keynes. Gradually, however, he became more interested in questions related to the choice among alternative economic systems, and in this area he became known as the foremost spokesman for

Mises's side in the systems debate, and as the strongest critic of Lange's views. In the postwar period his interests turned more in the direction of general social philosophy, with a strong focus on the methodological problems that he saw as specific to the social sciences.

It was Hayek who took the initiative to have Mises's article translated into English. With time, he himself came to believe that Mises's views on prices and markets paid insufficient attention to two important aspects of the market mechanism—incentives and information. When private firms and their owners strive to maximize profits, it is because the profits accrue to themselves; they have therefore a strong personal incentive to make decisions which, under perfect competition, are in the interests of society. By contrast, in Lange's socialist system the profit is collected by the state and this weakens the link between private interests and the good of society. The officials of the central planning bureau will have no personal incentives to ensure that the public companies actually maximize profit.

Equally important was Hayek's analysis of the problems of information. In his view the major part of the economically relevant information in society is private in character. Consumers' knowledge of their preferences and resources and firms' insights in the technology of production are as a rule unavailable to outside observers like a state planning bureau. It is through their market transactions that individuals provide information about technology and preferences to the rest of the economy, and the fundamental role of prices is therefore to be carriers of information. The fact that economic agents take prices as given reflects the fact that they do not have any information about the economy beyond their own private sphere. In fact, they have also limited information about their own situation; in Hayek's vision of the economic system, consumers and firms are permanently searching for new information, also about their own preferences and technology. The price system develops spontaneously as a result of the actions of individual agents, and such a system cannot possibly be replicated by bureaucratic processes.

Probably the best expression of Hayek's views is to be found in his article "The Use of Knowledge in Society" (1945). Here he asks the question of what we mean by a rational economic system or, as he prefers to put it, a rational economic order. He points out

327

that if we are in possession of all relevant information in the form of preferences and resources, then the solution to the problem of economic allocation is a matter of pure logic, and mathematical economists have shown us the conditions that must be satisfied to achieve an efficient allocation. However, according to Hayek, this is definitely not the economic problem with which society is in fact confronted:

> The peculiar character of the problem of a rational economic order is determined precisely by the fact that the knowledge of the circumstances of which we must make use never exists in concentrated or integrated form but solely as the dispersed bits of incomplete and frequently contradictory knowledge which all the separate individuals possess. The economic problem of society is thus not merely a problem of how to allocate "given" resources—if "given" is taken to mean given to a single mind which deliberately solves the problem set by these "data." It is rather a problem of how to secure the best use of resources known to any of the members of society, for ends whose relative importance only these individuals know. Or, to put it briefly, it is a problem of the utilization of knowledge not given to anyone in its totality. (Hayek 1945, pp. 519–520)

Prices transmit information to the individual economic agent, and this induces him to make socially rational decisions, even if his own information about the economy as a whole is severely limited. Hayek illustrates this point by the following example: let us assume that somewhere in the world there emerges a new industrial use of tin, or as an alternative assumption, that the estimated reserves of tin have been significantly reduced. In a market economy the individual user of tin will typically not know whether the increased scarcity of tin is due to the first or the second of these causes; neither is it important for him to know it. What is important is that a higher price of tin sends him a signal that it would be profitable for him to cut back on his own use of tin, and this would also be in society's interest.

The problem that is solved by the market cannot, Hayek maintains, be solved by a planning process of the type that Lange had in mind. The amount of information required for the problem to be solved by central planning is too dispersed and personalized to be made available to a central planning bureau. Economists like Lange and Lerner had been misled by formal analytical models that completely disregarded the problem of information.

Many economists in the 1950s and 1960s thought that it was obvious that Lange had won the debate with Mises and Hayek. There were at least two reasons for this. One was that Lange had based his arguments on existing economic theories, so that market socialism emerged as a direct application of the theories of welfare economics and general equilibrium. The firmer theoretical foundation lent a degree of scientific legitimacy to his ideas that the less formalized arguments of Mises and Hayek appeared to be lacking. The other main reason was the general planning optimism of the first couple of decades of the postwar period, which was derived both from the successes of wartime planning and from what was perceived as the great economic progress of the Soviet Union under its regime of central planning. More recently, this view of the debate has changed. On the one hand, the collapse of the socialist system in the Soviet Union and Eastern Europe seemed to lend support to Mises's and Hayek's views of the inherent weaknesses of central economic planning. On the other hand, modern developments in economic theory have taken a course that is much closer to Hayek's emphasis on the importance of incentives and information in the market economy.

In the middle of the Second World War, while still living in England, Hayek wrote *The Road to Serfdom*, which came out in 1944. This book represents a significant extension of the framework for discussion of alternative economic systems. Hayek maintains that the conditions for economic and political freedom in reality are closely connected, and that the restrictions on economic freedom that would follow from the extension of government control would necessarily also involve a loss of political freedom. From this point of view fascism and communism are no longer polar cases in political terms but closely related systems whose common contrast is the free market system and the liberal political order. Hayek therefore warned against the trend toward expansion of the public sector and central economic planning that he felt was so evident in Britain, and he argued that this development would necessarily imply a weakening of political democracy; this was the road to serfdom.

Joseph Schumpeter

Like Mises and Hayek, Joseph Schumpeter (1883–1950) was Austrian by birth, although he was born in a part of the Habsburg Empire that is now a part of the Czech Republic. He studied law and economics at the University of Vienna, where Wieser and Böhm-Bawerk were among his teachers. After completing his doctorate in law, he tried to establish himself in the legal profession, but he also began to write a book about research methods in economics, and on the basis of this book he obtained an academic position first in Czernowitz (a city now in the Ukraine) and later in Graz. In 1912 he published *Theorie der Wirtschaftlichen Entwicklung* (*The Theory of Economic Development*) where for the first time he presented his theories of the sources of economic growth. The book was soon translated into English and made Schumpeter an internationally recognized economist. But he had difficulties settling into academic life. He was an active participant in the political life of Austria, where his public image to many was a confusing mixture of conservative and socialist. After the First World War he was appointed Minister of Finance, but after just a few months he was forced to resign. He then became the managing director of a private bank, but this attempt at a new career ended in disaster for both him and the bank. He gradually returned to academic life as professor of economics at the University of Bonn in Germany. In 1932 he moved to the United States where he became a professor at Harvard University, and this became his academic home for the rest of his life. While at Harvard he published two major books, *Business Cycles* (1939) and *Capitalism, Socialism, and Democracy* (1942). His great work on the history of economic thought was incomplete at the time of his death but appeared as *History of Economic Analysis* in 1954.

Schumpeter said that in his youth he had set three goals for himself—to become the greatest lover in Austria, the greatest horseman in Europe, and the greatest economist in the world—but that he had only achieved two of them. A witty remark and an interesting glimpse of a personality with ambitions that were in part very modern and in part derived from premodern times. In this context we will leave aside his achievements in the first two areas, but there is no doubt that he became a very prominent and important economist. However, it is not easy to define the exact nature of his contribution to economics. Through much of his life he had an unhappy love affair with mathematical economics. He was convinced of the superiority of the mathematical method, but he did not possess the skills that were required to make a contribution of his own to formal economic analysis. What he has left to posterity is above all a particular vision of the economic system as an organism in continuous development. Many have therefore maintained that Schumpeter is the founder of what is sometimes called evolutionary economics, an approach that in their view is neglected by mainstream economics.[4]

Schumpeter's contributions to the great systems debate are closely related to his view of the driving forces in the development of the market economy. The main role in this process is played by the *entrepreneur*, the agent who introduces innovations in economic activity:

> The function of entrepreneurs is to reform or revolutionize the pattern of production by exploiting an invention or, more generally, an untried technological possibility for producing a new commodity or producing an old one in a new way, by opening up a new source of supply of materials or a new outlet for products, by reorganizing an industry and so on. (Schumpeter 1942; 1947, p. 132)

Inventions and discoveries occur continuously, but their transformation by entrepreneurs into innovations that alter the preconditions for productive activities happens in waves because of the social resistance to change. Innovations break through when the accumulation of inventions and discoveries has reached a critical mass. With a change of technology—in a broad sense—there will be opportunities for new products and new techniques of production; new firms and industries emerge while some of the old ones vanish. This dynamic process Schumpeter called *creative destruction*. In his book *Business Cycles* he claimed that the theory was supported by statistical evidence. He found empiri-

---

[4] An international Schumpeter Society attempts, through conferences and publications, to keep his vision alive in modern economic research.

cal support for the existence of three cycles of unequal length: a short-run cycle of about five years; a medium-run, ten-year cycle; and a long-run cycle of approximately sixty years.[5]

What kind of market economy is it that provides the best framework for the innovative entrepreneur? In spite of Schumpeter's admiration for Walras's general equilibrium theory, he believed that its idealized picture of the nature of competition was quite misleading as a description of an actual market economy, which always finds itself at a particular stage of a dynamic development process. In the real world, the static efficiency of the Walrasian equilibrium was much less significant than the dynamic efficiency that resulted in creative destruction. This process could hardly be imagined without deviations from perfect competition. To an increasing degree, a characteristic feature of a dynamic market economy will be concentration of market power with monopoly and oligopoly as the dominant market forms.

The development of a market economy dominated by large companies will, however, result in an economic system where the role of the entrepreneur becomes bureaucratized. Innovation becomes routine work rather than the outcome of genuine individual creativity:

> Economic progress tends to become depersonalized and automatized. Bureau and committee work tends to replace individual action. (Schumpeter 1942; 1947, p. 133)

This development will also undermine the social status of the entrepreneur; the mystique and glory that were attached to it in former times will disappear. The great masses of the people will no longer accept the role of the entrepreneurs as social and political leaders, and they no longer feel any emotional attachment to the system that they represent. At the same time there emerges a new class of intellectual idealists—educated at the institutions of learning created by the capitalist system—who are critical to

---

[5] These cycles, or "waves," had been suggested earlier, however. Thus, the medium-run cycle is associated with the French statistician Clément Juglar (1819–1905), while the long wave has been supported by references to the work of the Russian economist Nikolai Kondratief (1892–1931?). Kondratief vanished during Stalin's purges, and the year of his death is therefore uncertain.

an economic system based on self-interest. Their critical attitudes will encourage a policy that gradually transfers private firms to public ownership and "social control."

This theory of the eventual victory of socialism is clearly reminiscent of Marx's analysis of the development and decline of the capitalist system and the rise of the proletariat. The similarity appears above all in the broad sweep through economic, sociological, and political causes. But there are also a number of dissimilarities between the two perspectives. Marx predicted a development toward class war and revolution. Schumpeter, on the other hand, foresaw a gradual development whereby bureaucratic socialism would come to take the place of a capitalist system lacking in social legitimacy.

Would the transition to socialism be of benefit to society? In his comparison between socialism and capitalism (the market economy) Schumpeter takes a different viewpoint from that of Mises, Lange, and Hayek. The brand of capitalism that is relevant for the comparison is not the perfectly competitive economy of Walras and Pareto. Instead it is the capitalism of oligopolies and monopolistic competition;[6] this is both a more realistic vision and, by force of its dynamic efficiency, a more viable one. This implies that the fear of increasing bureaucracy that would follow the transition to socialism is without foundation:

> I for one cannot visualize, in the conditions of modern society, a socialist organization in any form other than that of a huge and all-embracing bureaucratic apparatus. ... But surely this should not horrify anyone who realizes how far the bureaucratization of economic life ... has gone already and who knows how to cut through the underbrush of phrases that has grown up around the subject. (Schumpeter 1942; 1947, p. 206)

Even if Schumpeter's writing expresses a general skepticism toward bureaucratic decision processes, whether they occur in the public or private sector, he takes the view that the problem of bureaucratization cannot be used as a point against either social-

---

[6] In this connection Schumpeter writes very positively about the work of Chamberlin and Robinson, but his own interpretation of their theories emphasizes the dynamic aspects of competition to a much larger extent than these writers did themselves.

ism or capitalism. He believes that a form of decentralized socialism of the Lange type would be feasible in practice. One of his arguments in favor of such a system is that the solution of fundamental economic problems would in some respects actually be easier than in the market economy. He compares the situation facing a manager in either of the two systems. One of the major difficulties of being the manager of a company is how to take account of the uncertainty that surrounds decision making in a market context. A very important source of uncertainty lies in the lack of knowledge about the behavior of competitors and about "how general business conditions are going to shape." This type of uncertainty would be eliminated under decentralized socialism, where the central planning agency, through its responsibility for determining prices, would take on the task of coordinating decisions between companies. Other types of uncertainty would remain and be basically the same as in a system of free markets, but the elimination of the uncertainty about the actions of others would radically reduce the complexity of the manager's work.

Schumpeter's analysis of the relationship between socialism and the market economy is complex and difficult to summarize. More than the other participants in the systems debate he emphasizes the importance of noneconomic factors, and his view of the inevitable victory of socialism is more reminiscent of Marx than of the Lange-Hayek debate over the price system. While Lange and Hayek discussed the *choice* between economic systems according to their ability to generate good outcomes for society, Schumpeter took an entirely different approach:

> Value judgments about capitalist performance are of little interest. For mankind is not free to choose. This is not only because the mass of people are not in a position to compare alternatives rationally and always accept what they are being told. There is a much deeper reason for it. Things economic and social move by their own momentum, and the ensuing situations compel individuals and groups to behave in certain ways whatever they may wish to do—not indeed by destroying their freedom of choice but by shaping the choosing mentalities and by narrowing the list of possibilities from which to choose. If this is the quintessence of Marxism then we all of us have got to be Marxists. (Schumpeter 1942; 1947, p. 129)

His comparison of his own analysis with that of Marx is obviously to the point. For in this reasoning it is not a question of a choice between systems on the basis of rational scientific discourse and informed political decisions; history has already decided the future course of events.[7] It should be noted that Schumpeter did not look forward to the future that he predicted, for he found his own vision of the transition to socialism to be unattractive. His prognosis for the development of society was quite different from his own wishes, which rather went in the direction of the liberal order in the Austria of his youth. But that was "the world of yesterday," which could not be restored.

Some words should also be said about Schumpeter as a historian of economic thought. This was an interest that had developed in his youth, and in his later years he worked on an extensive review of the history of economics from antiquity to modern times. He was unable to finish his *History of Economic Analysis* (1954), but his wife, Elizabeth Boody Schumpeter, who was an economic historian, edited the manuscript on the basis of Schumpeter's chapter drafts and notes, and the book was published four years after his death. It is a display of the strong sides of Schumpeter's talent: his wide reading, his personal and colorful style of writing, and his ability to draw out the long lines in the history of ideas. It is not a textbook in the usual sense. As his other books describe his visions of economic life, the *History* offers his vision of the history of economics, and this vision is so strong and personal that it often rises above narrow concerns like chronology. An example of this is the presentation of Cournot's theory of duopoly (Cournot 1838) in the part of the book entitled "From 1870 to 1914 and After." We can only guess at his reasons for organizing the material in this way, but a possible explanation is that he thought that Cournot's work could be seen as a further development of Alfred Marshall's theories of competition and monopoly. The reader may at times be somewhat frustrated by the difficulties of finding one's way in the book, but there are also new insights to be gained by the many

---

[7] In Schumpeter as well as in Marx there is an unresolved tension between the decisive role that they ascribe to the creative individual—Marx's capitalist and Schumpeter's entrepreneur—and their deterministic view of economic and political development.

unexpected connections drawn between topics and authors belonging to different time periods.

Overview of the Systems Debate

The great systems debate is an interesting episode in the history of economics. The debate about the relative merits of markets and socialism and of decentralization and central planning is naturally not limited to the relatively short time during which this particular debate took place. The systematic investigation of the pros and cons of alternative economic systems has been a central topic in the literature of economics both before and after this episode. The special urgency that the debate acquired in the 1930s and 1940s can be explained both by factors internal to the discipline and by external events.

The development of the theories of general equilibrium and welfare economics had led to a much clearer understanding of the efficiency properties of the market mechanism than had been the case before. At the same time, the stylized picture of the market economy that had been drawn by Walras had made many economists aware of the contrast between this picture and the real economy in which they lived. Among some of them, like Mises and Hayek, the dissatisfaction with the formalized theory of the market economy created an ambition to formulate a new theory of markets that more realistically captured their true efficiency properties. To economists like Lange and Lerner, on the other hand, the challenge became instead to explore alternative economic systems that could realize the potential for efficiency that was indicated by the theory of perfect competition. The discussions and controversies about the role of prices for efficient resource use, about incentives and information, and the relationship between politics and economics led—at least in the long run—to a clearer understanding of the role that economic theory could play in the debate about alternative economic and political systems.

In the period between the two world wars the choice between alternative systems was a problem of far more than academic interest. Socialist and communist parties and organizations had acquired considerable political influence, and the Russian revolution of 1917 had convinced many that communist seizure of power had become a real possibility in other countries as well. Communist and socialist ideology was strongly based on economic arguments, and it was natural that many economists should feel the need for a scientific scrutiny of them. But the contributions to the debate were hardly examples of detached evaluations. Without doubt, both Mises and Hayek on their side of the controversy and Lange and Lerner on the other saw their theoretical contributions as being in service to their political convictions. But this should not lead us to brush off their theories as poorly disguised political propaganda. None of them tries to hide the nature of their political sympathies; nevertheless, their theories can be evaluated on a purely scientific basis. We may consider Hayek's view of prices as carriers of information without having taken a stand in favor of his political libertarianism. We may also study Lange's theoretical model of decentralized socialism without being disturbed by our knowledge of his political support for a communist dictatorship.

The intensity of the debate was also a reflection of the personal experiences of the main actors. The most prominent among them were all people who left their home countries, which they saw as threatened by fascist or communist revolutions. Mises and Hayek immigrated to the United States, which seemed to them to offer the best prospects for a liberal political and economic order. Lange, after his American exile, moved back to his native Poland when its government seemed likely to carry out his ideas for economic reform. They must all have felt that the great systems debate concerned issues that were of central importance in their own lives.

FURTHER READING

The early contributions to the systems debate by Barone and Mises were translated into English and published in Hayek (1935). Mises's 1920 article is also available at the web site of the American Ludwig von Mises Institute (http://www.mises .org). This web site provides much interesting information about Mises, even if the contents have a strong ideological bias.

Oskar Lange's ideas about market socialism are presented in Lange and Taylor (1938). His life and writings are described in

Kowalik's article about him in *The New Palgrave*. Abba Lerner's *The Economics of Control* can still be read with profit as an introduction to welfare economics. Tibor Scitovsky writes about his life and work in *The New Palgrave*.

Hayek's book *The Road to Serfdom* (1944) is well worth reading even today. It contains many important insights into the relationship between economics and politics, even if most modern readers may feel that his dark prophecies concerning the effects of public sector expansion in a market economy are a bit overdone. As a summary of his views on the essential nature of markets and prices, the article on "The Use of Knowledge in Society" (Hayek 1945) can be strongly recommended. A recent biography is Caldwell (2004).

Anyone who is interested in the history of economic thought must get acquainted with Schumpeter's *History of Economic Analysis* (1954); in addition, *Capitalism, Socialism, and Democracy* (1942) is fascinating reading. Thomas McGraw (2007) has written an excellent biography that covers both Schumpeter's eventful life and his contributions to economics. For a shorter account, one may consult Heilbronner (1999) who has a lively and amusing chapter about his contradictory visions. Samuelson (1951), who followed Schumpeter's lectures as a student at Harvard, gives a vivid impression of his personality.

The systems debate also continues in more modern forms. Bardhan and Roemer (1992) argue that market socialism should still be taken seriously as an economic system, while counterarguments are presented by Shleifer and Vishny (1994). A wide-ranging modern analysis of the relative merits of markets and socialism is Stiglitz (1994), although the discussion is not closely related to the earlier debate. Gregory and Harrison (2005) provide a fascinating description of actual socialist planning as it was practiced in the Soviet Union in Stalin's times.

John Maynard Keynes
and the Keynesian Revolution

Looking back at the preceding chapters it may seem strange that we have hardly referred to the distinction between micro- and macroeconomics. This distinction plays an important role in modern expositions of economics and is considered of such significance that authors of introductory textbooks often divide their material into two parts of roughly similar length, one microeconomic and one macroeconomic. The microeconomic part covers the theories of consumer and firm behavior and of the functioning of markets, leaving to macroeconomics issues like unemployment, inflation, the business cycle, and economic growth. However, this partitioning of the field was unknown to earlier generations of economists.[1] Thus, for most of them the question of the driving forces behind the economic growth process could not be separated from the analysis of the efficiency of the market mechanism; growth theory—to use a modern term—was intimately connected with the theory of markets. There did exist a theory of the role of money in the economy, but since the main message of this theory, at least among a majority of writers, was that in the long run the quantity of money had no effect on the real economy, monetary matters were considered to be subordinate to the analysis of the real economy. Although there could be some real effects in the short run, these were widely considered as frictions that would be neutralized by market adjustment after a relatively short time.

A similar view was adopted with respect to the "crises" that were a recurrent experience of economic life. It was acknowl-

---

[1] The origin of the terms *micro-* and *macroeconomics* is not quite clear, but much suggests that they are due to the Norwegian economist Ragnar Frisch who in a 1933 article used the concepts of micro- and macrodynamics. The words *microeconomics* and *macroeconomics* were later used by the research group surrounding the Dutch economist Jan Tinbergen, who in his early work was strongly influenced by Frisch (see chapter 16).

edged that such crises resulted in unemployment, but the common attitude among economists was that unemployment was due to short-run market imperfections, especially in the labor market. In the long run, unemployment would be eliminated through the adjustment of the markets to new conditions. In particular, by a lowering of wages the demand for labor would increase until it was equal to supply. In other words, unemployment would vanish or at least be reduced to the unavoidable frictional amount that would always exist in a dynamic economy where some sectors expand while others are in decline.

This, admittedly, is a simplified review of the attitude to unemployment in earlier times. But it remains true that most economists' views concerning the causes of the business cycle and of policies against unemployment and inflation did not rest on a commonly accepted theoretical basis. However, during the 1930s this state of affairs underwent a radical change, and the person who more than anyone else is associated with the theoretical reorientation is the English economist John Maynard Keynes.

LIFE AND WORK

John Maynard Keynes (1883–1946) was born into the university environment in Cambridge, and Cambridge remained his spiritual and partly also his physical home throughout his life. His father, John Neville Keynes, also began his career as an economist and wrote a book about methodological issues,[2] but he gradually came to give up his scientific work, devoting his professional life to university administration. Maynard—the name used by family and friends—was educated at Eton, one of the elite public schools, and later at the University of Cambridge. He first specialized in mathematics, but under the influence of Alfred Marshall he took up economics as his main—but far from only—academic field of interest. As a matter of fact, his study of economics was short and unsystematic; most of his knowledge of the field was

---

[2] John Neville Keynes's *The Scope and Method of Political Economy* (1891) was a systematic comparison of the historical and theoretical approaches to the study of economics. This topic was closely related to the German-Austrian *Methodenstreit* that was described in chapter 8.

acquired by reading and gradually by his own teaching. Having completed his university education, he took the so-called Civil Service Examination in order to qualify for a position in the government service. Keynes did very well, ending up as number 2 of the 104 who sat for the exam, but, interestingly, his weakest scores were in mathematics and economics.

As a result of his examination performance Keynes obtained a position in the Ministry of Indian Affairs ("India Office") and later in the Ministry of Finance ("Treasury"). In parallel with his work in the India Office he studied probability theory and wrote a thesis, *A Treatise on Probability*, which in 1909 he submitted to King's College in Cambridge as a "fellowship dissertation," roughly corresponding to a doctoral thesis. It was published as a book in 1921 and has obtained a place in the history of probability theory. Thematically, it lies on the borderline between mathematics and philosophy.

A high point in Keynes's administrative career occurred when, at the end of the First World War in 1918, he was appointed a member of the British delegation to the Peace Conference in Versailles. Here he soon became uneasy about the policy pursued by the allied powers toward the vanquished Germany, especially about the amount of war reparations that in his view would cause severe damage both to the economy of Germany and the rest of Europe. His book *The Economic Consequences of the Peace* (1919), which combined economic analysis with vivid and provocative descriptions of the negotiation process, caused great public attention and made him world famous. By this book Keynes achieved a position as one whose opinions carried weight on all issues of economic policy.

With this incident, Keynes's bureaucratic career came to an end, at least temporarily, and he returned to Cambridge as teacher and researcher. At first he did not distinguish himself as an innovative theorist. In terms of his basic approach to economic theory, he was a faithful disciple of Marshall, while his research interests lay in the study of money and financial markets. He never held a professorial chair in Cambridge; his official title was simply Fellow of King's College. (As a matter of fact, there was only one chair of economics in Cambridge, and this was held by Pigou who was known as "the Prof.") This position gave him considerable freedom to write, to speculate on the stock exchange, to take part in cultural life, and to be active as a political advisor.[3] During a usual week he divided his time between London and Cambridge. Most workdays were spent in London, while he travelled to Cambridge for the weekends. On Monday mornings he gave a lecture course in monetary theory that was attended by students, university teachers, and visiting economists. On Monday evening, before returning to London, he presided over the meetings of his Political Economy Club in King's College, where the members were mostly his most promising students. From 1911 to 1945 he was in charge of the *Economic Journal*, first together with Edgeworth and later as its sole editor.

Keynes's first real contribution to his field of research was the book *A Tract on Monetary Reform* (1923). It shows him as an economist with great practical insight in the workings of the financial markets, but it does not have high academic pretensions. A much more ambitious work was his next major publication, *A Treatise on Money* (1930), which clearly aimed to give an original contribution to economic theory. However, most experts on Keynes consider the book to be less than successful in terms of its theoretical ambitions, especially because it tries to derive a dynamic macroeconomic theory from a set of equations that must mainly be regarded as accounting identities. Interestingly, this view appears to have been shared by the author, who in his preface wrote that he could have written both a shorter and better book if he were now to start afresh. And this is what he did; almost immediately he began writing the book that became his major work, *The General Theory of Employment, Interest, and Money* (1936), which will be discussed in more detail below. It is on this book that Keynes's fame as an economic theorist rests.

Toward the outbreak of the Second World War Keynes was once more drawn into political life as an advisor to the British government. In this role he made a number of significant contributions in several areas, but the most important was perhaps

[3] Keynes had strong literary and artistic interests and was a prominent member of the so-called Bloomsbury Circle that consisted of many well-known artists and intellectuals. He also became involved with the administrative and financial side of cultural life, and after his marriage in 1925 to the Russian ballerina Lydia Lopokova he developed a particular interest in the art of the ballet.

his efforts to establish the system of international exchange rate cooperation that became known as the Bretton Woods system. He had been in poor health after suffering a heart attack in 1937, and when he died at the relatively early age of sixty-three it may well have been caused by the heavy work load and extensive travelling that he had taken on during the war years.

THE GENERAL THEORY

When the *General Theory* was published, Keynes was already a famous and influential economist both in Britain and abroad, but his earlier work would hardly have qualified him for a place among the great names of economic science. His reputation did not primarily rest on his work in economic theory, and on this background it is quite remarkable that he managed to produce a theoretical contribution that many of his contemporaries regarded as the most important book on economics since the *Wealth of Nations.* During his work on the book Keynes received frequent suggestions and comments from a small circle of younger economists that became known as the "Cambridge Circus"; this included people who later became famous in the profession, like Dennis Robertson, James Meade, and Joan Robinson.

Many writers have stressed the continuity in Keynes's thought about monetary questions and emphasized the influence that Marshall had on him. Still, there can be no doubt that Keynes considered his *General Theory* to be a definitive break with established views in the area, including those that he had himself advanced in the *Treatise on Money* six years earlier. What was his own view of the pathbreaking nature of the book?

Popular views of what the *General Theory* is all about are often based on the political implications of the analysis, especially the recommendation that the government should try to stabilize employment by influencing aggregate demand. The policy tools to be used should primarily be changes in public expenditure and the level of taxation. And because Keynes wrote, and the book was read, during the period of the Great Depression and mass unemployment in the 1930s the essence of the book was naturally interpreted as a proposal to increase public spending and lower taxes, in other words to engage in deficit spending. Both in Keynes's own time and later this was widely regarded as his central message.

However, whether this view is historically correct is open to discussion, at least if we interpret it as a hypothesis of what was Keynes's real concern in the book. First of all, Keynes's contemporaries among the leading economists were not against proposals to stimulate demand by increases of public spending. In this connection, it is interesting to note that Keynes was one of six prominent economists who on October 17, 1931, published a letter to the editor in *The Times* urging the government to increase the demand for labor by an expansion of public expenditure. It is even more interesting that one of the other signatories was Pigou, for in the *General Theory* he was to be taken as the representative of the conventional view, or the "school" that Keynes referred to as "the classical economists."[4] One possible explanation of this apparent paradox is that Keynes was so concerned to emphasize the difference between himself and his predecessors that he overlooked the fact that Pigou agreed with him on crucial issues of economic policy. An alternative explanation is that he believed that the fundamental difference between him and the "classics" appeared not on the level of practical economic policy but on that of the underlying theory. The view that the second interpretation is the correct one receives support in the preface to the book where Keynes writes:

> This book is chiefly addressed to my fellow economists. I hope that it will be intelligible to others. But its main purpose is to deal with difficult questions of theory, and only in the second place with the applications of this theory to practice. (Keynes 1936, p. v)

On the other hand there can be no doubt that the *General Theory* does provide a theoretical foundation for the recommendation of a more active government policy to ensure full employment,

---

[4] Keynes writes (1936, p. 3) that he is aware of the common understanding of this concept, but that he has become accustomed to use it in a more general sense to include those that he calls "the *followers* of Ricardo"—as for example Mill, Marshall, Edgeworth, and Pigou. This definition is based on the view that the most important distinction between classical and modern economists lies in the modern view of unemployment as an equilibrium phenomenon in contrast to the disequilibrium perspective of the classics. Such a distinction becomes almost the same as the classification of all economists before Keynes as "classics," while Keynes stands out as the only modern economist.

which had indeed been a main concern of the author since the 1920s.[5] When economists with a background in "classical theory" suggested increased public spending as a remedy for unemployment, this recommendation was mostly justified by the particular features of the current state of the economy. By contrast, Keynes's analysis led him to believe that the state had to undertake a more permanent responsibility for carrying out an economic policy that ensured full employment.

The central theoretical message of the book is that the price and wage mechanism does not function in a way that leads to full employment. When the economy is exposed to shocks, particularly in the form of demand failures, it is quantities, not prices and wages that bear the brunt of adjustment to a new equilibrium. Instead of lower prices and wages, with a continuation of full employment at a lower level of real wages, we get excess production and unemployment in the new equilibrium. It is obvious that Keynes saw this as a theoretically revolutionary breakthrough which ought to lead all economists to rethink their theoretical position from first principles. This is how he expresses it in the preface to the book:

> The composition of this book has been for the author a long struggle of escape, and so must the reading of it be for most readers if the author's assault upon them is to be successful,—a struggle of escape from habitual modes of thought and expression. The ideas which are here expressed so laboriously are extremely simple and should be obvious. The difficulty lies, not in the new ideas, but in escaping from the old ones, which ramify, for those brought up as most of us have been, into every corner of our minds. (Keynes 1936, p. viii)

KEYNES AND THE CLASSICS ON LABOR AND WAGES

Keynes begins his analysis in chapter 2 of the *General Theory* by summarizing the classical economists' view of the labor market.[6] As a general reference for the nature of the classical view he re-

---

[5] See, e.g., the articles on "Inflation and Deflation" in part 2 of Keynes (1931).

[6] In the following, the concepts of the "classics" and the "classical economists" will be used in Keynes's sense, which should not be confused with the meaning of the term elsewhere in this book.

fers particularly to Pigou's recent book *Theory of Unemployment* (1933). According to Keynes, the classical theory of employment is based on two fundamental postulates:

1. The wage is equal to the marginal productivity of labor.
2. The wage is equal to the marginal (dis)utility of labor at any given volume of employment.

From the viewpoint of the history of thought, this is a good illustration of Keynes's peculiar use of the concept of "classical" economics. Naturally, we do not find any such postulates in the work of Smith, Ricardo, or Mill, who did not know the meaning of terms like *marginal productivity* and *marginal utility*. However, they are to be found in the writings of Marshall and Pigou, so that it is these economists and their contemporaries who are the real targets of Keynes's polemics.

Keynes now defines equilibrium as a state where the demand price of labor is equal to its supply price for all levels of output and employment. This definition of labor market equilibrium is obviously inspired by Marshall's general characterization of market equilibrium. If Keynes instead had been inspired by Walras a more natural definition would have been that at the ruling wage, the demand for labor is equal to its supply. In both cases the implication of the classical view is that the labor market tends toward a competitive equilibrium. Just "tends," for Keynes acknowledges that a realistic interpretation of the classical theory takes account of the frictional unemployment that arises because of various imperfections in the market mechanism that prevent continuous full employment (Keynes 1936, p. 6). But the essential feature of the theory, he says, is that employment can only be increased through organizational changes in the labor market that reduce frictional unemployment or through measures that either increase the marginal productivity of labor or decrease the marginal (dis)utility of labor—or that, in other words, increase labor demand or decrease supply.

Later in the same chapter Keynes confronts the classical theory of labor market equilibrium with the fact that according to him people rarely work as much as they would like at the current rate of wages. This implies that an increase in the demand for labor leads to increased employment, even with no change in wages. He says that the classical school is aware of this, and that it explains it by the observation that workers, especially through the influence of the unions, manage to sustain a level of wages that is so high that it results in unemployment. According to the classical view, therefore, this type of unemployment should be characterized as being voluntary.

Keynes has two objections to this theory. First, he maintains that the supply of labor depends *both* on the real and the nominal wage rate, that is, both on the purchasing power of wages and on its money value. This argument leads to a fundamental thesis of the book, which is that the nominal wage level is inflexible downward. An interesting justification for the assumption of nominal wage rigidity has to do with the workers' comparison of their own wage with that of others. If the workers in a particular industry or profession are asked to accept a reduction of their own nominal wage this will imply that their own wage is reduced relative to other groups, and this, Keynes argues, is a sufficient reason for them to resist the proposed reduction. On the other hand, a decrease of real wages that is due to increasing prices of consumer goods will meet with less resistance because it has the same effect on workers in all industries and professions.

The second objection to the classical view of unemployment is according to Keynes more fundamental. The classics had argued that it is the wage contract between workers and employers that determines employment. Keynes points out, however, that falling wages will lead to falling prices or at least to expectations of falling prices in the future. For this reason there will be little effect on real wages in the short run, so that one fails to achieve an increase in the demand for labor. The expectation of falling prices will also reduce the profitability of new investment so that the effects through this channel also fail to reduce unemployment. These objections clearly imply that one has to think about the labor market within a much broader framework where the whole demand side of the economy must be taken into account to a much larger extent than had been done in the classical theory. The causes of unemployment and the policies to combat it cannot be studied by means of a partial equilibrium analysis of the labor market.

The hypothesis of wage rigidity is a fundamental one in the context of Keynes's theory. This hypothesis was not entirely foreign to the classical economists that he criticized; as a matter of fact, the lack of wage flexibility was according to classical thinking one of the crucial factors for the explanation of unemployment. The difference between Keynes and the classics on this point was that while the classics thought of wage rigidity as a feature that delayed the normal adjustment to equilibrium in the labor market, Keynes considered it to be an equilibrium phenomenon. However, it is clearly untenable to claim that real wages are completely and permanently rigid downward; a long-lasting failure in the demand for labor must in the sufficiently long run lead to lower wages. In this perspective, the contrast between Keynes and the classics becomes a matter of degree rather than of fundamental disagreement.

DEMAND AND EMPLOYMENT

Since wages are not flexible downward the normal situation in the labor market will be one where the wage is too high to be consistent with full employment. Labor supply is greater than labor demand; consequently, it will be the demand for labor that determines the actual amount of employment. The demand for labor is determined by the demand for consumption and investment goods, and it is therefore the sum of these two components of demand that determines the demand for labor and thereby the amount of employment. Keynes had different ideas about the determinants of consumption and investment demand, and he formulated his ideas at the macroeconomic level: in other words, as theories of what determines *aggregate* consumption and investment goods demand. Aggregate income was in his view the main determinant of aggregate demand and therefore of employment and unemployment.

The idea that there exists a stable relationship between aggregate income and aggregate demand was one of Keynes's important contributions to economics. But the foundation for the hypothesis, at least as it appears in the book, is actually quite slender. Keynes refers neither to theory nor to empirical knowledge as justification of the hypothesis. He says (1936, p. 96) that there is a "fundamental psychological law" which implies that when income increases people's consumption will also increase, but by less than the increase in income. The ratio of the two increases is the *marginal propensity to consume*, which accordingly lies between zero and one and is probably decreasing with income. He is also of the opinion that the *average propensity to consume*—the ratio of total consumption to total income—also lies between zero and one and is decreasing with income.

With regard to investment, Keynes adopted the assumption that society's capital stock could be taken as given. The time perspective of the analysis was assumed to be so short that there was no time for new investment to affect it, so that in the short run the production capacity of the economy as a whole was fixed. (In this definition of the short run, the influence from the theoretical framework of Marshall is especially clear.) However, capital owners will wish to increase the capital stock as long as the expected yield on new investment is higher than the market rate of interest; investment demand will therefore be a decreasing function of the interest rate. This part of his analysis has much in common with what we find in the work of Irving Fisher. But Keynes also puts great emphasis on expectations and uncertainty as factors that must be taken into account in the study of investment demand. The foundation for opinions about the yield on investments just five or ten years hence is actually very weak, and investors must therefore base many of their decisions on quite different considerations:

> Businessmen play a mixed game of skill and chance, the average results of which to the players are not known by those who take a hand. If human nature felt no temptation to take a chance, no satisfaction (profit apart) in constructing a factory, a railway, a mine or a farm, there might not be much investment merely as a result of cold calculation. (Keynes 1936, p. 150)

But the uncertainty that surrounds investment activity not only relates to external events in the economy; uncertainty could also concern the likely behavior of other investors. In order to make profitable investments one has to make guesses about the decisions of others, and Keynes compared the situation of the individual investor with a type of competition that was popular among newspaper readers at the time:

> Professional investment may be likened to those newspaper competitions in which the competitors have to pick out the six prettiest

faces from a hundred photographs, the prize being awarded to the competitor whose choice most nearly corresponds to the average preferences of the competitors as a whole; so that each competitor has to pick, not those faces which he himself finds prettiest, but those which he thinks likeliest to catch the fancy of the other competitors, all of whom are looking at the problem from the same point of view. It is not a case of choosing those which, to the best of one's judgement, are really the prettiest, nor even those which average opinion genuinely thinks the prettiest. We have reached the third degree where we devote our intelligences to anticipating what average opinion expects the average opinion to be. And there are some, I believe, who practice the fourth, fifth and higher degrees. (Keynes 1936, p. 156)

In brief, Keynes's view of consumption and investment demand is that while there is a stable relationship between consumption and national income, investment demand is characterized by fluctuations that stem from the fact that expectations about the future are constantly changing, being strongly influenced by speculative considerations.

Consumers decide on the allocation of their income between consumption and saving, while firms decide on the amount of private investment. Because national income also represents the value of society's output, aggregate demand must in equilibrium be equal to output. Denoting the national income or product by Y, consumption by C, and investment by I, we can write the condition for equilibrium between production and demand as $Y=C+I$. But since saving, S, is defined as income minus consumption, we may alternatively write the equilibrium condition as $S=I$. The planned amount of saving must accordingly be equal to planned investment.

However, this equality between production and demand will not necessarily coincide with a state of full employment. For a given wage the demand for labor will be determined by the sum of consumption and investment demand, but there is no guarantee that this demand will correspond to the supply of labor at the same wage. In this perspective, equality of supply and demand for labor becomes the special case on which the classical theory focused, while Keynes's analysis becomes "the general theory."

How will fluctuations in investment demand transmit themselves to national income and employment? The answer to this
question Keynes provided in his theory of the investment multiplier. This had been formulated by one of the young economists
in the "Cambridge Circus," Richard Kahn, in an article published
a few years earlier (Kahn 1931), but Keynes gave it the form that
is familiar today. The intuition is simple: an increase in investment of 1 million pounds will increase national income by 1 million *plus* the secondary increase in consumption that is generated
by the increase in income. How large the secondary and therefore
the total increase will be depends on the marginal propensity to
consume; the higher is the marginal propensity to consume, the
larger is the multiplier that expresses the total increase as a mul-
tiple of the original increase of investment. In terms of mathematics this can be expressed as follows: suppose that investment
(I) increases by ΔI, where the symbol Δ represents a change.[7] Then
the national income (Y) will increase by $\Delta Y = \Delta I + c \Delta Y$, where c is
the marginal propensity to consume. When we solve this equa-
tion for ΔY, we get $\Delta Y = k \Delta I$, where the multiplier k is equal to
$1/(1-c)$. Since c is a number between zero and one, the multiplier
will be greater than one. Suppose as an example that $c=2/3$, and
that $\Delta I = 1$ million. Then it follows that $k=3$ and the increase in
income becomes $\Delta Y = 3$ million pounds.

We may summarize Keynes's view of the macroeconomic
functioning of the market economy as follows: fluctuations in
investment demand transmit themselves via their effects on consumption to fluctuations in income that are larger than those of
investment. The changes in income will lead to changes in the
demand for labor and therefore—because wages are rigid—to
changes in employment. Full employment becomes the special
case where the demand happens to coincide with the supply of
labor, but the normal state of the market economy is one of less
than full employment.

---

[7] While Keynes presents these concepts in mathematical terms, he does not
show the actual derivation of the multiplier, although this, from a mathematical point of view, is almost trivially simple. The explanation may be, as Robert
Skidelsky (1992, p. 471) has pointed out, that Keynes in spite of his mathematical training was remarkably insecure when he engaged in even quite simple
mathematical problems.

THE ROLE OF MONEY

The discussion so far has focused on the connection between aggregate demand and the volume of employment; in terms of the title of Keynes's book we have considered his views on employment but not on interest and prices. The link that Keynes established between the real and the financial side of the analysis appears in the form of his theory of the demand for money or, as he called it, the theory of liquidity preference.

The demand for money depended, in Keynes's view, both on the rate of interest and on real income. The interest rate represented the cost of holding financial assets in liquid form, so the higher was the rate of interest the lower was the demand for money. But money is also needed to carry out transactions so that the demand is an increasing function of aggregate income in society. The general public's demand for money must in equilibrium be equal to the supply of money as determined by the central bank via the structure of the banking system. In the Keynesian perspective, an expansionary monetary policy consists in an increase of the money supply by the central bank. For the general public to wish to hold the larger amount of money, the rate of interest must fall. This acts as a stimulus to investment and leads to increased output and employment.

On the whole, however, Keynes was skeptical about monetary policy as a means of counteracting fluctuations in investment and employment. There were particularly two reasons that made him believe that variations in money supply would be of little importance for macroeconomic stabilization. One was that he considered investment to be relatively insensitive to variations in the rate of interest. If, as an extreme case, one were to assume that this effect was zero, monetary policy would be unable to influence demand, and the only result of expansionary monetary policy would be a lower interest rate. The other reason was that he believed that when the rate of interest became sufficiently low an increase of the money supply would be unable to depress it further;[8] in that case also there would be no effect on investment demand. But if monetary policy was inef-

---

[8] This case later became known as "the liquidity trap," a term coined by Keynes's Cambridge colleague Dennis Robertson.

fective as a tool of stabilization policy, what other policies were available to replace it?

KEYNESIAN STABILIZATION POLICY

Keynes's answer to this question was to focus on fiscal policy. Fluctuations in private investment demand could be counteracted by variations of public expenditure in the opposite direction. Negative multiplier effects of failing private investment could be neutralized by positive multiplier effects of increased public spending. As an alternative, private consumption demand could be stimulated by lower taxes which would have their own multiplier effects on national income. To the extent that the "classics" had a well defined view of this issue, the usual attitude had been that an increase of public expenditure would push up the rate of interest and reduce private investment, possibly by so much that there would be no net effect on demand and employment. Keynes, on the other hand, was more optimistic with regard to the potential of fiscal stabilization, but the consequences in the form of fiscal deficits during periods of unemployment were unacceptable to many economists and politicians who were used to thinking of the balanced budget—equality between public spending and tax revenue—as an inviolable rule of economic policy.

Another controversial aspect of Keynes's analysis of the market economy was that he not only emphasized the unpredictability of private investment; he also believed that private investment was on a long-run declining trend as a result of a decreasing rate of return on capital. The reform required to stop this development, which would gradually lead to a fall in national income and employment, was an increasing degree of socialization of investment, implying more public ownership of capital. This aspect of Keynes's thought made many of his readers regard him as a sort of "Marx light," someone who believed that the market economy was doomed to collapse if it did not receive assistance in the form of substantial growth of the public sector and more central planning. There is obviously something in this view of Keynes, but it is no more than a half-truth. In the concluding chapter of the *General Theory*, "Concluding Notes on the Social

Philosophy towards which the General Theory Might Lead,"
he writes:

> If we suppose the volume of output to be given, *i.e.* to be deter-
> mined by forces outside the classical scheme of thought, then
> there is no objection to be raised against the classical analysis of
> the manner in which private self-interest will determine what in
> particular is produced, in what proportions the factors of produc-
> tion will be combined to produce it, and how the value of the final
> product will be distributed between them. . . . Thus, apart from
> the necessity of central controls to bring about an adjustment be-
> tween the propensity to consume and the inducement to invest,
> there is no more reason to socialise economic life than there was
> before. . . . When 9,000,000 men are employed out of 10,000,000
> willing and able to work, there is no evidence that the labour
> of these 9,000,000 men is misdirected. The complaint against
> the present system is not that these 9,000,000 men ought to be
> employed on different tasks, but that tasks should be available for
> the remaining 1,000,000 men. (Keynes 1936, pp. 378–379)

So Keynes was not an adversary of the market economy; his argument was just that the market system alone was incapable of
achieving a state of full employment. The markets were in need
of the helping hand of the government to reach this state, but
once this had been done the markets could on the whole be left
to do their work according to the classical recipe for an efficiently
functioning economy.

KEYNES AND THE KEYNESIANS

Keynes's *General Theory* is a brilliant book. It is written with great
literary skill by an author who is set on convincing the reader
that his vision of the economy is the right one and that the world
would be a better place for all if his views were generally accepted. It is full of striking formulations that show deep insight
and understanding. However, it has one rather obvious weakness: it never assembles the various parts of the analysis to a
consistent whole. Although it became usual to talk about "the
Keynesian model," it is clear that Keynes never wrote down a
formal model that could capture the essence of his vision. This

became a challenge for other economists who felt that Keynes's analysis was in need of clarification and increased precision. The first to suggest a more formal representation of Keynes's theory was the English economist John R. Hicks in his article "Mr. Keynes and the Classics" (1937).[9]

Hicks begins with some critical comments on Keynes's style of scientific debate. Even the most skeptical reader must concede, he says, that "the entertainment value of Mr. Keynes's *General Theory of Employment* is considerably enhanced by its satiric aspect" (Hicks 1937, p. 147). He goes on to argue that it is a paradox that Keynes lets Pigou's book *The Theory of Unemployment* (1933) be his representative of conventional "classical" thought, for this book is both quite new and besides "exceedingly difficult." To most people, Hicks says,

> its doctrines seem quite as strange and novel as the doctrines of Mr. Keynes himself; so that to be told that he has believed these things himself leaves the ordinary economist quite bewildered. (Hicks 1937, p. 147)

Hicks proceeds to construct a mathematical model that aims to provide a compact summary of the *General Theory* and at the same time illuminate the relationship between Keynes and the "classical" economists. Hicks's model can be written in terms of two equations. The first shows the combinations of national income and the rate of interest that are consistent with equilibrium in the real economy in the sense that planned saving is equal to investment. The second equation similarly shows which combinations of the national income and the rate of interest create equilibrium in the money market, that is, equality between money demand and supply. With these two equations we are able to determine the two unknowns of the model—national income and the rate of interest—and thereby also the equilibrium values of consumption and investment.[10] As an illustration of his mathematical model Hicks drew a diagram that

---

[9] Hicks's work will be further discussed in chapter 17.

[10] The first equation may be written as $I(i)=S(Y)$, where i is the rate of interest and the other symbols have the same meaning as before. The second equation is $L(i, Y)=M$, where $L(i, Y)$ is the demand function for money and M is the money supply.

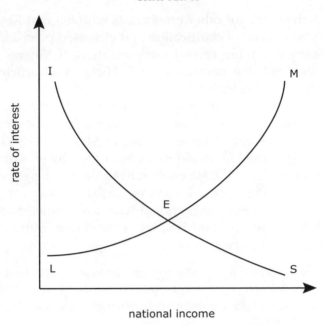

Figure 15.1. Hicks' IS-LM diagram. The point of intersection E between the IS and LM curves represents the equilibrium values of the national income (or national product) and the rate of interest.

later became known as the IS-LM diagram and which is shown in figure 15.1.

The IS curve describes the first of the two equilibrium equations. The lower is the rate of interest, the greater is the demand for investment and the higher must the national income be in order to generate an amount of saving that corresponds to the volume of investment; thus, the curve must be decreasing. The LM curve is a representation of the second equilibrium condition. The higher is the rate of interest, the lower is the demand for money and the higher must the national income be to create a demand for money that absorbs the supply; this implies that the curve must be increasing. At the point of intersection between the two curves we find the equilibrium solution of the model. The Keynesian and classical views can now be illustrated as special cases with regard to the shape of the two curves. The classical view was, according to Hicks, that the LM curve was almost vertical because money demand was independent of the interest rate. By contrast, Keynes's view was that money demand was very sensitive to changes in the rate of interest; in fact, so sensitive that the LM curve as a special case—the liquidity trap—was practically horizontal for sufficiently low interest rates. In the classical case, an expansionary monetary policy would, by shifting the LM curve to the right, increase total output in the economy, while fiscal policy by moving the IS curve to the right would have no effect on output and employment. In the Keynesian limiting case of the liquidity trap monetary policy would be ineffective while an expansionary fiscal policy would increase demand and employment.

Hicks's analysis greatly influenced the common view of the theoretical core of the *General Theory*, and the popularity of the IS-LM model grew so as to establish it as a standard component of every textbook in macroeconomics. But was it a good description of what Keynes really meant? This has been a much disputed question in the literature ever since the article was published. Keynes himself reacted positively to the draft of the article that Hicks sent to him, writing back that he had only minor objections to it. On the other hand, there are indications that he regarded Hicks's article as just a formal exercise that was not particularly interesting. Others, like Joan Robinson, reacted negatively to it, arguing that Hicks failed to bring out the essence of Keynes's analysis of the instability of the market economy and its sensitivity to uncertainty and changing expectations. The controversy reemerged in the theoretical literature in the 1960s and has been a recurrent theme in the debate over the true core of Keynes's theoretical message.[11]

In the United States the major proponent of Keynesian theory was Alvin Hansen (1887–1975) who was professor at Harvard University and who to begin with had been skeptical to the *General Theory* when it was first published. But he changed his views, and especially his book, *A Guide to Keynes* (1953), did much to spread the knowledge of Keynesian thinking in the United States. Probably of even greater importance was the fact that Paul Samuelson gave the new macroeconomics a prominent place and extensive coverage in his pathbreaking textbook *Economics: An In-*

[11] The modern debate on this issue was launched by the Swedish-American economist Axel Leijonhufvud (1968).

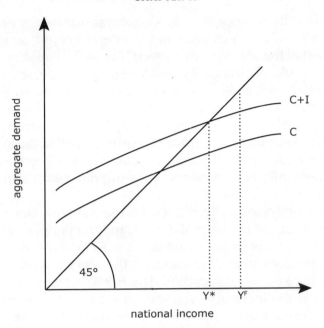

Figure 15.2. Samuelson's 45° diagram. Aggregate demand determines the equilibrium value of national income, which in this case is too low to generate full employment.

troductory Analysis, which came out in the first of many editions in 1948.[12] Here he introduced the so-called 45° diagram that was designed to demonstrate how national income in the short run was determined by aggregate demand. This diagram is shown in figure 15.2.

The lower of the two curves shows consumption (C) as a function of national income or product (Y) and implies a marginal propensity to consume that is less then one. On the top of consumption demand one adds on the demand for investment (I), which is assumed to be given by external (exogenous) factors. The 45° line represents the equality between aggregate demand and income or production, and at the point of intersection between the curve of aggregate demand (C+I) and the 45° line we find the equilibrium value of the national product Y^*, while the case of full employment corresponds to the national product Y^F.

[12] We come back to Paul Samuelson in chapter 17.

The diagram is a further simplification of Hicks's model. One interpretation of it is that the effect of the interest rate on investment and consumption is so weak that it can be disregarded, which was a view that some empirical studies that were published at the time seemed to support. In other words, the 45° diagram is a representation of the case where Hicks's IS curve is vertical, so that the level of national income is determined exclusively by the condition of equality between planned saving and planned investment.

It is remarkable that both of the two simplifying versions of Keynes's theory neglected the analysis of the labor market that Keynes gave such a prominent place in the *General Theory*. The basic assumption of the lack of wage flexibility was therefore difficult to perceive in the formal models of Hicks and Samuelson. The result was that generations of economics students were introduced to Keynesian macroeconomics without any discussion of the nature of the labor market. The first introduction was received in the form of the 45° diagram and the second as the IS-LM model. Many never got so far in their studies as to get acquainted with Keynes's theory of the labor market—a paradox, given that the problem of unemployment was the point of departure of the whole analysis. Those who maintained that both simplifications gave misleading interpretations of Keynes's own thinking, could with some justification point out that Hicks's article did not touch on the problem of wage formation, while Samuelson's 45° diagram apparently disregarded the whole triple of "employment, interest, and money."

The Long-run Development of the Market Economy

The core of Keynes's theory is related to the short run. It is true that he analyzes the investment decision in a long-run perspective, but it is the *demand* for investment that plays the main role. The effect of investment on the capital stock and on the production capacity of the economy is neglected. However, Keynes also had a long run, more loosely sketched theory of the development of the market economy, which is described in chapter 16 of the *General Theory*.

This theory is based on two elements. On the one hand, as capital accumulates the marginal return on it will decline, and this weakens the private incentives to carry out new investment projects. At the same time, the decreasing average propensity to consume means that with a growing national income the share of saving goes up. This leads to an increasing gap between saving and investment with a corresponding tendency to long-run permanent unemployment. Even though Keynes elsewhere maintains that it is in the case where public policy ensures full employment that the classical analysis becomes valid, he also emphasizes that the relative decline of private investment must be compensated by increased public investment. This long-run theory of the crisis of the market economy was overshadowed by the short-run stabilization analysis, and it also occupies much less space in the General Theory. But it was taken sufficiently seriously for many economists and politicians to believe that the Western world would be hit by mass unemployment after the Second World War when the soldiers were demobilized and the activity in the armaments industry was drastically reduced. However, such an effect on production and employment did not materialize, and it became clear that Keynes's views of the long-run development of private demand would have to be revised. This provided the inspiration for the development of new and more complex theories of the consumption function, which had both more solid theoretical foundations and were better supported by empirical research.

The Keynesian Revolution

"The Keynesian revolution" is a term that was first used by the American economist Lawrence Klein (1947) in one of the early book-length expositions of the Keynesian system. The expression caught on, especially because the economists that were active at the time actually experienced the breakthrough of Keynesian ideas as a revolution both in economic theory and policy. Mark Blaug has vividly described the reactions to the *General Theory* as

one of the most remarkable episodes in the entire history of economic thought: certainly never before and perhaps never since has the economics profession been won over so rapidly and so massively to a new economic theory. Those who lived through it felt themselves impelled to repudiate virtually the whole of received economic doctrine, and many took up the Keynesian system with an ardor that is more commonly associated with religious conversions. (Blaug 1991, p. 171)

There is actually little foundation in the *General Theory* for the view that one should feel an obligation to reject *all* other economic theory, so at this particular point Blaug's description may be an exaggeration. But on the other hand there is little doubt that the economics profession felt that it had entered a period of radical reorientation.

Was the Keynesian revolution in fact a scientific revolution in the sense that the concept has been used by Thomas Kuhn (1962)? There may be better reasons to answer this question in the affirmative in this case than with regard to the alleged marginalist revolution of the 1870s. The economic depression in the 1930s was so universal and deep that many felt that economics had failed both because it had no satisfactory theoretical explanation of the depression and because it did not provide constructive policy advice; there was in other words a genuine perception of a *scientific crisis*. Neither can there be any doubt that many economists in the years after 1936 felt that they were experiencing a revolution that called for a new agenda for research and a new framework for what Kuhn calls "normal science." An important part of Keynes's influence on the research agenda came through his hypotheses about the relationships between macroeconomic variables like income, consumption, investment, and money demand. On the one hand, his ideas inspired the development of a more solid theoretical foundation for his theories than he had provided; on the other hand, they gave a strong stimulus to empirical research. Thus, Keynes influenced the development of economics in ways that went far beyond his own specific contribution to theory and policy.

Later in the postwar period Keynesian economics gradually became exposed to serious criticism, and macroeconomic theory has in several ways changed in a direction that at least in part leads back to the economists that Keynes referred to as the classics. But whatever stand one takes on the claims of the different

361

schools of thought, it is obvious that *The General Theory of Employment, Interest, and Money* is one of the most influential books in the history of economics, that it established macroeconomics as a separate field of research and thinking, and that it acted as an encouragement to further research as have few other single contributions in the history of the subject.

KEYNES'S OTHER WRITINGS

It is evident that Keynes's reputation as an economic theorist is almost exclusively based on the importance of the *General Theory*. But in addition to this book, he has also made many other valuable additions to the literature of economics. Thus, among the economists whose work we have discussed in this book, he is one of the most prominent historians of thought as well as an outstanding commentator on current economic and political events. His essays on Marshall, Malthus, Edgeworth, and Jevons in his *Essays in Biography* (1933) are gems of the historical literature, and the wide-ranging articles in *Essays in Persuasion* (1931) are fascinating reading.

Keynes also contributed to the development of economic theory in ways that were more indirect. In his polemics against the Versailles peace treaty he had argued that the large amounts of war reparations that were imposed on Germany would have as a secondary effect that the terms of trade (the price of exports relative to the price of imports) would turn against Germany, thereby placing a burden on the country's economy that came in addition to the direct payments of reparation. This led to a debate in the *Economic Journal* with the Swedish economist Bertil Ohlin. Ohlin showed that Keynes's reasoning was not sufficiently general and that as a result of transfer payments the terms of trade could in principle develop both in favor and disfavor of the paying country, in this case Germany. A line of reasoning that had first been formulated by Keynes as part of an economic policy polemic was thereby transformed to a general theoretical issue, which came to be known in the literature as "the transfer problem." In this process, it was broken loose from the specific historical context that formed the basis for Keynes's original discussion.

An example of Keynes's ability to comment on and encourage the research of others concerns the mathematician, philosopher, and economist Frank Ramsey (see chapter 11). In his article on optimal saving, "A Mathematical Theory of Saving" (1928), the problem is formulated as follows: "How much of its income should a nation save?" Ramsey constructs a mathematical model of utility maximization over time and solves it by means of the so-called calculus of variation, an advanced mathematical technique that was mastered by few economists at the time. In his obituary article on Ramsey (reprinted in the *Essays in Biography*) Keynes says that this article is "terribly difficult reading for an economist." But it was Keynes who in his capacity as editor of the *Economic Journal* accepted the article for publication, an interesting decision by someone who at that time was not known as an economic theorist. Moreover, not only had he read the article, he had really understood the depth of its analysis. Ramsey, after having set out the assumptions on which the analysis is based, writes: "Mr Keynes has shown me that the rule governing the amount to be saved can be determined at once from these considerations" (Ramsey 1928, p. 545). Still, he says, it is best to develop the theory mathematically. Having done this, he then describes Keynes's intuitive mathematical reasoning in detail and shows that it leads to exactly the same solution as his own optimality condition, given a further simplifying assumption. The story shows that Keynes must have had a gift for theoretical abstraction and analysis which he may not have fully exploited when writing the *General Theory*.

How Original Was Keynes?

There can be no doubt that Keynes as a person was a highly original thinker and writer. A more interesting question is whether the theoretical perspective in his *General Theory* was really as original as the author suggested (as in the formulations in the preface that were quoted above), and as many of his disciples enthusiastically endorsed. Keynes was not only an academic researcher; he was also very much a political activist with a strong wish to influence policy and with a well-developed sense of the convincing and striking formulation.[13] He had cultivated his ability to write over many years of journalism and popular writing, and he brought it with him for use in his academic texts. In order to arrive at a balanced view of the significance of his contributions, it is therefore reasonable to take a skeptical attitude to some of his self-assessment.

It is not very difficult to find examples in the earlier literature that reflect many of Keynes's general views and ideas; in fact, Keynes uses a whole chapter in the *General Theory* to write about forerunners of his own theoretical approach. But the authors that he discusses either belong to a much earlier age (like Malthus) or are outside the field of scientific economics. However, there were in fact academic economists both in the relatively recent past and in Keynes's own time who had formulated theories that were close to his. Thus we find the theory of the multiplier in several publications of the German economist Nicholas Johannsen three decades earlier as well as in an article by the Danish economist Jens Warming (1932) who set up a multiplier model for an open economy. However, none of these succeeded in fitting the theory of the multiplier into a larger theoretical framework comparable to that of Keynes.

A theoretical approach that had some features in common with the Keynesian one became known as the Stockholm School, a group of Swedish economists who worked closely together for a period beginning in the late 1920s. The leading names in this group were Gunnar Myrdal (1898–1987), Bertil Ohlin (1899–1979), and Erik Lindahl (1891–1960). They were concerned with many of the same problems as Keynes, while in their theoretical contributions they aimed to integrate the analysis of short-run macroeconomic problems with a theory of the business cycle. However, the work of the school achieved little international importance. Its theories were not formulated in a way that made it easy for others to develop it further, and its most important work was not published in English until after the publication of the *General Theory*. By that time, the Stockholm School had ceased

---

[13] A famous example is the pronouncement in the *Tract on Monetary Reform* that "in the long run we are all dead." The context in which the phrase appears is a warning against an economic policy that places a great burden on present generations in order to obtain an uncertain gain in the long run.

to exist as an active macroeconomic research program.[14] Keynes had already won the struggle for attention and recognition in the international economic profession.

Even if is easy to find traces of Keynes's thought in the work of other authors, there can be no doubt that both the general approach to macroeconomic analysis and many of the more specific components of the *General Theory* are highly original. It is not surprising, therefore, that so many contemporary economists felt that they had been presented with a novel and significant breakthrough in scientific economics.

FURTHER READING

The Collected Economic Writings of John Maynard Keynes was published by the Royal Economic Society during the 1970s and 1980s with Donald Moggridge as chief editor. The edition contains all Keynes's books and published articles and in addition his correspondence with other economists, politicians, and people from cultural life. It also includes much previously unpublished material, for instance, notes written during his work on the *General Theory*, and a series of memoranda related to his activities during the Second World War.

The *General Theory* is such an important book in the history of economic thought that one should at least use some hours or preferably days by browsing and reading in it. It contains passages that are difficult and unclear, but for this one is more than compensated by the many examples of deep economic insight and understanding and the outstanding quality of the author's writing. For those to wish to enjoy Keynes's literary skill at its peak level the collections *Essays in Persuasion* and especially *Essays in Biography* are strongly recommended.

---

[14] The three most prominent members of the Stockholm School all made important contributions to economics, but they are better known for their work in other fields than macroeconomics. Erik Lindahl's work in public economics has been mentioned in chapter 12. Myrdal's interests gradually shifted to economic sociology and development studies. Ohlin's fame rests mainly on his contributions to the theory of international trade, where he is one of the originators of what is now known as the Heckscher-Ohlin model.

CHAPTER 15

There are three full-length biographies of Keynes: Harrod (1951), Moggridge (1992), and Skidelsky (1983–2000). Roy Harrod's book has a special position by having been written by a colleague who knew him personally, but the material on which it is based is so limited relative to what is now available that in important respects it must be considered as dated. Moggridge's and Skidelsky's books provide portraits of Keynes that cover all aspects of his activities—as researcher and teacher, political advisor and journalist, cultural personality, and private individual. A shorter exposition that focuses on Keynes's contribution to economic theory is Patinkin's article about him in *The New Palgrave*.

The Israeli economist Don Patinkin is also the author of one of the most influential books on macroeconomics and monetary theory of the postwar period. His *Money, Interest, and Prices* (1956; 1965) was an attempt to reconcile the Walrasian general equilibrium approach with Keynesian insights concerning the effects of macroeconomic policy. The book is also notable for its historical perspective on monetary economics from Hume to Samuelson.

Keynes's *General Theory* remains a central reference in modern macroeconomic textbooks, but the growth both of competing theoretical approaches and empirical research has naturally made it relatively less important than it was some decades ago. In this connection, it is instructive to consult a textbook from the golden age of Keynesian economics, for instance, Ackley (1961), to see the dominating position that Keynes's theories had at that time.

Frisch, Haavelmo, and the
Birth of Econometrics

E MPIRICAL RESEARCH in economics goes back a long time. We have already seen that the scholastics took a keen interest in studying actual market transactions, that Quesnay had ambitious plans for charting the many interindustry relationships in the French economy, and that Malthus based his theory of population on detailed observations from many countries. From the nineteenth century we have numerous examples of economists who did serious empirical work; Thünen recorded production and resource use on his East Prussian farm, and Jevons spent much of his time doing pathbreaking work on the construction of price indices. But in most of the books and articles that attempted to discuss the relationship between economic theory and real world observations, empirical data served simply as illustrations of the importance of the issues that were being discussed. There were no serious discussions of how economic theories could be systematically *tested* and little awareness of the problems that such tests would raise.

For a theory to be subjected to empirical tests in the statistical sense, a precise formulation of the theory would be required, and this presupposed the use of mathematical formulations. Such formulations were uncommon in the early days of economics, but there were exceptions. One of these was Cournot's "law of demand" (see chapter 7), which was the hypothesis that the demand for any particular consumer good was a decreasing function of its price: the higher the price, the lower the demand. Although our intuition may tell us that this hypothesis is "obviously true," it is not so trivial that it is without interest to seek empirical confirmation of it. Moreover, for many applications it is interesting to know more about the demand function than the fact that it is decreasing. If the government increases the tax on sugar, it may be interested in knowing whether and by how much the tax increase raises more revenue, and the answer to this question hinges on the magnitude of the price elasticity of demand. To find the form of the function, one possibility is, as Cournot suggested, to make observations of prices and quantities in a particular market, plot them in a diagram, and connect them with a curve; this curve arguably represents the mathematical relationship that we seek. But it is easy to see that there are a number of problems with this procedure.

One obvious question that is raised by Cournot's suggestion is how the required price-quantity observations are to be collected. There are two main procedures that one might adopt. One is to collect observations from different localities—for instance, cities or countries—during the same period of time; in modern jargon this is known as cross-section data. The alternative is to collect observations for the same locality at different points or periods of time, so-called time series data. In both cases, the underlying assumption is that prices and quantities vary across observations so that we get a number of price-quantity points in the diagram that enable us to draw the demand curve with some degree of confidence. However, whether we choose one or the other of these procedures, we face the difficulty that there is likely to be a number of other factors—such as income and population structure—that also affect the demand and that vary across localities or over time. These effects therefore need to be separated from the price effect that is our main object of interest in order to draw firm conclusions about the demand curve. Another problem is that the price-quantity observations that we make are not in general determined by demand alone. If we take the perspective of Alfred Marshall and assume that demand is determined in a competitive market by the intersection of the demand and supply curves, the question arises whether our observations reflect properties of the demand function, the supply function, or both. It appears, therefore, that the design of tests of economic relationships needs to be much more sophisticated than the one outlined by Cournot.[1]

[1] Cournot (1838; 1960, p. 52) hints at these complications when he writes that "the price of an article may vary notably in the course of a year, and, strictly speaking, the law of demand may also vary in the same interval, if the country experiences a movement of progress or decadence."

It was considerations like these that were later to give birth to what is known as *econometrics*, the systematic application of mathematical and statistical methods to the study of economic relationships. But before turning to an account of some features of this development, we first discuss some examples of empirical research in economics in the preeconometric era .

EARLY APPLICATIONS OF STATISTICAL METHODS

The first studies of the pattern of consumption across income classes were motivated by a concern with social inequality. English clergymen of the late eighteenth century collected budget data for poor families with the aim of throwing light on their vulnerability to increases in the prices of food, clothing, and fuel.[2] Toward the middle of the next century, following a period of social unrest and socialist agitation, there was renewed interest in the living conditions of the poor, and this time the budget studies took on a more systematic character. This line of work is exemplified by the studies of Ernst Engel and his forerunner Edouard Ducpetiaux (see the discussion in chapter 8). In the latter half of the nineteenth century the analysis of budget data became more sophisticated: researchers in the area were no longer content to construct tables that showed the variation of consumption outlays with income, but began to fit mathematical functions to their statistical data. This enabled them to compute what we would now call the income or Engel elasticity (although Engel himself did not use the notion of elasticity). The Italian economist Gustavo Del Vecchio, writing in 1912, on the basis of about fifty studies of consumer budgets fitted a mathematical function to the data and concluded that the magnitude of the income elasticity for food was about 0.6 (meaning that as income rose by 10 percent, the expenditure on food went up by 6 percent). This, of course, was a confirmation of Engel's Law.

Much of the work in this field was carried out without any connection with the theory of demand, which had focused its interest on the effects of price, not income, variations. The neglect of price effects was gradually rectified, and an important,

[2] A more detailed account can be found in Stigler (1954).

although little-known contributor to the empirical literature on demand functions was the French economist Marcel Lenoir.[3] In his 1913 doctoral dissertation, Lenoir fitted regression equations to data for the price and consumption of coffee and calculated price elasticities in the range of 0.4–0.6 (meaning that if the price of coffee rose by 10 percent demand would fall by 4–6 percent). Lenoir also considered the methodological problems involved in identifying the market observations of the volume of coffee traded with the amount of consumption; in his reflections on this issue, he was far ahead of his time.

Another important area of application of statistical methods to economic problems was the study of the business cycle. While explanations of the business cycle led an uneasy life on the outskirts of economic theory, empirical economists were well aware of the importance of the changes in economic life between good and bad times. In chapter 8 we saw that Jevons aligned his sunspot theory of the business cycle with astronomical data, and his line of investigation was taken up by the American economist Henry Ludwell Moore (1869–1958). Like Jevons, Moore was convinced that the final cause of the business cycle must be sought in factors outside the economic system, and in his first book (Moore 1914) he saw variations in the weather as the basic source of economic fluctuations. He investigated the empirical data showing the connection between rainfall and grain production in various parts of the United States and concluded that variations in rainfall could indeed explain a good deal of the observed fluctuations. In a later book (Moore 1923) he connected variations in the weather with the position of the planet Venus, which occupied a position between the earth and the sun with a periodicity of eight years, thus linking his analysis up with Jevons's sunspot theory. Although Moore's extensive use of mathematical and statistical methods marks an important step forward in the early development of econometrics, his Venus theory was met with a good deal of skepticism among academic economists.

Other economists felt that the primary task in the study of the business cycle lay not in the construction of formal theories

[3] Little seems to be known about Lenoir, who died as a young man in World War I. His work on demand functions is reviewed in Stigler (1954); see also the discussion in Morgan (1990).

but in the systematic and careful collection of data. Prominent among these was the American economist Wesley Clair Mitchell, commonly regarded as a member of the institutional school of economics (see chapter 13). His most important book is *Business Cycles and their Causes* (Mitchell 1913) in which he begins by reviewing a number of theories about the business cycle and finds them all wanting. The main task for business cycle research, he argues, is to get a clear view of the actual cyclical fluctuations in the economy, and with this object in mind he collected detailed statistical evidence for the United States, England, Germany, and France. He accepted that economic theory had a role to play in this research by directing attention to the variables that were of crucial importance, but he did not work with formal mathematical models, nor did he use the methods of mathematical statistics. He did argue that the data could be used to formulate and test theories, although he also maintained that each cycle had individual features that could only be discovered by historical research.[4]

Many of the problems that arose in the early applications of statistical methods to economic data clearly called for a more systematic approach to the problems of how to combine mathematical and statistical methods in the study of actual economic data. On of the pioneers in this line of work was Ragnar Frisch.

RAGNAR FRISCH

Ragnar Frisch (1895–1973) was born in Oslo (or Christiania, as the Norwegian capital was then called) where his father was a goldsmith. The family's intention was that Frisch would in time take over his father's business, and with this in mind he became a qualified goldsmith in 1920. However, he also had strong academic interests, and especially his mother urged him to begin university studies. In consultation with her he decided in favor

[4] The empirical approach of Mitchell and his followers was subjected to detailed criticism in Tjalling Koopmans's (1947) review of the later volume by Burns and Mitchell (1946). Koopmans's article was written from an econometric point of view, and its title "Measurement without Theory" became a compact statement of the econometricians' criticism of traditional approaches to empirical research in economics.

of economics; according to his own recollections, this was because the economics program at that time provided the shortest
and easiest way to a degree at the University of Oslo. He passed
his examinations with outstanding results in 1919 and the next
year he embarked on several years of further studies of economics and statistics abroad. In 1926 he received his doctorate in
Oslo on the basis of a dissertation in mathematical statistics and
then went abroad again, this time as a visiting lecturer at Yale
University where Irving Fisher was at his most active. In the Norwegian academic environment people became aware that Frisch
was a rising star in economics and were afraid that he would receive an offer that would make him stay abroad on a permanent
basis. It was decided to create a special chair for him, which he
held from 1931 until his retirement in 1965. In 1969, together with
Jan Tinbergen, he became the first recipient of the Nobel Prize
in Economics.[5]

At the personal level, Frisch had an enormous vitality and enthusiasm for his work. In addition to his research, he put a great
deal of effort into teaching, modernizing the economics program
at the University of Oslo in line with his own scientific priorities
with emphasis on the use of mathematical and statistical methods. During the 1930s he also became an active participant in the
public debate about economic policy, advocating expansionary
macroeconomic policy to fight the economic depression. In the
postwar period, he became a strong advocate of economic planning and critic of the market economy, which in his later years he
used to refer to as "unenlightened financialism." He was a strong
opponent of Norwegian membership in the European Economic
Community (later the European Union) whose economic system
he saw as the antithesis of rational economic planning.

Frisch was firmly convinced of the necessity to adopt mathematical and statistical methods both in economic research
and teaching. At the international level, this conviction led him
in 1930 to become one of the founders—together with Joseph

[5] The prize was founded on the initiative of Swedish academic economists
through a donation from the Bank of Sweden (Sveriges Riksbank) in 1968. It
is accordingly not one of the original prizes that were established by Alfred
Nobel's will and awarded for the first time in 1901. However, the procedure for
the selection of the prize winners is the same as for the prizes in the natural sciences and is administered by the Royal Swedish Academy of Sciences.

Schumpeter, Irving Fisher, and others—of the Econometric Society, and he became the first editor of its journal *Econometrica*. During his twenty-one years as editor, it became established as one of the leading international scientific journals, a position that it has kept since then. Throughout his career in teaching and research, Frisch emphasized the importance of economics as a quantitative science, although in his later years he also warned against the trend toward excessive formalization that he saw as characteristic of the younger generation of economists.

Consumption and Production Theory

Frisch was scientifically active in a number of areas.[6] In the theory of consumer demand, he was one of the first to develop an axiomatic foundation for utility theory that showed how the utility function could be derived from more elementary hypotheses about preferences and consistent choices. The type of utility function that Frisch preferred was defined as being cardinally measurable; it implied in other words that utility was measurable in the same way as temperature. His approach was accordingly the same as that of Edgeworth and stood in contrast to the assumptions adopted by Pareto (see the discussion of this in chapter 11). Frisch had a firm belief in utility as a measurable concept and in the importance of utility measurement. He also wrote a small book about it, *New Methods of Measuring Marginal Utility* (1932), but this has left few traces in modern work on consumer theory where the main view is that the measurement of utility is superfluous as long as one's main interest lies in the implications of utility maximization for the demand functions. More influential was a much later article, which studied the implications of utility theory for the various price and income elasticities of demand (Frisch 1959).

If asked to name a field where their teacher had made a particularly significant contribution, Frisch's old students might well have answered "the theory of production," since his lecture

---

[6] Not all of his fields of interest will be discussed here. He did important work in areas like oligopoly theory and the construction of index numbers, and he also wrote with great insight on the contributions of other economists like Alfred Marshall, Knut Wicksell, and Irving Fisher.

notes on this topic were required—and very difficult—reading at an early stage of their studies in economics. The first version of the notes was written during Frisch's stay at Yale University in the 1920s, and if they had been published then they would undoubtedly have been hailed as a pioneering contribution to economic theory. But publication was continually being postponed, and Theory of Production did not appear in book form until 1965 (as a translation of the 1962 Norwegian edition). By that time a number of other treatments of the same topic had long since been published and it did not receive much attention. The book discusses the representation of production processes by means of production functions in great detail and derives the conditions for optimal production and factor use under a variety of market forms. As a textbook for beginning students it was rather special; the treatment of the material was highly mathematical and based on a complicated conceptual apparatus. One might reasonably ask whether this was a rational use of the students' time and attention, but Frisch defended his approach by arguing that it provided training in rigorous reasoning and the use of analytical methods. This would give the students "command over a powerful tool that is of much use in a number of fields." But whatever the pedagogical justification of the approach, it is not on the theory of production that Frisch's fame rests.[7]

Dynamics and Business Cycles

Frisch's view of research methods in economics was inspired by the natural sciences, and this led him to formulate a precise distinction between static and dynamic economic theory that was borrowed from mechanics.[8] In a 1929 article he presents a brilliant exposition of the distinction. He asks the reader to imagine an economist who wishes to investigate the relationship between the price of a good and the quantity traded. The economist makes

[7] An interesting application of his approach to the theory of production appears in an article on nutrition problems that Frisch wrote in Norwegian and published as a chapter in a book by Knut Getz Wold in 1941. Frisch's analysis of this problem is original and is in several respects a forerunner of modern theoretical developments; see Sandmo (1993b) for further discussion of this contribution.

[8] See chapter 5 for a similar distinction that was drawn by John Stuart Mill.

observations of the data over a certain period, and for each time point of observation he writes down the price and quantity on a separate card.

> When he believes that he has obtained a sufficiently large material he collects his cards. The *description of the phenomena* is finished and the *analysis* begins. If during the analysis he disregards the time sequence of the cards, if in other words the analysis is of the kind that he might as well "shuffle the cards" before beginning the analysis, then the analysis is static. ... If on the other hand he designs the analysis so as to make the time sequence of the cards a factor of special importance, the analysis is dynamic. In the former case, therefore, time is just a kind of auxiliary variable. In the latter case the time pattern itself is of central importance. (Frisch 1929, p. 323)

At this time there were few examples of dynamic models in economic theory. The need for a more rigorous dynamic analysis was perhaps most pressing with respect to the explanation of the variations in the aggregate economic activity of society. As we have seen, there was considerable interest in business cycle studies at the beginning of the twentieth century and a number of empirical investigations were carried out in order to discover the "laws of motion" in economic life. There was, however, no really convincing theoretical hypothesis that could help to explain the time patterns observed in the data. This caught Frisch's interest and his contribution to business cycle theory is probably the field in which his work has exerted its greatest influence on modern economics. His reputation in this area rests on a single article, "Propagation Problems and Impulse Problems in Dynamic Economics" (Frisch 1933). He constructs a macroeconomic model that describes the demand for money as a function of consumption and investment, consumption as a function of the quantity of money, and investment as a function of the growth of consumption (what later became known as the acceleration hypothesis) together with an equation that describes how new investment projects are spread over time. From the present point of view, the individual elements of the model—such as its consumption function—are not always convincing, but the model as a whole is of major theoretical interest. On the one hand, it is an early example of a macroeconomic theory that aimed to explain aggregate

economic activity by means of a model with only a few variables
and equations; it is notable that it was published four years before
Hicks's (1937) two-equation model of Keynes's General Theory.
The model also had the property of showing how random shocks
could determine economic development over time so as to lead
to regular wavelike movements in activity; it was, in other words,
able to generate business cycles. By choosing plausible values of
the constants of the model, Frisch was able to demonstrate the
emergence of three different cycles with a periodic length of 8.57,
3.50, and 2.20 years, respectively, and these accorded well with
the empirical findings of business cycle research.

Econometric Methods

Frisch made his first scientific contributions in the area of mathematical statistics, and it was natural for him to become interested in the problems that are raised when one attempts to test
theoretical hypotheses by the use of empirical data. He was the
first to propose the use of the term *econometrics* to describe a research program that consisted in (1) mathematical formulations
of economic theories and (2) systematic tests of the theories using
the methods of mathematical statistics.[9] In Frisch's view, the two
components of the research program were closely interwoven.
Statistical analysis of economic relationships was in his opinion
meaningless unless it was based on rigorous theoretical reasoning, that is, on a mathematically formulated theoretical model.

Theory, he argued, also played an essential role for our ability
to critically interpret empirical observations. This view emerges
especially clearly in Frisch's analysis of what later became known
as the *identification problem*. Suppose that we are interested in
charting the connection between the price and the quantity demanded for a single commodity. Let us imagine that we have collected monthly data for a number of price-quantity combinations
and plotted them in a diagram. On the basis of these observations
we may compute a statistical regression line and draw it in the

[9] In the more recent literature, the interpretation of the concept of econometrics has become narrower. It now usually refers only to the statistical testing
of economic relationships and excludes the mathematical formulation of the
theoretical model.

diagram.[10] Suppose that the line slopes downward to the right. Is this a confirmation of the theory that demand increases with a decline in the price? Frisch's answer was: not necessarily. If the market that we study can be described as one of perfect competition, each price-quantity observation that we make corresponds to a point of intersection between a supply curve and a demand curve. Each pair of observations is therefore both a point on the supply curve and a point on the demand curve, and it therefore becomes difficult to decide whether our observations relate to one or the other of the two curves. Nevertheless, it is possible that the regression line that we have estimated does represent the demand curve and not the supply curve. To see this, we may take the case where consumers' demand, reflecting their incomes and preferences, is relatively stable over the period of observation while supply is influenced by external factors such as changes in the weather (as would be the case for agricultural commodities). In that case, each pair of observations would correspond to a point of intersection between the same demand curve and a supply curve that would be shifting over time. Consequently, all points of observation that we have plotted in the diagram lie on the demand curve, so that it is in fact this that we have found in the regression line that we have estimated. This is illustrated in figure 16.1.

Obviously, the example does not show that it is *always* the demand curve that we find by this procedure. For other commodities it may be reasonable to assume that it is the supply curve that is stable while the demand fluctuates, or that both curves change their positions from one month to the other. Frisch and other econometricians developed statistical methods that were designed to *identify* each individual relationship (such as demand and supply) from data observations that simultaneously represented different relationships between the same set of variables—confluence analysis, as Frisch called it.

Frisch put down a great deal of work in the development of statistical test methods, but it did not result in many scientific

[10] The standard procedure for the estimation of a regression line is the method of least squares. This consists in calculating a set of coefficients that minimize the sum of the squared deviations between the points of observation and the regression line.

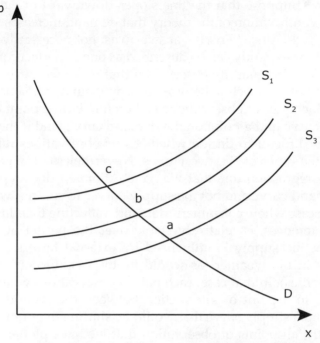

Figure 16.1. Estimating the demand curve. Each price-quantity observation (e.g. a,b,c) lies at the intersection of a demand and supply curve.
While the demand curve (D) is stable over the period of observation,
the supply curve (S_1, S_2, S_3) is shifting. Consequently, a regression line
based on the points of observation corresponds to the demand curve.

publications, nor can it be maintained that his published articles in this field had much direct and immediate effect. In Mary
Morgan's book (Morgan 1990) on the history of econometrics
she points out that a reason for this is that the articles even today are difficult to read because of Frisch's peculiar terminology
and his lack of references to the work of others. In spite of this,
Frisch is an important figure in the history of econometrics. His
article on the theory of the business cycle was a milestone in the
development of economics by its formulation of a model that
could be directly related to empirical data. Moreover, through
his speeches, lectures, and more popular writings he was an in-
defatigable propagandist for the necessity of using econometric
methods to better understand the functioning of the economy

and design a rational economic policy. His significance for this branch of economic science is probably much greater than indicated by the number of his publications and references to them in the literature.

National Accounting and Economic Planning

Another of Frisch's central areas of interest was the construction of a system of national accounts, a topic that he started to work on as early as the 1920s. Concepts like income and consumption, investment, imports, and exports for a nation as a whole had been in use for a long time, but there was no recognized set of definitions of the accounting relationships between them. Frisch was convinced that the scientific study of economic life was impossible without the establishment of a set of accounts for the national economy. This should be designed according to the rules of double book-keeping, as these were used in a private company. He was not alone as regards this conviction; internationally, the leading and most influential work on national accounting was done by the British economist Richard Stone (1913–91) who was particularly active in this area during World War II, although important work was also done in countries like the United States and the Netherlands.

In addition to the accounting rules for basic macroeconomic concepts, it was important to construct a system that showed the interrelationships between the various sectors of the economy.[11] This would allow one to study questions like how an increase in the consumption of a particular commodity would affect production and factor use in the industry and how this would spread to influence the activity in other sectors that supplied inputs to the industry in question. This type of system became known as input-output analysis and became a central element in macroeconomic planning in the postwar period. However, in spite of Frisch's contributions, the main honor for having constructed this tool of analysis should go to the Russian-born American economist Wassily Leontief (1906–99), whose book *The Structure of the American Economy* (Leontief 1941) became extremely influ-

[11] This ambition reminds one of Quesnay's 1759 work *Tableau Economique* that was discussed in chapter 2.

ential in this area. Over time, the input-output model became an important component of the large numerical models that came to be used by a number of governments in the postwar period.[12]

Frisch considered the development of national accounting as a necessary part of a much larger project, which was to establish an economic and political system based on economic planning. He had little faith in the market mechanism, although he never spelt out his objections to it in any analytical detail,[13] and it may appear is if—almost by definition—he identified a rational use of resources with the outcome of national economic planning. Frisch's own ambitions for his work went far beyond those of most other advocates of an increased role for economic planning. His view was that the national planning models that described the structure and functioning of the economy ought to be supplemented by a so-called macroeconomic preference function that was intended to represent the preferences of politicians regarding goals such as consumption, investment, income distribution, and employment. The task of the politicians ought to consist in the specification of their preferences so that in collaboration with the economic experts they would be able to construct their preference function. Once this function had been established, the experts— that is, the economists—would be able to calculate the socially optimal economic policy by use of the numerical model. This process evidently called for some education of the politicians, whose understanding of this way of thinking would at least initially be quite limited. With his characteristic enthusiasm Frisch set out to interview Norwegian politicians (among them Trygve Bratteli who later became prime minister) in order to establish their pref-

[12] In addition to the input-output description of the production side of the economy, these models also contain a set of demand equations to study the role of consumption. The models were further developed to take account of economic growth, regarding both production and consumption in a dynamic setting. An important influence on this development was the book *A Multi-Sectoral Study of Economic Growth* (Johansen 1960) by Frisch's former student Leif Johansen (1930–82). Johansen succeeded Frisch in his chair of economics at the University of Oslo.

[13] In a more popular context he expressed his market skepticism in a radio talk that he gave in 1947: "The study of the modern economic machinery has made me completely convinced that, if left to itself, this machinery must by its very nature become subject to the most violent convulsions and periodically spread sorrow and misfortune to large groups of the population."

erence functions, but the project never led to any practical results. From the present perspective, Frisch's line of thought testifies to his enormous ambitions for the social role of economics but clearly also shows him to have been politically rather naive.

Ragnar Frisch and the Systems Debate

Frisch never joined the great systems debate of the 1930s and 1940s. However, he was an active participant in the economic and political debate in Norway, often on the issue of socialism versus the market economy. As a polemicist Frisch had both strong and weak sides. He was often impressive in his ability to go to the core of an economic and political issue, and his style of writing could be forceful and to the point. But he was sometimes also arrogant and patronizing toward his opponents, and in his propaganda for the causes that he believed in he did not always adhere to academic standards of debate. An example of this is the preface that he wrote to a pamphlet by Leif Johansen, *Norway and the Common Market* (Johansen 1961). The main alternatives in terms of economic systems, he argued, are the unenlightened financialism in the Common Market and the "rule of social planning." While the former term was meant to signify the market economy, the latter was a system characterized by rational economic planning, in fact, quite similar to the system of centralized planning in the Soviet Union. The rule of social planning, Frisch argues, has to be adopted for the sake of the future of the Western economies, even if at present there are few who realize it:

> The scales will fall some time at the end of the 1960s (maybe earlier). By that time the Soviet Union will have surpassed the United States in terms of industrial output. *But then it will be too late for the West to realize the truth.*

> In saying this, I do not intend to declare myself as an adherent of a dictatorial form of a planned economy as in the Soviet Union under Stalin, when hundreds of thousands were left to die of hunger while food was exported in order to import machinery for the development of heavy industry (even if this laid the foundation for the present increased concern in the Soviet Union for the consumers and the standard of living). (Johansen 1961, pp. 9–10)

To these remarks he added a diagram, which in his opinion illustrated the possibilities for economic development under the alternatives of the market economy and a system of centralized planning. The diagram contained two growth curves where the one representing central planning showed both a significantly higher rate of growth and far smaller fluctuations around the trend than the corresponding curve for the market economy. The curves were not based on actual data but demonstrated nevertheless, according to Frisch, some "basic structural relationships," and those who did not realize this were unable or unwilling to face economic reality.

With our present knowledge of the actual development of the Soviet Union one may perhaps come to judge Frisch too harshly for his view of the growth possibilities under the two systems. In fact, there were a number of Western economists at the time who believed that the communist countries had the economic potential to overtake the market economies of the West. Still, there were few who professed such omniscience in this matter as did Frisch.

However, it is not Frisch the polemicist who occupies a prominent place in the history of economic thought. His position is based on his original contributions to economic theory and econometrics, and as an enthusiastic spokesman for the use of mathematical and statistical methods in economics he exerted a strong influence on the direction taken by economic science in the second half of the twentieth century.

MACROECONOMICS AND THE KEYNES-TINBERGEN DEBATE

Frisch's model of the business cycle was a significant contribution both in terms of its theoretical perspective and because it had a form that made it possible to submit it to examination via empirical data. However, because of its small scale, it had not reached the stage where it could be used to give a picture of the actual development of a real economy. The first to construct a model of this kind was the Dutch economist Jan Tinbergen (1903–94). Tinbergen was originally trained as a physicist but moved into economics because he considered it to be a more useful science. His career was divided between academia and government affairs and in 1945, as a professor at the Netherlands School of Economics, he became the director of the government's Central Planning Bureau. He had a strong background in theoretical statistics and became deeply interested in the emerging field of econometrics.

Tinbergen's first effort in the area of macroeconomic model building was an attempt to construct a numerical model of the Dutch economy that could be used as a foundation for anti-depression policies (Tinbergen 1937). The model consisted of twenty-two equations that were numerically estimated by using the technique of statistical regression analysis. The equations described the various components of investment and consumption demand as well as other features of the structure of the economy. He extended his work in a two-volume treatise that was published a few years later (Tinbergen 1939) in which he also presented a related macroeconomic model of the United States economy (comprising forty-eight equations). Tinbergen's work was a significant step forward both for the discipline of econometrics and more generally for applied economics. It laid the foundation for the work on large numerical models of the economy, which at present play an important role for business cycle forecasts and public policy design in many countries.

At this time many economists had begun to get familiar with mathematical models of the whole economy or with particular sectors of it. However, existing models were on a small scale, using only a few equations and variables. The small scale meant that it was easy to grasp the economic intuition behind the analysis, but this was different when it came to models on the scale represented by Tinbergen's work. To most economists, it was impossible to get an intuitive understanding of the working of the model as a whole, and this was especially true when it came to its dynamic properties, that is, the picture that it gave of the movements of central economic variables over time. The crucial test of its realism would therefore have to be whether it was consistent with the facts or, in other words, how the predictions of the model fitted the observation of the variables in the real economy. By feeding real economic data into his models, Tinbergen was able to show that they generated cyclical movements that corresponded well with empirical experience.

Given the novelty and complexity of Tinbergen's approach, it was not surprising that his work should initially have been met with a good deal of criticism. The most famous of his critics was no less than John Maynard Keynes, who wrote a long review of the first volume of his 1939 book in the *Economic Journal* (Keynes 1939). Keynes showed little appreciation of the nature of Tinbergen's pioneering contribution, focusing instead on what he perceived as a lack of reflection on the logical foundations of his program of research:

> The worst of him is that he is much more interested in getting on with the job than in spending time in deciding whether the job is worth getting on with. He so clearly prefers the mazes of arithmetic to the mazes of logic, that I must ask him to forgive the criticisms of one whose tastes in statistical theory have been, beginning many years ago, the other way round. (Keynes 1939, p. 559)

Tinbergen (1940) replied to the criticism by pointing out that a number of the critical questions that Keynes raised had already been answered in the book and that some of the other objections in the review were based on "a number of evident misunderstandings of Mr. Keynes's on mathematical questions." At a more general level, Keynes had taken a very strong position on the precedence of theory over statistical tests, arguing that if the data did not confirm a theory that one somehow knew to be right, then the fault lay in the data and in the nature of the statistical analysis. Tinbergen, on the other hand, allowed for the power of empirical analysis to lead to modifications of the theory, thereby making it more realistic.

In retrospect, the Keynes-Tinbergen debate is an interesting testimony to the reception of the new direction of quantitative work. In his readers' minds, Keynes may by means of his literary skills as a polemicist have scored a short-run victory over Tinbergen, whose reply in comparison is rather dry and technical. In the long run, however, it is quite clear that it was Tinbergen's approach to applied quantitative economics that won the day.

TRYGVE HAAVELMO

There are many points of similarity between Ragnar Frisch and Trygve Haavelmo. They were both professors at the University of Oslo and colleagues for a number of years. They both had a very strong quantitative orientation and became, each in his way, spokesmen for the new econometric approach to empirical economic research. Both of them did some of their best and most significant work in the United States. But their personalities were very different. While Frisch had a strong ambition to contribute to economic reform both by his participation in public debate and by more direct attempts to influence the political process, Haavelmo's working day concentrated on his academic activities as researcher and teacher. Frisch was an enthusiast, Haavelmo a skeptic. When in 1989 he was awarded the Nobel Prize in economics most people in Norway had no idea who he was, and his first reaction to the award indicated that he saw this as a piece of bad news that would be an unwelcome disturbance of his private life. In a memorable television interview immediately after the announcement of the prize he characterized the event as "a hell of a shock."

Trygve Haavelmo (1911–99) studied economics at the University of Oslo and after his graduation started to work as a research assistant for Ragnar Frisch, choosing econometrics as his field of specialization. In 1939 he received a grant for further study in the United States and began a stay that because of the outbreak of war and for other reasons came to last until 1947. During the war he worked mainly for the Norwegian exile government, having his basis in New York, but he also kept in close touch with various American research institutions. After the war, he was for a couple of years associated with the Cowles Commission at the University of Chicago, an institute that at the time was the world's leading center for research in mathematical economics and econometrics, and it was in econometrics that Haavelmo would come to make his most important contributions.[14] He was professor of economics at the University of Oslo from 1948 to 1979.

Econometric Theory

It was Haavelmo's contributions to econometrics that laid the foundations for his Nobel Prize award. These contributions were

[14] The Cowles Commission (which later moved to Yale University where it became the Cowles Foundation) has its name from the businessman Alfred Cowles who founded the institution in 1932.

mainly published during the years 1943–47 while he was still in the United States. His main work in the area is the monograph *The Probability Approach in Econometrics* (1944), which came out as a supplement to the journal *Econometrica* and which Haavelmo submitted as a doctoral dissertation to the University of Oslo in 1946. The focus of this work as well as a series of articles from the 1940s is on fundamental methodological issues, and his most important message is that economic theory and the statistical estimation of theoretical relationships must be regarded in close connection with each other. On the one hand, statistical estimation must take account of the restrictions that theory places on the relations that one wishes to test; without a theoretical hypothesis there is nothing to test. On the other hand, to be empirically useful the theory must be reformulated in probabilistic terms, for it must allow for the fact that the theoretical relationships will not hold in an exact sense when we attempt to test them against data.

In his *Probability Approach* Haavelmo discusses the question of what it is that makes a mathematical model into something more than pure mathematics. Maybe, he suggests rhetorically, it is simply because we denote x as consumption and y as price? But he soon rejects this view as being too simple:

What makes a piece of mathematical economics not only mathematics but also economics is, I believe, this: When we set up a system of theoretical relationships and use economic names for the otherwise purely theoretical variables involved, we have in mind some actual *experiment*, or some *design of an experiment*, which we could at least imagine arranging, in order to measure those quantities in real economic life that we think might obey the laws imposed on their theoretical namesakes. For example, in the theory of choice we introduce the notion of indifference surfaces, to show how an individual, at given prices, would distribute his fixed income over the various commodities. This sounds like "economics" but is actually only a formal mathematical scheme, until we add *a design of experiments* that would indicate, first, what real phenomena are to be identified with the theoretical prices, quantities and income; second what is to be meant by an "individual"; and, third, how we should arrange to observe the individual actually making his choice. (Haavelmo 1944, p. 6)

Experiments in the form that we know them from the natural sciences play little role in economic research but the principles of experimental design are nevertheless valid for the economist's selection of the data that he uses to test the predictions of economic theory.[15] The test of an economic theory by the use of empirical data requires therefore that one reflects on the relationship between the variables of the theory and the real-life data that we select to represent them. As an example, in the study of consumer demand it is important to consider critically the theoretical construction of the individual consumer who chooses his preferred composition of consumption goods: Can we test this theory by using data from budget surveys when we know that these data originate from decisions taken in households with several members?

In his work on the principles of econometrics, Haavelmo discusses a number of issues that have achieved the status of classical problems in the field. A careful presentation of all of these easily becomes very technical, and the exposition here must by necessity be very summary.[16] One important concept that he introduced was that of *autonomy*. An economic relationship is said to be autonomous when its character is unaltered with changes in the other relationships that characterize the economy; consequently, it is by estimating autonomous relationships that we can hope to uncover economic "laws." Haavelmo also made important contributions to the understanding of the identification problem, where he extended the analysis of Frisch and others. Finally, he contributed a pathbreaking analysis of what became known as the problem of *simultaneity*. In an economic model consisting of a set of n equations between n variables Haavelmo showed that it leads to erroneous conclusions if we try to estimate one of the equations in isolation from the $n-1$ other equations in the model; ideally, therefore, one ought to estimate all equations in the model simultaneously. His analysis of this problem had a great influence on later research in econometrics.

[15] This was true both in Haavelmo's time and for many years thereafter. But the situation is changing: in recent decades there has been a significant growth in experimental work whereby theories of economic behavior have been tested under laboratory conditions.

[16] An excellent survey of Haavelmo's contributions to econometrics, set in a historical context, can be found in the book by Mary Morgan (1990).

CHAPTER 16

Trygve Haavelmo as an Economic Theorist

When after the war he returned to Norway and started teaching at the University of Oslo Haavelmo more or less abandoned his work on the statistical and empirical aspects of econometrics and concentrated instead on economic theory. He had done theoretical work also during his stay in the United States; thus, one of his most cited articles is a study of the multiplier effects of a balanced increase of taxes and public expenditure in the context of a Keynesian macroeconomic model (Haavelmo 1945).[17] He argued that theory was the weakest link in economic science and therefore ought to be given the highest priority; in addition, one may speculate that the loss of the stimulating environment for econometric work in the United States contributed to the change in his research interests.

Haavelmo's studies of economic theory resulted in two books. The first, *A Study in the Theory of Economic Evolution* (1954), is a contribution to the theory of economic growth that is notable both as a forerunner of the later work by Solow (1956) and others and as an echo of themes that were prominent in the work of the classical economists, especially Malthus's work on the population question. His second book was *A Study in the Theory of Investment* (1960), which is a critical review of a series of models of capital accumulation, concluding that these models—particularly the neoclassical theory of the demand for capital goods—do not provide the foundations for a theory of investment demand. The crucial point of the argument is that while capital is a stock, investment is a flow; it is the change of capital over time, and this requires a different analysis from that of the demand for capital as such. Although the contribution of the book is critical rather than constructive, it has nevertheless exerted some significant influence on the empirical study of investment demand.

---

[17] Intuitively, it might be natural to believe that an increase of public spending financed by a corresponding increase of taxes would have no effect on the national income but simply reduce private spending by an equal amount. However, Haavelmo showed that the multiplier effect would be positive and under certain assumptions equal to unity. The reason is that the increase of public spending leads to an equal increase of aggregate demand, while the increase in taxation reduces private demand by less than the amount of tax, since part of the decline of private disposable income would be at the expense of saving.

The Progress of Econometrics

Over the course of the twentieth century econometrics developed from being the field of research of a relatively small group of avant-garde specialists in mathematical and statistical methods to become a standard set of tools to be used in almost any kind of empirical research. During this process, however, there has been a notable time pattern in the development of scientific specialization. The nineteenth-century economists who specialized in the study of consumer budgets had little contact with the theorists who worked on the determinants of consumer demand. Similarly, statistically inclined economists who were concerned with the time pattern of the business cycle were not close to the leading theoretical economists of their time. In the view of the early econometricians like Ragnar Frisch this situation was unfortunate; economic theories ought to be formulated in mathematical terms, and once this had been achieved, theoretical development and statistical testing ought to be carried out as a joint undertaking. Gradually, however, with the increasing scientific specialization that took place during the second part of the twentieth century, the situation tended to move back to what it had been before with a clearer separation between economic theorists and econometricians.

In spite of this, there can be no doubt that the emergence of the econometric approach has had a deep influence on theoretical and empirical economics. Theorists are more concerned with how their models can be confronted with empirical data, and those who engage in empirical work strive, to a much larger extent than before, to base their hypotheses on the insights that can be derived from economic theory.

Further Reading

With the exception of Niehans (1990), most general works on the history of economic thought pay little or no attention to the methodological issues that arise in empirical economic research. The reader who wishes to pursue the topic therefore has to consult the more specialized literature.

The history of econometrics until about 1950 as well as that of empirical work in the last part of the nineteenth and the early years of the twentieth century is discussed in the highly readable book by Morgan (1990). Some of the material in the book is unavoidably a bit technical, but these passages can easily be skipped by the reader who is primarily interested in the more general features of the story. Stigler's article (1954) is an informative and enjoyable history of the early work on the study of consumer behavior.

A number of Frisch's articles can be found in a collection edited by Olav Bjerkholt (Frisch 1995). An article by Leif Johansen (1969), marking the award of the Nobel Prize, surveys Frisch's most central scientific contributions, and the same issue of the *Swedish Journal of Economics* includes an evaluation by Bent Hansen (1969) of the work of Jan Tinbergen. A number of essays that were presented at a conference to mark the one hundredth anniversary of Frisch's birth have been collected in Strøm, ed. (1998); among these, Edmond Malinvaud's article about Frisch's views on development planning is of particular interest from the point of view of the history of thought. Andvig (1981) discusses Frisch's work on business cycles and relates it to other research in this area in the interwar period.

Haavelmo's *Probability Approach* is a highly technical piece of work, but the first chapter, entitled "Abstract Models and Reality," is also of interest to the more general reader. The story of Haavelmo's years in the United States, when he produced his most important work in econometrics, has been told in Bjerkholt (2007). Moene and Rødseth (1991) consider Haavelmo's main contributions to economics, giving priority to his work on economic theory rather than his contributions to econometrics.

The Modernization of Economic Theory
in the Postwar Period

Nᴇᴡ ᴍᴀᴛᴇʀɪᴀʟ for the history of economic thought is being produced daily in the form of books and articles, and it is not easy to decide where to draw the dividing line between the past and the present. In this book the line has been drawn roughly at the year 1970. The choice of such a date must necessarily be a little arbitrary, but there are also some good reasons to end the main part of the story at that point in time.

One reason is that the books and articles that have been published since 1970 still form part of contemporary economics in a way that is different from the role of the older literature. They remain references that are read not because of their historical interest but from a desire to learn about modern economics. It is evident, however, that this division must not be taken too literally. There are examples of older work that remains modern in the sense that there is nothing more recent that is obviously better in terms of providing insights and understanding with respect to modern thinking. There are also examples of more recent literature that must already be classified as being mostly of historical interest. But all things considered, 1970 seems a fairly reasonable choice of a date to define the dividing line between the past history and the present state of economics.

A related argument concerns our own distance to the literature under review. What is seen as especially important in the literature of a particular age is to a large extent determined by our knowledge of what came after. When at the present time we look on Cournot's theory of oligopoly as so important, this is to a large extent due to our knowledge of its influence on researchers who took up related ideas many decades later.[1] The classi-

---

[1] However, our evaluation of the scientific *quality and originality* of past theories should in principle be independent of our knowledge of later developments. We hold Cournot in so high regard not only because he is a forerunner of modern theories, but also because his main work scores so highly on the scales of quality and originality.

cal economists' distinction between productive and unproductive labor was a theoretical idea that turned out to be less than fruitful, but it nevertheless took a long time before it vanished from the literature. Taking a long-run historical perspective, the economics of the last three or four decades is still so close to us in time that it is difficult to distinguish between that which is important and that which is probably of less significance. But it should be emphasized again that the choice of 1970 has an element of arbitrariness and perhaps with equal justification one could choose 1980 as the year of demarcation for the era of contemporary economics. Admittedly, there may also be a subjective element in the picture: it is in some respects more difficult for an author to write about his own time and contemporaries than about the more distant past.

In the period after the Second World War the economics research community grew at an unprecedented pace, and the volume of new literature expanded correspondingly. During the period that we discuss in this chapter and the next there are therefore more important economists that "deserve" a place in the history of thought than is the case for any earlier period. But to include all those who have made significant contributions to knowledge would obviously be beyond the scope of a relatively short exposition. In these chapters we shall therefore be selective and concentrate on a few of the main themes from the period that from the present perspective appear to be among the most significant. Within each of the themes we shall further focus on one or a few especially prominent economists. When one considers the enormous growth of the literature of economics during this period, it is clear that there are several ways in which this can be done, and other writers on the history of thought have chosen different ways to organize their expositions and focused on other lines of development. Readers who wish to obtain a broad perspective should therefore consult several sources of information for the literature of this period.

JOHN HICKS AND GENERAL EQUILIBRIUM THEORY

The Keynesian revolution of the 1930s led to a strong increase of the interest in macroeconomic problems. But what academic economists regarded as the core of economic theory remained microeconomic and was based on the analysis of individual behavior. Keynes also anchored his theory in hypotheses about the motivation of individual economic agents, although his microeconomic theory was rather sketchy, being mainly the partial equilibrium analysis that he had been taught by Marshall. General equilibrium theory, as it had been developed by Walras and Pareto, was still relatively unknown to the great majority of economists, and some of the young theorists of the 1930s and 1940s became convinced that both the theory of individual behavior and the theory of markets were in need of modernization and upgrading. The pioneers in this process were the English economist John Hicks and the American Paul Samuelson.

John Hicks (1904–89) attended Oxford University where he began as a student of mathematics before switching his interests to the social sciences. The nature of his education in economics was historical rather than theoretical, and it was only after he started to teach at the London School of Economics that he became seriously interested in theory. From 1938 to 1946 he was professor at the University of Manchester before returning to Oxford in 1946.

A senior colleague at the London School of Economics had encouraged him to read Pareto, and Hicks became convinced that a further development of Pareto's theories should be a main priority of economic research. However, his first book was about labor economics. *The Theory of Wages* (1932) was a study of wage formation with emphasis on imperfect competition, including an extensive discussion of the role of trade unions. The book came out four years before Keynes's *General Theory*, and it is interesting to note that not all pre-1936 theorists believed that the labor market could be studied in terms of the theory of perfect competition, which was the impression given in Keynes's book. As by-products of his labor market analysis, Hicks introduced some new theoretical ideas and concepts that were to become highly influential beyond the specific context in which he used them. In particular this was the case for his analysis of technological progress. Technological progress was defined by the notion that the same quantity of output can be produced with less input of labor and capital than before. What would the consequences of technological progress be for the distribution of income in soci-

393

ety? Hicks introduced a classification of technological progress according to the way in which it influenced the so-called functional distribution of income, that is, the distribution of income between labor and capital. If the functional distribution remained unchanged, technical progress was defined to be neutral, while it was classified as labor saving or capital saving according to whether it lowered or raised labor's share of income.

After having written some important articles on the new Keynesian macroeconomics, Hicks published the book that was to become his most influential work, *Value and Capital*, in 1939.[2] This is an ambitious attempt to integrate a number of elements from different parts of economic theory. Hicks begins with a discussion of the theory of consumer demand. Having pointed out that Marshall's formulation of this theory has some evident shortcomings he gives an exposition of the theory as developed by Pareto. In the main text of the book he gives an elegant diagrammatic presentation of the theory, while the more general mathematical version is in an appendix. Hicks emphasizes that Pareto's formulation rests on a more solid foundation than Marshall's by making less demands on the utility theoretic foundations; one needs only some assumptions about the nature of preferences as expressed in the shape of the indifference curves. Hicks takes up the thread from Slutsky (1915) and shows graphically how the effect of a price change can be decomposed into income and substitution effects (see figure 17.1). His treatment of the model of consumer behavior has been extremely influential: the style of exposition is in essence exactly the same as we find in modern textbooks of microeconomics.

Following his study of consumer theory, Hicks extends the analysis to a general equilibrium model where consumers buy and sell goods under conditions of perfect competition. He goes on to analyze firms' decisions about production and factor use and to consider general equilibrium in an economy with production. In the second part of the book, he generalizes the framework further to a dynamic setting: the development of the economy over time, the accumulation of capital, and the movements of the business cycle. A fascinating aspect of the book is the way in which he explains his integration of elements from Marshall,

[2] See the discussion of his IS-LM model in chapter 15.

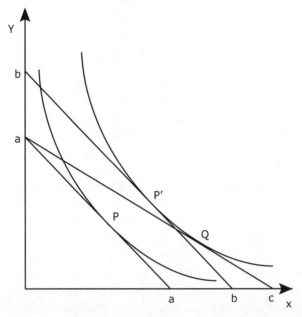

Figure 17.1. The income and substitution effects of a price change. A fall in the price of the X-good makes the budget line shift outward from *aa* to *ac*, so that the optimal consumption choice becomes Q instead of P. The increase in the consumer's utility level could alternatively have been achieved by an increase in income, shifting the budget line from *aa* to *bb* (touching the same indifference curve as *ac*) with the optimal choice of P'. The movement from P to P' is the income effect, while that from P' to Q is the substitution effect.

Pareto, Walras, and Keynes in a way that suggests that they all fit together. In his own words:

> It is one of the most exciting characteristics of the method of analysis we are pursuing in this book that it enables us to pass over, with scarcely any transition, from the little problems involved in detailed study of the behaviour of a single firm, or single individual, to the great issues of the prosperity or adversity, even life or death, of a whole economic system. (Hicks 1939; 1946, p. 245)

The explanation of why the book became so influential must be sought in part in the unitary perspective on economics that it provided, but to a large extent it was also due to the style of presentation. Even if one were unable to follow the dynamic analysis in the second part of the book the chapters on consumer theory alone were of major interest; they communicated the advanced analysis of Pareto and Slutsky without making demands on the reader's knowledge of mathematics (if one possessed this knowledge one could proceed to the mathematical appendix). Other parts of the book could be similarly characterized: Hicks managed to impart the essence of abstract theoretical topics like market stability in general equilibrium without demanding more of the reader than his full attention on the text and the ability to understand relatively simple diagrams.

Value and Capital is a very different book from Keynes's *General Theory*. Keynes's aim was to develop a theory that laid a better foundation for economic policy. Hicks's ambition was to create unity and coherence within the theoretical literature as it existed at the end of the 1930s. The application of the theory to practical problems of policy would have to be treated as a separate matter. According to Hicks, the theorist could obviously be of assistance to those in charge of economic policy, but his role would mainly have to consist in the clarification and explanation of the actual functioning of the economic system.

Hicks did research in a number of different areas of economic theory. Among his early contributions were important articles on welfare economics, where he strove to reconcile Marshall's theory of consumers' surplus with the more general analysis of Pareto. Later he published books on business cycle analysis (*A Contribution to the Theory of the Trade Cycle*, 1950) and consumer theory (*A Revision of Demand Theory*, 1956) before turning his attention to the theory of economic growth in the 1960s (*Capital and Growth*, 1965). But nothing of what he did later turned out to be as important for the development of economic theory as *Value and Capital*.

Paul Samuelson and the Foundations of Economic Theory

Paul Samuelson (1915–2009) is one of the most versatile and influential figures in the history of economics. He began his studies at the University of Chicago and continued to do graduate work at Harvard University. The education that he received at these institutions was probably the best that a young economist could get at that time. The economics departments at Chicago and Harvard had assembled many of the world's leading economists—some of them emigrants from Hitler's Germany—and especially Harvard also attracted some of the most promising economists in the United States. It was a stimulating environment for a gifted student, and Samuelson began early to write theoretical articles that were published in some of the world's leading scientific journals. He had a solid grounding in mathematics and was soon convinced that large parts of economic theory rested on inadequate logical foundations. Further theoretical progress would therefore require a substantial increase in the use of mathematics. His book *Foundations of Economic Analysis* (1947) and a long series of articles on topics ranging over the whole of economic theory soon established him as one of the world's leading economists. As professor at the Massachusetts Institute of Technology (MIT) he helped its economics department achieve a leading position both in the United States and in the world at large.

The question that Samuelson raises in the first part of the *Foundations of Economic Analysis* is this: What is the empirical content of the economic theories of consumer and firm behavior? With regard to the theory of the consumer he pointed out that while a number of economists from the time of Gossen and Jevons had postulated that consumers maximize utility, they had not clarified the consequences that the postulate has for observable market behavior. By studying the behavior of consumers we cannot observe whether or not they are maximizing utility, and such a conclusion would not in itself be very interesting either. What we do observe and what economists are basically interested in is the consumers' demand, and an important task for economic theory must therefore be to clarify which hypotheses about demand follow from the postulate of utility maximization. This clarification is one of Samuelson's main achievements. He formulates the problem of utility maximization with a high degree of generality and mathematical rigor and derives its consequences for consumer behavior. Here he follows in the footsteps of Slutsky and Hicks but with a greater degree of mathematical precision. He also demonstrates how mastery of the general theory of consumer choice may lead to deeper insights in more special topics like the effects of rationing and the construction of price indices.

Samuelson carries out the same type of analysis for the case of the competitive firm and shows that the postulate of profit maximization implies a number of hypotheses about the firm's supply of output and its demand for factors of production. He also emphasizes that the fundamental logic underlying the theories of consumer and firm behavior is the same: it is the idea that the decision maker maximizes something—utility or profit—that gives the theory a structure that makes it possible to derive hypotheses about behavior. Starting from the mathematical conditions for a maximum, one can investigate how the solution to the problem depends on variables that consumers or firms must take as given, in particular prices and (in the case of consumers) income. This is *comparative statics analysis*; a method that since Samuelson wrote about it has constituted the core of the theory of economic behavior.[3]

Foundations also contains a pathbreaking analysis of dynamic economic models, that is, models that describe the development of an economic system over time. In this context he argues that for a model to give a realistic description of the real world it must have an equilibrium solution that is *stable*. For an unstable solution cannot be sustained over time and can therefore rarely be observed. "How many times," he asks rhetorically, "has the reader seen an egg standing upon its end?" He also shows how the conditions for stability are essential for the conclusions that can be drawn from the model.

Wedged in between the static and dynamic parts of the book, Samuelson also has a chapter on the theory of welfare economics that is a masterly synthesis of the literature from the breakthrough of marginalism to the middle of the 1940s. He provides a rigorous exposition of Pareto's welfare theory and points out that the conditions for Pareto optimality define the limits to how far we can stretch the idea of social optimality without comparing the utility levels of different persons. Should we wish to go further, it requires us to introduce what Samuelson calls a *social*

---

[3] The analysis of production decisions in the *Foundations* is based on neoclassical production functions in the tradition founded by Wicksell (see chapter 12). In Dorfman, Samuelson, and Solow (1958) the analysis of production was extended to the case of linear models using the then new optimization technique of linear programming.

welfare function, a function that shows how aggregate welfare depends on the utility levels of all individuals that make up society. This theoretical construction made an important contribution toward the clarification of the normative content of economic theory and the distinction between efficiency and distributive justice as criteria for optimal resource use.[4] The chapter also testifies to Samuelson's deep interest in the history of economic thought, which has resulted in a large number of articles about important economists of the past.[5]

Foundations is above all a book about analytical methods, and many of Samuelson's scientific articles also have a strong focus on questions of method. This is particularly the case for the papers that lie within the core areas of economic theory—demand theory, welfare economics, and the theory of capital and growth. But in addition to this he has also explored a number of special areas, and of these his contributions to the theory of international trade and public finance or public economics deserve special mention.

In the field of international economics Samuelson is best known for his work on the connection between commodity and factor prices. The point of departure for his contributions in this area was the so-called Heckscher-Ohlin model, first formulated by the Swedish economists Eli Heckscher and Bertil Ohlin.[6] In his analysis of the determinants of international trade, David Ricardo had assumed that while commodities were mobile between countries, factors of production were not. This assumption was taken over by the large majority of later contributors to the international trade literature. But whereas Ricardo had assumed that technologies of production differed between countries, Heckscher (1919; 1950) and Ohlin (1933) assumed instead that technologies were the same while countries differed in terms of their endowments with factors of production. Some countries were relatively well endowed with labor, others with capital. In

[4] The concept of the social welfare function had earlier been introduced by Abram Bergson (1938), but Samuelson's exposition was more transparent and became more influential.

[5] See the references for a selective list of some of these articles.

[6] Eli Heckscher (1879–1952) was both a theorist and economic historian and most of his work is in the area of economic history. His best-known contribution in that field is the book *Mercantilism* (1931).

the Heckscher-Ohlin model, commodity prices were determined in world markets while factor prices were formed in the domestic markets for capital and labor. In an article written jointly with Wolfgang Stolper, Samuelson analyzed the effects of commodity price changes on factor prices and found that an increase in the price of a commodity leads to an increase in the price of the factor of production that is used intensively in the production of that commodity; for instance, an increase in the world market price of a labor-intensive good will raise domestic wage rates. This is known as the Stolper-Samuelson theorem (Stolper and Samuelson 1941).

To take the analysis a step further, suppose that there are two countries in the world, one of which is richly endowed with labor and the other with capital. In the absence of trade, wages will be low in the labor-rich country and high in the capital-rich country while the reverse would be true for the price of capital. With the opening of trade, the labor-rich country will find its comparative advantage to be in labor-intensive products, and with the expansion of output of these products the demand for labor will increase and wages rise. In the capital-rich country, on the other hand, wages will fall and the price of capital rise. Thus, through the effect of international trade in commodities, the prices of the factors of production will be brought closer together. How close? Samuelson (1953–54) showed that under certain conditions the theory implied that factor prices would be completely equalized and that this result was valid beyond the simple case of two factors and two goods. This result is known as the factor price equalization theorem.

In the area of public economics or public finance Samuelson's most important single contribution is the theory of public goods (Samuelson 1954). His definition of this concept is that a public good is one that is simultaneously available to all, so that the consumption of one person does not reduce its availability to others (as in the case of national defense). He also showed how one could derive conditions for the optimal allocation of resources to public goods. The central optimality condition contrasted sharply with the social efficiency condition for the supply of private goods. In the latter case, each consumer's marginal willingness to pay for the good—his marginal benefit—should be equal to its marginal cost. In the case of public goods, the *sum* of all consumers' marginal benefits should be equal to the marginal cost of production. In symbols,

$$MB_1 + MB_2 + \ldots + MB_n = MC.$$

Here the symbol MB stands for the marginal benefit and subscripts denote the individual consumers in the economy—n in all. This optimality condition, often referred to as the Samuelson rule, is of fundamental importance for the analysis of the expenditure side of government budgets and the development of cost-benefit analysis for public sector projects.[7] At the same time the theory pointed to a fundamental problem of incentives in that the motivation of a single agent to provide a public good is very weak, since the agent would bear the whole cost of production but only receive a small fraction of the benefits. This type of good is therefore poorly suited for the market mechanism, and its provision is a natural task for the public sector.

In addition to his many scientific contributions Samuelson has also had an important influence on the teaching of economics through his textbook *Economics: An Introductory Analysis*, which was first published in 1948 and has by 2009 appeared in nineteen editions (in recent years with William Nordhaus as coauthor).[8] It has been translated into more than forty languages and has been printed in millions of copies, making it the most influential textbook on economics ever written.[9] Its commercial success may to

[7] However, the "rule" assumes that public expenditure is financed by nondistortionary taxes, so that it has to be modified to allow for more realistic cases of tax finance. See the discussion of Pigou's analysis of this problem in chapter 11.

[8] The scope and volume of his scientific output is overwhelming. The five volumes of his collected articles that have so far been published (Samuelson 1966–86) contain almost 400 articles, and a significant number of new papers have been published since then.

[9] The only other candidate for this distinction would in a historical perspective have to be Marshall's *Principles*. Obviously, in a smaller and less globalized world it did not reach the same number of readers; on the other hand, it was a book that also addressed itself to other economists and became very influential with respect to the future development of economics. But times had changed between 1890 and 1948. Samuelson's *Economics* was a book for undergraduate students; academic economists seeking inspiration for their own research would be more likely to consult the *Foundations*, a book that was quite inaccessible to beginning students. A direct comparison of the influence of the two books is therefore hardly possible.

some extent be ascribed to the prestige of its author, but there are also many more substantial reasons for its popularity. It is written in a lively and amusing style, it has a good balance between theory and applications, and it explains advanced theoretical insights in a simple and accessible form. There is no doubt that it has helped to form modern economists' views of what their subject is all about.

One of the book's very influential ideas was the concept of the "neoclassical synthesis." As a result of the world economic depression in the 1930s many had come to view the theories of the classical economists—"classical" in the sense of Keynes—as being of little relevance for a world of overproduction and mass unemployment. But this attitude, according to Samuelson, is without foundation. Keynes's theories have shown us how to use sensible macroeconomic policies to stabilize the economy at a state of full employment. Once this has been achieved, the classical analysis of markets and prices is fully valid; this is the fruitful synthesis of Keynes and the classics.

KENNETH ARROW AND THE FOUNDATIONS OF WELFARE ECONOMICS AND GENERAL EQUILIBRIUM

The work of Hicks, Samuelson, and others during the 1930s and 1940s had helped place the theories of general equilibrium and welfare economics in the center of modern economics. But there remained some fundamental problems in these areas that had not been sufficiently clarified and that appeared as exciting challenges to economic theorists, especially those with a strong mathematical background. Prominent among these were the American economist Kenneth Arrow, who made important contributions both to the foundations of welfare economics and to the theory of competitive equilibrium. In the latter area another important contributor was the French economist Gérard Debreu.

Kenneth Arrow (1921–) began his university studies at City College in New York and went on to Columbia University where he specialized in mathematics. However, Harold Hotelling, who was one of his teachers at Columbia, convinced him that he ought to switch to economics. His education was interrupted by the war, but afterward he resumed his doctoral studies at Columbia while he also spent considerable time at the Cowles Commission in Chicago. From 1949 he has been associated with Stanford University except for the years 1968–79, when he taught at Harvard.

Arrow's doctoral studies resulted in a dissertation that was published in book form as *Social Choice and Individual Values* (Arrow 1951a). The book is a theoretical study of collective or social choice mechanisms; the question that it raises is what demands we should make on such a mechanism, given that it is designed to work in a democratic society or in a democratically organized group of individuals. Suppose that a committee is about to choose between a certain number of alternatives. Each member of the committee is rational in the sense that he has a preference ordering that ranks the alternatives. Will the collective choice that the committee makes also satisfy the demands of rationality? It had long been known that there were special cases where the answer to this question was no. The best known of these was Condorcet's voting paradox, which shows that majority voting does not necessarily generate a collective preference ordering (the paradox was presented in chapter 2). A natural question to ask is whether the paradox is just a curiosity or an illustration of a deeper and more general problem.

Arrow demonstrated that the example was far more than a curiosity.[10] He approached the issue in a systematic way by setting up a number of conditions or axioms that a social preference ordering ought to satisfy. Very briefly, these axioms can be stated as follows: (1) The social preference ordering should be derived from the preference orderings of the individuals in society, whatever form these might have. (2) If one or more individuals change their ordering of alternatives A and B in favor of A, the social preference ordering should not change in the reverse direction. (3) The social ordering of alternatives A and B should be independent of whether or not C is an available alternative. (4) The social ordering should not be imposed from outside. (5) No one should be a dictator; it should not be the case that one

---

[10] It is an interesting point that in 1951 Arrow did not know Condorcet's analysis; however, he was acquainted with other discussions of the paradox of voting.

individual's preferences determine the social ordering whatever the preferences of the others. On the nature of these axioms Arrow remarked:

> These conditions are, of course, value judgements and could be called into question; taken together they express the doctrines of citizens' sovereignty and rationality in a very general form, with the citizens being allowed to have a wide range of values. (Arrow 1951a; 1963, pp. 30–31)

Arrow's main result was now that there is no social preference ordering that satisfies all the axioms at the same time. It is this result that is known as the Arrow impossibility theorem. Accordingly, the paradox of voting is not a peculiar and exceptional case; it is an example of a far more general problem.

There are few individual contributions to economic theory that have had an impact comparable to this book.[11] Among other things, it raised the issue of how the impossibility theorem should be seen in relation to welfare theory as presented, for example, in Samuelson's *Foundations*. Did Arrow's result prove that Samuelson's social welfare function was a logically untenable construction?[12] Did it show that rational collective decisions in a democratic society were impossible? Or was it the case that the five axioms contained implicit assumptions that actually made the result far less destructive than it appeared? Later research in this area has attempted to study how sensitive Arrow's result is to reformulations of the axioms, but the literature on this topic is far too extensive to be surveyed here.

---

[11] The study of collective decision making is not only of interest to economists but also to other social scientists, and the influence of *Social Choice and Individual Values* has been widespread and particularly strong within political science.

[12] This question became especially pressing because Arrow referred to his social preference ordering as a social welfare function, suggesting that it was precisely the same as Samuelson's concept of the same name. The common view is now that the two concepts are not identical; Samuelson's social welfare function is not assumed to be derived from individual preferences by a collective choice mechanism. In the *Foundations* he remarks that he does not go into the issue of where his welfare function stems from, but that it should be interpreted as an expression of ethical values that can be ascribed to "a benevolent despot, or a complete egotist, or 'all men of good will,' ... God, etc." (Samuelson 1947, p. 221.)

Arrow's interest in welfare economics also led him to develop a mathematically more general and rigorous analysis of the connection between general equilibrium and Pareto optimality than had so far been available in the literature (Arrow 1951b). Earlier studies had, for example, been based on the stylized assumption that all individuals consumed positive quantities of all commodities and that all prices were positive. Using more advanced mathematical methods, Arrow showed that these restrictive assumptions were unnecessary for the main results of the theory. Through this article and simultaneous and later work by Gérard Debreu, the relationship between equilibrium and optimality became known as the *two main theorems of welfare economics:* (1) A competitive equilibrium is a Pareto optimum. (2) Any Pareto optimum can be sustained as a competitive equilibrium.[13]

Arrow and Debreu had a common interest in establishing general equilibrium theory on a firmer logical and mathematical foundation. The theory as formulated by Walras had an obvious weakness in that it did not contain a proof of the existence of an equilibrium solution to his model. The problem of constructing such a proof had been studied by several economists and mathematicians in the interwar period, but it was not until the joint work of Arrow and Debreu (1954) that it received a satisfactory solution.

It is perhaps not immediately clear why the problem of existence of equilibrium should be of interest to economic theorists. It might actually be tempting to argue that the problem is uninteresting: we *know* that equilibrium exists because the model of competitive markets actually shows us how the market economy functions. Quite apart from the question of whether the last part of this statement is a realistic one, the argument is based on a fundamental misunderstanding. We cannot by the use of theoretical methods prove the existence of an equilibrium "out there"; we can only prove that it exists in the *model* that we

---

[13] Gérard Debreu (1921–2004) was born in France but spent most of his academic life in the United States, and it was during his stay at the Cowles Commission in the early 1950s that his collaboration with Arrow began. His 1959 book *Theory of Value* became an influential reference for the extensive research on general equilibrium theory that took place in the 1960s and 1970s.

have constructed. To be able to show this is very important, for if the model does not have an equilibrium solution, the conclusions that one attempts to derive from it will lack logical foundation. To be certain that equilibrium exists is therefore important for our conviction of the internal logic of the model. Walras and his successors had argued that the model was logically consistent from the fact that the number of equations was equal to the number of unknowns. But as demonstrated in chapter 9, this is no guarantee of an economically meaningful solution to the system of equations.

Arrow and Debreu gave a mathematically precise and general form to the assumptions that it had been usual to make in general equilibrium models. They assumed that there were constant or decreasing returns in production, that consumers had convex indifference curves, and that there were no external effects on the consumption or production side of the economy. They further assumed that firms maximized profit and that consumers maximized utility, taking prices as given. On the basis of these assumptions they showed the existence of equilibrium in the sense of existence of a set of prices that were such as to make demand equal to supply in all markets.[14]

Seen from a later perspective it is easy to realize that this proof was a major theoretical achievement, but both at the time and later there were clearly many economists who felt that the proof of existence of equilibrium was of little importance for their own work. However, an interesting aspect of the proof was that it showed that economists who worked with general equilibrium models that were based on "the usual assumptions" could now be assured that equilibrium actually existed in the model that they worked with. The general proof of existence made it superfluous to provide proofs of existence for more specialized models as long as these models could be regarded as special cases of the Arrow-Debreu model.

Arrow's research interests gradually came to extend over a large area. A main focus of his work became the theory of economic decisions and resource use under uncertainty. Starting

---

[14] For some goods, however, it could be the case that equilibrium occurred at a point where supply exceeded demand. In such a case the price of the commodity in question would be zero.

from the Neumann-Morgenstern expected utility theorem (see below), he clarified the role of risk aversion for the understanding of economic behavior and showed how further assumptions about attitudes to risk could generate interesting hypotheses about behavior in areas like portfolio choice, insurance, and business organization (Arrow 1963a). He also showed how the theory of general equilibrium could be generalized to take account of uncertainty: assume that there exists a set of markets in which one can buy claims conditional on the occurrence on some specific event or state of the world; so-called state contingent claims. It can then be shown that the two main theorems of welfare economics hold for this case, so that the formal incorporation of uncertainty has indeed been achieved (Arrow 1953; 1964). Although the theory is obviously far from being a realistic description of real world risk markets, the analysis has come to serve as an important theoretical benchmark for the study of more realistic cases like stock markets and regular insurance contracts.

Arrow has also been a pioneer in the analysis of situations with asymmetric and incomplete information, particularly in markets where the agents do not have the same information about the quality of the goods or services that are traded. Especially well known is his theoretical analysis of the health sector (Arrow 1963b), which provided the foundation for a completely new analytical approach to the study of health economics. This paper is remarkable both for its inventive use of the theoretical tools of uncertainty theory and for the careful attention to the institutional characteristics and social norms of the health sector. For example, Arrow shows convincingly how the trust relationship that is characteristic of many patient-physician relationships can be interpreted as a substitute for ideal insurance markets.

John von Neumann and Oskar Morgenstern and the Theory of Games

The point of reference for the modernization efforts of Hicks, Samuelson, Arrow, and Debreu was the theory of perfect competition. Imperfect competition plays a very minor role in their work, even if important progress had been made in this area during the 1920s and 1930s (see chapter 13). However, there were others who believed that the focus on perfect competition was a very unfortunate one for economists who wished to understand the functioning of real markets, where the interaction between firms involving active competitive strategies was of central importance. But while the strength of the theory of perfect competition was its firm logical structure, the theory of imperfect competition consisted of a number of different analytical models that had not been derived from a common set of fundamental assumptions. One of the critics of the established theory in this regard was the German economist Oskar Morgenstern (1902–77), who in the 1930s wrote several articles that were extremely critical to the existing theory of economic behavior and competition; however, he did not possess the analytical skills that were required in order to create an alternative to the dominant theoretical approach. The turning point came when after Hitler's annexation of Austria he was dismissed from his position at the University of Vienna and decided to immigrate to the United States. At Princeton University he became acquainted with another immigrant, the Hungarian-born John von Neumann (1903–57), who was among the most prominent and respected mathematicians and physicists of his time. The collaboration between the two of them resulted in a completely new approach to the study of economic behavior: the theory of games.

At an early stage of his career, Neumann had developed a fascination for economics, which he regarded both as an interesting field of application and as a source of inspiration for mathematical analysis. He wrote an early study of the problem of existence of equilibrium in competitive models, but an even more important contribution was his article (Neumann 1928) on the analysis of games between two players. The games that he had in mind in this article were social games (*Gesellschaftsspiele*) like chess, but in a footnote he mentioned the possibility of application of his approach to economic problems. It was through discussions with Morgenstern that he came to realize the potential fruitfulness of economic applications of the theory of games, and the discussions led them to plans to write a broad exposition of the theory with applications to central economic problems. In the course of two years they completed their book *The Theory of Games and Economic Behavior*, which came out in 1944; a revised edition appeared in 1947. During the two years of writing the project grew considerably; their initial plan was to write a long journal article, which gradually changed to a vision of a short book, but the final product had become a book of more than six hundred pages.

Like the work by Arrow and Debreu on general equilibrium theory, *The Theory of Games and Economic Behavior* represented a significant extension of the use of mathematics in economic theory. From its beginnings in the first part of the nineteenth century, the mathematics that economists employed was chiefly differential and integral calculus, while the new approaches employed more advanced mathematics like set theory. The formal development of the theory of games was the work of Neumann, while Morgenstern's contribution was to build a bridge between the new mathematical models and the criticism of economic theory that he had formulated in his early papers.

The core of the theory of games is the analysis of individual decisions in situations where each individual ("player") must make decisions knowing that the outcome for him depends on the actions that other individuals take—and where he is aware that the others think in the same way. We have already encountered this type of setting in the context of Cournot's duopoly theory (see chapter 7), where the firms find themselves in the same kind of strategic situation that Neumann and Morgenstern analyzed. Cournot cut his way through the complexity of the problem by assuming that each of the competitors takes the other's output as given. But this may seem like a rather arbitrary assumption that is not founded on any deeper analysis of the strategic situation of the players. Neumann and Morgenstern set themselves the task of erecting the theory of games on an axiomatic foundation and began by analyzing very simple games.

The simplest of all games is called a zero-sum game between two players. "Zero sum" refers to the assumption that the gain of one player is equal to the loss of the other. Let us call the players A and B and imagine that each of them can choose between two decisions or strategies: A can choose strategy a_1 or a_2, and B's possible strategies are b_1 and b_2. The result for A will then depend not only on whether he chooses a_1 or a_2, but also on the choice made by B. What is rational behavior for the two players, and what will be the outcome or equilibrium of the game?

There are four possible outcomes, and these are illustrated by the example in table 17.1.

TABLE 17.1
A Zero-sum Game for Two Players

	Strategies for B	
	b_1	b_2
Strategies for A		
a_1	−1	+2
a_2	0	+3

The numbers in the table show the possible outcomes for A. If, as an example, he chooses strategy a_1 while B chooses his strategy b_1 the outcome for A is equal to -1 (which could, for example, be interpreted as minus 1 million dollars). But since the game is zero-sum it means that the outcome for B in this case becomes +1 (or plus 1 million dollars). What should A do? Neumann and Morgenstern postulated that A will choose the strategy that makes his minimal gain as large as possible (or his maximal loss as small as possible). From inspection of the table it is easy to see that this implies that he will choose strategy a_2, where the worst that can happen to him is the outcome of 0. Had he instead chosen a_1 he might have risked the loss of −1. What will B do? Because the numbers show the gain for A, they also show the loss for B. If B reasons in the same way as A, he is interested in choosing the strategy that minimizes his loss, and this implies that he will choose b_1 which guarantees him an outcome that is no worse than 0. Once these strategies have been chosen, neither player has an incentive to change his strategy. In this game, therefore, there is an equilibrium given by the strategies a_2 and b_1 with an outcome for each of the players equal to 0.

A zero-sum game between two players is in itself of little economic relevance, and the interesting feature of the game is therefore mainly that it shows the basic structure of game theory. Most situations that can be described in terms of strategic interaction between economic agents involve more than two persons. Moreover, situations like contract negotiations and market competition can rarely or never be described as a zero-sum game, since the outcome as a rule is either that both parties get a positive gain, or that the gain to the winners is greater than the loss of the losers. Accordingly, Neumann and Morgenstern went on to analyze more general games, and it turned out that there was frequently a confusing multiplicity of equilibria. Those who had expected that game theory would provide a unique equilibrium concept for situations of strategic interaction were therefore disappointed. With time, however, it came to be realized that the chief contribution of game theory to economics was to establish a general structure for the analysis of this kind of problem where old and new theories of strategic behavior could find their place within a general theoretical framework.

An important contribution to this understanding of the theory of games was given by a young American mathematician, John Nash (1928–). In a short article (Nash 1950a) he showed that any game with an arbitrary number of players, where every player chooses his own best strategy given the strategies adopted by the other players, had an equilibrium solution. The Nash equilibrium, as it came to be called, can be interpreted as a generalized version of Cournot's theory from 1838 which postulates this type of behavior for oligopolistic markets but without a more general and deeper justification. At the same time Nash's analysis showed that market equilibrium under perfect competition could be regarded as the outcome of a game with a large number of players.[15]

The Prisoners' Dilemma

Following Neumann and Morgenstern's work, game theorists turned their attention to the development of a number of more specific games, and some kinds of games have turned out to be of particular interest to both economists and other social scientists. Among these a prominent example is *the prisoners' dilemma*, which is an interesting case of a non-zero-sum game.[16] The structure of the game is as follows: two prisoners, A and B, are interrogated separately (so that there is no communication between

[15] Nash's other important contribution to economic theory was his axiomatic analysis of the problem of negotiation between two agents and his proposal for an equilibrium solution for such situations (Nash 1950b).

[16] The game was invented by mathematicians studying game theory around 1950; see Dixit and Nalebuff (2008), p. 66.

TABLE 17.2
The Prisoners' Dilemma Game

	Strategies for B	
	confess	not confess
Strategies for A		
confess	5, 5	2, 10
not confess	10, 2	3, 3

them) on the suspicion of having committed a crime. Their shared understanding of their situation is that if both refuse any knowledge of the crime, they will only get a relatively light sentence. If, for instance, A confesses both will be convicted, while the length of A's sentence will depend on whether or not B also confesses; his sentence will be shorter if he is the only one to confess. The strategic situation can be illustrated in table 17.2.

Here the entries in the table represent the number of years in prison with the first number representing the sentence for A and the second that of B. Thus, if A confesses he gets five years in prison if B also confesses and two if he does not. If he does not confess, he gets ten years' imprisonment if B confesses and three if B also does not confess. For prisoner B the situation is symmetrical. What is the rational strategy for prisoner A? It is easy to see that A's best choice is to confess, for whatever B does, A is in a better situation if he has chosen to confess. B is in the exact similar situation, so his best strategy is also to confess. The strategy "confess" is said to be a *dominant strategy* for both players and the equilibrium outcome is five years in prison for both. However, the result of individually rational decisions is not collectively rational, for both would have been better off had they decided not to confess, which would have led to the outcome (3, 3). This is the equilibrium that would presumably have been established if the players had been able to communicate and cooperate; (3, 3) is therefore said to be the *cooperative equilibrium* in contrast to the *non-cooperative equilibrium* (5, 5).

Much of the interest in this game comes from the insight that individually rational behavior does not always result in an outcome that is good for society; "society" in this context meaning the community of the two prisoners. Economists have found that the prisoners' dilemma game provides a fruitful framework for studying a number of problems where the individual choice of dominant strategies leads to socially inferior outcomes.[17] Examples include a variety of economic and social issues ranging from advertising and price wars to resource depletion and environmental pollution. It is a good example of how game theory has contributed a structural framework for the study of the strategic interaction between economic agents.

The Expected Utility Theorem

A very important innovation that Neumann and Morgenstern introduced in the second edition of their book—which, however, has no direct connection with game theory—was a theory of rational decision making under uncertainty. As early as 1738 Daniel Bernoulli (see chapter 2) had proposed that a rational person ought to maximize expected utility in the sense of the weighted sum of the utility of every possible outcome, using the probabilities as weights. Over the years, several economists had referred to this principle,[18] but it had never been derived as a consequence of more fundamental principles of rational behavior. This is just what Neumann and Morgenstern did; they formulated a series of axioms about rational behavior and showed that the theory of maximization of expected utility followed as a result of the axioms.

In the theory of rational choice among certain outcomes, which goes back to the work of Pareto (see chapter 11) the basic axioms of rational choice are *completeness* and *transitivity*. Completeness means that when faced with any two alternatives A and B, the rational agent will always be able to decide whether he prefers A to B, B to A, or whether he is indifferent between them. Transitivity means that if the agent prefers A to B and B to some third

[17] Note that the outcome represented by the lower-right-hand corner of table 17.2 is the Pareto optimal outcome; both players are better off than in the non-cooperative equilibrium in the upper-left corner.

[18] One of them was Jevons (1871), who suggested several examples of application of the principle but without any further justification for it.

alternative C, he will also prefer A to C. Neumann and Morgenstern required that these axioms also hold for the choice between uncertain outcomes or "lotteries" and with some additional axioms they were able to show that preferences between uncertain outcomes could be represented by an expected utility function. To be more precise, let us assume that the outcomes can be represented by the value of consumption for every possible event or state of the world. If p_s is the probability of this state and c_s is consumption, then the agent's expected utility is

$$E[u] = p_1 u(c_1) + p_2 u(c_2) + \ldots + p_n u(c_n),$$

assuming that there are n states or events altogether.

The expected utility theorem, as the principle is now called in the literature, was quickly recognized as a major contribution and came in the following decades to form the foundation for theoretical studies of insurance and financial markets as well as a number of other areas where the existence of uncertainty was judged to be of essential practical importance. These developments will be discussed further in chapter 18.

Further Reading

When it comes to the more recent period that we have discussed in this chapter, it is far easier to read the original literature, since the terminology and conceptual framework are much closer to what we find in current literature. All economists who are interested in the history of thought should have some acquaintance with Hicks's *Value and Capital* and Samuelson's *Foundations*, even if they do not read them from beginning to end. One gets a good impression of Hicks's expository style by reading part 1, "The Theory of Subjective Value," which might lead to a taste for more. *Foundations* has a mathematical structure that is not always easy to penetrate, but one can skip many of the details and still share in Samuelson's inspiring vision for economic theory. Arrow's *Social Choice and Individual Values* can be read with profit even if one does not see through all the details in the proof of the impossibility theorem. That some parts of the book are in the borderland between economics and philosophy should for many be an extra attraction. Arrow's most important contributions to the theory of risk and uncertainty have been collected in Arrow (1974).

The Theory of Games and Economic Behavior is not an easy read, but the sixtieth anniversary edition from Princeton University Press is nevertheless worthy of attention by the reader with a more general interest in the topic. The edition contains interesting forewords and postscripts by prominent game theorists and in addition a selection of reviews of the original edition.

The biographical and historical literature about the economists of this period is expanding quickly. Here are a few examples: an interesting picture of Hicks emerges in an interview done by Arjo Klamer (1989) shortly before Hicks's death. An article by Samuelson (1998) gives a lively perspective on his time as a student and the writing of the *Foundations*. The story of the work on the proof of existence of competitive equilibrium has been told by Weintraub (1983), and the early history of game theory is related by Leonard (1995). Oskar Morgenstern (1976) has described the nature of his collaboration with Neumann on the theory of games. Sylvia Nasar (1998) has written a best-selling biography of John Nash that also provided the basis for the movie *A Beautiful Mind*.

Further Developments in the Postwar Period

T HE WORK DISCUSSED in chapter 17 focused mainly on basic research in microeconomics and general equilibrium theory. The present chapter continues the account of developments from the time of Keynes until about 1970. It begins with an account of the work of two economists whose contributions were to a large extent inspired by Keynes: Milton Friedman opposed the Keynesian view both of the fundamental mechanisms at work in the economy and of the best policies for economic stabilization while Robert Solow extended the work of Keynes by constructing macroeconomic models designed to analyze the long-run growth process of the economy. We continue in the present chapter with a description of developments in the area of public finance before reverting to the microeconomic perspective with a discussion of the area of uncertainty and information.

MILTON FRIEDMAN AND THE CRITIQUE OF KEYNESIAN POLICIES

The Keynesian revolution in macroeconomic thinking was extremely influential both in economic theory and policy in the first couple of decades after the Second World War. Keynesian models dominated the textbooks, and the Keynesian perspective was the central source of inspiration for theoretical and empirical research. However, toward the end of the 1960s the Keynesian approach was losing ground, partly because the development of the Western economies took a direction that seemed to indicate that the theory had some serious shortcomings, partly because the logical foundations of Keynes's theory became subject to critical evaluation. On the one hand, the phenomenon of "stagflation"— a combination of high unemployment and high inflation—that several countries started to experience in the 1960s caused many economists to doubt whether Keynesian stabilization policy led to acceptable results. On the other hand, there was a growing awareness that the Keynesian theory of macroeconomic equilibrium was too sketchy to be theoretically convincing and that there was a need to rethink the theoretical foundations of macroeconomic policy. A large number of economists contributed to the reorientation that was to follow, but among Keynes's critics none was more influential than the American economist Milton Friedman (1912–2006).

Milton Friedman was educated at Rutgers University and the University of Chicago before receiving his Ph. D. from Columbia University in 1946. After having held several jobs both in government and research organizations, Friedman began teaching at the University of Chicago in 1946 where he remained for a period of thirty years. There he became a prominent member of the group of economists known as the Chicago School, characterized on the one hand by a strong belief in the power of economic theory to illuminate a wide range of social issues and on the other hand by a firm conviction of the benefits of free markets and small government.

Friedman's first serious attack on the Keynesian theoretical framework came with his work on the theory of the consumption function, which was one of the most important components of Keynesian macroeconomics. Keynes had assumed that aggregate consumption demand was a function of total income in society, but he had presented no theoretical justification for this hypothesis, nor had he discussed what precise definitions of income and consumption one ought to use in attempts to confront the hypothesis with statistical data. The postwar development did not seem to be in accordance with Keynes's hypothesis of decreasing average propensity to consume, and Friedman became convinced that both the theoretical and empirical research that were inspired by Keynes's work rested on much too weak foundations. This conviction motivated him to develop a new theory of the consumption function, the so-called permanent income hypothesis (Friedman 1957).

The basic theoretical hypothesis was based on an analysis inspired by the work of Irving Fisher (1930) who had assumed that consumers maximize utility over time subject to a given level of lifetime income (see chapter 12). Friedman pointed out that an implication of this view was that consumption was related to permanent income—a long-run expected normal level of income—and not to current income, which may deviate from permanent income both in positive and negative directions. He went on to demonstrate that this theory was able to reconcile two apparently conflicting sets of empirical observations. The first is that in a cross-section of the population at a given time one observes a relationship between consumption and saving that fits with the Keynesian hypothesis: the rich consume a smaller share of their income than the poor. The second is that in time series data for the long run there is proportionality between consumption and income. Friedman's hypothesis was that the time series data reflected the relationship between consumption and permanent income. The cross-section data, on the other hand, contained components of so-called transitory income (positive or negative) that would not have appreciable effects on consumption. In the short run, therefore, the average propensity to consume is decreasing while in the long run it is constant. This has an important implication for economic policy: attempts to stabilize the economy through short-run fiscal policy measures like variations in public spending and the tax level will be ineffective or at least off target. In order to influence consumption demand, the government must be able to influence permanent income, while short run increases or decreases of taxes that are expected to be reversed when the business cycle turns will have little effect. The theory and empirical analysis of his book together led to a more critical view of the Keynesian recommendation to stabilize aggregate demand and employment by means of countercyclical fiscal policy.

Another area in which Friedman became very influential was the analysis of the causes of inflation and the role played by changes in the quantity of money, a relationship that in the Keynesian literature had been largely neglected. Friedman became a spokesman for a modern version of the quantity theory of money. In the long run money was neutral: the quantity of money was of no importance for the "real" side of the economy—production, consumption, and economic growth—while the long-run rate of inflation was determined solely by the growth of money supply. In the short run, however, neutrality did not hold, so that monetary policy would normally have effects on demand, production, and employment. But in Friedman's view the time pattern of these effects was so complex that any attempt by the government to fine-tune economic activity by monetary measures might easily destabilize the economy rather than contribute to increased macroeconomic stability, and he substantiated his view by a detailed empirical analysis of American monetary history (Friedman and Schwartz 1963). The Keynesian recipe for macroeconomic policy that called for careful adjustment of policies to the various phases of the business cycle—a so-called discretionary policy—should be rejected in favor of a system of *policy rules*; in the case of monetary policy Friedman recommended a rule of 4 percent annual growth in money supply. The choice of percentage was based on the assumption that it corresponded roughly to the real growth rate of the economy, so that the 4 percent increase of money supply would imply an approximately constant price level over time. Friedman's ideas about policy rules had great influence both on macroeconomic research and practical policy design.[1]

Friedman was among the twentieth-century economists who were best known among the general public, mainly in his role as a strong spokesman for the free market economy and as a critic of public ownership and market regulation. His writings in this area began with his book *Capitalism and Freedom* (1962), and he was also known for his role as commentator in a series of popular television programs on economics developed together with his wife Rose Friedman, who was also an economist. Entitled *Free to Choose,* the series became extremely popular and was also developed into a best-selling book with the same title (Friedman and Friedman 1979).

Friedman's message in these books is that economic freedom is of crucial importance for society in two respects: it is an essential part of the more general concept of freedom that is associated with a democratic society and is therefore of value in and of itself. But it also has instrumental value since it is an indispensable condition for securing political and intellectual freedom; at this point there is a close similarity between his ideas and those

[1] An account of Friedman's views on monetary economics and policy can be found in Friedman (1969). A famous example of an analysis that shows that a policy by rules may frequently yield better results than discretionary policy is the article by Kydland and Prescott (1977).

of Friedrich von Hayek (see chapter 14). In addition, Friedman puts great weight on the market as an institution that works to avoid social conflict:

> The widespread use of the market reduces the strain on the social fabric by rendering conformity unnecessary with respect to any activities it encompasses. The wider the range of activities covered by the market, the fewer are the issues on which explicitly political decisions are required and hence on which it is necessary to achieve agreement. In turn, the fewer the issues on which agreement is necessary, the greater is the likelihood of getting agreement while maintaining a free society. (Friedman 1962, p. 24)

While Friedman acknowledges the necessity of public sector decisions in situations where public goods are involved ("neighbourhood effects" as he calls them), he is a strong advocate of the use of the market mechanism wherever possible, even if the market deviates considerably from the ideal of perfect competition. Thus, he recommends a strongly reduced role for government in the area of education and a program of downsizing a large number of market regulations, for example, those relating to occupational licensing.

It is tempting to draw a clear distinction between Friedman as a researcher and as an ideological spokesman for the market economy. However, there is clearly a unity of thought that runs through all his work, characterized by his skepticism toward the exercise of government authority and the emphasis on the need to limit discretionary policy actions. Obviously, however, the empirical foundations for his policy recommendations are much stronger in the area of fiscal and monetary policy, where they are backed up by theoretical models and empirical research, than in many of the other areas covered in his more popular writings. But in general, his policy recommendations have had a strong influence on policymakers in many countries, particularly during the last quarter of the twentieth century.

ROBERT SOLOW AND GROWTH THEORY

Keynes's macroeconomic theory was set in a short-run framework. The demand for investment goods played a crucial role in Keynesian models, but investment had on the other hand no effect on production capacity or productivity. This type of theoretical model could not, therefore, be used to study the long-run development of the economy, which depends in a crucial way on the accumulation of capital. The English economist Roy Harrod (1948) and the American Evsey Domar (1946) had constructed closely related models of economic growth that showed how the economy could expand by means of saving and investment, which increased the stock of capital and thereby the national product. However, the Harrod-Domar model had some serious shortcomings. First, it assumed that there was no possibility of substitution between capital and labor in production, and second, it did not show how the growth rate of the economy adjusted itself to growth in those factors of production that did not expand via saving and investment. These shortcomings were overcome in a pathbreaking article by Robert Solow (1956).

Robert Solow (1924–) studied at Harvard University where, after having served in the Second World War, he obtained his Ph.D. in 1951. He joined the faculty of the Massachusetts Institute of Technology in 1950 and remained there throughout his academic career. His research interests have been mainly in the area of macroeconomics where he has written a large number of extremely influential papers, some of them coauthored by Paul Samuelson. But no other single paper of his has been as influential as the 1956 article. The model that he developed there has later become known as "the neoclassical growth model."

The model follows in a certain sense in the tradition from Keynes insofar as it is based on a few relationships between a small number of variables. There is one commodity in the economy that can be used either for consumption or investment and two factors of production, labor and capital. The relationship between aggregate output (the national product) and factor use can be described by a production function with constant returns to scale: an increase of the use of both capital and labor by 1 percent will lead to a 1 percent increase in output. The supply of labor increases at a constant growth rate that is determined by factors outside the model, and there is full employment; here there is accordingly a marked difference with Keynesian theory. The stock of capital increases with the amount of investment. Investment is at any time equal to saving, which is assumed to be proportional to national income or product.

Solow now showed that the rate of growth of national product is the sum of two terms that are related to the growth rates for each of the two factors of production. The first term is the rate of growth of population, while the second term reflects the growth of capital per worker. Solow's analysis implies that the economy in the long run will converge to a growth path on which the second term becomes equal to zero. In other words, the long-run growth rate for the economy will equal the rate of growth of population. This he calls the *natural rate of growth* of the economy.

If the national product grows at the same rate as population, income per head will obviously be constant. A remarkable feature of Solow's analysis is therefore that in the long run there will be no increase in the average standard of living. The reason for this is the assumption that the technological relationship that transforms labor and capital into output is constant over time; there is in other words no technological progress. Solow modified the model by assuming the existence of technological progress that makes labor more productive and showed that it implied that the natural growth rate became equal to the sum of the growth rates for population and the level of technology. This implies that the long-run growth of per capita standard of living is solely due to technological progress. An increased rate of saving and investment may also contribute to growth, but this effect is temporary; in the long run the economy will return to the natural rate of growth, although with more capital per worker and therefore with higher per capita income and standard of living.

Solow's analysis established the study of economic growth theory as a separate branch of economics. From his first paper he went on to study both further theoretical refinements of the original model and the empirical facts of economic growth. In a further contribution, taking his point of departure from the 1956 article, he considered the sources of growth on the basis of historical data (Solow 1957). His central finding was that most of the growth in aggregate output could be explained by technical progress while only a small part was due to capital accumulation. This article marked the beginning of a long line of studies of "growth accounting" that were undertaken for many countries and different time periods. Many of these studies confirmed Solow's conclusion about the importance of technical progress for the understanding of growth, but there was also a suspicion that the methods used tended to underestimate the role of growth in capital per worker. In another influential article (Solow 1960), Solow pointed out that new technology tends to be embodied in new capital equipment, and he developed models that showed how new technologies enter the production process through investment in new capital goods, implying a more important role for capital accumulation than indicated by the earliest studies of growth accounting.

In the work of the classical economists, the causes of growth were closely tied to the development of the market economy, for instance through increased specialization and division of labor. Although their analysis was less rigorous in logical and mathematical terms, their perspective on economic growth and development was a broader one. The nature of Solow's model was such that there was little room for the broader view. Solow has been very much aware of this and has emphasized that simple models of this type had a limited but important role to play. In a survey exposition some years later (Solow 1970; 2000), he remarked that he did not believe that this kind of model could be used for realistic analyses of the causes of economic growth or for making firm policy recommendations. But work on the models, he argued, is still more than an intellectual game, for they provide us with important suggestions for the design of more detailed and realistic studies.

Solow's work was an important source of inspiration for the many economists who engaged in studies of economic growth during the 1950s and 1960s. What emerged from this research was partly the construction of new variants of the Solow model, using more general assumptions about the number of the sectors of production, the structure of capital, technological progress, population growth, or saving behavior. There was also a renewed interest in the problem first posed by Frank Ramsey in 1928: What is an optimal allocation of national income between consumption and investment when capital accumulation increases the production possibilities in the future?[2] Solow has himself made important contributions to the literature on optimal economic growth, particularly in the context of the exploitation of natural resources.

---

[2] See chapter 15 for a presentation of Ramsey's work.

Solow has also made a number of important contributions to short-run macroeconomic analysis. While his "neoclassical" growth model seemed to signal an adherence to pre-Keynesian economics, his research on short-run problems of unemployment and stabilization policy has definitely a Keynesian flavor, and in recent decades he has taken a very critical view of the attempts to restore a modern version of the neoclassical theory of the market economy as basically a self-adjusting mechanism, even in the short run. In his 1987 Nobel Lecture he expressed this view as follows:

> The markets for goods and for labor look to me like imperfect pieces of social machinery with important institutional peculiarities. They do not seem to me at all like transparent and frictionless mechanisms for converting the consumption and leisure desires of households into production and employment decisions. (Solow 1970; 2000, p. xvi)

This is a view of the market mechanism that is markedly different from the opinions expressed by Milton Friedman. In the interpretation of the insights of economic theory as well as the results of empirical research there still remains considerable scope for economic judgment concerning the workings of the real economy.

PUBLIC FINANCE AND THE THREE BRANCHES OF GOVERNMENT

The analysis of public sector policies relating to resource allocation and the distribution of income has played a prominent role in economic research since the time of Adam Smith. The problems that have been studied within this branch of economics are partly positive or descriptive: How does an income tax affect labor supply? What effects does the introduction of social security have on private saving? But as we have seen, there are also economists who have concerned themselves with normative issues. A good example of this is Dupuit (see chapter 7). He raised the question of the best way to calculate the social profitability of public projects and of the right prices to charge for public services. John Stuart Mill and others concerned themselves with the design of a just tax system.

In his 1959 treatise on public finance that was a summary of the current state of the subject, Richard Musgrave suggested a way of thinking about the role of the public sector that became very influential (Musgrave 1959, chapter 1).[3] He proposed that one ought to think about the economic role of government as being organized in three branches: the allocation branch, the distribution branch, and the stabilization branch. The task of the allocation branch should be thought of as the determination of public expenditure and the design of the tax policy required to finance it. The task of the distribution branch was to bring about a socially desirable distribution of income, while finally the objective of the stabilization branch was to ensure price stability and full employment. The three objectives taken together clearly reflected a *normative* perspective on the public sector, although in order to understand the welfare effects of taxes and public expenditure one also had to go into the *positive* issues of policy effects on individual and firm behavior as well as the questions related to the incidence of taxes and public spending, in other words, the study of policy effects on commodity and factor prices.

Positive and normative issues cannot be studied in isolation from each other. Thus, in order to determine whether direct or indirect taxation is the best alternative from the point of view of social welfare, one has to know something about the effects that the two systems actually have on saving, labor supply, and the distribution of income as well as the possible effects of tax reform on unemployment and inflation. These are obviously matters for positive theory and empirical research. Because of the close relationship between the issues that are of concern to the three branches of government, the division of labor between them cannot be absolute.[4]

---

[3] Richard Musgrave (1910–2007) was born in Germany but immigrated to the United States where he received his Ph.D. from Harvard University and later taught at several American universities. His best-known work, in addition to the 1959 book, is the innovative analysis of taxation and risk-taking in Domar and Musgrave (1944).

[4] Musgrave actually suggested that the "manager" of each of the three branches "ought to plan his job on the assumption that the other two branches will perform their respective functions properly" (Musgrave 1959, p. 5). But this particular idea has not found much favor with later public finance economists.

Musgrave's survey was an authoritative statement of the contents of this field of research in the 1950s. An interesting reflection of this was the space given to the tasks of the stabilization branch, which occupied more than a third of the book. This consisted mostly in the analysis of tax and expenditure effects on national income and employment within the context of Keynesian macroeconomic models. In the following decades this part of public finance—or public economics, as the field also came to be called—tended to become redefined as part of the core of macroeconomic theory while public finance proper concentrated on issues related to resource allocation and income distribution.[5]

Regarding the relationship between normative and positive approaches to problems of allocation and income distribution, an interesting case is provided by the debate over the relative merits of direct and indirect taxes. In chapter 13, we saw that Harold Hotelling (1938) considered this issue and concluded that if an individual is to pay a given amount of tax, it is best both for him and society that taxation is direct rather than indirect. For indirect taxation means that consumer prices no longer reflect the marginal costs of production, and this leads to a loss of social efficiency. Direct taxation, according to Hotelling, involves by contrast no such costs. However, it was pointed out by Little (1951) that this conclusion rested on an implicit and unrealistic assumption, namely, that the income tax did not affect the amount of labor supplied. In the special case of fixed labor supply the income tax would indeed be in the nature of a lump sum tax, that is, a tax defined as a fixed amount to be paid. Obviously, such a tax does not affect the prices, wages, or interest rates with which the taxpayer is faced on the margin, so that a competitive equilibrium in the commodity, labor, and capital markets is efficient both before and after the imposition of the tax. But in general, as Little pointed out, a tax on income would reduce the wage rate that the individual received and so act as a tax on labor or a subsidy to leisure. The implication of this is that there is no purely theoretical case against indirect taxes. Whether direct and indirect taxes are best from a social point of view becomes basically an em-

---

[5] Thus the book by Atkinson and Stiglitz (1980), which reflects the development of the area through the 1960s and 1970s, contains no discussion whatever of Musgrave's stabilization branch.

pirical question whose answer will depend on the magnitudes of demand and supply elasticities. The natural next step would seem to be the development of a theory of optimal taxation that would clarify the precise roles of the various elasticities. Such a theory did not materialize until almost two decades after Little's analysis. In the meantime, however, considerable progress was achieved in the related field of public sector pricing.

Public production raised two sets of issues related to economic welfare. First, what were the conditions that justified nationalization and public production? Second, once it had been decided that production was to take place in the public sector, which prices should be charged for the goods and services provided? Hotelling had concentrated on the latter question, taking public ownership of the railways and other public utilities as an institutional and historical fact, but the justification of public ownership was closely related to the problem of optimal price policies. With decreasing average costs as in large parts of sectors like transport and energy supply, prices equal to marginal cost would result in an accounting deficit, and this would be inconsistent with private ownership under competitive conditions. In such industries, if left in the private sector, decreasing average cost would lead to monopoly with prices above the marginal costs of production.

Public ownership could solve this problem by charging prices equal to marginal cost and cover the deficit through government transfers (assuming as before that the taxes required would not distort competitive prices), and this insight provided the basic case for socialization and public production.[6] As it was expressed by the English economist James Meade in 1943:

> Where a community needs only one gasworks, or electricity station, or railway network, monopoly must obviously exist. In these cases, socialisation in one form or another, of the industries concerned, is the only radical cure to ensure that they are run in such a way as to equate marginal costs to prices ... rather than to make a profit. (Meade and Fleming 1944, p. 322)

However, one problem with this argument concerns the government transfer required to cover the total costs of production. In practice, a public utility would often be required to finance its

---

[6] This had also been emphasized by earlier economists, e.g., by Knut Wicksell.

total costs from its own revenue, but then it would have to raise prices above marginal costs. In that case a new problem arose: a railway or energy company that produced a number of different services would have to decide whether prices should be raised by the same percentage markup on all services or whether the markup on marginal costs should vary from one commodity to another. A group of French economists associated with the energy company Electricité de France who worked on practical problems of pricing started to interest themselves in the theory of efficient prices when the public company is subject to the condition that revenue must cover total costs. Marcel Boiteux (1956; 1971) demonstrated that such a "second-best" price system would imply that the percentage deviation between prices and marginal costs should be inversely proportional to the elasticity of demand. The more inelastic the demand the larger ought to be the difference between price and marginal cost.

This result is reminiscent of Ramsey's (1927) analysis of the problem of optimal indirect taxes (see chapter 11), and this is obviously no coincidence, since the difference between price and marginal cost can in fact be considered as a tax levied on the consumers of the services provided by the public utility. In the 1960s there emerged a new interest in the more general problem of optimal taxation that had been raised by Ramsey. The problem was now referred to as the choice of a second-best optimal tax system. The expression "second best" alluded to the insight that the ideal tax system would be one of individualized lump sum taxes, but such a system was in practice infeasible unless the lump sum was such as to levy the same amount of tax on everybody, which would have unacceptable distributive effects. The problem of optimal tax policy must therefore be a choice of the best among a number of imperfect alternatives; a "choice of evils" as Ricardo had said.

A modern reconsideration of Ramsey's problem from this point of view was presented in an article on optimal commodity taxation by Peter Diamond and James Mirrlees (1971) that inspired a large literature on the normative aspects of taxation. The theory confirmed and generalized the conclusion of Ramsey and Boiteux that the highest taxes ought to be levied on goods that were inelastic in demand, although the optimal tax rate would have to be decided not only on the basis of the own price elasticity but also on the cross price elasticities of demand. Moreover, the elasticity rules might have to be modified for the purpose of redistribution: a government with egalitarian preferences might wish to impose lower taxes on commodities primarily consumed by the poor.

A similar breakthrough occurred in the theory of optimal income taxation. In chapter 11 we saw that Pigou argued in favor of egalitarian income redistribution provided that this did not lead to "a contraction in the size of the national dividend." But an income tax with a positive marginal rate on income from labor would be likely to reduce labor effort, so that the design of an income tax schedule would have to strike a compromise between redistribution and the concern for efficiency. As early as 1945, William Vickrey had formulated an analytical model that showed how in principle one ought to construct an income tax system that represented a rational trade-off between efficiency and distributive justice. However, the analysis did not lead to very clear conclusions, and it was not until an article by Mirrlees (1971) that the theory achieved a form that allowed other economists to build on it in more applied work on problems of tax policy.[7]

The Mirrlees model is based on a number of simplifying assumptions. All individuals have identical preferences over consumption and leisure. They differ only in terms of their productivity per hour worked; some have high, some have low productivity, and this is reflected in their market wages. Their incomes consist only in their earnings from labor. The government has to raise revenue through a tax on income and chooses the income tax schedule that maximizes the sum of utility in society (or minimizes the loss in utility from income taxation). Since everyone is supposed to have the same utility function with decreasing marginal utility of consumption, one might expect that the result of the analysis would be a progressive tax schedule with an increasing marginal tax rate. Interestingly, this turned out in general not to be the case. Mirrlees's numerical experiments with the model indicated that the marginal tax rate in the optimal solution tended to decrease toward the top of the income

[7] For a more detailed presentation of the work of Vickrey and Mirrlees, who shared the Nobel Prize for economics in 1996, see Sandmo (1999).

distribution. The natural interpretation of the result was that while the redistributive gain from taxing the top income earners was small, the efficiency loss would be substantial because of the high labor productivity of these individuals. Clearly, the special assumptions on which the model is built—e.g. competitive labor markets and no income from capital—imply that the analysis cannot be the last word on the normative theory of tax progressivity, but it is an important input into the more systematic thinking about this issue.

A DISSENTING VIEW: JAMES BUCHANAN AND PUBLIC CHOICE THEORY

These studies of public sector pricing and tax policy were applications of welfare economics to practical problems for the public sector, and many economists were enthusiastic about a development that allowed them to use abstract and rigorous theory to derive conclusions that appeared to be of direct relevance for economic policy. However, there were others, like the American economist James Buchanan, who regarded the new theories with a good deal of skepticism.[8] Buchanan argued that the conclusions inspired by welfare economics were founded on some implicit and unconvincing assumptions about the behavior and motivation of public sector bureaucrats and politicians. This point is perhaps most easy to understand with reference to the earlier quotation from James Meade. Meade says that public production will *ensure* that prices will be set equal to marginal costs; the decision makers are assumed as an empirical hypothesis to act in accordance with the best interests of society. By contrast, the common assumption about private sector agents is that they act in accordance with their personal interest. Is there any reason to believe, Buchanan asks, that agents in the public sector are essentially different? One of his main points was that the analysis of a reform that transfers an activity from the private to the

---

[8] James Buchanan (1919–) received his Ph.D. from the University of Chicago in 1948 and has taught at several universities, mainly in Virginia. Most recently, he was professor and director of the Center for Study of Public Choice at George Mason University. He received the Nobel Prize for economics in 1986.

public sector should not—as Meade does—compare the actual functioning of private markets with the ideal world of welfare economics but rather with a realistic theory of the behavior of public sector agents based on their self-interest. Policy recommendations must be based on realistic theories of individual behavior not only for the private but also for the public sector. This was the central message in the book by Buchanan and Tullock (1962) that marked the beginning of a direction of research commonly referred to as the public choice school.

Another of Buchanan's messages is that normative economic analysis should concentrate on the design of laws and institutions within which bureaucrats and politicians act; this framework should be designed in such a way as to provide these agents with incentives that to the largest extent possible led them to take actions that promoted the public interest. An interesting application of this idea concerns the design of the tax system. Buchanan was critical to the approach taken in the theory of optimal taxation, arguing that a realistic analysis of the public sector could reverse its conclusions about the tax structure. Politicians who find themselves at "the constitutional stage," meaning a stage where they are able to reflect on the long-run interests of society, should design a set of rules for tax policy that limit the tendencies to overexpand the public sector that are likely to characterize day-to-day politics. This view implies that one should be cautious about allowing the taxation of goods that are inelastic in demand. By restricting the tax available to politicians of the future to a tax base that shrinks when taxes go up, one makes it costly for them to increase the tax level and puts a brake on their desire for expansion of the public sector and thereby of their own role in society. This recommendation is obviously in direct contradiction to those that can be derived from optimal tax theory.[9]

Both Buchanan and some other economists of the public choice school take a skeptical view of the public sector in general; the state represents primarily a concentration of power against which the citizens need protection. They have also tended to characterize representatives of the welfare theoretic approach as politically naive in their alleged belief that the state will neces-

---

[9] The central reference regarding Buchanan's views on the issue of taxation is the book by Brennan and Buchanan (1980).

sarily adopt the policies that theory recommends (a belief that is considerably less widespread today than in the immediate postwar period). But the contrast between the two approaches may easily be exaggerated. The theory of public choice is a useful corrective to simplistic interpretations of welfare economics, but on the other hand there is little basis for the view that economists should limit themselves to only one of the two approaches. In terms of research strategies it is obviously both possible and fruitful to switch between a positive and normative perspective on the public sector. In this view, the two approaches are complements, not substitutes.

The Economics of Uncertainty and Information

We have already on several occasions touched on the analysis of uncertainty in economics. From Bernoulli's analysis of the St. Petersburg paradox (see chapter 2) we saw that he was led to propose expected utility as the basic principle that should guide rational behavior, or—in an alternative interpretation—as the objective that best explained actual behavior in situations comparable to that involved in the tossing of pennies. With the Neumann-Morgenstern proof that the maximization of expected utility followed from a set of axioms of rationality, the stage was set for the exploration of a whole set of questions related to markets and institutions whose existence in an essential way is due to the existence of uncertainty in economic affairs.

Before describing some of the applications of the expected utility approach, it may be useful to consider some more basic aspects of the expected utility theorem. When Bernoulli suggested his principle of rational behavior, the hypothesis of *risk aversion* was at the center of his analysis, for his objective was to explain how a rational player would only be willing to pay less than its expected value to be allowed to participate in a game of gambling. But risk aversion is no part of the expected utility hypothesis as such; it is an additional hypothesis that is introduced to explain important aspects of utility. Risk aversion corresponds to a particular property of the Neumann-Morgenstern utility function that can be illustrated by means of some simple mathematics. Suppose that an individual with income y is invited to participate in a gamble that involves either the gain or the loss of an amount x, each with probability 0.5. No doubt a common reaction would be to refuse the invitation, and the hypothesis that an individual would in most cases prefer a certain income to an uncertain income with the same expected value defines the notion of risk aversion. If we now assume that the individual evaluates the game by means of a utility function with income as its only argument, we can represent the individual's preferences by the inequality

$$u(y) > 0.5u(y+x) + 0.5u(y-x).$$

If we now multiply both sides of this inequality by 2 and rearrange the terms we can rewrite it as

$$u(y+x) - u(y) < u(y) - u(y-x).$$

The last inequality says that the increase in utility involved in going from income y to $y+x$ is less than the increase that follows from going from $y-x$ to y. In other words, risk aversion is represented by the property of diminishing marginal utility. If the inequality sign had been reversed, this individual instead of being a *risk averter* had been a *risk lover*, while if the sign had been one of equality he would have been risk *neutral*.

It might seem obvious that of the three possibilities regarding the shape of the utility function, the economist should definitely opt for the assumption of risk aversion. There is not only the example of the St. Petersburg paradox to suggest this; there is also the economically much more important case of the insurance industry that would support this choice. From the insured person's point of view, insurance involves giving up a certain amount (the insurance premium) in exchange for an uncertain payment whose expected value is less than the premium. His willingness to engage in this exchange can only be explained if it is assumed that he is risk averse.

However, risk aversion does not explain all aspects of behavior under uncertainty. It is a fact of life that individuals also participate in gambling activities, in which they engage in a risky undertaking with negative expected value. In order to explain this type of behavior, it seems that we must assume these individuals to be risk lovers, but we then face the empirical paradox that many people both buy insurance and participate in gambling activities. How can they be risk averters and risk lovers at the same time?

Milton Friedman and the statistician Leonard Savage (Friedman and Savage 1948) made an early attempt to resolve this paradox. They did this by postulating that consumers were risk averse over the range of incomes below their current income while being risk lovers with respect to incomes above their actual income, with a return to risk averse attitudes at sufficiently high incomes. This article has become a classic in the economics of uncertainty, although its direct influence on the literature has been modest, probably due to the rather complex nature of the hypothesis and the limited interest that economic theorists have taken in the explanation and understanding of gambling. Instead, applications of the expected utility theorem have been almost exclusively based on the hypothesis of risk aversion.

The most obvious field of application is insurance. Here risk averse individuals and firms pay insurance companies to take on some of the risk that they carry with respect to life and property. The insurance companies can take on these risks because they have a diversified portfolio of insurance contracts; in addition, they can spread their risks further by reinsuring their contract with other insurance companies. The equilibrium in this type of market was studied by the Norwegian economist Karl Borch (1962), who showed that it implied a Pareto optimal allocation of risk among the insurance companies. A related development came in the study of asset markets with the development of the so-called capital asset pricing model by Sharpe (1964), Lintner (1965), and Mossin (1966), which did much to integrate financial economics with the main body of economic theory. In public finance the expected utility approach was used by Mossin (1968) and Stiglitz (1969) in a more general treatment of the problem of taxation and risk-taking that was first discussed by Domar and Musgrave (1944).[10]

---

[10] Mossin and Stiglitz showed that capital income taxation with loss offset tended to encourage risk-taking because the government took on some of the risk that would otherwise have been born by the investor. A similar conclusion had been derived by Domar and Musgrave, but because of its foundation in the expected utility theorem the Mossin-Stiglitz result carried greater conviction.

The theory of expected utility maximization with risk aversion was gradually applied to a number of other problems in economics: portfolio and saving decisions, labor supply and occupational choice, and production and investment decisions in firms. From being a somewhat esoteric topic on the fringes of economics, by the early 1970s the tools of the economics of uncertainty had become part of the standard equipment of the economic theorist.

Uncertainty about the outcome of economic decisions reflects the imperfect information economic agents have about their economic environment. This information need not be symmetric; people may have different probabilities concerning the different outcomes. But uncertainty theory did not really take the case of asymmetric information seriously until about 1970, and the most influential single contribution to the new area was an article by George Akerlof (1970). The intriguing title of this paper, "The Market for Lemons," was a reference to the used car market; a "lemon" is an American term for a bad car. Suppose that there exists a market for used cars without any private or public regulation. The seller of a used car knows whether the car is a good car or a lemon, while the buyer can only acquire this knowledge after having owned the car for some time. However, the buyer does know the fraction of good cars in the market, and he uses this as his probability that the car that he is considering is a good car. Since good and bad cars cannot be identified by the buyers they must sell at the same price. Suppose to begin with that the common price reflects the expected value of the car; this is accordingly higher than the true value of a lemon and lower than the value of a good car. If this price were established, what would be the reaction of the owners and prospective sellers of good cars? Obviously, if the price that they can get is lower than the true value of their car, they will withdraw it from the market. The average value of the cars that are for sale will fall and so will the price. Then more good cars will be driven out of the market until the only cars that are for sale are the lemons.

The used car market is obviously of some independent interest, but Akerlof's theory would not have become so influential if it had not been for the fact that the basic theory is applicable to a wide range of important economic problems. In insurance, the problem that Akerlof described is known as *adverse selection*; insurance premiums may be set at levels where only high-risk in-

435

dividuals will be willing to pay them. Akerlof also described several other areas in which this problem arises, such as the employment of minorities and credit markets in developing countries. He also argued that the problem of adverse selection provided an explanation of institutional arrangements that so far had not received any attention in economic theory: quality guarantees, restaurant chains, and professional licensing may all be seen as attempts to overcome the problem related to asymmetric information about product quality.

Another concept that entered into the standard vocabulary of economists at about this time (although it had long been used in the insurance industry) was that of *moral hazard*. This refers to the hypothesis that insurance may change the behavior of the insured in a direction that makes the event for which he is insured more likely to happen—such as when car insurance makes the owner less careful to check whether he has locked the car. Arrow (1963b) had discussed this problem in the context of medical insurance, and it soon found applications in labor economics and in the more general area of the study of contracts.

As this survey of the economics of uncertainty and information has shown, the expected utility theorem has had a great influence on economic research over a wide range of issues. However, there have also been economists who have been in doubt as to whether the concept of rationality that it embeds is a realistic one or whether it makes unrealistic demands on peoples' ability to think in a consistent manner about uncertain events. Prominent among the skeptics was the French economist Maurice Allais (1953). He conducted an experiment—among a group of subjects that included some prominent economists—that was an attempt to test whether the choices that people made conformed to the consistency requirements of the expected utility theorem. The experiment is intriguing and worth considering in more detail. The subjects were confronted with the following two problems:

Problem 1. State your preference between the following two alternatives:

  A. $1 million with probability 1 (i.e., with full certainty).
  B. $5 million with probability 0.10, $1 million with probability 0.89 or nothing with probability 0.01.

Problem 2. State your preference between the following two alternatives:

C. $1 million with probability 0.11 or nothing with probability 0.89.
D. $5 million with probability 0.1 or nothing with probability 0.9

The majority of the subjects expressed a preference for alternative A over B and for D over C (the reader might consider whether he or she would do the same). However, if we assume that the subjects have based their choices on the axioms of the expected utility theorem, there is a problem. For a preference for A over B implies

$$u(1) > 0.1u(5) + 0.89u(1) + 0.01u(0)$$

while a preference for D over C must imply

$$0.1u(5) + 0.9u(0) > 0.11u(1) + 0.89u(0).$$

Since the sum of the left-hand sides of the two inequalities must obviously be greater than the sum of the right-hand sides, we can write their sum as

$$u(1) + 0.1u(5) + 0.9u(0) > 0.1u(5) + 0.89u(1) + 0.01u(0) \\ + 0.11u(1) + 0.89u(0).$$

When we collect and rearrange the terms we can rewrite this inequality as

$$0.1u(5) + 0.9u(0) > 0.1u(5) + 0.9u(0),$$

The last inequality says that a lottery that offers $5 million with probability 0.1 and nothing with probability 0.9 is preferred to itself, which is clearly a meaningless proposition. The contradiction shows that the subjects who chose A over B and D over C were inconsistent when judged by the rationality criteria of the expected utility hypothesis: having chosen A in the first question they should have chosen C in the second question.

The so-called Allais paradox should be interpreted with some care. It does not necessarily imply that the expected utility theorem is useless as a guide to rational action; however, it shows that it is *difficult* to choose rationally. On the other hand, it is more disturbing when considered as a positive theory of how people actually make choices. It does seem perfectly reasonable to choose alternatives A and D, and this observation has led to a number of suggestions for alternative concepts of rationality for choice under uncertainty. So far, however, none of these attempts have succeeded in replacing the expected utility theorem as the dominant approach to the analysis of risky choices.

FURTHER READING

Milton Friedman's *Capitalism and Freedom* as well as his later book *Free to Choose* provide interesting and provocative reading. Many will find the insistence on the message of market liberalism to be politically annoying, but Friedman's ideas always have a background in economic reasoning and cannot be easily rejected. Those who wish to train themselves to argue against this message will find that Friedman is a tough sparring partner, and if one feels in need of a second, James Meade's book *The Intelligent Radical's Guide to Economic Policy* (1975) provides good support.

Robert Solow has given an excellent account of growth theory in his book *Growth Theory: An Exposition* (Solow 1970; 2000). The second edition contains in addition to the original 1970 version several additional chapters that comment on the developments in the intervening period as well as the text of his 1987 Nobel Lecture.

Richard Musgrave's *The Theory of Public Finance* (1959) is a good source of information about the state of public finance at the end of the 1950s. An account of Musgrave's life and work and his place in the history of public finance can be found in Sinn (2007). Some of Buchanan's most influential articles have been collected in Buchanan (1989). This book and other articles are reviewed in Sandmo (1990), while a survey of Buchanan's contribution as a whole has been provided by Atkinson (1987). The different approaches that Musgrave and Buchanan have taken to the study of the role of the state can be studied in a book based on a joint series of lectures that they gave in 1998 (Buchanan and Musgrave 1999). The lectures also testify to the authors' broad historical perspective on the economics of the public sector.

Drèze (1964) reviews the work by postwar French economists on public utility economics and macroeconomic planning. The work by Vickrey and Mirrlees that led to their Nobel Prize award is described in broad terms in Sandmo (1999). More detail on Vickrey is provided by Drèze (1997) and on Mirrlees by Dixit and Besley (1997).

The state of the economics of uncertainty at the end of the 1960s has been described in the book by Karl Borch (1968), himself one of the leaders in the field. A good textbook exposition of the economics of asymmetric information is Kreps (1990).

Many of the economists whose work we have discussed in this and the preceding chapter have won the Nobel Prize in Economics (or, officially, The Sveriges Riksbank Prize in Economic Sciences in Memory of Alfred Nobel). The home page of the Swedish Nobel Foundation, www.nobel.se, is a good source of information about the prize winners, for example, in the form of autobiographical essays and links to other material about them. Breit and Spencer (1997) have edited a collection of essays where thirteen American prize winners tell the stories of their backgrounds and academic careers.

Long-term Trends and New Perspectives

H AVING DESCRIBED the history of economic ideas from the eighteenth century to the beginning of the 1970s it is natural to conclude with some reflections on the long lines in the history of thought. Is it possible to offer some broad generalizations on the development of the science of economics? What are the most pronounced trends in modern economics, and what are their historical roots? Is it possible to predict the course that the subject will take in the twenty-first century? A discussion of these issues in the course of a few pages must necessarily be superficial and selective as well as speculative. However, it might stimulate the reader to further thoughts on the matter, both on the background of the previous chapters and the experience that he or she might have with the economics of our own time.

The history presented in this book has been the account of the development of economic ideas and theories. But underneath the surface of this account lies another story that has only surfaced occasionally: the story of economics as a profession. This story cannot be entirely separated from the history of thought, and in the following we shall therefore discuss long-term trends both from the point of view of the history of ideas and the history of the economics profession.

NEW PERSPECTIVES IN ECONOMIC THEORY

In the foregoing chapters we have seen that a large number of what we regard as the main issues in economic theory have been discussed in the academic literature at least from the time of Adam Smith and David Ricardo. What are the determinants of relative prices? What are the causes of economic growth? Which are the factors that determine the distribution of income between individuals and classes in society? These and some other questions are so fundamental and many-dimensional that economists have continued to analyze them for more than two hundred years. The answers have been modified or changed over time both because the theoretical perspective has become broader and deeper and because the structure of the economy and society is subject to continuous change.[1]

A bird's-eye view of the history of economics shows that it has been characterized by a broadening and deepening of its perspective. An example of scientific progress that can be described as a broadening of the view is the great breakthrough for theories of imperfect competition in the 1930s by which economic theory was able to capture a new part of the realities of economic life. An example of progress by deepening of the analysis is the research on the existence of competitive equilibrium in the 1940s and 1950s. In this case it was not a question of extending economists' view of economic reality but of exploring the logical foundations of existing theories. Even if most examples of scientific breakthroughs have elements both of broadening and deepening it may be of interest to ask what kind of development we have seen in recent years. Has economic theory expanded primarily by broadening its perspective or exploring its foundations? This is not the type of question that has a definitive answer, since the two perspectives are frequently so interwoven that it is difficult to say which is which. We shall attempt to throw light on this question by means of some examples.

Theoretical research that is predominantly deepening takes its point of departure from existing economic theories and models and tries to reestablish them on more solid logical foundations or on the basis of more general assumptions. It is not difficult to

---

[1] Some may have heard the story of the former student who after many years visits his old professor of economics and is invited to take a look at the exam questions that the professor has just set. "But," he says, "these are the same questions that we had thirty years ago!" "Yes," answers the professor, "for in economics we do not change the questions, only the answers." The story is obviously not intended as a positive judgment on economics as a science; however, most of those who laugh at it have not seen its true significance. In fact, the professor has a good point, even if he expresses it a little too categorically. Taking a broad view, the central questions that economists study remain the same. And it would indeed be remarkable if an active professor in an evolving field of research did not after thirty years find that many of the old exam questions required new answers.

find examples of this type of research from recent decades. One is the study of markets with asymmetric information, which was discussed in chapter 18. Another example is the research on the microeconomic foundations of macroeconomic theories. Keynes had postulated that the labor market was characterized by wage rigidity, but was it possible to derive the lack of wage flexibility as the result of the interplay between employers, workers, and trade unions? An extensive recent literature has explored this and similar problems within macroeconomics. A third example concerns the foundations for the variety of theories of imperfect competition, where it has turned out that the more general perspective of game theory has created a better understanding of the multitude of concepts and hypotheses in this area of economic theory.

However, the expansion of economics in recent years has also taken the form of broadening the definition of the scope of the subject. This is demonstrated through the emergence of specialized fields with their own educational courses, textbooks, and academic journals. The classical economists treated areas like international trade and public finance as integrated parts of the core of economics, while today these tend to be defined as areas of specialization. In addition, a number of new fields have been added: financial economics, the economics of health and education, law and economics, and environmental economics are just a few examples. Some of this development should be seen as driven by demand: thus, with a growing health sector there arises a need for more research on the economic aspects of health care and for more economists with a specialized competence in the area. However, part of the explanation is also that economics has become more applicable to a number of real-world problems. The theory has become more operational and adaptable to the study of practical problems, while there has also emerged better and more accessible methods for empirical analysis. Part of the move toward increased specialization should therefore be seen as driven by supply: economists have become more productive in offering research-based services to practical decision makers.

Both the broadening and deepening processes have led to a renaissance of the interest in the study of institutions in economic life. In the work of the classical economists like Smith and Mill, the description and analysis of central economic institutions received considerable attention, but with the advent of marginalism and general equilibrium theory the institutional perspective was gradually pushed aside. Instead, the view emerged that a preoccupation with institutions was antitheoretical. This was a theme both in the German-Austrian *Methodenstreit* (see chapter 8) and in the recurrent discussions about the use of mathematics in economics. General equilibrium theory created an image of the market economy as directed by anonymous "forces." But studies of markets with asymmetric information—like Arrow's (1963) analysis of the market for health care and Akerlof's (1970) study of the used car market—demonstrated that realistic theories had to take account of the institutional realities of these markets. In a similar vein, attempts to understand the mechanisms that create unemployment led to a stronger theoretical interest in understanding the role of trade unions in the labor market.

The increased attention to the economic importance of institutions has also been nourished by developments in the global economy. In the postwar period, development economics emerged as a new field of research with a strongly practical agenda: how to promote economic growth in the poor countries (or the underdeveloped countries, as they were called in the 1940s and 1950s)? For many years, the planning approach was the dominating one. The two central issues appeared to be, first, to promote structural change in the poor economies; to achieve this it was essential to establish—primarily under public ownership—the sectors that the rich countries had and the poor had not, above all large-scale manufacturing. Second, it was important to promote economic growth, and this was to be achieved by increasing the rate of saving and investment. Efforts in these directions gradually turned out to have limited success, and the new view that with time came to dominate development economics laid much greater emphasis on the study of incentives and institutions within the economic and social framework that actually existed in the poor countries. The new emphasis was reinforced by the experience of the breakdown of the communist system of central planning in the Soviet Union and Eastern Europe in the 1990s. The analysis of the crisis of the old system as well as the construction of a new turned out to require more than theoretical insight in the conventional sense; in addition, there was a need for understanding the functioning of institutions both under the old and the new systems.

Economic theory has, therefore, developed both in terms of broadening and deepening in recent years. In some areas existing theories have become more deeply rooted in assumptions about human behavior. In other areas we observe that the theory has become more specialized with a view toward application to a number of different applied problems. Even if we have witnessed a continued growth of pure theory in the sense of Walras we have also seen a marked tendency to let theory merge with the study of institutions. This tendency may well come to change the character of economic analysis in the twenty-first century. The English economist Frank Hahn (1925–), himself a distinguished contributor to economic theory, has given an intriguing expression to this prospect:

> Instead of theorems we shall need simulations, instead of simple transparent axioms there looms the likelihood of psychological, sociological and historical postulates. These new roads will find willing and happy travellers, but it is unlikely that those with the temperament and facilities of mid-twentieth-century theorists will find this a congenial road. There will be a change of personnel, and economics will become a "softer" subject than it now is. (Hahn 1991, p. 47)

To what degree this prediction will turn out to be correct is obviously an open question. But an interesting aspect of Hahn's vision of the future is the idea that economics will move closer to the other social sciences. There is actually some support for this view in aspects of the development of modern economics.

"Imperialism" and Multidisciplinary Approaches

Alfred Marshall said that economics was the study of men "in the ordinary business of life," and Lionel Robbins defined it as the study of the allocation of scarce resources among alternative uses. Neither of these definitions is sufficiently precise to allow us to draw clear limits between what is and what is not economics. Moreover, it is far from obvious that there are or that there ought to be any fixed limits to the subject. Experience has shown that accepted limits have been extended as economic researchers have attempted to apply their tools of analysis to new areas, and both Marshall's and Robbins's definitions could be interpreted to refer to areas that have not traditionally been considered parts of economics. Particularly in recent times, we have seen a clear trend toward the extension of the scope of economic analysis, which by some has been referred to as "economic imperialism" (Lazear 2000). At the same time, many economists have attempted to increase the explanatory power of their theories by adopting ideas from other sciences, sometimes through interdisciplinary cooperation with researchers from other scientific fields.

The work of the American economist Gary Becker (1930–) is one of the most obvious examples of economic imperialism.[2] In the course of his career, Becker has studied a number of areas of social life that before his time were not considered to be part of the natural habitat of economists. Among his early work were innovative studies of discrimination—in particular racial discrimination—in the labor market and of education and human capital formation. More controversial was his theory of crime and punishment (Becker 1968), where he ventured into the area of criminology. The picture he draws of the criminal is that of a person who commits his crime on the basis of a rational calculation of the probability of getting caught and the resulting punishment against the gain if he escapes. He also derives the implications of this hypothesis for a rational administration of justice, which often turn out to consist of low probabilities of discovery combined with severe punishment. Yet another area where Becker has practiced economic imperialism is the study of the family (Becker 1981). He applies relatively simple theoretical models to the question of parents' choice of the number of children and how much to invest in them in the form of time and educational resources ("the quantity and quality of children"). He has also studied the importance of economic factors for the marriage contract, maintaining, for example, that the economic approach is able to explain whether a society practices monogamy or polygamy, how high the divorce rate is, and how many children that are born outside of marriage. Like his work on crime, this part of his research has been both influential and controversial. His

---

[2] A more detailed review of Becker's work with further references can be found in Sandmo (1993a). Becker received the Nobel Prize for economics in 1992.

writings have opened up new areas for economic analysis and yielded much new and interesting insight. On the other hand, his critics have maintained that the one-sided economic approach to this class of problems implies that one's understanding of society as well as one's view of public policy comes to rest on a foundation that is at once too narrow and too unrealistic.

Economic imperialism has also made itself felt in a several other areas. The growth of academic literature in areas like health economics and the economics of the environment can clearly be considered from this angle: economists have invaded areas that were previously occupied by physicians and biologists. In the study of political decision making, where Arrow and Buchanan made pathbreaking contributions, economists have taken up issues that were previously considered to belong to the exclusive domain of political scientists. A good example of the positive, or descriptive approach, to the study of political processes is the book by Avinash Dixit whose work has in part been carried out in close collaboration with political scientists (Dixit 1996). This is an illustration of the fact that not all applications of economic theory to new problems take the form of imperialism. They may also be the result of cooperation between researchers from different academic areas who try to illuminate problems of mutual interest by joining their fields of expertise and competence. The applications of economic theory and econometrics to problems of historical research belong in the same class. Such ventures into new fields, whether they take the form of aggressive imperialism or multidisciplinary cooperation, have at times caused criticism both from other economists and from others who feel that their areas have been invaded by enemy forces. Some economists hold the opinion that the use of economic analysis beyond its traditional boundaries is of doubtful value and gives economics a bad name, especially among the other social sciences. Moreover, other social scientists have criticized the economic approach for being too narrow, neglecting important aspects of the complexity of social and economic life. Edward Lazear has given a balanced comment on this controversy:

> The strength of economic theory is that it is rigorous and analytic. . . .
> But the weakness of economics is that to be rigorous, simplifying
> assumptions must be made that constrain the analysis and narrow

the focus of the researcher. It is for this reason that the broader-thinking sociologists, anthropologists, and perhaps psychologists may be better at identifying issues, but worse at providing answers. (Lazear 2000, p. 103)

This is a thoughtful argument in favor of interdisciplinary cooperation, which should be seen in connection with Hahn's forecast for the development of economics in the direction of closer collaboration with the other social sciences.

It should also be noted that the use of economic analysis in other academic fields has not only been the result of "economic imperialism"; there are also a number of examples of researchers in other disciplines who have adopted concepts and theories from economics for use in their own field of work. One example of this is the philosopher John Rawls (1972) who has employed economic concepts like indifference curves and social welfare functions to illuminate central questions of moral philosophy. Another example is Jon Elster whose work in the borderland between philosophy, sociology, and political science makes extensive use of economic theory (see e.g. Elster 1989).

INCREASING FORMALIZATION

In the eighteenth century economics was a "literary" field of study. Those who wrote about it did not, as a rule, use any formalized methods of analysis (Malthus's arithmetic and geometric series can hardly count as mathematical economics). In spite of exceptional cases like Cournot, it is reasonable to say that this was a situation that lasted until well beyond the middle of the nineteenth century. However, some modifications of this statement may be in order. Ricardo's *Principles* has a form of exposition that is different from that of the *Wealth of Nations*; the stylized form of reasoning and the numerical examples lie closer to the language of mathematics than is the case in Smith's work. Some passages of John Stuart Mill's *Principles* go even further in this direction. His theory of price formation in international trade has such a highly formalized structure that it can almost directly be translated into mathematics. However, it was with the marginalist breakthrough in the 1870s that the formalization of economic theory began in earnest. It became increasingly common to use diagrams and equations in academic books and articles, even if many authors (like Alfred Marshall) chose to reserve them for footnotes and appendices. Nevertheless, if we go back to volumes of leading journals like the *Economic Journal* and the *American Economic Review* from the 1920s and 1930s we will still find that only a minority of the articles makes use of mathematical methods. In the period after the Second World War, however, the use of mathematical and statistical formalization was increasingly accepted, and if we take a look at the latest issues of the two journals we will discover that it is actually hard to find an article that does *not* employ mathematical methods. A similar development can be seen in the textbook literature, and in most Western countries it is hardly possible to study economics, even at a rather elementary level, without at least some previous knowledge of mathematics.

Is this progress? It is at any rate a development that has not taken place without considerable resistance. At regular intervals in the past we have witnessed debates about the use of mathematics in economics. The critics of mathematics have focused on two main arguments. First, they have pointed out that mathematical models must by necessity build on so many conceptual simplifications that they are unable to capture the complexity of human relationships and the structure of social and economic life. Second, they have maintained that the increasing standard of theoretical formalization has led to unfortunate consequences for economists' choice of topics for their research. Those who strive to achieve status and prestige among their academic colleagues will have an incentive to choose research problems that are easy to formalize rather than being related to important problems in the real world.

This criticism should clearly be taken seriously, and several counterarguments have been advanced. As regards the first point, it is clear that *any* attempt at careful analysis of an economic problem, whether it be "literary" or mathematical, must be based on simplifying assumptions. The advantage of a mathematical formulation is that both the assumptions and the reasoning that leads from assumptions to conclusions become more transparent. A theory that builds on patently unreasonable assumptions or faulty logic cannot be a good theory, whether or not it has been formulated in mathematical language. It is not the mathematics as such that makes a theory unrealistic.

A further and related argument in favor of the mathematical approach concerns the relationship between theoretical and empirical research. The empirical testing of economic theories is to a large extent based on statistical methods. A statistical test employs mathematics, typically in the form of regression equations. But if we are to be able to judge the theoretical basis for these equations we must be able to refer to a theory that has also been formulated mathematically.

The second objection to mathematical formalization is more difficult to reject, since it assumes that we can somehow observe the motivation and thought processes of the individual researcher. Some would argue that the objection is of little significance since long-run status and prestige also depend very much on the economic importance of the problems that one studies, not only on the element of advanced mathematics. However, it is certainly possible to find examples of economists who have applied exciting new mathematical methods to problems that in the long run have turned out to be of only marginal interest; in that case their prestige becomes very short-lived. However, the objection does point to an interesting general feature of the research process. The researcher chooses his or her problems not only for their intrinsic economic interest but according to whether they are researchable: Is it possible to structure a theoretical problem so that one arrives at interesting and testable results? Are there data that allow for the hypotheses to be tested empirically? If the researcher finds that the answer is no, he is likely to drop the problem. However, some economists have instead risen to the challenge of developing theories and finding data that can open up new areas for academic research.

The increasing formalization both of theoretical and empirical economics has also had important consequences for the relationship between academic economists and the outside world. Adam Smith's *Wealth of Nations* was at the same time a theoretical treatise, a textbook, and a work that aimed to reach the general reading public. In contrast, a modern economist with similar ambitions would have to write one book of each type. The treatise would be too specialized to be read by students and the general public, and the textbook would have too much of the character of a learning aid to appeal to the general reader. But there are modern economists who write all three types of books, so that economics continues to be accessible to a wide readership even if the average citizen is unable to read Samuelson's *Foundations* or Debreu's *Theory of Value*.

Possibly the most problematic aspect of the increasing formalization of the subject is the barrier that has grown up for students whose interest is limited to a fairly short introduction to the field. This may be less of a problem in the teaching tradition of the United States than in many European countries, and it is clearly open to discussion whether training in mathematics and statistics should be required by students at the elementary level. A broad and relatively nontechnical introduction to economics is a valuable supplement to courses of study with focus on the other social sciences or the humanities. This could also contribute to a reduction of the isolation of economics from the rest of the social sciences, which is frequently mentioned as a serious problem for economics.

A Greater Role for Empirical Research

A striking feature of modern economics, whether one compares it with the situation of two hundred, one hundred, or fifty years ago, is the increased importance of empirical research. If as an example we consider the state of economics one hundred years ago journal articles that treated a problem in economic theory would only rarely include empirical analysis that could be said to constitute a test of the theory. Empirical contributions would as a rule take the form of a rather informal presentation of statistical data in combination with a similarly informal discussion of possible theoretical explanations. Today, the situation is entirely different. Both theoretical and empirical methods have become much more rigorous, and the empirical analysis is subject to much higher standards both as regards the quality of the data and the econometric techniques that are used to analyze them.

There are several reasons for this development. The availability of data has been radically improved ever since the systematic collection of economic statistics started in earnest in the first half of the nineteenth century. When Adam Smith made statements about the national income, he did not have in mind a precisely defined concept as we have it today in our system of national accounts, and he could have no clear conception of the magnitude of the national income of Great Britain or any other country. With time, as statistical data became available in more systematic forms, economists (as shown in chapter 16) became more conscious of the need to develop a more reflective and critical view of the relationship between theoretical concepts and their empirical counterparts. Another reason for the stronger position of empirical research is the great progress in econometrics that implies that economists stand on firmer ground in their efforts to confront theories with data. A third and obvious reason is the development of data processing technology, which implies that the individual researcher has access to enormous masses of data and to analytical techniques that enable him more or less single-handedly to carry out research projects that only a few decades ago would have required the efforts of several research assistants over a long time—assuming that the projects were at all feasible.

The greater empirical strength of economics as a science also has another aspect, as demonstrated by the emergence of economic models that provide direct support for economic planning and practical decision making both for the economy as a whole and for individual industries and firms. The formation of economic policy is to an increasing degree based on large numerical models that have been designed with a view to providing answers to specific questions that are of interest to policymakers: What happens to inflation and the rate of interest if the government's budgetary surplus drops by 50 billion euros? What are the consequences for the structure of Norwegian industry of a permanent strengthening of the value of the krone by 5 percent relative to the euro? Similar models have also been extensively used at the sectoral level, for instance, in the analysis of energy supply. This kind of application of economics was unthinkable given the state of the subject before the Second World War. The development that has occurred as a consequence of the progress in economic theory, econometric methods, data collection, and technology is certain to continue during the twenty-first century.

An interesting new source of data for economic research is evidence from experimental research. An oft-repeated statement used to be that "economics is not an experimental science." This is no longer quite true, since laboratory experiments where individuals encounter problems and choices similar to those that exist in real markets or other economic settings have recently become widely used as a source of information about individual behavior. Laboratory research has, for example, tested hypotheses about behavior in different competitive settings as well as the more general issue of people's behavior in situations involving strategic decision making. Experimental researchers have also been concerned with the study of decision making under uncertainty and the attitudes that people have to problems related to distributive justice. The experimental work can be seen as part of a wider move towards what is called behavioral economics where the aim is to base the study of individual behavior on empirical generalizations from observed choices and attitudes rather than from a set of axioms for rational choice. The rapid growth of research in this area may possibly come to confirm Frank Hahn's conjecture about the changing nature of economics in the twenty-first century, although it is still too early to tell.[3]

Economics Becomes a Profession

A striking feature in the story of the development of economics from the days of Adam Smith until the present time is the altered institutional framework in which the central characters of the story have carried out their work. At least until the middle of the nineteenth century a university affiliation was the exception rather than the rule for the leading economists of the time. Ricardo was a "gentleman of leisure" with a practical background from the financial sector and Thünen was a landowner while Mill and Dupuit were affiliated with public or semipublic institutions where their work was of an administrative nature. True,

---

[3] A leading researcher in the field of experimental studies has been Vernon Smith, while Daniel Kahneman has made pioneering contributions to behavioral economics. For samples of their work one may consult Smith (2000) and Kahneman and Tversky, eds. (2000). Smith and Kahneman shared the Nobel Prize for economics in 2002.

Smith and Cournot were at least for parts of their lives university professors—but not in economics in the more specific sense. As we have seen, Malthus was the first professor of economics in Britain, but he was employed by an institution that had no environment for academic research. None of these had a formal training in economics as a basis for their scientific writing. It is also remarkable that most of them only used a relatively small fraction of their time on academic research and writing. Ricardo and Mill were both intensely occupied with economics for some years of their lives, but for the most part they were busy with other tasks. Men like Thünen and Dupuit were so busy pursuing their practical careers that the time left over for research was severely limited.

This situation underwent a radical change around the time of the marginalist breakthrough. All the three main characters in this episode in the history of economic thought—Jevons, Menger, and Walras—were university professors who could pursue their study and research full time. Moreover, even if the local environments for some of them could be perceived as narrow and provincial, more than the economists of fifty to a hundred years earlier they saw themselves as members of an international community of scholars. The latter half of the nineteenth century also saw the development of the institutions that we now associate with an academic profession. Economics was established as a separate field of study at a number of universities where groups of economists began to form small clusters of researchers, and specialized institutes like bureaus of statistics offered new job openings for trained economists. Separate organizations were formed with the purpose of promoting the development of the subject and provide services to members such as conferences and the publication of academic journals. The British organization, the Royal Economic Society, and its *Economic Journal* were both founded in 1890–91. The society's American counterpart, the American Economic Association, was founded in 1885, while the publication of its journal, *American Economic Review*, did not begin until 1911. However, some of the European countries were earlier than this. In Germany, the Verein für Sozialpolitik (Association for Social Policy) was founded in 1873. In Denmark the journal of the national association of economists, *Nationaløkonomisk Tidsskrift*, began publication in 1873, and a Norwegian journal followed in 1886; some German journals are even older. That the economics profession itself organized a system for scientific publication led by degrees to an increase in the quality of published articles and books. When submitting an article to one of the leading journals the author could expect to receive a critical evaluation by the editor and perhaps also by a referee that the editor had appointed. When publishing a book with scientific pretensions, the author could expect that it would be reviewed in one or more of the academic journals. The system of "peer review" had made its entry in economics.[4]

As late as at the end of the nineteenth century the most prominent writers in the field had usually a very modest amount of formal education in economics before they entered a career as active researchers, and even after the turn of the century there are many similar cases. Keynes had devoted about half a year to serious study of economics before he embarked on a career of teaching and research, and a generation later we have seen that both Joan Robinson and John Hicks had only taken a bachelor's degree before they published their first books. This is in marked contrast to their American contemporaries. Edward Chamberlin and Paul Samuelson are representative of the new generations of American economists who laid the foundation for an academic career by going through an academic program that led in the end to a doctor's degree. In recent decades this has become the established pattern in the training of economic researchers all over the world. Through years of formal education followed by the writing of a doctoral dissertation under supervision the student is brought to a level where he or she should be able to produce independent and original work. The time of the amateurs is definitely over.[5]

[4] While the system of refereeing of articles was adopted by virtually all academic journals in economics during the twentieth century, the publication of book reviews became less common. Several journals that previously published a number of book reviews in every issue have closed down this part of their activities.

[5] This type of professional development is naturally not limited to the field of economics. In other disciplines one will find similar processes, although at different periods of time. Some sciences entered early into this process, others later.

The Globalization of Economics

From the time of Adam Smith until the beginning of the twentieth century Great Britain was the leading country in the development of economics as a scientific discipline. It was there that the classical economists had laid the foundation for academic economics, and through the work of Jevons the country also played a leading role during the early marginalist breakthrough. It was also in Britain far more than in Austria and Switzerland that the next generations of economists extended and refined the new theoretical approach. But some time into the twentieth century Britain's position began to be less dominant. New environments for economic research started to grow up in several other European countries, but above all there was a distinct movement of the center of gravity toward the United States. This development was to have wide-ranging consequences for the discipline and it can be ascribed to several causes.

One of these has already been mentioned. American universities succeeded in establishing a structure of education and academic degrees that was to prove superior to the traditional European system of university education, particularly in regard to the training of academic researchers. Although the individual European countries had different academic traditions, their systems had nevertheless some features in common. Formal education typically came to an end at the master's level or earlier, even for persons who had ambitions to pursue an academic career. The work required for a doctoral dissertation—to the extent that this degree was a precondition for academic employment—was often carried out over a long time and without systematic supervision by a senior researcher. At the end of the nineteenth and beginning of the twentieth century young American economists, as a part of their advanced academic training, would study at the leading European universities, particularly in Germany. However, after the Second World War, the flow rapidly started to move in the opposite direction. Because of the efficient program of study at American universities and the opportunities offered for getting in contact with a large and active research community, young European economists realized that it was at the large American universities that they got the best opportunity for modern research training. Some of them spent several years at an American university to obtain a Ph.D., while others stayed for shorter periods as part of their doctoral work at their home universities.

The process of the development of American universities toward increasing quality and prestige was assisted by global political events. In many European countries—above all in Russia, Germany, and Italy—the emergence of dictatorship led to severe restrictions of academic autonomy and freedom of speech. This together with the persecution of the Jews and other minorities caused many academics including a number of economists to leave their countries and move to the United States, where some of them obtained positions at the best universities. When Paul Samuelson was a doctoral student at Harvard in the late 1930s his teachers included Joseph Schumpeter from Austria, Wassily Leontief from Russia, and Gottfried Haberler (known among other things for his contributions to international trade theory) from Germany.

In the postwar period, some of the young European economists who came to study in the United States chose to remain there, but most of them returned to their own countries. Many of these became ardent spokesmen for reform of university education and research organization in their own countries; they emphasized the importance of organized research training and of increased ambitions to contribute to the research frontier through publication in the leading international journals. As their ideas gradually gained acceptance, many European countries became integrated in the international community of economic research. In some countries such as the Netherlands and Norway this development began at an early stage while some of the larger countries were latecomers to the process of globalization. Today, however, the international orientation has taken hold in all the major research communities in Europe, and European economists from many countries are regular contributors to the leading academic journals. This development has also led to a strengthening of graduate studies, and several of the European doctoral programs are now able to compete with the American universities for the most promising students. Nor have the American influence and the following internationalization of domestic universities and research institutes been limited to Europe; universities in countries like Israel, Japan, Korea, and India have undergone a similar process, and China is on its way.

456

The leading journals are all published in English, and it is English language publication that defines the concept of "international publication." During the latter half of the twentieth century, English has become the international scientific language of economics, its *lingua franca*. Although Knut Wicksell read the economics literature in English, German, and French (in addition to the three main Scandinavian languages), a modern economist seldom feels the need to master any other foreign language than English. This development has also changed the role of the economic journals. A Scandinavian economist who believes that he has made an original theoretical contribution will now wish to have his paper published in an English-language journal in order to reach an international public. In Sweden, one consequence of this was that the journal *Ekonomisk Tidskrift*, which in its time published original contributions by economists like Wicksell and Myrdal, was no longer able to attract submissions of general theoretic interest. It closed down in order to reemerge as the *Scandinavian Journal of Economics*, where both Scandinavian and other economists publish papers that are deemed to be of interest to an international readership. Articles that aim to reach a broader readership or to analyze specific problems of the Swedish economy have instead found a new outlet in the more popular journal *Ekonomisk Debatt*. A similar development has occurred in a number of other European countries.

With English as the common language of scientific communication and the international journals as a common platform of publication for the world's economists, economics has become a global area of research, very much different from what was the case as late as the 1930s. The growth of international conferences and the improved possibilities of international mobility have further contributed to this process. In more recent years, the Internet has become an important new source of rapid dissemination of new research results. The opportunities for keeping abreast with the most recent developments have accordingly been radically improved, but at the same time it is evident that the individual economist's capacity to absorb the increasing flow of scientific information has not expanded to the same degree. What the implications of this will be for the future of the subject is an open question. However, one consequence is clearly a move toward increasing specialization, since it is in nobody's power to follow the growth of knowledge across the entire discipline, as it was possible to do in earlier times. A related consequence is that a demand has arisen for books and journals that can communicate new scientific insights to nonspecialists who are interested in what happens in other fields but do not have the time or the ability to read the most specialized research papers. An interesting example of a journal that was founded specifically to meet this demand is the American *Journal of Economic Perspectives*, which publishes articles on a broad range of subjects, written by specialists for nonspecialists. In time, perhaps, being a generalist—someone who is able to absorb and synthesize the general development of economics—will become recognized as a genuine form of scientific specialization.

Do Economists Agree on Fundamental Issues?

When Winston Churchill was minister of finance (chancellor of the exchequer) in Great Britain in the 1920s he is said to have remarked that whenever he asked two economists for advice he could count on getting three answers, "two of them from Mr. Keynes." It seems to be a widespread belief that economists have widely different views on important issues and one may wonder if there is a real basis for this view. From the point of view of the history of ideas it would perhaps be more reasonable to believe that after two and a half centuries of academic economic research economics would have reached a state of consensus rather than disagreement. Is it possible to come to a conclusion about the real state of affairs?

First of all, it is necessary to straighten out a certain vagueness in the question regarding the lack of consensus among economists: Who are the economists that are supposed to disagree so much? In this book we have used the concept of economist to denote a researcher, someone who concerns himself or herself with extending and communicating the scientific basis for our knowledge about the functioning of the economy. However, in the media and public debate the term *economist* is sometimes used in a much wider sense; frequently, indeed, so wide that it includes persons with little or no formal training in economics, far less with any background in research. Nobody should be surprised at the existence of considerable disagreement in such a widely defined group. But if it were to turn out to be the same extent of disagreement among researchers and academic economists it would be more disturbing, since this would raise the question of whether the scientific insights of economists provides them with any foundation at all for making pronouncements about the functioning of the economic system.

The alleged disagreement among economists is especially linked to their analyses and recommendations regarding economic policy. If we consider a case where economists do not agree on the best choice of policy there are at least two possible sources of this disagreement. One is that our factual knowledge about the effects of a particular policy is uncertain. Consider the question of whether lower taxation of labor income will increase the supply of labor. A lot of research has been done on this issue, but there is some variation in the results, and the economists who wish to extract the essence of the results have to use their judgment in weighing the various pieces of evidence, and on the basis of different personal judgments they could easily come to arrive at different conclusions. The other possible source of disagreement is that a policy recommendation must be based not only on scientific theories and evidence but also on ethical judgments and political ideology. Would it be a good idea to move some of the burden of personal taxation from wages to income from capital? Some economists think that such a reform would lead to a less efficient tax system and take this as a sufficient reason to oppose it. Others would take the view that any loss of efficiency from the reform would be unlikely to be large enough to outweigh what they consider to be its positive redistributive effects. Even if both groups of economists are careful to present the basis for their respective conclusions (which in policy debates they sometimes neglect to do) the impression left in the mind of the general public is often simply that there are disagreements about policy in the economics profession.

But how large is the disagreement in practice? There have been several attempts to measure this. One example is a study by Alston, Kearl, and Vaughan (1992), who distributed a questionnaire to 1,350 American economists asking them to indicate "general agreement," "agreement with provisos," or "general disagreement" with forty different statements about policy-related questions. For some of the statements, the amount of agreement was remarkably high. In 1990, only 6 percent of those asked indicated that they were in general disagreement with the statement, "Tariffs and import quotas usually reduce general economic welfare," while 76 percent were in general agreement. The response to statements about the effect of minimum wages on unemployment and about whether social assistance should be given in cash or in kind also demonstrated a high level of consensus. This is particularly remarkable since both sources of possible disagreement could be expected to be present: uncertainty about factual relationships and different value judgments. On the other hand, there was a considerable lack of consensus regarding more theoretical statements, especially when they were formulated in rather general terms, such as the statement, "Inflation is primarily a monetary phenomenon." On this issue, value judgments are hardly relevant; on the other hand, the statement can be interpreted in so many different ways that it comes as no surprise that the responses are fairly uniformly distributed among the three alternatives. A corresponding study undertaken among British economists, as presented in an article by Ricketts and Shoesmith (1992), gave very similar results. These opinion polls do not suggest, therefore, that there is a good basis for the view that economists are in general disagreement about important issues, at least not more than could be expected given the complexity of the questions. Unfortunately, there is no investigation of this kind from the time when Winston Churchill made his famous remark, so that we cannot know if economists' views have become more uniform over time.[6] But if what Churchill said was in fact a true report on his own experiences and not just an example of his pleasure in a good turn of phrase (which one might perhaps suspect), the results of the empirical studies certainly indicate that the degree of consensus must have increased significantly.

---

[6] Alston, Kearl, and Vaughan (1992) compare the results of their 1990 investigation with a similar study of responses in 1976. The difference in the distribution of responses between the two years is relatively small, however, and the time span may also be too short to expect any clear trends in opinions and attitudes.

Planning and the Market

A recurrent theme in the literature of economics since the age of Adam Smith—and accordingly also in this book—has been the question of which economic system is best in terms of reaching the two fundamental goals of efficient use of resources and just distribution of income between individuals. Is it bureaucracy and planning that yield the best results, or can we rely on the invisible hand of the market as the system best suited to further the common good?

Smith himself was well aware that the right answer to this question had to include elements of both alternatives. In his view, markets should occupy a dominant place in the economic system, while the state or the public sector had an important role to play in the areas of economic life where there were inconsistencies between private incentives and the public interest. Over the course of the nineteenth and twentieth centuries, the interpretation of these conclusions became increasingly sophisticated. The conditions required for the invisible hand of the market to do its work became more rigorously formulated and better understood. At the same time, the case for justifiable public intervention in the economy became more clearly defined and the analysis of the aims and means of economic policy was significantly improved. Nevertheless, there have been considerable differences among economists regarding the proper balance between planning and the market. The disagreements became particularly visible during the great systems debate in the interwar period, as discussed in chapter 14. Even if most economists both then and now have adopted less extreme views than Mises and Hayek or Lange and Lerner, there has always remained considerable scope for differences of opinion on this issue.

With the breakdown of the communist economic system of the Soviet Union and the countries of Eastern Europe around 1990, Western spokesmen for central planning lost an important benchmark case. It was no longer possible to refer to the Soviet Union as a case of a successful and sustainable planned economy. The previously communist countries reformed their economic systems by allowing a greater role for free markets, and so did many of the developing countries that had based their economic systems on government planning and regulation. In addition, most

461

Western countries also began to move in the direction of more reliance on the market mechanism, including areas that had traditionally been regarded as belonging in the domain of the public sector. Privatization, deregulation, and competition became important reform strategies in sectors like communications, energy supply, and health care. In this turnaround of economic policy, the politicians in power could on the whole count on the support of academic economists who during the 1970s and 1980s had often been sharp critics of market intervention and regulation. But there have also been economists who worry that the change of course from planning to markets might go too far and too fast, and that the theoretical insights in what kind of problems the market *cannot* solve will get lost in the revived understanding of the problems that it *can* solve.

At the turn of the millennium it was suggested that the market economy had won its final victory over the system of central planning. However, it should be kept in mind that even in the Western economies that rely most on the functioning of private markets, there is considerably more central planning than was the case in the first half of the twentieth century. The public sector is much larger, whether one looks at its share of employment or gross national product. Macroeconomic policy is to an important extent based on large planning models, and private economic activity is subject to legal regulation, for example, with regard to health, the environment, and safety at work, to a much larger extent than was the case before. A certain amount of market deregulation and downsizing of government planning could therefore take place without the Western economies ending up in the "night watchman state" of the golden age of economic liberalism at the end of the nineteenth century.

Moreover, it may be doubtful whether the global trend toward more heavy reliance on markets and private incentives that has been so marked during the last few decades will continue for the foreseeable future and finally become consolidated. The American economist and sociologist Albert Hirschman (1982) has advanced a theory of "frustration cycles" in the choice among alternative economic systems. The theory is based on the idea that one tends to compare the actual version of the current system with an ideal version of the alternative. The existing system necessarily suffers from a number of imperfections that one becomes more aware of the longer they last. An alternative system that promises to provide better solutions to these problems therefore becomes increasingly attractive until widespread dissatisfaction results in a change of system or at least in radical reform. However, with the passage of time it will turn out that the new system has imperfections that were not so visible in the idealized version of it. At that stage memories of the shortcomings of the previous system have been weakened, and once again one tends to judge it on the basis of the idealized version of theory rather than on practical experience. This releases a new wave of reform in the opposite direction of the previous one.

Hirschman believes that this mechanism goes far toward explaining the fluctuations in the support for private and public solutions to economic problems. It is not easy to pass judgment on the theory's explanatory power, but it is at least a reminder of the fact that ideas are important, and that the history of economic thought is also a story of ideas that have had major if sometimes indirect influence on economic and social development. John Maynard Keynes has given an eloquent expression of this view:

> The ideas of economists and political philosophers, both when they are right and when they are wrong, are more powerful than is commonly understood. Indeed the world is ruled by little else. Practical men, who believe themselves to be quite exempt from any intellectual influences, are usually the slaves of some defunct economist. Madmen in authority, who hear voices in the air, are distilling their frenzy from some academic scribbler of a few years back. I am sure that the power of vested interests is vastly exaggerated compared with the gradual encroachment of ideas. (Keynes 1936, p. 383)

Skeptics may ask whether this is a testable hypothesis. But at the end of our story of the history of economic ideas I believe we should be broad-minded enough to let Keynes have the last word.

Further Reading

Since the present chapter has discussed contemporary trends in economic research, the relevant literature is no longer limited to the field of the history of thought in the more specific sense. Current trends in economics are best studied by reading surveys and expositions of the recent literature. A good place to look for this is the *Journal of Economic Literature*. In each issue of this journal there are three or four survey or review articles, many of them in a nontechnical style, that have been written by experts in the field.

Anniversaries provide one with good opportunities to take a broad view of the development of economics. When the *Economic Journal* marked its one hundredth anniversary, it asked a number of well-known economists to speculate on the theme of "the next hundred years." The result has been published in the form of twenty-two short and readable articles in the January issue for 1991. A few years later, the turn of the millennium inspired the editors of the *Quarterly Journal of Economics* to commission a series of articles that would discuss the development of economics taking Marshall's *Principles of Economics* as their point of departure. William Baumol (2000) considers the development of microeconomic theory, Samuel Bowles and Herbert Gintis (2000) write about general equilibrium theory, Edward Lazear (2000) on economic imperialism, and Olivier Blanchard (2000) on macroeconomics.

The debate about the role of mathematics in economic theory can hardly be said to be of much significance in the modern literature, since there are no longer any leading economists who believe that academic economics can be a nonmathematical discipline. A classical discussion of the place of mathematics with references to the earlier debate can be found in the book by Tjalling Koopmans, *Three Essays on the State of Economic Science* (1957), essays II and III. In the 1950s, when Koopmans wrote, the use of mathematics in economics textbooks was less common than it now is, and there were separate courses and texts in mathematical economics as a special and supplementary field of study. An excellent and historically interesting example of such a book is Allen (1956).

National histories of economic thought and of the contributions of economists to policy debates in their own countries is a field that is too large to be surveyed here. The interest in the national histories lies less in the individual country's contributions to theory and more in the applications of theory to particular problems of domestic economic policy. This implies that individual economists who are neglected in general histories of economic thought because they have not made any contributions that are of international interest may still be important figures in their own countries, and the same goes for books and articles related to domestic economic problems.

A good impression of modern economics as an academic discipline can be gained from two books edited by Michael Szenberg, *Eminent Economists* (1992) and *Passion and Craft: Economists at Work* (1998). The first of these contains autobiographical articles by prominent economists who were born during the period 1910–30. They write partly about their lives and careers, partly about their scientific attitudes and priorities. In the second book, economists born one generation later reflect on their interests and their methods of work.

* References *

Ackley, Gardner (1961), *Macroeconomic Theory*. New York: Macmillan.

Akerlof, George A. (1970), "The market for 'lemons': Quality uncertainty and the market mechanism." *Quarterly Journal of Economics 84*, 488–500.

Aldrich, John (2004), "The discovery of comparative advantage." *Journal of the History of Economic Thought 26*, 379–399.

Allais, Maurice (1953), "Le comportement de l'homme rationnel devant le risque: Critique des postulats et axiomes de l'école americaine." *Econometrica 21*, 503–546.

Allen, R. G. D. (1956), *Mathematical Economics*. London: Macmillan.

Allen, Robert Loring (1993), *Irving Fisher: A Biography*. Oxford: Blackwell.

Alston, Richard M., J. R. Kearl, and Michael B. Vaughan (1992), "Is there a consensus among economists in the 1990's?" *American Economic Review 82, Papers and Proceedings*, 203–209.

Andvig, Jens Christopher (1981), "Ragnar Frisch and business cycle research during the interwar period." *History of Political Economy 13*, 695–725.

Arrow, Kenneth J. (1951a), *Social Choice and Individual Values*. 2d ed. New York: Wiley, 1963.

———. (1951b), "An extension of the basic theorems of classical welfare economics." *Proceedings of the Second Berkeley Symposium on Mathematical Statistics and Probability*. Berkeley: University of California Press.

———. (1953), "Le role des valeurs boursières pour la repartition la meillure des risques." *Econometrie*. Paris: Colloques Internationaux du Centre National de la Recherche Scientifique. Translated as "The role of securities in the optimal allocation of risk-bearing." *Review of Economic Studies 31*, 1964, 91–96.

———. (1963a), *Aspects of the Theory of Risk-Bearing*. Helsinki: Yrjö Jahnsson Foundation. Reprinted in Arrow (1974).

———. (1963b), "Uncertainty and the welfare economics of medical care." *American Economic Review 53*, 941–973.

———. (1974), *Essays in the Theory of Risk-Bearing*. Amsterdam: North-Holland.

Arrow, Kenneth J., and Gérard Debreu (1954), "Existence of an equilibrium for a competitive economy." *Econometrica 22*, 265–290.

Atkinson, Anthony B. (1987), "James M. Buchanan's contributions to economics." *Scandinavian Journal of Economics 89*, 5–15.

Atkinson, Anthony B., and Nicholas H. Stern (1974), "Pigou, taxation and public goods." *Review of Economic Studies 41*, 119–128.

Atkinson, Anthony B., and Joseph E. Stiglitz (1980), *Lectures on Public Economics*. Maidenhead: McGraw-Hill.

467

REFERENCES

Auspitz, Rudolph, and Richard Lieben (1889), *Untersuchungen über die Theorie des Preises*. Leipzig: Duncker & Humblot.

Backhouse, Roger E. (2002), *The Ordinary Business of Life*. Princeton: Princeton University Press.

Bardhan, Pranab, and John E. Roemer (1992), "Market socialism: A case for rejuvenation." *Journal of Economic Perspectives 6(3)*, 101–116.

Barone, Enrico (1908), "Il ministro della produzione nello stato collettivista." *Giornale degli Economisti*. Translated as "The ministry of production in a collectivist state" in Hayek (1935).

Baumol, William J. (2000), "What Marshall *didn't* know: On the twentieth century's contributions to economics." *Quarterly Journal of Economics 115*, 1–44.

Becker, Gary S. (1965), "A theory of the allocation of time." *Economic Journal 75*, 493–517.

———. (1968), "Crime and punishment: An economic approach." *Journal of Political Economy 76*, 169–217.

———. (1981), *A Treatise on the Family*. Cambridge, Mass.: Harvard University Press.

Bergson, Abram (1938), "A reformulation of certain aspects of welfare economics." *Quarterly Journal of Economics 52*, 310–334.

Berlin, Isaiah (1939), *Karl Marx: His Life and Environment*. 4th ed. Oxford: Oxford University Press, 1978.

Bernoulli, Daniel (1738), "Specimen theoriae novae de mensura sortis." *Commentarii Academiae Scientiarum Imperiales Petropolitanae*. Translated as "Exposition of a new theory on the measurement of risk." *Econometrica 22*, 1954, 23–36.

Bjerkholt, Olav (2007), "Writing 'The Probability Approach' with nowhere to go: Haavelmo in the United States, 1939–1944." *Econometric Theory 23*, 775–837.

Black, R. D. Collison (1972), "W. S. Jevons and the foundation of modern economics." *History of Political Economy 4*, 364–378.

Blanchard, Olivier (2000), "What do we know about macroeconomics that Fisher and Wicksell did not?" *Quarterly Journal of Economics 115*, 1375–1409.

Blaug, Mark (1962), *Economic Theory in Retrospect*. 5th ed. Cambridge: Cambridge University Press, 1997.

———. (1972), "Was there a marginal revolution?" *History of Political Economy 4*, 269–280.

———. (1991), "Second thoughts on the Keynesian revolution." *History of Political Economy 23*, 171–192.

Böhm-Bawerk, Eugen von (1884–1889), *Kapital und Kapitalzins*. Jena: Fischer. Translated as *Capital and Interest*. South Holland, Ill.: Libertarian Press, 1959.

———. (1896), "Zum Abschluss des Marxschen Systems." O. von Boenigk, ed., *Staatswissenschaftliche Arbeiten: Festgabe für Karl Knies*. Berlin: Haering. Translated as *Karl Marx and the Close of His System*. New York: Kelley, 1949.

Boiteux, Marcel (1956), "Sur la gestion des monopoles publics astreints a l'équilibre budgétaire." *Econometrica* 24, 22–40. Translated as "On the management of public monopolies subject to budgetary constraints." *Journal of Economic Theory* 3, 1971, 219–240.

Borch, Karl H. (1962), "Equilibrium in a reinsurance market." *Econometrica* 30, 424–444.

———. (1968), *The Economics of Uncertainty*. Princeton: Princeton University Press.

Boulding, Kenneth E. (1971), "After Samuelson, who needs Adam Smith?" *History of Political Economy* 3, 225–237.

Bowles, Samuel, and Herbert Gintis (2000), "Walrasian economics in retrospect." *Quarterly Journal of Economics* 115, 1411–1439.

Breit, William, and Roger W. Spencer, eds. (1995), *Lives of the Laureates: Thirteen Nobel Economists*. 5th ed. Cambridge, Mass.: MIT Press, 2009.

Brems, Hans, and Henning Friis (1959), "Frederik Zeuthen." *National-økonomisk Tidsskrift 97*, 1–22.

Brennan, Geoffrey, and James M. Buchanan (1980), *The Power to Tax: Analytical Foundations of a Fiscal Constitution*. New York: Cambridge University Press.

Buchanan, James M. (1989), *Explorations into Constitutional Economics*. College Station: Texas A&M University.

Buchanan, James M., and Richard A. Musgrave (1999), *Public Finance and Public Choice: Two Contrasting Visions of the State*. Cambridge, Mass.: MIT Press.

Buchanan, James M., and Gordon Tullock (1962), *The Calculus of Consent*. Ann Arbor: University of Michigan Press.

Burns, Arthur F., and Wesley C. Mitchell (1946), *Measuring Business Cycles*. New York: National Bureau of Economic Research.

Cairnes, John E. (1874), *Some Leading Principles of Political Economy Newly Expounded*. London: Macmillan.

Caldwell, Bruce (2004), *Hayek's Challenge: An Intellectual Biography of F. A. Hayek*. Chicago: University of Chicago Press.

Cantillon, Richard (1755), *Essay sur la nature de la commerce en général*. Translated as *Essay on the Nature of Commerce*. London: Macmillan, 1931.

Capaldi, Nicholas (2004), *John Stuart Mill: A Biography*. Cambridge: Cambridge University Press.

Chamberlin, Edward H. (1933), *The Theory of Monopolistic Competition*. 6th ed. Cambridge, Mass.: Harvard University Press. 1948.

Chipman, John S. (1965), "A survey of the theory of international trade, Part 1: The classical theory." *Econometrica 33*, 477–519.

———. (1976), "The Paretian heritage." *Revue Européenne des Sciences Sociales, T. 14, no. 37*, 65–173.

Condorcet, Marquis de (1785), *Essai sur l'application de l'analyse à la probabilité des décisions rendue à la pluralité des voix*. Paris.

———. (1994), *Foundations of Social Choice and Political Theory*. Translated and edited by Iain McLean and Fiona Hewett. Aldershot: Edward Elgar

Cooter, Robert, and Peter Rappoport (1984), "Were the ordinalists wrong about welfare economics?" *Journal of Economic Literature 22*, 507–530.

Cournot, Antoine Augustin (1838), *Recherches sur les principes mathématiques de la théorie des richesses*. Paris: M. Rivière & Cie. Translated as *Researches into the Mathematical Principles of the Theory of Wealth*. New York: A. M. Kelly, 1960.

Debreu, Gérard (1959), *Theory of Value*. New York: Wiley.

de Marchi, Neil B. (1972), "Mill and Cairnes and the emergence of marginalism in England." *History of Political Economy 4*, 344–363.

Dempsey, B. W. (1960), *The Frontier Wage: The Economic Organization of Free Agents*. Chicago: Loyola University Press.

Diamond, Peter A., and James A. Mirrlees (1971), "Optimal taxation and public production I–II." *American Economic Review 61*, 8–27, 261–278.

Dixit, Avinash K. (1996), *The Making of Economic Policy: A Transaction-Cost Politics Perspective*. Cambridge, Mass.: MIT Press.

Dixit, Avinash K., and Timothy Besley (1997), "James Mirrlees' contributions to the theory of information and incentives." *Scandinavian Journal of Economics 99*, 207–235.

Dixit, Avinash K., and Barry J. Nalebuff (2008), *The Art of Strategy*. New York: Norton.

Domar, Evsey D. (1946), "Capital expansion, rate of growth, and employment." *Econometrica 14*, 137–147.

Domar, Evsey D., and Richard A. Musgrave (1944), "Proportional income taxation and risk-taking." *Quarterly Journal of Economics 58*, 388–422.

Dome, Takuo (1994), *History of Economic Theory. A Critical Introduction*. Aldershot: Edward Elgar.

Dorfman, Robert (1986), "Comment: P. A. Samuelson, Thünen at two hundred." *Journal of Economic Literature 24*, 1773–1776.

———. (1989), "Thomas Robert Malthus and David Ricardo." *Journal of Economic Perspectives 3(3)*, 153–164.

Dorfman, Robert, Paul A. Samuelson, and Robert M. Solow (1958), *Linear Programming and Economic Analysis*. New York: McGraw-Hill.

Drèze, Jacques H. (1964), "Some postwar contributions of French economists to theory and public policy." *American Economic Review 54(4)*, part 2 (Supplement), 1–64.

———. (1997), "Research and development in public economics: William Vickrey's inventive quest of efficiency." *Scandinavian Journal of Economics 99*, 179–198.

Dupuit, Jules (1844), "De la mésure de l'utilité des travaux publics." *Annales des Ponts et Chaussées*. Translated as "On the measurement of the utility of public works." Kenneth J. Arrow and Tibor Scitovsky, eds., *Readings in Welfare Economics*. London: Allen & Unwin, 1969.

———. (1849), "De l'influence des péages sur l'utilité des voies de communication." *Annales des Ponts et Chaussées*. Translated as "On tolls and transport charges." *International Economic Papers, no. 11*. London: Macmillan, 1962.

Edgeworth, Francis Ysidro (1877), *New and Old Methods of Ethics*. Oxford: James Parker.

———. (1881), *Mathematical Psychics*. London: Kegan Paul.

———. (2003), *Mathematical Psychics and Further Papers on Political Economy*, edited by Peter Newman. Oxford: Oxford University Press.

Ekelund, Robert B. (2000), "The economist Dupuit on theory, institutions, and policy: First of the moderns?" *History of Political Economy 32*, 1–38.

Ekelund, Robert B., and Robert F. Hébert (1990), "Cournot and his contemporaries: Is an obituary the only bad review?" *Southern Economic Journal 57*, 139–149.

———. (1997), *A History of Economic Theory and Method*. 4th ed. New York: McGraw-Hill.

Elster, Jon (1985), *Making Sense of Marx*. Cambridge: Cambridge University Press.

———. (1989), *Nuts and Bolts for the Social Sciences*. Cambridge: Cambridge University Press.

Engels, Friedrich (1845), *Die Lage der arbeitenden Klassen in England*. Translated as *The Condition of the Working Class in England*. Oxford: Oxford University Press, 1993.

Feiwel, George R., ed. (1989a), *Joan Robinson and Modern Economic Theory*. New York: New York University Press.

———, ed. (1989b), *The Economics of Imperfect Competition and Employment: Joan Robinson and Beyond*. New York: New York University Press.

Fellner, William (1949), *Competition among the Few*. New York: Knopf.

Fisher, Irving (1892), *Mathematical Investigations in the Theory of Value and Prices. Transactions no 9 of the Connecticut Academy of Arts and Sciences*. Republished, New Haven: Yale University Press, 1926.

———. (1906), *The Nature of Capital and Income*. New York: Macmillan.

Fisher, Irving. (1907), *The Rate of Interest.* New York: Macmillan.

———. (1930), *The Theory of Interest.* New York: Macmillan.

Fisher, Irving, and Herbert W. Fisher (1942), *Constructive Income Taxation: A Proposal for Reform.* New York: Harper.

Friedman, Milton (1957), *A Theory of the Consumption Function.* Princeton: Princeton University Press.

———. (1962), *Capitalism and Freedom.* Chicago: University of Chicago Press.

———. (1969), *The Optimum Quantity of Money, and Other Essays.* Chicago: Aldine.

Friedman, Milton, and Rose Friedman (1979), *Free to Choose.* New York: Harcourt Brace Jovanovich.

Friedman, Milton, and Anna J. Schwartz (1963), *A Monetary History of the United States, 1867–1960.* Princeton: Princeton University Press.

Frisch, Ragnar (1929), "Statikk og dynamikk i den økonomiske teori." *Nationaløkonomisk Tidsskrift 67*, 321–379. Translated as "Statics and dynamics in economic theory." *Structural Change and Economic Dynamics 3,* 1992, 391–401.

———. (1932), *New Methods of Measuring Marginal Utility.* Tübingen: Mohr.

———. (1933), "Propagation problems and impulse problems in dynamic economics." *Economic Essays in Honour of Gustav Cassel.* London: Allen & Unwin.

———. (1950), "Alfred Marshall's theory of value." *Quarterly Journal of Economics 64*, 495–524.

———. (1959), "A complete scheme for computing all direct and cross demand elasticities in a model with many sectors." *Econometrica 27*, 177–196.

———. (1965), *Theory of Production.* Chicago: Rand McNally.

———. (1995), *Foundations of Modern Econometrics: The Selected Essays of Ragnar Frisch.* Edited by Olav Bjerkholt. Aldershot: Edward Elgar.

Galbraith, John Kenneth (1958), *The Affluent Society.* Boston: Houghton Mifflin.

———. (1967), *The New Industrial State.* Boston: Houghton Mifflin.

Gårdlund, Torsten (1956), *Knut Wicksell. Rebell i det nya riket.* Stockholm: Bonniers. Translated as *The Life of Knut Wicksell.* Stockholm: Almquist & Wicksell, 1958.

Godwin, William (1793), *Enquiry Concerning Political Justice.* London: G. G. J. and J. Robinson.

Gossen, Hermann Heinrich (1854), *Entwickelung der Gesetze des menschlichen Verkehrs und der daraus fliessenden Regeln für menschliches Handeln.* Braunschweig: Friedrich Vieweg & Sohn. Translated as *The Laws of Human Relations and the Rules of Human Action Derived There-*

from, with an introduction by Nicholas Georgescu-Roegen. Cambridge, Mass.: MIT Press, 1983.

Grampp, William D. (2000), "What did Smith mean by the invisible hand?" *Journal of Political Economy 108*, 441–465.

Gray, Alexander (1931), *The Development of Economic Doctrine: An Introductory Survey*. 2d ed., revised by Alan Thompson. London: Longman, 1980.

Gregory, Paul, and Mark Harrison (2005), "Allocation under dictatorship: Research in Stalin's archives." *Journal of Economic Literature 43*, 721–761.

Groenewegen, Peter (1995), *A Soaring Eagle: Alfred Marshall, 1842–1924*. Aldershot: Edward Elgar.

Haavelmo, Trygve (1944), *The Probability Approach in Econometrics*. *Econometrica 12*, Supplement.

———. (1945), "Multiplier effects of a balanced budget." *Econometrica 13*, 311–318.

———. (1954), *A Study in the Theory of Economic Evolution*. Amsterdam: North-Holland.

———. (1960), *A Study in the Theory of Investment*. Chicago: University of Chicago Press.

Hahn, Frank (1991), "The next hundred years." *Economic Journal 101*, 47–50.

Hansen, Alvin H. (1953), *A Guide to Keynes*. New York: McGraw-Hill.

Hansen, Bent (1969), "Jan Tinbergen: An appraisal of his contribution to economics." *Swedish Journal of Economics 71*, 325–336.

Harrod, Roy F. (1948), *Towards a Dynamic Economics*. London: Macmillan.

———. (1951), *The Life of John Maynard Keynes*. London: Macmillan.

Harsanyi, John C. (1955), "Approaches to the bargaining problem before and after the theory of games: A critical discussion of Zeuthen's, Hicks's, and Nash's theories." *Econometrica 24*, 144–157.

Hayek, Friedrich A., ed. (1935), *Collectivist Economic Planning*. London: Routledge.

———. (1944), *The Road to Serfdom*. Chicago: University of Chicago Press.

———. (1945), "The use of knowledge in society." *American Economic Review 35*, 519–530.

Heckscher, Eli (1919), "Utrikeshandelns verkan på inkomstfördelningen." *Ekonomisk Tidskrift 21*, Part 2. Translated as "The effect of foreign trade on the distribution of income," in Howard S. Ellis and Lloyd A. Metzler, eds., *Readings in the Theory of International Trade*. Homewood, Ill.: Richard D. Irwin, 1950.

———. (1931), *Merkantilismen*. Stockholm: Norstedt. Translated as *Mercantilism*. London: Allen & Unwin, 1935.

Heilbroner, Robert L. (1999), *The Worldly Philosophers*. 7th ed. New York: Simon & Schuster.

Hicks, John R. (1932), *The Theory of Wages*. London: Macmillan.

———. (1937), "Mr. Keynes and the 'classics'; a suggested interpretation." *Econometrica 5*, 147–159.

———. (1939), *Value and Capital*. 2d ed. Oxford: Oxford University Press, 1946.

———. (1950), *A Contribution to the Theory of the Trade Cycle*. Oxford: Oxford University Press.

Hicks, John R. (1956), *A Revision of Demand Theory*. Oxford: Oxford University Press.

———. (1965), *Capital and Growth*. Oxford: Oxford University Press.

Hirschman, Albert (1982), *Shifting Involvements: Private Interest and Public Action*. Princeton: Princeton University Press.

Hollander, Samuel (1979), *Economics of David Ricardo*. London: Heinemann.

Hotelling, Harold (1929), "Stability in competition." *Economic Journal 39*, 41–57.

———. (1931), "The economics of exhaustible resources." *Journal of Political Economy 39*, 137–175.

———. (1938), "The general welfare in relation to problems of taxation and of railway and utility rates." *Econometrica 6*, 242–269.

Hume, David (1752), *Political Discourses*. Edinburgh: Kinkaid.

Hutchison, T. W. (1953), *A Review of Economic Doctrines 1870–1929*. Oxford: Oxford University Press.

Jaffé, William, ed. (1965), *Correspondence of Léon Walras and Related Papers I–III*. Amsterdam: North-Holland.

———. (1972), "Pareto translated: A review article." *Journal of Economic Literature 10*, 1190–1201.

———. (1983), *William Jaffé's Essays on Walras*, edited by Donald A. Walker. Cambridge: Cambridge University Press.

James, Patricia (1979), *Population Malthus: His Life and Times*. London: Routledge and Kegan Paul.

Jevons, William Stanley (1865), *The Coal Question*. London: Macmillan.

———. (1871), *The Theory of Political Economy*. London: Macmillan. Pelican Classics Edition, edited by R. D. Collison Black. Harmondsworth: Penguin Books, 1970.

———. (1884), *Investigations in Currency and Finance*, edited by H. S. Foxwell. London: Macmillan.

Johansen, Leif (1960), *A Multi-Sectoral Study of Economic Growth*. Amsterdam: North-Holland.

———. (1961), *Norge og Fellesmarkedet* (Norway and the Common Market). Oslo.

———. (1965), *Public Economics*. Amsterdam: North-Holland.

————. (1969), "Ragnar Frisch' contributions to economics." *Swedish Journal of Economics 71*, 302–324.

Kahn, Richard F. (1931), "The relation of home investment to unemployment." *Economic Journal 41*, 173–198.

Kahneman, Daniel, and Amos Tversky, eds. (2000), *Choices, Values, and Frames*. New York: Cambridge University Press and the Russell Sage Foundation.

Keynes, John Maynard (1919), *The Economic Consequences of the Peace*. London: Macmillan.

————. (1921), *A Treatise on Probability*. London: Macmillan.

————. (1923), *A Tract on Monetary Reform*. London: Macmillan.

————. (1930), *A Treatise on Money*. London: Macmillan.

————. (1931), *Essays in Persuasion*. London: Macmillan.

————. (1933), *Essays in Biography*. London: Macmillan.

————. (1936), *The General Theory of Employment, Interest, and Money*. London: Macmillan.

————. (1939), Review of Tinbergen. *Economic Journal 49*, 558–574.

————. (1971–1989), *The Collected Writings of John Maynard Keynes 1–30*, edited by Elizabeth Johnson and Donald Moggridge. London: Macmillan.

Keynes, John Neville (1891), *The Scope and Method of Political Economy*. London: Macmillan.

Klamer, Arjo (1989), "An accountant among economists: Conversations with Sir John Hicks." *Journal of Economic Perspectives 3(4)*, 167–180.

Klein, Lawrence R. (1947), *The Keynesian Revolution*. New York: Macmillan.

Konow, James (1994), "The political economy of Heinrich von Stackelberg." *Economic Inquiry 32*, 146–165.

Koopmans, Tjalling C. (1947), "Measurement without theory." *Review of Economics and Statistics 29*, 161–172.

————. (1957), *Three Essays on the State of Economic Science*. New York: McGraw-Hill.

Kowalik, Tadeusz (1987), "Lange, Oskar Ryszard." *The New Palgrave, Vol. 3*, 123–129.

Kreps, David M. (1990), *A Course in Microeconomic Theory*. Hemel Hempstead: Harvester Wheatsheaf.

Kuenne, Robert, ed. (1967), *Monopolistic Competition Theory: Studies in Impact*. New York: Wiley.

Kuhn, Thomas S. (1962), *The Structure of Scientific Revolutions*. 2d ed. Chicago: University of Chicago Press, 1970.

Kydland, Finn E., and Edward C. Prescott (1977), "Rules rather than discretion: The inconsistency of optimal plans." *Journal of Political Economy 85*, 473–491.

Lange, Oskar, and Fred M. Taylor (1938), *On the Economic Theory of Socialism*. New York: McGraw-Hill Paperbacks, 1964.

Langholm, Odd (1998), *The Legacy of Scholasticism in Economic Thought: Antecedents of Choice and Power*. Cambridge: Cambridge University Press.

Lazear, Edward P. (2000), "Economic imperialism." *Quarterly Journal of Economics 115*, 99–146.

Leibenstein, Harvey (1950), "Bandwagon, snob, and Veblen effects in the theory of consumers' demand." *Quarterly Journal of Economics 64*, 183–207.

Leijonhufvud, Axel (1968), *On Keynesian Economics and the Economics of Keynes*. New York: Oxford University Press.

Leonard, Robert J. (1995), "From parlor games to social science: von Neumann, Morgenstern, and the creation of game theory 1928–1944." *Journal of Economic Literature 33*, 730–761.

Leonard, Thomas C. (2005), "Eugenics and economics in the progressive era." *Journal of Economic Perspectives 19(4)*, 207–224.

Leontief, Wassily W. (1941), *The Structure of the American Economy 1919–1939*. New York: Oxford University Press.

Lerner, Abba P. (1944), *The Economics of Control: Principles of Welfare Economics*. London: Macmillan.

Liedman, Sven-Eric, and Mats Persson (1993), "Anders Berch and the Uppsala University Chair in Economics." *Economics at Uppsala University*. Department of Economics, Uppsala University.

Lindahl, Erik (1919), *Die Gerechtigkeit der Besteuerung*. Lund: C. W. K. Gleerups förlag. Translated in part as "Just taxation—a positive solution" in Richard A. Musgrave and Alan T. Peacock, eds., *Classics in the Theory of Public Finance*. London: Macmillan, 1958.

Lintner, John (1965), "The valuation of risk assets and the selection of risky investments in stock portfolios and capital budgets." *Review of Economics and Statistics 47*, 13–37.

Little, Ian M. D (1951), "Direct versus indirect taxes." *Economic Journal 61*, 577–584.

Malthus, Thomas R. (1798), *An Essay on the Principle of Population*. London: J. Johnson. Pelican Classics Edition, edited by Anthony Flew. Harmondsworth: Penguin Books, 1970. ("First Essay").

———. (1803), *An Essay on the Principle of Population*. Edited with an introduction by Donald Winch. Cambridge: Cambridge University Press, 1992. ("Second Essay")

———. (1820), *Principles of Political Economy. Considered with a View to their Practical Application*. London: Murray.

———. (1966), *The Travel Diaries of Thomas Robert Malthus*. Edited by Patricia James. Cambridge: Cambridge University Press.

Marshall, Alfred (1890), *Principles of Economics*. 8th ed. Variorum Edition, Volumes 1–2, 1961. London: Macmillan, 1920.

———. (1919), *Industry and Trade*. London: Macmillan.

———. (1923), *Money, Credit, and Commerce*. London: Macmillan.

Marx, Karl (1867–1894), *Das Kapital I–III*. Abridged translation as *Capital*. Oxford: Oxford World Classics, 1995.

———. (1905–1910), *Theorien über den Mehrwert*, edited by Karl Kautsky. Translated as *Theories of Surplus Value*. Moscow: Foreign Language Press, 1963.

Marx, Karl, and Friedrich Engels (1848), *Manifest der kommunistischen Partei*. Translated as *The Communist Manifesto*. New York: Penguin Signet Classics, 1998.

McGraw, Thomas K. (2007), *Prophet of Innovation: Joseph Schumpeter and Creative Destruction*. Cambridge, Mass.: Harvard University Press.

McLelland, David, ed. (2002), *Karl Marx: Selected Writings*. Oxford: Oxford University Press.

Meade, James E. (1975), *The Intelligent Radical's Guide to Economic Policy*. London: Allen & Unwin.

Meade, James E., and J. Marcus Fleming (1944), "Price and output policy of state enterprise: a symposium." *Economic Journal 54*, 321–339.

Medema, Steven G., and Warren J. Samuels (2003), *The History of Economic Thought: A Reader*. London: Routledge.

Menger, Carl (1871), *Grundsätze der Volkswirtschaftslehre*. Wien: Braumüller. Translated as *Principles of Economics*. Glencoe, Ill.: Free Press, 1950.

———. (1883), *Untersuchungen über die Methode der Sozialwissenschaften und der politischen Ökonomie insbesondere*. Leipzig: Duncker & Humblot.

Mill, John Stuart (1843), *A System of Logic. Collected Works of John Stuart Mill*, Vols. 7–8. Toronto: University of Toronto Press, 1973–74.

———. (1844), *Essays on Some Unsettled Questions of Political Economy. Collected Works of John Stuart Mill*, Vol. 4. Toronto: University of Toronto Press, 1967.

———. (1848), *Principles of Political Economy. Collected Works of John Stuart Mill*, Vols. 2–3. Toronto: University of Toronto Press, 1965.

———. (1859), *On Liberty. Collected Works of John Stuart Mill*, Vol. 18. Toronto: University of Toronto Press, 1977.

———. (1863), *Utilitarianism. Collected Works of John Stuart Mill*, Vol. 10. Toronto: University of Toronto Press, 1969.

———. (1873), *Autobiography. Collected Works of John Stuart Mill*, Vol. 1. Paperback edition, Oxford: Oxford University Press, 1969.

———. (1963–85), *Collected Works of John Stuart Mill*. Toronto: University of Toronto Press.

Mirrlees, James A. (1971), "An exploration in the theory of optimum income taxation." *Review of Economic Studies 38*, 175–208.

Mises, Ludwig von (1920), "Die Wirtschaftsrechnung im sozialistischen Gemeinwesen." *Archiv für Sozialwissenschaften.* Translated as "Economic calculation in the socialist commonwealth," in Hayek (1935).

Mitchell, Wesley C. (1913), *Business Cycles and their Causes.* Berkeley: California University Memoirs, Vol. 3.

Moene, Karl Ove, and Asbjørn Rødseth (1991), "Nobel Laureate: Trygve Haavelmo." *Journal of Economic Perspectives 5(3)*, 175–192.

Moggridge, Donald E. (1992), *Maynard Keynes: An Economist's Biography.* London: Routledge.

Moore, Henry L. (1914), *Economic Cycles—Their Law and Cause.* New York: Macmillan.

———. (1923), *Generating Economic Cycles.* New York: Macmillan.

Morgan, Mary S. (1990), *The History of Econometric Ideas.* Cambridge: Cambridge University Press.

Morgenstern, Oskar (1976), "The collaboration between Oskar Morgenstern and John von Neumann on the theory of games." *Journal of Economic Literature 14*, 805–816.

Mossin, Jan (1966), "Equilibrium in a capital asset market." *Econometrica 34*, 768–783.

———. (1968), "Taxation and risk-taking: An expected utility approach." *Economica 35*, 74–82.

Mun, Thomas (1664), *England's Treasure by Forraign Trade.* London: Macmillan, 1895.

Musgrave, Richard A. (1959), *The Theory of Public Finance.* New York: McGraw-Hill.

Musgrave, Richard A., and Alan T. Peacock, eds. (1958), *Classics in the Theory of Public Finance.* London: Macmillan.

Nasar, Sylvia (1998), *A Beautiful Mind.* New York: Simon & Schuster.

Nash, John F. Jr. (1950a), "Equilibrium points in n-person games." *Proceedings of the National Academy of Sciences 36*, 48–49.

———. (1950b), "The bargaining problem." *Econometrica 18*, 155–162.

Negishi, Takashi (1989), *History of Economic Theory.* Amsterdam: North-Holland.

Neumann, John von (1928), "Zur Theorie der Gesellschaftsspiele." *Mathematische Annalen 100*, 295–320.

Neumann, John von, and Oskar Morgenstern (1944), *The Theory of Games and Economic Behavior.* 60th anniversary ed., Princeton University Press, 2004.

New Palgrave Dictionary of Economics 1–4 (1987), edited by John Eatwell, Murray Milgate, and Peter Newman. London: Macmillan. 2d ed., Vols. 1–8, edited by Steven N. Durlauf and Lawrence E. Blume. London: Macmillan, 2008.

Niehans, Jürg (1990), *A History of Economic Theory. Classic Contributions 1720–1980*. Baltimore: Johns Hopkins University Press.

O'Brien, Denis P. (2004), *The Classical Economists Revisited*. Princeton: Princeton University Press.

Ohlin, Bertil (1933), *Interregional and International Trade*. Cambridge, Mass.: Harvard University Press.

Pareto, Vilfredo (1896–97), *Cours d'économie politique*. Lausanne: Rouge.

———. (1909), *Manuel d'économie politique*. Paris: Giard & Brière, 1909. Translated as *Manual of Political Economy*. London: Macmillan, 1971.

———. (1916), *Trattato di Sociologia Generale*. Translated as *The Mind and Society: A Treatise on General Sociology*. New York: Dover, 1963.

Patinkin, Don (1956), *Money, Interest, and Prices: An Integration of Monetary and Value Theory*. 2d ed. New York: Harper & Row.

Persky, Joseph (1989), "Adam Smith's invisible hands." *Journal of Economic Perspectives 3(4)*, 195–201.

———. (1990), "A dismal romantic." *Journal of Economic Perspectives 4(4)*, 165–172.

Pigou, Arthur C. (1920), *The Economics of Welfare*. 4th ed. London: Macmillan, 1952.

___, ed. (1925), *Memorials of Alfred Marshall*. London: Macmillan.

———. (1928), *A Study in Public Finance*. 3d ed. London: Macmillan, 1947.

———. (1933), *The Theory of Unemployment*. London: Macmillan.

———. (1941), *Employment and Equilibrium*. 2d ed. London: Macmillan, 1949.

Quesnay, François (1759), *Tableau économique*. English translation (in parallel with the French text) by Marguerite Kuczynski and Ronald L. Meek. London: Macmillan, 1972.

Rae, John (1895), *Life of Adam Smith*. London: Macmillan. Reprinted with an introduction by Jacob Viner. New York: Augustus M. Kelley, 1965.

Ramsey, Frank (1927), "A contribution to the theory of taxation." *Economic Journal 37*, 47–61.

———. (1928), "A mathematical theory of saving." *Economic Journal 38*, 543–559.

Rawls, John (1972), *A Theory of Justice*. Oxford: Oxford University Press.

Ricardo, David (1810), *The High Price of Bullion, a Proof of the Depreciation of Bank Notes*. London: John Murray. *The Works and Correspondence of David Ricardo*, edited by Piero Sraffa, Vol. 3. Cambridge: Cambridge University Press, 1951.

———. (1817), *On the Principles of Political Economy and Taxation*. 3d ed. London: John Murray, 1821. *The Works and Correspondence of David Ricardo*, edited by Piero Sraffa, Vol. 1. Cambridge: Cambridge University Press, 1951.

REFERENCES

Ricardo, David. (1928), *Notes on Malthus*. Baltimore: Johns Hopkins University Press. *The Works and Correspondence of David Ricardo*, edited by Piero Sraffa, Vol. 2. Cambridge: Cambridge University Press, 1951.

———. (1951–55), *The Works and Correspondence of David Ricardo*, edited by Piero Sraffa, Vols. 1-10. Cambridge: Cambridge University Press.

Ricketts, Martin, and Edward Shoesmith (1992), "British economic opinion: Positive science or normative judgement?" *American Economic Review 82, Papers and Proceedings*, 210–215.

Robbins, Lionel (1932), *An Essay on the Nature and Significance of Economic Science*. London: Macmillan.

———. (1952), *The Theory of Economic Policy in English Classical Political Economy*. London: Macmillan.

Robbins, Lionel. (1998), *A History of Economic Thought. The LSE Lectures*, edited by Steven G. Medema and Warren J. Samuels. Princeton: Princeton University Press.

Robinson, Joan (1933), *The Economics of Imperfect Competition*. 2d ed. London: Macmillan, 1969.

———. (1956), *The Accumulation of Capital*. London: Macmillan.

Roemer, John E. (1988), *Free to Lose: An Introduction to Marxist Economic Philosophy*. Cambridge, Mass.: Harvard University Press.

———. (1994), *Egalitarian Perspectives: Essays in Philosophical Economics*. Cambridge: Cambridge University Press.

Ross, Ian S. (1995), *The Life of Adam Smith*. Oxford: Oxford University Press.

Rothschild, Emma (2001), *Economic Sentiments: Adam Smith, Condorcet, and the Enlightenment*. Cambridge, Mass.: Harvard University Press.

Samuelson, Paul A. (1947), *Foundations of Economic Analysis*. Cambridge, Mass.: Harvard University Press.

———. (1948), *Economics: An Introductory Analysis*. New York: McGraw-Hill.

———. (1951), "Schumpeter as a teacher and economic theorist." *Review of Economics and Statistics 33*, 98–103.

———. (1953–54), "Prices of factors and goods in general equilibrium." *Review of Economic Studies 21*, 1–20.

———. (1954), "The pure theory of public expenditure." *Review of Economics and Statistics 36*, 387–389.

———. (1962), "Economists and the history of ideas." *American Economic Review 52*, 3–18.

———. (1966–86), *Collected Scientific Papers*. Cambridge, Mass.: MIT Press.

———. (1967), "Irving Fisher and the theory of capital." William Fellner et al., eds. *Ten Economic Studies in the Tradition of Irving Fisher*. New York: Wiley.

———. (1971), "Understanding the Marxian notion of exploitation: A summary of the so-called transformation problem between Marxian values and competitive prices." *Journal of Economic Literature 9*, 399–431.

———. (1983), "Thünen at two hundred." *Journal of Economic Literature 21*, 1468–1488.

———. (1998), "How *Foundations* came to be." *Journal of Economic Literature 36*, 1375–1386.

Sandmo, Agnar (1990), "Buchanan on political economy: A review article." *Journal of Economic Literature 28*, 50–65.

———. (1993a), "Gary Becker's contributions to economics." *Scandinavian Journal of Economics 95*, 7–23.

———. (1993b), "Ragnar Frisch on the optimal diet." *History of Political Economy 25*, 313–327.

———. (1999), "Asymmetric information and public economics: The Mirrlees-Vickrey Nobel Prize." *Journal of Economic Perspectives 13(1)*, 165–180.

———. (2007), "Léon Walras and the Nobel Peace Prize." *Journal of Economic Perspectives 21(4)*, 217–228.

Say, Jean-Baptiste (1803), *Traité d'économie politique*. Translated as *A Treatise on Political Economy*. New York: Augustus M. Kelley, 1971.

Schumpeter, Joseph A. (1912), *Theorie der wirtschaftlichen Entwicklung*. Leipzig: Duncker & Humblot. Translated as *The Theory of Economic Development*. Cambridge, Mass.: Harvard University Press, 1934.

———. (1939), *Business Cycles: A Theoretical, Historical, and Statistical Analysis of the Capitalist Process*, Vols. 1–2. New York: McGraw-Hill.

———. (1942), *Capitalism, Socialism, and Democracy*. 2d ed. New York: Harper, 1947.

———. (1954), *History of Economic Analysis*. London: Allen & Unwin.

Schwier, Jerome F., and Ann S. Schwier (1974), "Pareto's three manuals." *Journal of Economic Literature 12*, 78–87.

Screpanti, Ernesto, and Stefano Zamagni (2005), *An Outline of the History of Economic Thought*. Oxford: Oxford University Press.

Sen, Amartya K. (1970), "The impossibility of a Paretian liberal." *Journal of Political Economy 78*, 152–157.

Sharpe, W. F. (1964), "Capital asset prices: A theory of market equilibrium under conditions of risk." *Journal of Finance 19*, 425–442.

Shleifer, Andrei, and Robert W. Vishny (1994), "The politics of market socialism." *Journal of Economic Perspectives 8(2)*, 165–176.

Sinn, Hans-Werner (2007), "Please bring me the *New York Times:* On the European roots of Richard Abel Musgrave." *International Tax and Public Finance 16*, 124–135.

Skidelsky, Robert (1983–2000), *John Maynard Keynes*. Volume 1, *Hopes Betrayed 1883–1920* (1983). Volume 2, *The Economist as Saviour 1920–*

1937 (1992). Volume 3, *Fighting for Britain 1937–1946* (2000). London: Macmillan/Penguin Books.

Skinner, Andrew S., and Thomas Wilson (1975), *Essays on Adam Smith.* Oxford: Oxford University Press.

Slutsky, Eugen (1915), "Sulla teoria del bilancio del consumatore." *Giornale degli Economisti.* Translated as "On the theory of the budget of the consumer" in G. J. Stigler and K. E. Boulding, eds., *Readings in Price Theory.* Chicago: Irwin, 1952.

Smith, Adam (1759), *The Theory of Moral Sentiments.* London: Millar. Glasgow Bicentenary Edition, edited by D. D. Raphael and A. L. Macfie. Oxford: Oxford University Press, 1976.

———. (1776), *An Inquiry into the Nature and Causes of the Wealth of Nations.* London: Strahan and Cadell. Glasgow Bicentenary Edition, edited by R. H. Campbell and A. S. Skinner. Oxford: Oxford University Press, 1976.

Smith, Vernon L. (2000), *Bargaining and Market Behavior: Essays in Experimental Economics.* Cambridge: Cambridge University Press.

Solow, Robert M. (1956), "A contribution to the theory of economic growth." *Quarterly Journal of Economics 70,* 65–94.

———. (1957), "Technical change and the aggregate production function." *Review of Economics and Statistics 39,* 312–320.

———. (1970), *Growth Theory: An Exposition.* 2d ed. Oxford: Oxford University Press, 2000.

Spiegel, Henry William (1991), *The Growth of Economic Thought.* 3d ed. Durham, N.C.: Duke University Press.

Stackelberg, Heinrich von (1934), *Marktform und Gleichgewicht.* Wien: Julius Springer.

———. (1948), *Grundlagen der theoretischen Volkswirtschaftslehre.* Bern: Francke. Translated as *The Theory of the Market Economy.* London: W. Hodge, 1952.

Stigler, George J. (1941), *Production and Distribution Theories: The Formative Period.* London: Macmillan. Republished as *Production and Distribution Theories.* New Brunswick, N.J.: Transaction, 1994.

———. (1954), "The early history of empirical studies of consumer behavior." *Journal of Political Economy 62,* 95–113.

———. (1955), "The nature and role of originality in scientific progress." *Economica 22,* 293–302. Also in Stigler (1965).

———. (1958), "Ricardo and the 93 % labor theory of value." *American Economic Review 48,* 357–367. Also in Stigler (1965).

———. (1965), *Essays in the History of Economics.* Chicago: The University of Chicago Press.

———. (1990), "The place of Marshall's *Principles* in the development of economics." Chapter 1 in Whitaker (1990).

Stiglitz, Joseph E. (1969), "The effects of income, wealth and capital gains taxation on risk-taking." *Quarterly Journal of Economics 83*, 262–283.

———. (1994), *Whither Socialism?* Cambridge, Mass.: The MIT Press.

Stolper, Wolfgang F., and Paul A. Samuelson (1941), "Protection and real wages." *Review of Economic Studies 9*, 58–73.

Strøm, Steinar, ed. (1998), *Econometrics and Economic Theory in the 20th Century: The Ragnar Frisch Centennial Symposium.* Cambridge: Cambridge University Press.

Szenberg, Michael, ed. (1992), *Eminent Economists.* Cambridge: Cambridge University Press.

___, ed. (1998), *Passion and Craft: Economists at Work.* Ann Arbor: University of Michigan Press.

Thünen, Johann Heinrich von (1826, 1850), *Der isolierte Staat in Beziehung auf Landwirthschaft und Nationalökonomie,* Vols. 1–2. Translated in part as *von Thünen's Isolated State,* edited by Peter Hall. Oxford: Pergamon Press, 1966.

Tinbergen, Jan (1937), *An Econometric Approach to Business Cycle Problems.* Paris: Hermann & Cie.

———. (1939), *Statistical Testing of Business-Cycle Theories,* Vols. 1–2. Geneva: League of Nations.

———. (1940), "On a method of statistical business-cycle research: A reply." *Economic Journal 50*, 141–154.

Turgot, Anne Robert Jacques (1766), *Réflexions sur la formation et la distribution des richesses.* Translated as *Reflections on the Formation and Distribution of Wealth.* London: Good, 1774. Electronic version at http://www.econlib.org/library/Essays/trgRfl1.htm.

Veblen, Thorstein (1899), *The Theory of the Leisure Class.* New York: Macmillan.

———. (1904), *The Theory of Business Enterprise.* New York: Scribner.

Vickrey, William (1945), "Measuring marginal utility by reactions to risk." *Econometrica 13*, 319–333.

Walker, Donald A. (2006), *Walrasian Economics.* Cambridge: Cambridge University Press.

Walras, Léon (1874–1877), *Éléments d'économie politique pure.* Lausanne: L. Corbaz. *Elements of Pure Economics,* translated and with an introduction by William Jaffé. Homewood, Ill.: Irwin, 1954.

———. (1886), *Théorie de la monnaie.* Lausanne: L. Corbaz.

Warming, Jens (1932), "International difficulties arising out of the financing of public works during depression." *Economic Journal 42*, 211–224.

Weintraub, E. Roy (1983), "On the existence of a competitive equilibrium: 1930–1954." *Journal of Economic Literature 21*, 1–39.

Whitaker, John K., ed. (1975), *The Early Economic Writings of Alfred Marshall, 1867–1890,* Vols. 1–2. New York: The Free Press.

———. (1977), "Some neglected aspects of Alfred Marshall's economic and social thought." *History of Political Economy 9,* 161–197.

___, ed. (1990), *Centenary Essays on Alfred Marshall.* Cambridge: Cambridge University Press.

Wicksell, Knut (1893), *Über Wert, Kapital und Rente.* Translated as *Value, Capital, and Rent.* London: Allen & Unwin, 1954.

———. (1896), *Finanztheoretische Untersuchungen.* Translated in part as "A new principle of just taxation" in Richard A. Musgrave and Alan T. Peacock, eds., *Classics in the Theory of Public Finance.* London: Macmillan, 1958.

Wicksell, Knut. (1898), *Geldzins und Güterpreise.* Jena: Gustav Fischer. Translated as *Interest and Prices.* London: Macmillan, 1936.

———. (1901), *Föreläsningar i nationalekonomi, Första delen.* 3d ed. Lund: Gleerup, 1928. Translated as *Lectures on Political Economy,* Vol. 1. *General Theory.* London: Routledge and Kegan Paul, 1934.

———. (1906), *Föreläsningar i nationalekonomi, Andra delen.* Lund: Gleerup. Translated as *Lectures on Political Economy,* Vol. 2. *Money.* London: Routledge and Kegan Paul, 1935.

———. (1958), *Selected Papers on Economic Theory,* edited with an introduction by Erik Lindahl. London: Allen & Unwin.

Wieser, Friedrich von (1889), *Der natürliche Wert.* Wien: Hölder. Translated as *Natural Value.* New York: Kelley & Millman, 1956.

———. (1914), *Grundriss der Sozialökonomie.* Tübingen: Mohr. Translated as *Social Economics.* London: Allen & Unwin, 1928.

Wildasin, David E. (1990), "R. M. Haig: Pioneer advocate of expenditure taxation?" *Journal of Economic Literature 28,* 649–660.

Zeuthen, Frederik (1928), *Den økonomiske fordeling.* København: Nyt Nordisk Forlag.

———. (1930), *Problems of Monopoly and Economic Warfare.* London: Routledge.

* Index *

485